BOOLEAN SEMANTICS FOR NATURAL LANGUAGE

SYNTHESE LANGUAGE LIBRARY

TEXTS AND STUDIES IN
LINGUISTICS AND PHILOSOPHY

VOLUME 23

EDWARD L. KEENAN

University of California at Los Angeles

and

LEONARD M. FALTZ

Arizona State University

BOOLEAN SEMANTICS

FOR

NATURAL LANGUAGE

D. REIDEL PUBLISHING COMPANY

A MEMBER OF THE KLUWER ACADEMIC PUBLISHERS GROUP

DORDRECHT / BOSTON / LANCASTER

Library of Congress Cataloging in Publication Data

Keenan, Edward L. (Edward Louis), 1937–
      Boolean semantics for natural language.

      (Synthese language library ; v. 23)
      Bibliography: p.
      Includes index.
      1. Semantics (Philosophy)   2. Logic.   3. Algebra, Boolean.
I. Faltz, Leonard M., 1940–   .   II. Title.   III. Series.
B840.K43   1984   160   84–22349
ISBN 90–277–1768–0
ISBN 90–277–1842–3 (pbk.)

Published by D. Reidel Publishing Company,
P.O. Box 17, 3300 AA Dordrecht, Holland.

Sold and distributed in the U.S.A. and Canada
by Kluwer Academic Publishers,
190 Old Derby Street, Hingham, MA 02043, U.S.A.

In all other countries, sold and distributed
by Kluwer Academic Publishers Group,
P.O. Box 322, 3300 AH Dordrecht, Holland.

Printed in The Netherlands

To our parents
Edward L. Keenan, Edith C. Keenan,
Joseph Faltz, Charlotte L. Faltz

TABLE OF CONTENTS

PART I: THE EXTENSIONAL LOGIC

B. *Extending the Core Language*

PART II: THE INTENSIONAL LOGIC

PREFACE

In the spring of 1978, one of the authors of this book was sitting in on a course in logic for linguists given by the other author. In attempting to present some of Montague's insights in an elementary way (hopefully avoiding the notation which many find difficult at first), the authors began discussions aimed towards the construction of a simple model-theoretical semantic apparatus which could be applied directly to a small English-like language and used to illustrate the methods of formal logical interpretation. In these discussions two points impressed themselves on us. First, our task could be simplified by using boolean algebras and boolean homomorphisms in the models; and second, the boolean approach we were developing had much more widespread relevance to the logical structure of English than we first thought. During the summer and fall of 1978 we continued work on the system, proving the more fundamental theorems (including what we have come to call the Justification Theorem) and outlining the way in which an intensional interpretation scheme could be developed which made use of the boolean approach (which was originally strictly extensional). We presented our findings in a monograph (Keenan and Faltz, 1978) which the UCLA Linguistics Department kindly published as part of their series called Occasional Papers in Linguistics; one of the authors also presented the system at a colloquium held at the Winter Meeting of the Linguistic Society of America in December 1978.

On the basis of encouragement from colleagues as well as our own sense of the value of the boolean semantic approach, the authors decided to publish the system in book form. Originally we had hoped to create a reworked version of the 1978 monograph, improving on matters of exposition and clarity only. As we progressed, however, we found more and more ways to extend and improve the theory, so that the present book is to all intents and purposes an entirely new work. Herein will be found, for example, a way of defining an ontology without the need of a set (the 'domain of discourse' U) whose elements are not directly denotable by expressions in the language; a deeper discussion of determiners; a deeper and more general presentation of the interpretation of modifiers; a more general discussion of the theorems relating to the intensional system; a discussion of case marking; and, generally, what we hope is a clearer picture of the pervasiveness of boolean structure in the semantics of natural language.

Loose ends remain; however, we have resisted the temptation to delay publication of the book until all the developments and extensions we could possibly conceive of were worked out and included. As it is, we have delayed this book enough; it seemed high time to make available to the scholarly community a complete presentation of the current state of our system, since so much had been developed beyond the versions hitherto available. We hope that this book may be the foundation for further work on and in the boolean semantics framework.

During the time that we have been working on the theory of boolean semantics, we have been fortunate to have had the help and advice of friends and colleagues. It is our pleasure to thank the following people for their contributions, criticisms, and encouragement: Emmon Bach, Filippo Beghelli, Scott Busby, David Gil, William Ladusaw, Susan Mordechay, Larry Moss, Richard Oehrle, Barbara Partee, Stan Peters, Maureen Schmid, and Jonathan Stavi. Our apologies to any persons we may have inadvertently omitted. Our special thanks to Vimal Graham and Cathy Mullins for typing the manuscript, and to the National Science Foundation for funding portions of the work herein under grant BNS 79–14141.

July 1983

BOOLEAN SEMANTICS: AN OVERVIEW

Much of this work uses the notation and concepts of boolean algebra. Neither the notation nor the concepts are particularly difficult to learn, nor does this work presuppose any basic familiarity with them. Nonetheless a sudden immersion might prove chilling to some, so we are presenting here a rather lengthy introduction designed to explain what we think is most novel about our work and what the motivations were which led up to it.

Section 1 below concentrates on what we think are the most substantive aspects of our work which are new. These aspects primarily concern the nature of the denotations of natural language expressions and the semantic relations, such as entailment, which are defined in terms of them. They are largely, though not entirely, independent of the syntactic form of the English representations we propose. For this reason the semantic contribution of this work is rather naturally adaptable to other forms of natural logic, such as, by and large, the various proposals of Montague. (In fact, as noted in the text, we have relied on Montague at certain crucial points.)

Section 2 below concentrates on the syntactic form of our English representations which do contain some novel features, such as the absence of linear order of exrpessions.

Finally, Section 3 points out one difference between our work and all other semantic work for natural language, namely a change in the basic ontology of standard logic, one which has no effect on which expressions entail which others, but which does pertain to the formal elegance and linguistic suggestiveness of the system.

1. SKETCH OF THE SEMANTICS

1.1. *Characterizing English Denotations and Entailments*

Our work situates itself squarely within the tradition of model theoretic semantics for natural language: we provide semantic representations for a fragment of English and interpret them in such a way so as to account for our pretheoretical judgments of semantic relatedness of English expressions. More explicitly, the basic criterion in terms of which our proposals, and those

1

of any form of model theoretic semantics for natural language, are to be evaluated is given by:

(1)   *Criterion of Logical Adequacy*
       Expressions e and e' of a natural language are judged by speakers to be semantically related in a certain way if and only if their formal representations are provably related in that way.

The fundamental relation we, and others, endeavor to represent is the *entailment* (= *logical implication, logical consequence*) relation. Classically it holds between expressions e and e' of category Sentence. Pretheoretically we say that sentence e entails a sentence e' if and only if (iff) e' is true whenever e is; that is, whenever the world is the way e says it is then it is also the way e' says it is. For example, trivially we judge pretheoretically that (2b) below is true whenever (2a) is.

(2)   a. John is a linguist and Mary is a biologist.
       b. John is a linguist.

Thus, given that (2a, b) lie in the fragment of English we intend to represent, it follows that our system would be descriptively inadequate if we could not show that our representation for (2a) formally entailed our representation for (2b).

In fact, anticipating slightly, we may note here that one novelty in our semantics is that it permits a natural and intuitive generalization of the entailment relation to expressions of category other than Sentence. To see this pretheoretically, let us slightly reformulate the intuition of entailment as follows: e entails e' iff e contains all the information in e' (and possibly more). In the case where e and e' are sentences, this intuition tells us that e claims everything that e' does, and possibly more. So if the world is the way e says it is we are guaranteed that it is the way e' says it is; that is, e entails e' on the original intuition. And conversely, if the world is the way e' says it is whenever it is the way e says it is, then clearly e has all the information of e' (and possibly more). So the intuition in terms of informativeness coincides with the standard one for the case where e and e' are sentences.

But the intuition now covers expressions of other categories as well. Pretheoretically, for example, the one place predicate (P_1) in (3a) below contains all the information in (3b). In particular,

(3)   a. walk and talk
       b. walk

whatever (3b) claims of an individual is claimed as well by (3a), and, in fact, more is claimed by (3a).

Similarly, the two place predicate (P_2) *hug and kiss* is more informative than the P_2 *hug* in the sense that, whenever two individuals are related in the way that *hug and kiss* says they are, then they are also related in the way *hug* says they are.

Our examples suggest that for most any category C, a conjunction of expressions e and e' of category C is more informative than (more exactly: at least as informative as) either of the conjuncts taken alone. And this is basically correct. Thus the compound Adjective Phrase in (4a) is more informative than that in (4b) in the sense that for any noun n, an individual which has the property expressed by *tall and handsome n* of necessity has the property expressed by *tall n*.

(4) a. tall and handsome
     b. tall

Similarly the compound determiner in (5a) below is more informative than that in (5b) in the sense that for any noun n, the properties which *some but not all n*'s have must all be properties which *some n*'s have.

(5) a. some but not all
     b. some

Of course the expressions in a category which bear the informativeness relation to each other are not limited to conjunctions and single conjuncts. In general, for example, an expression e is more informative than a disjunction (e or e'). Classically for example a sentence e entails a disjunction (e or e') of sentences. And, for e, e' of category P_1, it is obvious that an individual which has the property expressed by e must have the property expressed by (e or e'); e.g., (6a) below entails (6b):

(6) a. John is crying.
     b. John is either crying or laughing.

Of somewhat greater linguistic interest is the fact that our pretheoretical intuitions of informativeness (or semantic containment) are not limited to expressions related by the traditional boolean connectives (*and, or,* and *not*). For example, modifiers create expressions which, typically, are intuitively more informative than the expressions they modify. Thus the P_1 in (7a) below is more informative than that in (7b): any individual of which the former holds must also be one of which the latter holds.

(7) a. sing loudly
     b. sing

Similarly the Common Noun Phrase *tall student* is more informative than *student*: the individuals with the former property must be a subset of those with the latter property. The AP phrase *very tall* is more informative than *tall*, etc.

Now, since the various pairs of expressions which bear the informativeness relation to each other are of quite different grammatical categories and thus are semantically interpreted in different ways, it is not obvious that we can represent the fact that these different pairs of expressions have a property in common (that of the first being at least as informative as the second) in a uniform way. However, the boolean approach to semantics taken here yields a completely natural solution to this problem, one which we explicate below.

Notice that the problem here is not substantially different from explicating the sense in which the boolean connectives *and, or*, and *not* have the same meaning regardless of whether they combine with Sentences, P_1's, AP's, full Noun Phrases (*John and every student*), or any other sorts of expressions. Within linguistics, early approaches to this problem claimed that we have only one *and, or*, and *not* by claiming that, in one way or another, sentences exhibiting conjunctions of expressions of category other than Sentence were somehow elliptical or shortened forms of more complex sentences in which the *and* overtly conjoined sentences. Thus (8a) below was to be transformationally derived from (8b) in early versions of transformational grammar.

(8) a. John (both) lives in New Jersey and works in New York.
     b. John lives in New Jersey and John works in New York.

However (as logicians realized much sooner than linguists) this approach cannot be successfully carried through for the general case where Noun Phrases other than ones denoting individuals are used, in the sense that the meaning of the derived or elliptical construction is not in general the same as that of the one it is elliptical for (derived from). Thus (9a) and (9b) below are not paraphrases:

(9) a. Some student (both) lives in New Jersey and works in New York.
     b. Some student lives in New Jersey and some student works in New York.

Obviously (9b) can be true in a situation in which (9a) is false and so is not a paraphrase of (9a).

The approach we take to this problem is substantially different from the syntactic shorthand approach sketched above. It involves what we consider a significantly 'deeper' analysis of the nature of the denotations (= interpretations) of natural language expressions. As this analysis provides the basis for the most significant innovations of our system as compared with other proposals for model theoretic semantics for natural language, we shall sketch it in outline here, leaving the full substance of the innovations to the body of this work.

The basic idea is the following. In all model theoretic approaches to natural language, we associate with each category C of expressions a set of possible denotations, here called T_C or *the type for C*, defined in terms of the semantic primitives of the model. In standard first order extensional logic (EL), the primitives of a model are two: a non-empty universe of discourse U, and a set of two truth values, taken here as $\{0, 1\}$. Models may thus differ according as they choose different U's. Once a universe U is chosen, however, the types (sets of possible denotations) for categories are fixed, for they are defined in terms of U and the set $\{0, 1\}$, henceforth called 2. The type for Sentence (and Formula) is taken to be 2, and the type for the individual constants and variables is taken to be U. The type for one place predicates is the power set of U; so a P_1 will be interpreted as a subset of U, intuitively the set of entities in U of which that P_1 holds in that model. Similarly, the type for P_2 would be the power set of $U \times U$, i.e. U^2, the collection of all sets of ordered pairs over U. In general, T_{P_n}, the type for the n-place predicates, is the power set of n-tuples over U, U^n. (Equivalently, we can think of T_{P_1} as the set of functions from U into 2; and more generally, T_{P_n} will be the set of functions from U^n into 2.) Finally, the type for the n-place function symbols is the set of functions from U^n into U.

Notice, now, that the semantic primitives of EL, namely U and 2, have quite different statuses. Since U is an arbitrarily selected set, required only to be non-empty, it cannot be assumed to have any structure at all. We cannot, for example, assume that the elements of U bear any given relation to each other. On the other hand, the set 2 is a set with a boolean structure

— one which is on some approaches made quite explicit and on others is just informally adumbrated by saying that the element 1 of 2 is understood as *true*, and the element 0 is understood as *false*. These latter informal remarks serve to ground our intuitive understanding of a formal statement that one or another formula is interpreted as 1 (or 0). But what do these statements mean interal to logic itself? One thing they mean is that a conjunction of formulas (or sentences) is interpreted as 1 just in case each conjunct is so interpreted; in all other cases a conjunction is interpreted as 0. This conforms to our pretheoretical intuitions in that a conjunction of formulas is only regarded as true if each conjunct is; otherwise it is false. Similarly, a disjunction of formulas will have value 1 iff at least one disjunct has value 1; and a negation of a formula has value 1 iff the formula negated is interpreted as having value 0.

A more mathematical way to say all this is just to say that the set of truth values must possess at least two distinct elements, call them the zero and unit elements, and must have two binary functions, called meet and join, and one unary function, called complement, defined on it. The meet and join functions are defined by the standard truth tables for conjunction and disjunction respectively, and the complement function is defined by the truth table for negation. Then, in defining how complex formulas take their denotations as a function of those of their parts, we stipulate that a conjunction of formulas is always interpreted as the meet of the interpretations of the conjuncts; that of a disjunction as the join, and that of a negation as the complement.

Basically what this says is that the type for formulas is a boolean algebra: it is a set with two distinguished elements on which are defined meet, join, and complement functions which satisfy the (very stringent) axioms of boolean algebra (which we give explicitly in Part I of this work); and these functions are used in giving the interpretations of conjunctions, disjunctions, and negations of formulas.

Now, on the approach we develop, in distinction to EL, essentially all types (with a few exceptions of some interest) are sets with a boolean structure. Thus, we can directly interpret conjunctions, disjunctions, and negations in most categories by taking them to be the appropriate meet, join, and complement functions of the interpretations of the expressions conjoined, disjoined, or negated. The sense in which we have only one *and, or*, and *not* is explicated on the grounds that they are always interpreted as the meet, join, and complement functions in whatever set we are looking at.

In a similar way we can now explicate what we mean by saying that the various pairs of expressions discussed earlier bear an informativeness relation one to the other. All boolean algebras exhibit a partial ordering relation defined on the domain of the algebra in terms of the meet (or join) operation. This relation is normally symbolized $\leqslant$ and pronounced 'less than or equals'. It may be defined as follows: for all x, y in the domain of a boolean algebra, $x \leqslant_{df} y$ iff the meet of x with y is in fact x. Equivalently, we could define x to be $\leqslant$ to y iff the join of x with y is y. (The equivalence of these definitions follows from the axioms which the meet and join functions are required to satisfy.)

Now, it turns out that the informativeness relation discussed earlier is in effect just the boolean less than or equals relation. More explicitly, for e and e' expressions in any boolean category C (one whose type is the domain of a boolean algebra), e *is at least as informative as* e' iff for every model, the denotation of e in that model is $\leqslant$ to the denotation of e' in that model. Thus, any boolean category will posses an 'entailment' relation among its expressions, and that fact is entirely due to the fact that the expressions of that category take their denotations in a set with a boolean structure — a structure which itself is motivated by the desire to directly interpret conjunctions, disjunctions, and negations of expressions in that category.

While the need to directly interpret boolean combinations of expressions in a category is the most obvious and direct motivation for taking the type for that category to be the domain of a boolean algebra, it turns out not to be the only motivation, nor even the 'deepest' one. 'Deeper', or perhaps more surprising, motivations concern the fact that we can say insightful things in boolean terms about the meanings of various expressions which are not obviously boolean in nature — that is, which do not involve *and, or,* or *not* or their various infinite analogues, such as *every, some, no, always, sometimes, never,* etc. As one sort of example, consider the semantics of Adjective Phrases (AP's).

The most productively formed AP's have the semantic property of being *restricting* in the sense that, booleanly speaking, *skillful artist* is $\leqslant$ to *artist* (but not *apparent artist* or *fake artist*). To say that the $\leqslant$ relation holds among the above expressions amounts to saying that in any model, every individual with the skillful (tall, female) artist property also has the artist property — something which need not be the case when *skillful* is replaced by AP's like *apparent* or *fake*; see Part II for details.

These facts are represented in our system as follows. The syntax of our logic uses subcategorization features such as +*restricting* to form subcategories of categories. Thus AP_{+rest} is a (sub) category of AP in our system, one to which *skillful*, etc. belong but *apparent, fake*, etc. do not. In general, as AP's syntactically combine with Common Noun Phrases, denoted simply N in our system, to form Common Noun Phrases, all AP's are semantically interpreted by functions from T_N into T_N. T_N, like most other types in our system, is a set on which boolean operations are defined. We then define the type for the restricting AP's to be the set of functions f from T_N into T_N such that for all $p \in T_N$, $f(p) \leqslant p$.

In this way, then, we say what makes restricting AP's different in meaning from non-restricting ones. Note that we say it directly in terms of what sorts of objects the restricting AP's may denote. Moreover, the constraint on their denotations is naturally given in purely boolean terms — it is thus something we could not say as easily if T_N were not a set with a boolean structure.

More of boolean interest can be said concerning AP's. For example, there is a naturally felt semantic distinction between 'merely' restricting AP's like *tall* and AP's we call *absolute* (or *intersecting*), such as *male* and *female*. Syntactically, the former naturally compare and have superlative forms (*taller than, less tall than, tallest, least tall*) whereas the latter do not naturally form comparatives and superlatives. (If we say that Mary is more female than Sue we shift our interpretation of *female* from an AP absolutely designating sex to one referring to properties characteristically or stereotypically associated with female individuals.)

Semantically, there is a marked difference in logical behavior between merely restricting AP's and absolute ones. Thus (10a) below entails (10b), whereas (11a) does not entail (11b).

(10) a. John is a female artist.
     b. John is a female individual.
(11) a. John is a tall artist.
     b. John is a tall individual.

It turns out (see Part I.B for details) that the constraint on the functions from T_N into T_N needed to interpret absolute AP's so that the entailment in (10) holds is again naturally given in boolean terms. In fact, an even more surprising result ensues: the type for the absolute AP's turns out, extensionally, to be isomorphic to the type for the Common Noun Phrases, N. So, up to isomorphism, we cannot distinguish absolute AP's from common nouns. This semantic fact correlates with some interesting syntactic properties of these AP's in English: namely, absolute AP's include those AP's which in many respects function syntactically like common nouns. For example, they combine with determiners to form full NP'S ($\bar{N}$'s in our notation). Thus, (12a) is acceptable English while (12b) is decidedly ungrammatical.

(12) a. Two males entered Mario's pizza shop at 6 p.m.
      b.* Two talls entered Mario's pizza shop at 6 p.m.

We have, then, a non-obvious correlation between English surface form and logical form (semantic representation) which, to our knowledge, has not been explicitly noticed before in the literature.

While much more could be said (and is, in the relevant sections of this book) concerning the boolean nature of AP meanings, let us turn to two other examples of semantically interesting properties of natural language expressions which are boolean, although not obviously so. Let us consider here first other extensional predicates and their full NP ($\bar{N}$) arguments.

Among the $\bar{N}$'s we treat in Part I, the Extensional Logic, are not only proper nouns like *John, Mary*, etc. but also $\bar{N}$'s formed from Determiners (Dets) and Common Nouns Phrases, N's, such as *every student, no student, at least three students*, etc. In addition, of course, boolean combinations of $\bar{N}$'s are $\bar{N}$'s, e.g. *John and every teacher, John and (but) not every student, either exactly two students or (else) exactly five students*, etc Classically, the proper nouns constitute a syntactically definable subcategory of full NP's (i.e. $\bar{N}$'s), denoted here $\bar{N}_{+\text{prop}}$. In our system, then, the set of possible proper noun denotations will be a subset of the possible $\bar{N}$ denotations. In fact, it turns out to be a subset with a very special semantic property, one naturally statable in boolean terms, and to our knowledge only statable in boolean terms. We can thus characterize the meaning of the subcategorization feature *+proper*, and this characterization turns out to be interesting in the intensional logic (formulated in Part II) where other argument categories (e.g. $\bar{S}, \bar{P}_1$) are used in addition to $\bar{N}$.

To get an informal feel for the semantically characteristic property of proper nouns consider first that we (extensionally) interpret proper nouns, following Montague (1970), as sets of common noun denotations, called here (extensional) *properties*. Loosely, we represent John as the set of 'his' properties, e.g. doctor, non-vegetarian, tallest surgeon, etc. Let us refer to these sets of properties as *individuals*. They are not arbitrary sets of properties, but rather must meet certain boolean conditions. For example, if John has the doctor property he cannot also have its boolean complement, the non-doctor property, and conversely. Further, if he has both the properties

p and q he must have the property of being both a p and also a q, and conversely. For example, John must have the doctor property and also the lawyer property iff he has the property of being both a doctor and a lawyer. A similar condition involving disjunctions holds, too. Note that the characterization of just which property sets constitute individuals (possible proper noun denotations) are given solely in terms of the boolean structure on T_N, the set of Common Noun Phrase denotations. We return to this point in a different context below.

Individuals, then, are sets of a certain sort, namely, sets of properties. It is natural to interpret conjunctions of individual denoting expressions as the intersection of the sets denoted by the two (or more) expressions. Thus, the expression *John and Mary* will denote the properties common to John and Mary. Similarly, we interpret *John or Mary* as denoting the union of the John individual with the Mary individual. And, *not Mary* (as it occurs for example in *John but not Mary*) will denote the set theoretic complement of the Mary individual, that is, the set of properties not in the Mary individual.

Clearly, then, the set of possible $\bar{N}$ denotations will include not only the sets which meet the conditions of being individuals, but also those sets obtainable from individuals by taking intersections, unions, and complements. Further, we want to be able to take arbitrary intersections and unions, not just finite ones. Thus, we want *every student* to denote the properties common to the individuals with the student property, that is, the intersection of all those individuals regardless of how many there happen to be. Similarly, *some student* will denote the union of the individuals with the student property.

We may naturally wonder just how many of all the sets of properties can be obtained from individuals by taking complements and arbitrary intersections and unions? The answer (Section A in Part I) is that any set of properties can be obtained in this way. So, we will want $T_{\bar{N}}$ to be the set of all sets of properties, that is, the power set of T_N.

We note further (Section A of Part I) that the power set of a non-empty set determines a paradigm case of a boolean algebra. Specifically, for A a non-empty set, the power set of A, which we denote by A^*, is the domain of a boolean algebra where the zero and unit elements are respectively the empty set, $\emptyset$, and A, and the boolean meet, join, and complement operations are respectively set theoretic intersection, union, and complement (relative to A). The boolean $\leqslant$ relation is provably just the subset relation.

Thus we have informally shown that the full set of possible $\bar{N}$ denotations is uniquely determined by the boolean operations (intersection, etc.) once the individuals are given. Somewhat more cognitively, we may say that a speaker can comprehend any NP denotation provided he knows what the individuals are and what it means to take boolean functions of them, that is, what it means to take intersections, unions, and complements.

More formally, to say that all sets of properties can be generated from the individuals by taking intersections, etc. is to say that the set of individuals, the possible proper noun denotations, is a set of (complete) generators (c-generators) for $T_{\bar{N}}$. Moreover, it turns out that the type for proper nouns is not merely a set of c-generators for $T_{\bar{N}}$, it is a minimal such set: provably, no subset of $T_{\bar{N}}$ which is strictly smaller than the set of individuals can be a set of c-generators for $T_{\bar{N}}$. We can, in fact, assess in a general manner just how small a subset of $T_{\bar{N}}$ the type for proper nouns is. It turns out that in a model of n individuals (n not necessarily finite) there are $2^{(2^n)}$ sets of properties, i.e. possible $\bar{N}$ denotations. So, in a world of only 4 individuals, there are over 65,000 possible $\bar{N}$ denotations (65,536 to be exact)! In general, then, the possible proper noun denotations constitute a very small portion of the complete set of possible $\bar{N}$ denotations. It is a sort of testimony to the power of boolean operations that from such a small set the entire large set can be computed.

Moreover, the proper noun denotations not only determine booleanly what sets of properties can be referred to by arbitrary $\bar{N}$'s, there is a sense which we can make explicit in which they also determine what we can say (in first order) about $\bar{N}$ denotations. What we can say about $\bar{N}$ denotations is given by the set of one place predicate denotations, T_{P_1}. Syntactically P_1's combine with $\bar{N}$'s to form Sentences, so semantically they can be represented by functions from $T_{\bar{N}}$ into the type for Sentence (extensionally, the set $\{0, 1\}$). In a model of n individuals, the total number of such functions would be 2 raised to the power $2^{(2^n)}$, an incomprehensibly large number even for very small values of n.

But are all such functions possible (first order) P_1 denotations? The answer is clearly no. Imagine, for example, a model in which *John* and *Mary* are interpreted as different individuals. Then it will follow that the expressions *John, Mary*, and *John and Mary* all have different denotations. If P_1 denotations were arbitrarily selected functions from $T_{\bar{N}}$ into the type for Sentence, T_S, then we might interpret a P_1 such as *sleep* by a function which assigned the *John and Mary* set of properties value 0 (false) but assigned the *John* set value 1 (true) and the *Mary* set value 1. But this is obviously not possible, for then (13a) below would be true and (13b) false.

(13) a. John is sleeping and Mary is sleeping.
      b. John and Mary are sleeping.

(NB: in our semantics we do not in fact represent tense and aspect. We have included it in our illustrative examples in this section, holding it constant across relevant examples, for naturalness.)

Obviously enough, (13a) and (13b) must have the same truth value. This amounts to saying that an arbitrary P_1 denotation cannot assign truth values arbitrarily to $\overline{N}$ denotations; i.e., not all functions from $T_{\overline{N}}$ into T_S are possible (first order) P_1 denotations. But how can we characterize which of these functions are possible P_1 denotations? The answer is surprisingly elegant in boolean terms. From the example given above we may observe that a P_1 denotation must assign to an intersection (meet) of $\overline{N}$ denotations the truth value obtained by applying the function separately to each of the $\overline{N}$ denotations over which the meet was taken — we obtain a truth value in each case — and take the meet of the resulting truth values in the truth value algebra T_S. Symbolically, we want to require that P_1 denotations *preserve meets*; i.e.

(14)   sleep(John and Mary) = sleep(John) and sleep(Mary).

Drawing the functions which can interpret *sleep* from those from $T_{\overline{N}}$ into T_S which meet this condition, we guarantee that (13a) and (13b) above are logically equivalent. Similarly, we want a possible *sleep* interterpretation to *preserve joins* (15) and to *preserve complements* (16).

(15)   sleep(John or Mary) = sleep(John) or sleep(Mary)
(16)   sleep(not(every student)) = not(sleep(every student))

Functions from a (boolean) algebra into another which preserve the boolean operations in the above sense are called *homomorphisms*. Thus, we take T_{P_1} to be the set of (complete) homomorphisms from $T_{\overline{N}}$ into T_S. How many of them are there? In a model of n individuals, there happen to be just 2^n such functions, the same as the number of (extensional) properties in a world of n individuals. This is exactly what we expect of first order predicates; that is, the first order predicates correspond one for one to sets of individuals, or equivalently to the functions from individuals into 2. More formally, we will prove (a generalized version of) the Justification Theorem given below:

(17)   For every function f from the individuals on $T_{\bar{N}}$ into 2 there
         is exactly one (complete) homomorphism from $T_{\bar{N}}$ into 2 whose
         values on the individuals are the same as f.

(To say that a homomorphism is complete is just to say that it preserves
arbitrary meets (intersections in the case at hand) and arbitrary joins (unions),
not just finite ones.) Thus any property of individuals uniquely determines
a possible P_1 denotation, and conversely.

It turns out then that the individuals, the possible proper noun denotations, are indeed an exceedingly special set of $\bar{N}$ denotations. They are not
only a set of complete (c) generators for $T_{\bar{N}}$, they are *free*, in that P_1 denotations can take their values freely, in any way we like, on individuals; then,
their values on all the other sets of properties are uniquely determined by
the fact that P_1 denotations are complete homomorphisms. Thus, modulo
the boolean operations, the proper noun denotations determine not only
what the full set of $\bar{N}$ denotations is, they also determine what can be said
about them (in first order — see Part I.B for a discussion of various sorts
of higher order predicates and their homomorphic nature).

Let us emphasize finally that the above discussion not only presents a
very special semantic property of proper noun denotations, that of being
a set of complete, free generators for $T_{\bar{N}}$, it has thereby also revealed a rather
special property of $T_{\bar{N}}$ itself, namely, that it is an algebra which has a set of
such generators. 'Most' boolean algebras do not have that property. In fact,
those which do are provably just those which are isomorphic to power sets
of power sets, and thus have cardinality $2^{(2^n)}$ for some cardinal n.

It is reasonable to ask whether the types for any other categories in our
system also have individuals (i.e. complete, free gnerators). In the extensional
logic in Part I the answer is no. In particular, the types of Modifier categories
like AP's and Adverb Phrases and Prepositional Phrases are not algebras
with individuals. Similarly the types for the n-place Predicates do have
individuals. And finally, the type for Determiner is not such an algebra.

However, the intensional logic in Part II does present some categories
whose types do have individuals. This is the case for the category $\bar{S}$, which
syntactically includes expressions like those italicized in (18) below:

(18) a. John believes *that Fred is a linguist*.
      b. John believes *either that Fred is a linguist or that Mary is a
         biologist*.
      c. John believes *that Fred is a linguist but not that Mary is biologist*.

Similarly the type for the category of infinitival nominals, which we represent formally as $\bar{P}_1$, and which includes the expressions italicized in (19) below, also have individuals:

(19) a. *To study in the summer* is difficult.
      b. *To (both) stand on your hands and sing the national anthem* is difficult.
      c. *(Both) to stand on your hands and to sing the national anthem* are difficult.

It appears then that categories which function as *arguments* of predicates are characterized by types with individuals (see Part II for a discussion of what the individuals are in the $\bar{S}$ and $\bar{P}_1$ algebras). Other major classes of categories such as Modifiers, Predicatives, and Specifiers (= Determiners) do not have types with that semantic property.

1.2. *Characterizing Possible Semantic Systems for Natural Language*

The above discussion provides the first step in characterizing constraints on possible semantic systems for natural language. Let us define a boolean algebra to be an *Argument algebra* iff it has individuals (a set of complete free generators). Then we can say of natural logics that they must include some Argument algebras among their types. Let us further define a category of a language to be an *Argument category* iff its type is an Argument algebra.

We can now state a non-obvious correlation between syntactic form and semantic representation: the categories whose types are Argument algebras ($\bar{N}$, $\bar{S}$, etc.) are just those which receive case marking, trigger verb agreement, and are affected by syntactic operations like Passive and Raising. Note that these latter two operations do in fact affect all the 'bar' categories we have discussed:

(20) a. The President is believed to be a jelly bean addict.
      b. That Fred stole the money is believed to be false.
      c. To study in summer is believed to be difficult.

Do the other sorts of categories we have consiered also have types with (booleanly) distinguished properties? The answer appears to be yes, though many specific points remain to be worked out. Consider for example the n-place predicates. Are there semantic properties which the types for P_1's,

P_2's, etc. have in common which distinguish these types from the types for other categories? We have already seen that the (first order extensional) P_1's are homomorphisms. In fact, the P_2's are homomorphisms as well. For example, the P_1's in (21a, b) below clearly hold of the same individuals and thus are extensionally the same, whence the P_2 *kiss* must preserve meets:

(21) a. kiss some student and every teacher
      b. kiss some student and kiss every teacher

Let us ask then what categories are such that their types are sets of homomorphisms (defined by their values on the individuals). We find not only the *n*-place Predicates among these, but a few other categories as well. In particular, the type for 'transitive' AP's like *fond (of)*, *jealous (of)*, etc. which combine with $\bar{N}$'s to form ordinary AP's such as *fond of John, jealous of some student*, etc. consists of homomorphisms. For example, the property a teacher has if he is fond of either John or Mary must be the same one he has if either he is fond of John or he is fond of Mary. Thus, loosely, we want the equation below to hold, whence *fond of* preserves joins:

(22)   fond of (John or Mary) = (fond of John) or (fond of Mary).

Similarly, 'transitive' common nouns, the 'relational' nouns of philosophers, such as *friend (of)*, *colleague (of)*, etc. are semantically homomorphisms. Thus, for example, an individual has the property of being a friend of either John or Mary iff he has the property of being a friend of John or a friend of Mary, so *friend (of)* preserves joins.

Finally, certain extensional prepositions seem to behave homomorphically on their $\bar{N}$ arguments. Thus, if someone works in [either New York or Chicago], then he works either in New York or in Chicago, and conversely. Hence, we want *in [New York or Chicago]* to be extensionally the same PP modifier of *work* as *in New York or in Chicago* whence *in* preserves joins. Similarly, taking *no* as short for *not a*, we have *in no bar* (i.e. *in [not (a bar)]*) = *not [in a (any) bar]*, so *in* preserve complements.

Let us define then a boolean algebra to be a *Predicative Algebra* iff its elements are homomorphisms. We may then by extension call a category a Predicative category if its type is a Predicative algebra. The (extensional) categories thus characterized as Predicatives then are the *n*-place Predicates, transitive AP, transitive Common Noun, and Preposition. This class does appear to be a reasonably natural syntactic class. For example, it largely coincides with those categories whose expressions may show agreement with features of Argument categories such as person, number, and gender.

We have then given two sorts of semantic types needed for a natural language semantics: Argument algebras (ones with individuals) and Predicative algebras (ones whose elements are homomorphisms). We note the Predicative algebras we use are not in general algebras with individuals, and that Argument algebras never have homomorphisms as elements.

Are there yet other types of algebras we need for natural language semantics? A reasonable place to look is at Modifier categories like AP, Adverb Phrase, and Prepositional Phrase. These categories are always interpreted by functions from one algebra into itself. These functions are most commonly, but not always, as we pointed out earlier, restricting; moreover, these algebras have subalgebras of absolute or intersecting functions which are isomorphic to the domain of the functions. If we define an algebra to be a Modifier algebra just in case its elements are restricting functions from an algebra into itself, and if we define a category to be a Modifier category just in case its type is a Modifier algebra, we find that extensionally we identify the AP's, Adverb Phrases, and PP's as modifiers. Again, this seems a rather natural syntactic class.

We note that algebras of restricting functions do not have individuals, nor are they algebras of homomorphisms (the only function which is both restricting and a homomorphism is the identity function). So, Modifier types are in principle distinct from the types of Argument categories and Predicatives.

Thus, we can begin to make some substantive claims about what sorts of denotation types we need in a natural logic: at the very least, we need Argument algebras, Predicative algebras, and Modifier algebras. Are there any others?

The only category with productively formed members in the extensional logic we propose which we have not yet considered is that of Determiner (Det). Syntactically, Dets combine with N's to form $\bar{N}$'s, and include expressions like *every, at least two and at most six, John's, no student's* etc. Semantically, then, Dets will be interpreted by functions from properties into sets of properties, i.e. from T_N into $T_{\bar{N}}$. But are just any such functions possible Det denotations in English? We argue here, based on Keenan and Stavi (1981) and Barwise and Cooper (1980), that only functions which meet a condition we call *conservativity* are possible Det denotations. Essentially, these are just the functions f which make the equation below true, thinking of *student* and *vegetarian* as arbitrary properties:

(23) f(students) are vegetarians iff f(students) are both students and vegetarians.

Obviously, every student is a vegetarian iff every student is both a student and a vegetarian; similarly, exactly two students are vegetarian iff exactly two students are both students and vegetarians; John's dog is a vegetarian iff John's dog is both a dog and a vegetarian, etc.

The conservativity condition appears to characterize elements of T_{Det}. Let us then (somewhat tentatively) define an algebra of functions from a set A into its power set A^* to be a *Specifier* algebra iff its elements are just the conservative functions from A into A^*.

On this definition, just what categories will turn out to be Specifier categories? So far, only Det itself. Therefore, it may be that Det is a rather special category and its type rather unique among the types we need to represent natural language denotations; or it may simply be that we have not looked hard enough to find other sorts of specifiers: or perhaps we have not yet formulated the notion of a Specifier with sufficient generality. A more general definition might allow us to represent Dets as simply a rather special case of Specifiers and yet include other categories as well. Complementizers such as *that, whether*, etc. show some similarities to Dets, but do not seem very productively formed; AP's also show some similarities to Dets and are more productively formed, but we have so far not found a convincing formulation to include Modifiers and Specifiers as special cases of something more general. (See Keenan and Stavi, *op. cit.*, for some discussion.)

2. ON THE RELATION BETWEEN ENGLISH FORM AND LOGICAL FORM

As indicated at the beginning of this Introduction we have emphasized initially the nature of the *objects* which interpret English expressions, as that is the aspect of our semantic proposals which is perhaps most new. That discussion may leave the reader with the (incorrect) impression that the purpose of our semantic work was to see just how much of English semantics we could squeeze into a boolean format. In fact, however, our motivation was quite other. The boolean nature of our semantics emerged slowly and painfully at first and then by leaps and bounds during the course of our work. Neither author began this enterprise with any particular awareness of boolean algebras.

Rather, our work began with a desire to provide a semantics for natural language which was comparable in expressive power to the intensional logic of Montague (1973) (henceforth PTQ) but which was explanatorily more adequate according to certain criteria we discuss briefly below.

In Section 1 above we formulated the basic criterion of Logical Adequacy for natural logics: they must correctly represent our pretheoretical judgments of semantic relatedness among the expressions of the natural language(s) we are studying. This criterion is basically the criterion of *descriptive adequacy* as the term is used in Linguistics (Chomsky, 1965). Given a semantic system of some reasonable degree of descriptive adequacy, we may consider it *explanatorily adequate* to the extent that it is useful in accounting for aspects of language other than the judgments of semantic relatedness which directly motivate the system.

What are some of these other aspects of language? The overwhelmingly most obvious one is that speakers use English expressions with the particular meanings they do in fact have. More specifically, speaker/hearers usually correctly understand the utterances they hear and produce, even though these are often novel in the sense of never having been heard or uttered by the relevant parties before. That is, in some reasonable sense, speaker/hearers have learned and can use the (by and large) correct meaning representations for English expressions; moreover they can do this in 'real time' — time spans appropriate for the conduct of everyday social intercourse. We might note as well, a point analogous to one stressed in the early syntactic literature in generative grammar, that children learn at a rather young age not merely to produce well formed i.e. grammatical expressions of English, they learn to use them meaningfully — to assert things they intend as true, to deny and contradict what other have said, to make inferences on the basis of what others have said, etc.

We should like then our semantic theory to represent explicitly the association between English expressions and the objects we use to represent their meanings, called here *logical forms* (LF's). Obviously, the most direct way of achieving this would be to use the English expressions themselves as the objects which we formally assign denotations to (interpret). The spirit of our proposals is thus more consonant with the approach taken in Montague (1970) (henceforth EFL) than with that of PTQ.

The LF's we use, then, will resemble ordinary English in a great many respects, which we discuss below. But our LF's are not identical to English surface forms (to the extent that we know what they are). The disparity is justified here on both practical and theoretical grounds. On practical grounds, we must acknowledge that the meaning system of English is much richer than we know how to represent, so some overtly expressed aspects of English meanings are simply ignored by us. In particular, this is true for tense and aspect marking. The reader may think of sentences in our formal system as being intended to hold at a point (or interval) of time. For cases where entailments are justified, the points (or intervals) of time are held constant across entailing and entailed sentences.

Of more theoretical and sometimes methodological import, there are two reasons why we have chosen to make our LF's distinct from English surface forms (SF's). First, it is our judgment that the SF's of different languages differ more than the minds of the speakers of those languages. It is thus reasonable, we feel, to expect that what we can say across languages is more similar than the specific means used to say it. Hence, we expect that LF's, for languages, that is, meaning representations, are more similar than their surface forms are. For example, we expect that the LF's needed for English and Japanese differ less than the SF's needed for English and Japanese. Consequently, we have tried to eliminate from our LF's properties of English SF's which are obviously not fairly general across languages — provided, of course, these properties are not semantically significant and so need not be referred to by the interpreting function. In particular, we do not represent in our LF's agreement phenomena, case marking on Argument categories (but see Part I.B for some discussion of case marking determination by predicates), or, more surprisingly perhaps, word order. Thus our LF's, while possessing a fairly rich constituent structure, do not define a linear (word) order relation on their terminal elements. Derived expressions in our system are formed by taking sets over simpler expressions. Thus, the LF we use to represent the meaning of (24a) is given in (24b), where, as usual, curly brackets are used as in set theory.

(24)   a. Every doctor likes some female patient
       b.

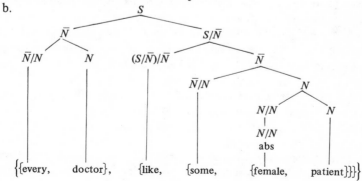

We note here that our logical syntax employs the slash notation in a standard way: expressions of category X/Y combine with ones of category Y to form ones of category X. In addition, however, we form derived categories in two other ways: first, we use (a limited set of) features to form subcategories, as in N/N_{abs}, abbreviated AP_{abs}, for *absolute adjective phrases*; and second, we have adopted (and adapted) the bar notation of current linguistic theory, thereby representing a category difference between e.g. {female, patient}, a N or Common Noun Phrase, and {some, {female, patient}}, a $\bar{N}$ or full Noun Phrase.

Note that while word order, case marking, and verb agreement are not marked in (24b) it is trivially easy (up to choice of tense) to construct the English sentence whose meaning is intended to be represented by (24b). We have not attempted in this work to rigorously define the *read out* function which would formally associate LF's with the English forms they are intended to represent. For most cases of LF's which illustrate what is new about our system, the value of that function at a given LF is obvious, as in (24b) above. Fully specifying that function, however, would require that we enter many details of agreement and word order phenomena which are irrelevant to our principle goal of representing English meanings. We note without example here that our logical syntax covers a larger fragment of English than e.g. PTQ, and that characterizing the corresponding SF's of English is considerably more difficult than in that work.

A second reason for a disparity between SF and LF here lies with the nature of English ambiguity. Semantically ambiguous forms, as judged pretheoretically, can not be directly interpreted. If a sentence S could be both true and false in a given state of affairs then we could not even define an entailment relation, since we could argue that the sentence both entailed itself (trivially, it is true if it is true) and that it didn't entail itself (since we have a case where it is true and also false). We must therefore associate different LF's with each 'reading' of an ambiguous expression. For example, we represent the classical quantifier scope ambiguities in sentences like (25a) below by the two LF's, (25b) and (25c).

(25) a. Every student read a book
      b. (every student) (read (a book))
      c. (a book) (λx ((every student) (read x)))

Note that here, and elsewhere, we normally use ordinary parentheses rather than curly brackets when using expressions of our formal language. The structure in (25b) above, basically isomorphic to that in (24b), represents the reading in which *every student* has wide scope over *a book*. For most speakers this is the most natural reading, and the structure we use for it corresponds very well to the observable English surface form.

(25c), on the other hand, represents the reading where *a book* has wide scope over *every student*. The syntactic structure of (25c) corresponds much less well to that of (25a) than does (25b), and is clearly syntactically more complex than (25b). The subexpression (λx ((every student) (read, x))) is a P_1, i.e. an expression of category $S/\bar{N}$; semantically it takes the denotation of *a book* as argument yielding as value a sentence denotation.

Despite this poor correspondence to SF, however, we have decided to live with structures like (25c) in our system. The reasons are largely, but not entirely, practical. The alternative, instantiated in PTQ, is to handle quantification or 'NP insertion' as a substitution rule, generating distinct LF's which grossly resemble (25b) but which code in some way the order in which the $\bar{N}$'s *every student* and *a book* are put into the structure. This would make the LF's and consequently the interpreting function for the language as a whole much more complicated. We chose not to countenance these complications (exemplified in the translation function of PTQ) since the focus and contribution of our monograph does not concern variable binding operators (though we include three such in our system). In short, we do not want to complicate the things we are interested in in favor of something we are not.

Note further that the substitution rule by itself, and the resulting analysis trees, still requires the use of variables or 'place holders' of infinite numbers (it obviously doesn't matter whether we write them as he_n or x_n), still requires some coindexing mechanism, and most awkwardly, still yields LF's which do not approximate well to the independently motivated SF's in English. As regards this latter point we refer the reader to Partee (1975) in which the attempt to relate the analysis trees of PTQ to the sort of labelled bracketings used in defining ordinary syntactic operations in English is unsuccessful. Both approaches, then, appear to yield LF's with poor correspondence to SF's. We feel that the reason for this poor correspondence is that NP scope differences in natural language are not in fact coded or in general reflected in the derivational history of an expression. If so, we have a situation where we need something in LF which really doesn't correspond to anything in SF.

Moreover, in (weak) favor of our approach we would like to suggest the following two points.

First, there does appear to be a correlation, in many simple cases, between the preferred reading of an expression and the LF which most closely corresponds to it syntactically. We have already illustrated this in (25a, b). A somewhat different case is that illustrated by:

(26)   John is looking for a unicorn.

(26) is arguably ambiguous according as *a unicorn* is within the scope of *look for* or not. The most natural reading is where it is in the scope of *look for*, in which case it is understood non-transparently (not implying the existence of a unicorn), and it is this reading which is represented by our LF (isomorphic to (25b)) which corresponds constituent for constituent to (26). The transparent reading of (26) in which *a unicorn* is outside the scope of *look for* is the one for which we must use the lambda operator.

If further investigation continues to support the claim that the less accessible readings are ones whose LF is more complicated, that fact may perhaps serve as an explanation for the lesser degree of accessibility.

A second possible advantage of using the lambda operator directly in our LF's is that the structures they create may prove to be useful in representing properties of natural language other than scope ambiguities. Note that our lambda operator syntactically derives an $n+1$ place predicative from an n-place one, where the argument category of the derived predicative is given by the type of the variable used with lambda. (We treat sentences as 0-place predicates — a sentence combines with zero arguments to form a sentence.) There appear to be a variety of cases where we want LF's for such derived $n+1$ place predicates which do not involve inserting $\bar{N}$'s into expressions.

One such case in English involves unbounded 'Tough Movement'. Sentences (27a, b) below illustrate respectively the case where we want predicates like *be tough, easy, difficult*, etc. to take P_1 infinitives as arguments yielding P_0's (Sentences) and where we want to allow them to take P_2 infinitives as arguments yielding P_1's whose argument category is the same as that of the P_2 from which it is derived.

(27)   a. To believe that Fred would steal the money is hard.
       b. That Fred would steal the money is hard to believe.

(Note then that $\bar{S}$'s as well as ordinary $\bar{N}$'s can undergo 'Tough'). We want, then, the expression following *hard* in (28a) below to be a P_2 infinitive, which it will be, semantically, if it is represented with the use of a lambda operator as in (28b).

(28) a. Fred is hard to believe that the University would fire.
      b. to (λx (believe that the University fire x)).

Another sort of case where we want lambda derived P_n's are the Raising to Object cases. Thus, following *believe* in (29) below, we have first an $\bar{N}$ and then a P_1 infinitive, of which the $\bar{N}$ is the understood argument.

(29)   John believes Fred to have stolen the money.

In several languages, however, the 'raised' $\bar{N}$, *Fred* above, need not function as the subject of the main predicate of the P_1 infinitive. Thus in languages as diverse as Chicewa (Trithart, 1977), Fijian (Gordon, 1978), and Kipsigis (Jake and Odden, 1979) we can form raising pairs like those illustrated in (non-) English below:

(30)   John believes the money that Fred has stolen it.

Note that a pronoun remains in the position from which *the money* was raised, the complementizer remains, and the clause is finite. In these respects, such clauses in those languages do not differ at all from the case where the embedded subject is raised. And these structures can be represented in the same way as the subject raising ones, provided we have a way of representing the expression following *the money* above as a P_1 (that would take *the money* as argument). And that is precisely what the lambda operator affords us: (31) below is such a P_1.

(31)   (λx (Fred stole x)).

There remains a final disparity between our LF's and SF's they are intended to represent, one which in English concerns only a limited range of structures. Consider that for three-place Predicates in English at least two of the arguments must linearize on the same side of the P_3 in surface structure. Different linear orders will be compatible with different constituent structures at LF, but since the preferred linear order often depends on the relative surface size of the arguments, it will happen that sometimes the constituent structure we assign to a LF does not match with the preferred linear order. Similar statements hold for various ways of forming syntactically complex P_2's — the preferred order of argument and modifier, for example, is again subject to very surfacy constraints.

For example, among the subcategories to which verbs like *find* and *consider* belong is one which combines with AP's to yield ordinary $\bar{N}$ taking P_2's. The orders illustrated in (32a, b) are both acceptable, but only (32a) is immediately compatible with the constituent structure of the LF we assign it.

(32) a. I find unacceptable the proposal put forward by the chairman.
      b. I find the proposal put forward by the chairman unacceptable.

In (32) the a-structure is perhaps somewhat better than the b-one, but as the $\bar{N}$ argument (*the proposal* . . .) is replaced by less 'heavy' ones the a-structure decreases in acceptability. For example, choosing *it* for the $\bar{N}$ argument renders the a-structure ungrammatical.

We are simply not concerned in this work with arguing whether one structure in (32) is more basic than the other. We refer the reader to Keenan (1982b) for evidence from universal grammar supporting the existence of a surface operation called *Argument Attraction* which reorders an argument of a headed P_n to be adjacent to the head. We note without example here that a considerable diversity of structures may, depending on word order conventions in the language, yield structures which are inputs to that reordering process. Various examples arise during the course of this work.

In summary then, our LF's do exhibit certain regular divergences in form from the SF's they represent, but typically these divergences are sufficiently regular to make the computation of the SF quite easy given a LF. Furthermore, we note below a variety of often non-obvious ways in which the LF's we employ do present properties of SF's, and thus we consider that we have achieved to a significant extent the goal of representing the association of (surface) form and meaning in English.

First of course, for a great many cases of even fairly complex SF's, we find that their constituents are in a one-to-one correspondence with those of the LF's we use to represent their meanings. Now, our LF's are compositional, in the sense that the interpretation of syntactically complex expressions is given as a function of the interpretations of their constituents. Consequently, we satisfy the following (strong) form of the Fregean condition to a large extent:

(33)   *The Fregean (Compositionality) Condition*
        An English expression e is derived from expressions $e_1, \ldots, e_n$
        if and only if the interpretation of e is explicitly given as a
        function of the interpretations of $e_1, \ldots, e_n$.

It is basically the satisfaction of this condition which allows us to account for how speakers comprehend novel utterances: if they know what the parts mean, and if they know how structures derived in that way take their meanings as a function of their parts, then they can figure out what the whole means. For example, as we mentioned earlier, we form boolean combinations (conjunctions, disjunctions, and negations) in almost all categories. The derived expressions are directly interpreted as a function of the interpretation of the conjuncts, disjuncts, etc. that they are derived from. If they were derived by 'reducing' sentences, we could not in general give the correct interpretation of the derived structure as a function of what it was derived from.

Secondly, syntactically similar structures are interpreted in semantically similar ways. This condition can be formulated more rigorously in a variety of special cases, but a few examples will be sufficient to indicate the non-trivial sorts of correspondences it covers.

As a first case, distinct expressions of English having the same grammatical category must be represented by expressions in the logic having the same category and thus interpreted as elements of the same type. So, items of the same category denote the same type of thing; and conversely, items in different categories denote differently. Thus, following the lead of Montague (1970) here, proper nouns and quantified noun phrases (*John* and *every man* respectively) are both expressions in category $\bar{N}$ in the logic and thus both denote sets of properties. Of course, since the proper nouns form a subcategory of $\bar{N}$, they take their denotations in a proper subset of $T_{\bar{N}}$. On the other hand (in distinction to some forms of Montague Grammar), since common nouns and P_1's are syntactically distinct categories in English, they will be syntactically distinct in the logic and thus have distinct types. (Extensionally, T_N and T_{P_1} are disjoint but isomorphic; this isomorphism does not hold in our intensional logic, though T_N there is isomorphic to a subcategory of P_1.)

As another somewhat more novel case (as compared to the semantics of PTQ) note that P_1's and P_2's are distinct but in many ways very similar categories in English. For example, lexically simple elements in both categories are traditionally called *verbs*; expressions in both categories commonly enough across languages exhibit agreement with their arguments (P_1's with their subjects, P_2's with their objects). Both may 'host raising' to their argument position; i.e. P_1's like *is certain*, raise to subject, and P_2's like *believe* raise to object. Similarly, the common forms of Equi are ones in which it is controlled by arguments of P_n's; i.e. it is the subject argument of the P_1 *want to leave* which controls the reference of the infinitival phrase, whereas in *persuade (John) to leave* it is the object of the P_2 which controls it. Both P_1's and P_2's in many languages undergo Passive, such as Latin, Turkish, commonly in Uto-Aztecan, etc. Finally, both accept certain sorts of adverbial modification. (34a) below illustrates the case where the P_1 *examine the patient* is modified by *individually* (i.e. the doctors acted individually); (34b) illustrates the case where the P_2 *examine* is so modified (so the patients were treated individually), and (34c) is properly ambiguous as to the scope of *individually*.

(34)   a.   The doctors examined the patient individually.
        b.   The doctor examined the patients individually.
        c.   The doctors examined the patient individually.

Given these strong similarities, then, we expect that P_1's and P_2's will be interpreted in semantically similar ways. And this is the case in our system. Extensionally, both are functions of a very similar sort, namely homomorphisms, with the same domain, $T_{\overline{N}}$. They differ only with regard to their range algebras. Consequently, we are able to formulate several of the processes mentioned above in a fully general way, that is, for P_n's in general, regardless of whether n has value 1 or value 2. (See e.g. the treatment of Passive in Part I.B.) Note that the uniform semantic treatment of P_n's is in marked distinction to the treatment in PTQ.

More generally, the classification of the sorts of algebras needed for natural language given earlier determine somewhat farther reaching correspondences between SF and LF. Thus, while Argument categories like $\overline{N}$, $\overline{S}$, and the various $\overline{P_1}$'s are syntactically distinct, they clearly exhibit, as pointed out earlier, syntactic similarities. And within our approach their types are semantically similar in a non-obvious way — they have free generators called individuals. Similarly, the various categories of Modifiers, e.g. AP, AdvP, and PP exhibit syntactic similarities (but also differences) which are represented in our system by the (semantic) similarities of their types — the major subcategories here are always interpreted by restricting functions, and subcategories of those by absolute (intersecting) functions. It is unsurprising, then, to find regular means of converting expressions in one category to another. For example, the *-ly* function in English (*slow → slowly*) basically expresses the isomorphism between restrictive AP's and restrictive Adverb Phrases.

A third and yet more general correspondence between SF and LF in our system concerns the regularity in surface coding properties — agreement and word order in particular — of the *function-argument* relation defined at the level of LF. As regards word order, not having marked it at LF allows us to state generalizations concerning the regularities in the ways in function-argument structures are linearized in the world's languages. For example, the most widespread word order type — the verb final languages — may be characterized as follows: Predicatives follow their arguments, Modifiers (and Dets) precede. Just the opposite word order assignment holds for the rigorous verb initial languages, viz VOS ones like Fijian, Ineseno Chumash, Malagasy. VSO and SVO languages generally follow the pattern for VOS ones with the exception of the position of the subject which occurs somewhat more to the left than predicted. Note that since we have many categories of Predicatives, Arguments, and Modifiers these generalizations represent a fairly large number of specific claims about word order regularities. And of course these generalizations are only possible if we can actually give properties that Predicatives, for example, have in common. This we have done in semantic, in fact boolean, terms. We refer the reader here to Keenan (1979) for more detailed discussion. Here we only stress that there are regularities in the way our function-argument structures are expressed in the SF's of the world's languages. So, to the extent that apprehending these function-argument relations is important to understanding the meaning of expressions we can say that languages do provide fairly regular observable means in surface for expressing these relations. (Needless to say, of course, other quite independent phenomena such as contraction and cliticization also affect word order regularities in surface.)

As regards agreement phenomena, the following claim receives good support from our function-argument assignment at LF: *Expressions of functions may agree with expressions of their arguments*. So Predicatives may show agreement with their Arguments (by '*may*' here we mean that there are some languages in which they do show such agreement), and Modifiers and Dets may show agreement with their arguments. We again refer the reader to Keenan (1979) for supporting data and justification for the claim that the agreement of function expressions with argument expressions is not an arbitrary regularity of natural language. There it is presented as a special case of the *Meaning-Form Correlation Principle* given below:

(35)   *The Meaning-Form Correlation Principle*
        For X and Y categories, the form of expressions of category X
        may depend on (vary with) the form of expressions of category

Y in a structure E if the meaning of the expressions of category X depends on (varies with) those of category Y in that structure.

Note that there is an intuitive sense in which the 'meaning' of a function expression may depend on that of its argument; namely, what the function 'does' to the argument may vary with properties of the argument. Standard examples from mathematics are, say, the absolute value function, where the value of the function varies systematically according as the argument is positive or negative. Similarly, rounding off functions are of this sort. A more arbitrary example would be a function f which sends a number x to x^2 if x is odd and to x^3 if x is even.

Similarly, in natural language we find that the expressions we have interpreted by functions exhibit this sort of variation with respect to their arguments. For example, a P_1 like *run* implies both internal movement and external movement (i.e. relative to other things) when the argument expression denotes animate things. So, if a horse runs we understand (without further qualification) that both his parts move and that he changes location relative to other things (however momentarily). But if the argument expression is a mechanical object, the sense of external movement is absent: watches or cars may run without changing location. And, for the rather more special cases of things like faucets and noses, neither internal nor external movement of the object is intended; rather something else of an appropriate sort is understood to move out of the object.

Analogous claims hold for modifiers. A strong animal is one which can exert a lot of force; but a strong chair or wall is an object that can withstand a lot of force, etc.

In general, then, we adjust our interpretation of function expressions to suit the nature of the argument they are applying to. Note the similarity here to the reinterpretation of expressions used in everyday metaphors, discussed in Faltz (1982). Typically it is the function expression which gets interpreted in some non-literal way rather than the argument expression. If we say that John exploded when he heard the news we do not alter our interpretation of *John* but we likely alter our interpretation of *explode* (though we could intend it literally). Similarly, in *a shaky proposal* it is the function expression *shaky* whose sense is adjusted to the nature of proposals; *proposal* is understood in its ordinary literal sense.

A further related class of cases here concerns various forms of 'fixed expressions' such as idioms and proverbs. Often enough all expressions are non-literal in proverbs, as in *the early bird gets the worm*. In many cases of idioms, however, we find that certain expressions are interpreted literally and others non-literally. However, the former are typically Argument expressions, the latter function ones. Thus, in *he jumped from the frying pan into the fire*, the entire P_1 is non-literally interpreted (usually) but its argument *he* is interpreted in an ordinary literal referential way.

3. AN ONTOLOGICAL INNOVATION

In one respect, namely, the choice of semantic primitives, our approach differs strongly from all other approaches to model theoretic semantics for natural language.

Recall that in EL (standard extensional logic, to which we limit ourselves here for illustrative purposes) a model contains two semantic primitives, the set of truth values and the universe of discourse U, in terms of which the possible denotations of all expressions in the language are defined. Now, EL has the property referred to in Keenan (1982b) as *ontological perfection*: the semantic primitives are themselves possible denotations for expressions in the language, truth values being denotable by sentences (formulas), and the elements of U (entities) being denotable by individual constants (proper nouns) and individual variables.

However, once EL has been enriched along the lines of Montague (1970, 1973) the resulting logic is no longer ontologically perfect. In particular, proper nouns and individual variables now take their denotations in the set of what we have called *individuals*, sets of properties (common noun denotations) which meet certain conditions. Thus, no expressions in English take their denotations (via the translation function, in PTQ) in U itself. This actually seems mysterious. Why should the meanings of expressions be defined ultimately in terms of something which we can not refer to in principle and so in some sense cannot know? Why should the denotation of a syntactically unanalyzable expression such as *John* be given as a function of an entity which no proper part of *John* denotes? (Extensionally recall, *John* is translated in Montague grammar as $(\lambda P)(P(j))$, where '*j*' denotes in U).

U then seems mysterious, a kind of noumenal world of entities which underlies the phenomenological world of individuals. On our approach, U has been eliminated altogether, and the resulting (extensional) logic is ontologically perfect. The key to eliminating U is, unsurprisingly perhaps, boolean. Recall that on Montague's (extensional) approach, the type for common nouns is the collection of subsets of U, and thus constitutes a power set boolean algebra. Individuals, proper noun denotations, are particular subsets of that algebra. It turns out that we can define those subsets in purely boolean terms without reference to U at all. Further, it is a standard theorem of boolean algebra (see Part I for details) that power set boolean algebras are completely characterized (i.e. up to isomorphism) by satisfying two additional boolean requirements: *completeness* and *atomicity*.

Thus, on our approach, the semantic primitives of a model are taken to be an algebra of truth values as before together with another algebra P of properties, required to be complete and atomic. Noting that the truth value algebra 2 is also complete and atomic, we now have a more uniform set of primitives — two boolean algebras of similar sorts. Moreover, the system is ontologically perfect, since the algebra P is the type for the common noun phrases. Individuals are defined as subsets of P which satisfy certain boolean conditions, and provably, as in the spirit of EL, P is isomorphic to the power set of the individuals on P. So up to isomorphism we can still think of a property as being a set of individuals; the only difference now is that individuals are defined in terms of properties, whose boolean nature is directly justified by judgments of entailment in natural language, rather than the other way around.

This approach then provides a simplification of the ontology (= semantic primitives) of a natural logic. Moreover, it suggests the following interesting question: is there any sense in which common noun denotations, properties, are linguistically more basic than proper noun ones, individuals? In Part I.A we answer this question in the affirmative.

PART I: THE EXTENSIONAL LOGIC

A. *The Core Language, L*

In this section we present an elementary formal language *L*, called the *core language*, whose associated semantics is rich enough to illustrate the major innovations we propose. Syntactically the language *L* is intended to represent the basic predicate-argument structure of (first order) English. The English categories represented in *L* are: Common Noun Phrase (*man, student*, etc.), Full Noun Phrase (*John, every man*, etc., a category which includes Proper Noun Phrase as a subcategory), Determiner (*every, some*, etc.), One Place Predicate (*sleep, walk*, etc.), Two Place Predicate (*hug, kiss*, etc.), and Sentence (sometimes referred to a Formula or as Zero Place Predicate). Essentially all categories of *L* are boolean in that complex members can be recursively formed from simpler ones by taking combination with *and, or*, and *not* all derived expressions are directly interpreted as a function of the interpretation of their immediate constituents.

1. SYNTAX OF THE CORE LANGUAGE *L*

To define the core language *L* we shall define first a set CAT of *category names*, and second, relative to a set *V* of *basic vocabulary* defined by listing, we shall define a set PE_V of *possible expressions over V*. Then we shall associate with each name *C* in CAT a set *n(C)* of possible expressions called *the category named by C*. A category then is a set of expressions, and *L* is defined to be the union of these sets.

Defining CAT

The elements of CAT are built up recursively from two primitive category names '*N*' and '*P*', which we may think of as *nominals* and *predicates* respectively. '*N*' for example will turn out to name the category of (zero place) *common noun phrases*. It will include expressions like *man, woman*, etc. '*P*' will name the category of *formulas*, which we regard as zero-place predicates. Complex category names are formed from simpler ones by the use of *slashes* (/), *bars* (‾), and *subcategorization features*. We provide a quick illustration of this notation below.

Given that N is a category name (we drop the use of single quotes where it is clear from context that we are talking about the symbol and not the category it names) we may form the category name $\bar{N}$ using the bar notation. $\bar{N}$ will name the category of full noun phrases, including members like *every man, John, John and every man*, etc. From the category name $\bar{N}$ we may form the name $\bar{N}_{\mathrm{prop}}$, which will name a subcategory of the category named by $\bar{N}$, namely the category of *proper noun phrases*, which includes expressions like *John, Mary*, etc.

Finally, given that N and $\bar{N}$ are in CAT, we may use the slash notation to form the category name $\bar{N}/N$ which names the category of expressions which combine with expressions of category N to form expressions of category $\bar{N}$. This category will include expressions like *some, all, some but not all*, etc. and will sometimes be abbreviated as *Det*, for *Determiner*.

Below we give a formal definition of CAT. We use $\emptyset$ to denote the empty set, and for any set W, W^* denotes the power set of W, that is, $W^* =_{\mathrm{df}} \{K : K \subseteq W\}$. And standardly, for any ordinal $n \geqslant 1$, W^n will denote the set of all sequences of n elements of W. We note that the full generality of the notation given below will not be utilized in the syntax of the core language itself, but it will be used in various of the extensions of that language to be proposed later.

DEFINITION 1. SF_L, or the set of *subcategorization features of L*, is $\{\{\mathrm{proper}\}\}$.

DEFINITION 2. CAT, or the set of *category names of L*, is the least set of finite sequences chosen from $\mathrm{SF}_L \cup \{\text{'}N\text{'}, \text{'}P\text{'}, \text{'}/\text{'}, \text{'}-\text{'}, \text{'})\text{'}, \text{'}(\text{'}\}$ which satisfies conditions (i) through (iv) below:

    (i)   'N' $\in$ CAT and 'P' $\in$ CAT
    (ii) if $X \in$ CAT and $f \in \mathrm{SF}_L$ then $\frac{X}{f} \in$ CAT, where $\frac{X}{f}$ abbreviates the sequence $\langle X, f \rangle$
    (iii) if $X \in$ CAT then $\bar{X} \in$ CAT, where $\bar{X}$ abbreviates the sequence $\langle X, - \rangle$
    (iv) if $X \in \mathrm{CAT}^n$ and $Y \in \mathrm{CAT}^n$, any ordinal $n \geqslant 1$, then $(X/Y) \in$ CAT

Discussion of the Definition

(i) The notation for subcategories mentioned in clause (ii) above requires that f be a non-empty set of features. In writings we shall normally omit the set brackets. As the core language L is extended we shall add more elements to SF_L robbing it of its currently trivial character (there is only one element, {proper}, in SF_L as currently defined).

(ii) In clause (iv) above X and Y are both n-ary sequences of elements of CAT. For the case where $n = 1$ this rule coincides with the standard one in categorial grammar, since then CAT^n is just CAT^1 which is in effect just CAT, so X and Y are elements of CAT and X/Y names the category of expressions which combine with ones of category Y to form ones of category X.

Consider now the case for $n = 2$. Then X is a sequence of two category names, say $\langle X_1, X_2 \rangle$. Similarly $Y = \langle Y_1, Y_2 \rangle$, and X/Y is $\langle X_1, X_2 \rangle / \langle Y_1, Y_2 \rangle$. Expressions in the category named by this complex symbol will combine with ones of category Y_1 to form expressions of category X_1, and they will combine with ones of category Y_2 to form expressions of category X_2. And more generally for $X, Y \in CAT^n$, expressions of category X/Y will combine with expressions of category Y_i to form expressions of category X_i, all i $(1 \leqslant i \leqslant n)$. The utility of this notation, which will not be used in the core language but will be used in various of its extensions, will be illustrated shortly.

(iii) In terms of the slash notation in clause (iv) we may define certain natural classes of category names which will be useful both in the syntax of L, and, more importantly, in the semantics for L, These classes will be called *predicative hierarchies*.

DEFINITION 3. For all $C \in CAT$ and all non-negative integers n,

(i) $C_0 =_{df} C$ and
(ii) $C_{n+1} =_{df} C_n/\bar{N}$

For each $C \in CAT$, the set of C_n as defined above will be called the *predicative hierarchy generated by* C and denoted PH_C.

The elements on the left side of the equality sign above are new category names introduced into our notation for convenience. Thus C_0 'abbreviates' C, C_1 abbreviates $C_0/\bar{N}$, etc. Intuitively an expression of category C_{n+1} will combine with an expression of category $\bar{N}$ to form a C_n. 'Ultimately' then a C_{n+1} combines with $n + 1$ expressions of category $\bar{N}$ to form a C_0, that is, a C. Thus C_n is the category of n-place C's. In particular P_n is the category name for n-place predicates. So P_0 $(= P)$ is the name for the zero place predicates, i.e. the formulas. P_1 $(= P_0/\bar{N})$ is the name for the one place predicates, P_2 $(= P_1/\bar{N})$ the name for the two place predicates, etc. And in general, the predicative hierarchy generated by P, namely $\{P_n : n \geqslant 0\}$ is the set of n-place predicate categories of L.

Notice of course that other categories besides P determine predicative hierarchies. That generated by N, namely $\{N_0, N_1, \ldots\}$ is the set of n-place common noun phrases. N_0 of course is just N. N_1 is $N_0/\overline{N}$. In the extensions of L we propose expressions like *friend (of)*, *cousin (of)*, etc. will have this category. They will thus combine with full noun phrases like *John, every student*, etc. to form N_0's like *friend of every student*, etc. And these expressions, like lexically simple N_0's, will combine with determiners like *a, every*, etc. to form $\overline{N}$'s, e.g. *a friend of every student*, etc.

Similarly in extensions of L the category N/N, abbreviated AP for Adjective Phrase, determines a predicative hierarchy. AP_1 for example will include 'transitive' adjectives like *fond (of)*, *jealous (of)*, etc., which combine with full noun phrases to form complex adjective phrases, AP_0's, like *fond of Mary*, etc.

The notion of a predicative hierarchy is both a technically useful one and one which makes a substantive suggestion concerning how complex expressions may be formed in semantically regular ways from simpler ones in natural language. Technically, it allows us to extend L by big steps easily giving a more adequate approximation to the complexity of natural languages. In particular once we have provided a semantics for a category C, we have a regular way to assign interpretations to C_n's for every n, regardless of what category C is. In particular given a semantics for C_n the semantics we associate with C_{n+1} is determined. We illustrate this in L with the most productive case of predicatives, the P_n's. In more substantive terms it seems that natural languages actually avail themselves of this operation of forming a C_{n+1} from a C_n, independently of the nature of C. Thus our notation suggests, correctly, that we may expect to find one place common nouns, one place adjectives, etc. in languages.

(iv) Let us consider now the advantages of our generalized notation for forming slash categories. In the simplest cases, subject to some restrictions, it allows us to represent expressions which, naively, have more than one category. Consider for example *be*. On the one hand it appears to be a P_2, combining with an $\overline{N}$ such as *a student* to form a P_1 *is a student* (which we write as *be a student* since verb agreement is not represented in the system). On the other hand it combines with AP's like *female* to form P_1's like *be female*. In our notation then we may assign *be* directly to the category $\langle P_1, P_1 \rangle / \langle \overline{N}, AP \rangle$ rather than having to say for example that English has two *be*'s, one which combines with $\overline{N}$'s to form P_1's, the other which combines with AP's to form P_1's. Moreover once *prepositional phrases* (PP's) such as *in the garden* are added to L it is a simple matter to extend the category of *be* to $\langle P_1, P_1, P_1 \rangle / \langle \bar{N}, AP, PP \rangle$. Somewhat more interestingly, consider the case of PP's themselves. They appear to combine with P_1's to form P_1's, i.e. *sing* and *sing in the garden* are both expressions of category P_1. We shall argue further that PP's should also be allowed to combine directly with P_2's to form P_2's, i.e. we shall treat both *find* and *find in the garden* as P_2's[1]. The natural suggestion then is that PP's may combine generally with P_n's to form P_n's. We may then assign such expressions to the category X/X, where X is the infinite sequence $\langle P_1, P_2, \dots \rangle$. More speculative but possibly deeper uses of this notation will be presented in the intensional logic (Section II).

(v) The notation in Definition 2 for deriving complex category names from simpler ones is semantically motivated. Specifically, in the semantics for L we will associate with each $C \in$ CAT a set of possible denotations (relative to a model) for expressions in the category named by C. This set will be called *the type for* C and denoted T_C. Now the types we associate with complex category names are defined in terms of those we associate with the names they are derived from. In general in L the following dependencies hold: the type for a category of the form $\frac{X}{f}$ will be a subset of T_X, the type for X; just which subset is determined by the interpretation of the features in f. The type for a category of the form $\bar{X}$ will be $(T_X)^*$, the power set of T_X. (This dependency will be somewhat generalized in the intensional logic.) And the type of a category of the form X/Y will be some set of functions f whose domain is the union of the T_{Y_i}, for all Y_i in the sequence Y, whose range is $\bigcup T_{X_i}$, and whose value at any y is in T_{X_i} if y is in T_{Y_i}.

(vi) Notice finally a technical usage in Definition 2. We define CAT to be the 'least' subset of a certain set satisfying certain conditions. Formally the least subset of a set A satisfying some conditions F is the intersection of all the subsets K of A satisfying these conditions. Having given the definition in this way we must of course show that the intersection is in fact a set satisfying F. In the case at hand the proof is easy and will be omitted.

In defining the language L itself we shall have occasion to use a somewhat more complicated form of taking 'least' sets. Specifically we shall define a naming functon n from CAT into the sets of possible expressions over the basic vocabulary V. n will be defined to be the least function satisfying certain conditions. In general the use of 'least' here is to be interpreted as follows. Given sets A and B, consider the set G of functions from A into B^*, the power set of B, which satisfy certain conditions K. The *least function* from A into B^* satisfying K is, by definition, that function f whose value at each $a \in A$ is the intersection of the $g(a)$, taken over all $g \in G$. This clearly defines f to be a function from A into B^*, but of course we must prove that f so defined satisfies K.

Defining V and PE_V

DEFINITION 4. V, or the *basic vocabulary* of L, is the set

> {*and, or, not, John, Mary, man, woman, student, bachelor, existent, sleep, exist, die, walk, laugh, kill, kiss, hug, be, every, all, a, some, no, the*}

To define the possible expressions over V recall from the Overview that derived expressions in this system, in distinction to many others, are not formed by concatenation but merely by taking sets of simpler expressions. Thus our representation for *John is sleeping* will be the set {*John, sleep*} and not the string (⌒John⌒sleep⌒).

DEFINITION 5. PE_V, or the set of *possible expressions over V*, is recursively defined by the following conditions:

(i) If $x \in V$ then $x \in PE_V$.
(ii) If $Y \subseteq PE_V$ is finite then $Y \in PE_V$.

Definition 5 could have been given somewhat more rigorously, but in fact its exact nature plays little role in what follows.[2] We need PE_V simply to provide a domain inside of which the categories of L may be defined.

Let us sketch the argument that {*John*, {*kiss, Mary*}} is an element of PE_V. From Definition 4 we have that *kiss* and *Mary* are elements of V and so in PE_V by (i). Thus {kiss, Mary} $\subseteq PE_V$ and so by (ii) is an element of PE_V. Since *John* $\in V$ and so in PE_V by (i), we have that {*John*, {*kiss, Mary*}} is a subset of PE_V and so in PE_V by (ii). On the other hand PE_V abounds with absurdities such as {and, {{{and}}}. Such possible expressions will not be in any category named by any $C \in CAT$ and thus will not be expressions in L.

Defining L

The categories of L will be those subsets of PE_V named by the naming function n defined below:

DEFINITION 6. n is the least function from CAT into $(PE_V)^*$ satisfying the conditions given in (i) through (iv) below:

- (i) *Lexical Conditions*
  $\{John, Mary\} \subseteq n(\bar{N}_{prop})$
  $\{man, woman, student, bachelor, existent, individual\} \subseteq n(N)$
  $\{sleep, exist, die, walk, laugh\} \subseteq n(P_1)$
  $\{kiss, hug, be, have, kill\} \subseteq n(P_2)$
  $\{every, all, a, some, no, the\} \subseteq n(\bar{N}/N)$
- (ii) *Subcategory Conditions*
  For all $C \in$ CAT and all $f \in SF_L$, $n(C) \subseteq n(C)$
- (iii) *Conditions on Functional Applications*
  For all ordinals $k \geqslant 1$, all $X, Y \in CAT^k$, and all $e, e' \in PE_V$, if $e \in n(X/Y)$ and $e' \in Y_i$, Y_i the ith term in the sequence Y, then $\{e, e'\} \in n(X_i)$, X_i the ith term in the sequence X.
- (iv) *Conditions on Boolean Combinations*
  For all $C \neq \bar{N}_{prop}$ in CAT, all $e, e' \in PE_V$,
  if $e \in n(C)$ and $e' \in n(C)$ then $\{e, and, e'\} \in n(C)$,
  $\{e, or, e'\} \in n(C)$, and $\{not, e\} \in n(C)$.

We note without proof that n as defined is in fact a function from CAT into $(PE_V)^*$ which satisfies conditions (i) through (iv).

DEFINITION 7. Cat, or the *categories* of L, = $\{n(C): C \in CAT\}$

DEFINITION 8. $L = \bigcup Cat$

Remarks on the Definitions

(i) We shall henceforth *use* the elements of CAT to refer to the categories (elements of Cat) which they name. Thus we shall write *man* $\in N$ rather than *man* $\in n(N)$.

(ii) Note that *and, or*, and *not* are not members of any category. Such expressions will be called *syncategorematic*. The only syncategorematic elements of V are *and, or*, and *not*.

(iii) It follows from Definition 6 that the only non-empty categories of L are N, $\bar{N}$, $\bar{N}_{prop}$, $\bar{N}/N$, P_0, P_1, and P_2. Of these, all but P_0 have lexical members, that is elements which are also in the basic vocabulary V. In the extensions of L we propose other categories will become non-empty in either of two ways: one, we shall add new items to V and new lexical conditions (rules) assigning them to categories currently empty, and two, a few new types of rules (conditions) will be added allowing us to form derived expressions in P_n for all finite n, as well as N_n for all finite n.

(iv) The categories mentioned in clause (iv) of Definition 6 will be called *boolean categories*. Thus all categories of L are boolean except $\bar{N}_{\text{prop}}$. Note that by the Subcategory rule (clause (ii) of Definition 6) all elements of $\bar{N}_{\text{prop}}$ are also elements of $\bar{N}$. Thus the expression $\{John, and, Mary\}$ is an element of $\bar{N}$ but not of $\bar{N}_{\text{prop}}$. The formal argument that this is so is as follows: By lexical rule both *John* and *Mary* are elements of $\bar{N}_{\text{prop}}$. By the subcategory rule then both are elements of $\bar{N}$; thus by the rule of boolean combinations $\{John, and, Mary\}$ is an element of $\bar{N}$. We may represent this argument informally by the following (unordered!) tree:

(1)

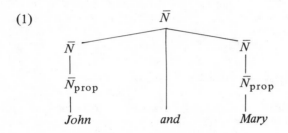

(v) Similarly the unordered tree in (2) below represents the argument that $\{\{every, student\}, sleep\}$ is an expression in L of category P_0 (Formula).

(2)

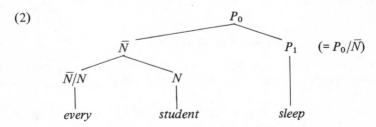

(vi) In presenting complex expressions of L certain liberties will be taken with our notation in the interests of readability. In particular we will commonly use ordinary parentheses instead of curly brackets; outer parentheses will often be omitted, as will commas. Thus the expression represented in (2) above will usually be presented informally simply as (*every student*) *sleep*.

Recalling that within a constituent linear order is not defined we might also represent this expression as *(student every) sleep* or *sleep (student every)*. But we could not use *every sleep student* or *student sleep every*.

(vii) In illustrating examples of complex expressions we shall sometimes use lexical items of English not included in *V* when it is obvious to which category they belong. Thus we may consider that English expressions like *John greeted and either hugged or kissed Mary* are represented in *L* as illustrated in (3):

(3)

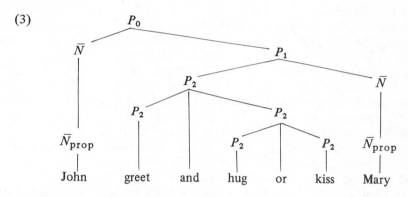

(viii) As an exercise in our notation the reader may find it instructive to construct representations for the following English sentences: *Not every student is sleeping, Every man kissed a woman, John is a man, John is not a man, John but not Bill read the book, Some student was singing and dancing, Some student was singing and some student was dancing.* Note that *not every student* may be generated in two different ways on our syntax: *(not (every student))*, in which *not* combines with an $\bar{N}$ to form an $\bar{N}$, or *((not every) student)*, in which *not* combines with a Det (= $\bar{N}/N$) to form a Det.

(ix) Finally it is instructive to contrast the syntax of *L* with that of standard first order logic (FOL) as regards its similarity to English.

(4) a. Eng: John loves no student
        L: (John (love (no student)))
        FOL: $(\forall x)$ (student $(x) \rightarrow$ not (love (John, x)))
     b. Eng: John but not Bill kissed Mary
        L: (John and (not Bill)) (kiss Mary)
        FOL: (kiss (John, Mary)) and (not (kiss (Bill, Mary)))

Intuitively L-representations of English correspond much more closely to English than do those of FOL. Perhaps the most striking difference is that 'Quantifiers' like *every, no*, etc. in L combine directly with common nouns to form full noun phrases as in English, whereas quantifiers in FOL are necessarily constructed with a variable and do not form constituents with common nouns. Thus (4a) and its L-representation contain no variables, whereas its FOL-representation does. Note that in this respect L resembles the languages used in Montague Grammar and this resemblence is not accidental: in the semantics we use for quantified $\bar{N}$'s we have availed ourselves of Montague's basic intuition which enabled him to treat *John* and *every man* as having the same (gross) logical category. Note also in this regard that treating quantifiers as formula level operators in FOL forces it to render complex noun phrases as formulas combined by logical connectives with others formulas. Thus the FOL-representation of (4a) uses a connective, $\rightarrow$ (if-then) not present in the English sentence or its L-representation. Note that the FOL-representation of (4a) contains four properly embedded formulas, whereas neither (4a) nor its L-representation contain any.

A second major difference between L and FOL concerns the productivity of the boolean operators *and, or*, and *not*. L, like English, allows essentially all categories to form complex members with these operators. FOL on the other hand, and by and large Montague Grammar as well, restrict these operators to formulas. Thus the L-representation of (4b) is largely isomorphic to (4b)[3] whereas its FOL representation again contains a multiplicity of properly embedded formulas. As noted in the Overview, one of the innovations of our semantics is the provision of a general method for interpreting *and, or*, and *not* regardless of the category of item they combine with. The semantics needed to do this turns out to be enlightening as regards the semantics of many categories not apparently related to the boolean operators, such as adjective phrases, n-place predicates, and predicative hierarchies generally.

In these respects, English resembles L more closely than it resembles FOL. On the other side of the ledger, English shares with FOL but not with L the structure of linear order. However, in the face of the massive differences between the syntax of English and the syntax of FOL, the presence of linear order in the latter does not seem to confer upon it a great deal of similarity to English.

Overall then, noting principally the absence of tense and aspect marking in L, it appears that the semantic structures represented by L can be integrated rather easily into a general grammar of English. Considering only the limited fragment of English we have (so far) intended to represent it should not be difficult for example to define an interpreting function from English into *L* which associates with English sentences *L*-structures which represent their meanings.

We turn now to the semantics of *L*.

2. THE SEMANTICS FOR *L*

We shall provide a semantics for *L* in two steps. First, we shall associate with each category *C* of *L* a set of possible denotations for expressions in that category called *the type for C* and denoted T_C. As indicated earlier, the types for complex categories will be given in terms of the types of those categories from which they are formed. The types for the primitive categories, N_0 (= *N*) or the zero place common noun phrases, and P_0 or the zero place predicates (formulas), are defined directly, not in terms of other types, and thus constitute the semantic primitives, or as we shall sometimes say, the *ontology*, of *L*.

Once the types are defined we shall define the notion of an *interpretation* of *L*. Basically this will be a function *m* which associates with each expression *e* in a category *C* some element of the set T_C subject of course to certain conditions. In particular the value of *m* at complex expressions such as *John and Mary, every student*, etc. will be determined by its values at the expressions the complex ones are formed from. On the other hand, the values of *m* at lexically simple expressions can be any element of the corresponding types, subject only to certain lexical constraints. Thus some lexical symbols, such as *every, exist*, etc. are intuitively logical constants, and will be interpreted by *m* as designated members of their types. Further, the value of *m* at certain lexical symbols is constrained relative to that of others, e.g. the interpretation of *bachelor* is not independent of that of *man*, etc.

As will be clear in what follows, the most fundamental step in defining a semantics for *L* lies in the definitions of the types. Once they are given, the interpretations of expressions by elements in the types is very largely obvious.

Before defining the types it will be well to recall the basic descriptive adequacy criteria in terms of which we evaluate whether a proposed semantics for a fragment of English is adequate or not. This criterion is simply that the entailment relations among sentences of English must be correctly characterized. For example, pretheoretically, (5a) below is judged to entail (5b), but the converse entailment fails.

(5)   a. Some student is both singing and dancing.
        b. Some student is singing.

Informally, to say that (5a) entails (5b) is just to say that (5b) is true whenever (5a) is; that is, if the world is the way (5a) says it is, we are guaranteed
that it is the way (5b) says it is. The converse, however, fails: it is certainly
possible that some student is singing without there being any student who
is both singing and dancing. Now L provides representations for these sentences, and in the semantics for L we formally define an entailment relation.
If our semantics is adequate for these English sentences it must be the case
that our formal representation of (5a) formally entails that for (5b) but not
conversely. To the extent that this is not the case our semantics is incorrect.

We might note here that one enlightening aspect of our semantics is that
it provides basic semantic relations (e.g. entailment) for essentially all categories, not just P_0. Thus a more general, informal, way of saying that (5a)
above entails (5b) is to say that the information in (5b) is contained in that
of (5a). To claim (5a) is to claim everything in (5b), and something more
besides. Let us say then that (5a) is *more informative* than (5b).

And notice now that in the same intuitive sense, the P_1 of (5a), namely
is singing and dancing, is also more informative than that in (5b), *is singing*,
i.e. *is singing and dancing* says more about an arbitrary individual than
does *is singing*. Similarly compare common noun phrases like *man* and *tall
man*. Intuitively the latter has more information in it than the former; any
individual which has the property expressed by *tall man* necessarily has the
property expressed by *man*.

Thus in the semantics we provide, we define an *informativeness* relation
which obtains among elements e and e' in any boolean category. This relation
coincides with classical entailment when e and e' are chosen from the category
P_0.

Defining the Types for L

Our definition of the types is given quite simply in a single paragraph (p.
103). That presentation, however, has two properties which will be unfamiliar
to some readers. First it uses certain elementary concepts of boolean algebra,
ones which in fact are all familiar from set theory, but which may appear
unfamiliar when given in the more general notation of boolean algebra.
Consequently our presentation of the types will include what we hope is
a minimally sufficient explication of the boolean concepts used.

Second, the ontological primitives of our system do not include entities or individuals, i.e. proper noun denotations. Proper noun denotations, henceforth called *individuals*, are characterized in terms of common noun denotations, henceforth called *extensional properties* (or more simply, *properties*, as these are the only kinds of properties considered in *L*). In our presentation of the types we shall provide a basic justification of this point. Here we simply note without discussion that taking properties rather than individuals (or entities) as primitive simplifies the ontology of *L* compared to that of other systems and permits a better correspondence between English forms and the logical forms of *L*. It does not however change the class of valid arguments representable in *L*. Thus *L* is a strictly first order extensional logic which differs from classical logic (for the moment) only in not providing for non-trivial uses of variable binding operators. We shall of course extend *L* to include these, in which case then all arguments shown to be valid in classical logic are valid in *L*. As we further extend *L* of course its expressive power will exceed that of classical logic.

The Type for P_0 or Formulas

In standard first order logic (FOL) the formula denotations are given by the set $\{0, 1\}$ of truth value ($0 = $ *false*, $1 = $ *true*). The identity of these two objects is irrelevant to the logic; it is sufficient that they are distinct and that one of them is designated as *true*, the other as *false*. It is important to realize however that the set of truth values in FOL is always treated as possessing a boolean structure, though different formulations of FOL differ with regard to how explicitly they codify this structure in the formal statement of the semantics for complex formulas. But all approaches must say in one way or another that a conjunction of formulas is true iff each conjunct is true, a disjunction is true iff at least one of the disjuncts is true, and a negation of a formula is true iff the formula negated is false. Thus, details of formalism aside, all approaches may be described as ones in which formulas are interpreted as truth values, i.e. an interpreting function for the language, which we call m, maps formulas into $\{0, 1\}$, a set we henceforth refer to simply as 2. And all approaches say in effect that where S and T are formulas, $m(S \text{ and } T)$, the interpretation of the conjunction of S with T, is given as some function, call it $\wedge$, of $m(S)$ and $m(T)$. The function is defined of course by the standard truth table for conjunction. Explicitly, writing the function symbol between its arguments, we have that $(1 \wedge 1) = 1$, and $(1 \wedge 0) = (0 \wedge 1) = (0 \wedge 0) = 0$. Then the definition of the interpretating function m applied to conjunctions of formulas is given by $m(S \text{ and } T) = m(S) \wedge m(T)$. Similarly the interpretation of disjunctions is given by $m(S \text{ or } T) = m(S) \vee m(T)$, where $\vee$ is the following binary function on truth values: $(0 \vee 0) = 0$ and $(0 \vee 1) = (1 \vee 0) = (1 \vee 1) = 1$. Finally, $m(not \ S)$ is defined to be $(m(S))'$, where the $'$ function (called complement) is defined by $1' = 0$ and $0' = 1$.

Thus in FOL, the set of truth values is taken to be a set with two distinct elements on which are defined two binary functions, $\wedge$ and $\vee$, which we shall call *meet* and *join* respectively, and one unary function $'$, called here *complement*. This just says that the type for formulas in FOL is a boolean algebra of a particularly simple sort. To see this let us give a formal definition of a boolean algebra:

DEFINITION 9. β is a boolean algebra iff β is a six-tuple $\langle B, 0_\beta, 1_\beta, \wedge_\beta, \vee_\beta, '_\beta \rangle$ where B is a non-empty set called the *domain* of the algebra β, 0_β and 1_β are elements of B, called the *zero* and *unit* elements respectively, $\wedge_\beta$ and $\vee_\beta$ are binary functions on B (i.e. functions from $B \times B$ into B) called *meet* and *join* respectively, and $'_\beta$ is a unary function on B called *complement*, which satisfy the following conditions. (We omit the subscript β in the statement of the conditions): For all $x, y, z \in B$,

(a) $0 \neq 1$
(b) $x \wedge y = y \wedge x$ (Commutativity Laws)
   $x \vee y = y \vee x$
(c) $(x \wedge (y \vee z)) = (x \wedge y) \vee (x \wedge z)$ (Distributivity laws)
   $(x \vee (y \wedge z)) = (x \vee y) \wedge (x \vee z)$
(d) *Complement laws*
   $(x \wedge x') = 0$
   $(x \vee x') = 1$
(e) *Laws of zero and unit*
   $(x \vee 0) = x$
   $(x \wedge 1) = x$

(We shall adopt here the common practice of referring to a boolean algebra by the name we use for its domain. In cases where we have different algebras with the same domain this would lead to confusion, but such cases will not arise in this paper.) The reader may easily verify that the set 2 (= $\{0, 1\}$) is (the domain of) a boolean algebra, where the zero and unit elements are 0 and 1 respectively, and the meet, join, and complement functions are defined by the standard truth tables for conjunction, disjunction, and negation respectively. Assuming these definitions we may state this formally as follows:

(6) $\langle 2, 0_2, 1_2, \wedge_2, \vee_2, '_2 \rangle$ is a boolean algebra.

To verify the truth of (6) we must show of course that the boolean axioms are satisfied. Clearly $0_2 \neq 1_2$ since we defined 0_2 to be 0 and 1_2 to be 1, and these two elements of 2 $(= \{0, 1\})$ were taken as distinct. So axiom (a) is satisfied. The other axioms are easily seen to hold by examining cases. For example, the first commutativity law states that for all $x, y \in 2$, $(x \wedge y)$ is the same element of 2 as $(y \wedge x)$. Clearly is both x and y are 1 then the definition of $\wedge$ in the algebra 2 tells us that $(x \wedge y) = 1$ and $(y \wedge x) = 1$, so they are equal. If either x or y are 0 then $(x \wedge y)$ is 0 and so is $(y \wedge x)$, so again $(x \wedge y) = (y \wedge x)$. The other axioms are easily checked the same way.

We might note in passing that 2 is the *smallest* boolean algebra, in the following sense. According to Definition 9, every boolean algebra B contains at least two elements, namely 0 and 1. The algebra 2 contains *only* these two elements. Any algebra which is fundamentally distinct from 2 must have some elements in addition to these two.[4]

We have just seen that the set 2 of the possible interpretations of formulas of FOL can be regarded as a boolean algebra. We now take this algebra 2 to be our set T_{P_0}, that is, the type for formulas for our language L.

We might ask, why go to the trouble of formally specifying T_{P_0} as a boolean algebra? One answer that we can give now (others will come later) is that boolean algebraic structure will represent the semantic generalization we need in order to interpret boolean combinations in essentially all categories in a uniform way. Whenever the type for a category C is a boolean algebra we will always interpret conjunctions of expressions in C as the meet of the interpretations of the conjuncts. Similarly disjunctions will be interpreted as joins, and negations as complements.

For example, if $T_{\bar{N}}$ is a boolean algebra, then the interpretation of the $\bar{N}$ *John and Mary* can be taken to be the meet of the interpretations of the $\bar{N}$'s *John* and *Mary*. Similarly, if T_{P_1} is a boolean algebra, then the interpretation of *sing and dance* can be taken to be the meet of the interpretations of *sing* and of *dance*. Similar statements can be made for expressions of various categories constructed with *or* and with *not*.

One consequence of such an approach can be seen immediately. Namely, the axioms of boolean algebra will guarantee that certain pairs of expressions will have identical interpretations. For example it follows from the first distributive law that the interpretation of (*John and* (*Bill or Harry*)) is the same element of $T_{\bar{N}}$ as the interpretation of ((*John and Bill*) *or* (*John and Harry*)). This is empirically correct; for example, because these two expressions must have identical interpretations, it will follow that the formulas ((*John and* (*Bill or Harry*)) (*read the book*)) and (((*John and Bill*) *or* (*John and Harry*)) (*read the book*)) must have the same truth value.

Note, therefore, that in L (and in English) the meaning of *and* (and *or* and *not*) is not simply some way of relating sentence meanings. Rather, the meaning of *and* is much more general and much more abstract, for it relates meanings drawn from essentially *any* type. Its meaning is category independent, since no matter what type is chosen, *and* relates pairs of meanings from that type in the same way, namely, in the way expressed by the meet operation in boolean algebra. Analogous claims hold of course for *or* and *not*. They express ways we think about things of whatever type rather than 'intrinsic' properties or relations of things themselves. This suggests that the meanings of *and, or*, and *not* are a direct reflection of properties of the human mind. As George Boole wrote many years ago, they represent 'Laws of Thought' (Boole, 1854). In any event, even if the reader is not prepared to extrapolate with us from the ubiquity of *and, or*, and *not* to laws of thought, he must concede that very few expressions of natural language may combine with elements of almost any category to form derived elements in that category, and that in consequence we are motivated to find an interpretation for these elements which does not depend on the specific denotations of the elements in the categories they combine with. We shall achieve just such a characterization of the meanings of *and, or*, and *not* by taking the types for most categories to be boolean algebras. The algebra used for formulas thus represents only a very special case of a general semantic property of human languages.

While we shall have more to say about the type for P_0 later let us now consider the somewhat trickier types for N, $\bar{N}$, and $\bar{N}_{\text{prop}}$.

The Types for N, $\bar{N}$, and $\bar{N}_{\text{prop}}$

To present these types let us consider first, in so far as possible, the corresponding types in FOL. In addition to 2, FOL takes as a semantic primitive a non-empty set U called the *universe of discourse*. Elements of U will be referred to here as *entities*. As U can be any non-empty set it possesses essentially no structure, in distinction to 2 which possesses a rich if minimal boolean structure. Semantically U is taken as the set of possible denotations of individual constants, approximately the proper nouns of natural languages, and the range of the individual variables. In our terminology then FOL takes the type for $\bar{N}_{prop}$ as U, a semantic primitive.

Common nouns, not distinguished from P_1's in FOL, are thought of as subsets of U, or equivalently functions from U into 2. On the former view, a N such as *man* will be interpreted as a subset of U and the predicate *man* will hold of an entity x just in case x is a member of that subset. On the latter view, *man* holds of x iff the function *man* is interpreted as maps x onto 1. For simplicity of presentation let us adopt for the nonce the former view, in which *man* is a subset of U. Then the set of possible denotations of N's (= P_1's) is U^*, the power set of U, that is the collection of all the subsets of U. Note that U^* includes both $\emptyset$, the empty set, and U itself, (taken $\neq \emptyset$). In our terminology, then, $T_N = T_{P_1} = U^*$ in FOL.

Notice, now, that power sets are examples of boolean algebras par excellence. Indeed much of the development of modern boolean algebra has been inspired by their use as abstractions or generalizations of ordinary set theory. Thus note:

(7)   For S a non-empty set, $\langle S^*, \emptyset, S, \cap, \cup, ' \rangle$ is a boolean algebra, where S^* is the power set of S, the zero element of the algebra is the empty set $\emptyset$, the unit is S itself, meet is ordinary intersection, join is union, and complement is set theoretic complement relative to S.[5]

To see that the six-tuple in (7) above is a boolean algebra note first that the zero and unit, $\emptyset$ and S respectively, are elements of S^*, the domain of the algebra, since each is a subset of S and S^* is the collection of all the subsets of S. Further $\cap$, $\cup$, and $'$ are functions of the right degree on S^*, e.g. $\cap$ maps pairs of elements $A, B \in S^*$ onto $A \cap B$, those elements of S which are in both A and B; thus $A \cap B$ is a subset of S and so an element of S^*. To see that the boolean axioms are satisfied we note first that since S was taken as non-empty, $\emptyset \neq S$, i.e. the zero and unit elements of the algebra S^* are distinct. The remaining axioms are elementary truths of set theory. E.g. the first distributivity law just states $(A \cap (B \cup C)) = (A \cap B) \cup (A \cap C)$ for all elements $A, B, C \in S^*$.

Consequently by taking T_N in FOL to be U^*, we have in effect taken it to be a boolean algebra, specifically a power set algebra. Again of course we might ask why go to the trouble to specify that U^* is a boolean algebra under the set theoretic operations given above. The answer is essentially the same as the one we gave earlier to the comparable question concerning T_{P_0}. Here we may only note that if, e.g., *sing* and *dance* are interpreted as subsets of U, then we can within the framework of FOL define boolean combinations of P_1's in a natural way. For example *sing and dance* would just be interpreted as the intersection of the set which interprets *sing* with that which interprets *dance*. Thus *sing and dance* would hold of an entity x iff x was in that set, which from the definition of intersection is so just in case x is in each of the sets over which the intersection is taken, that is, x is in the *sing* set and also in the *dance* set. And this is just to say that *sing and dance* holds of x iff both *sing* does and *dance* does. So taking the type for P_1 as a boolean algebra allows us to generate boolean combinations of P_1's and to directly interpret them as meets, joins, and complements.[6]

Consider now the more problematic type for $\bar{N}$. FOL as we have noted, has no such category, although it does have the equivalent of a subcategory of it, $\bar{N}_{\mathrm{prop}}$. It is clear however that we could not merely modify the syntax of FOL to create more complex elements in $\bar{N}_{\mathrm{prop}}$, however, since U, the type for $\bar{N}_{\mathrm{prop}}$, is simply not big enough to provide denotations for complex $\bar{N}$'s like *every man*. Imagine for example a U with just two members, say John and Bill, and let *man* be interpreted as U itself (so everything which exists in that universe is a man). Then if all complex $\bar{N}$'s were to take their denotations in U, *every man* would have to denote either John or Bill, say John. Then *every man is John* would be true, which it obviously isn't since Bill is a man and he is not John.

On the other hand, since *John* and *every man* are both syntactically $\bar{N}$'s we want them to take their denotations in the same type in order that we may give the interpretations of sentences as a function of their form.

A solution to this problem was provided by Montague (1970), a solution which we essentially adopt, but with certain changes. Let us, following Montague's intuition for the moment, think of proper nouns not as denoting elements of U, but rather as denoting the collection of subsets of U which contain a fixed element. Specifically, proper noun denotations, which we shall now call *individuals*, may be defined by the following temporary definition:

DEFINITION 10. For all $x \in U$, $I_x =_{\mathrm{df}} \{K \subseteq U: x \in K\}$. I_x will be called the *individual generated by* x. We then define $T_{\bar{N}\mathrm{prop}}$ to be $\{I_x: x \in U\}$.

Note that each element of an I_x is a subset of U, that is an element of $T_N = U^*$. So each I_x is itself a subset of T_N, and thus a member of $(T_N)^*$, the power set of T_N. Referring neutrally to the elements of T_N as (extensional) properties, we may thus think of the denotation of *John* as the set of properties which hold of some fixed element of U. And obviously enough the elements of U are in a one-to-one correspondence with the set of individuals. For given each x in U there exists an individual I_x. If x and y are distinct elements of U then I_x and I_y are distinct individuals, since I_x contains $\{x\}$ as a member but I_y doesn't, and I_y contains $\{y\}$ as a member, but I_x doesn't.

Now given this one-to-one correspondence it is trivial to modify the semantics of the P_n's. P_1's for example can be thought of as subsets of the set of individuals (rather than subsets of U, the set of entities): equivalently they are functions from the set of individuals into 2. Thus for each predicate of entities on the old view we have a corresponding predicate of individuals on the new view: we just replace the statements mentioning entities x by statements mentioning individuals I_x.

So far it just seems that we have copied over the old semantics in a more complicated notation. But now we can achieve the goal of interpreting proper nouns and complex $\bar{N}$'s in the same type. For example given that *John* and *Mary* are interpreted as individuals, say I_x and I_y respectively, we may now interpret John and Mary as $I_x \cap I_y$, the set of properties which I_x (John) and I_y (Mary) have in common. Similarly *John or Mary* can be interpreted as the union of I_x with I_y, the set of properties true of John or of Mary. Finally, *not John* can be interpreted as $(I_x)'$, the set of properties which John does not have.

Similarly, if we allow unbounded intersections and unions, we can interpret words like *every* and *a*. To see how this is done, let p be the subset of U which interprets *man*. Then *every man* will be the set of properties which all the individuals with the man property have in common. Formally, *every man* denotes $\bigcap\{I_x\colon p \in I_x\}$. In a parallel fashion, we can say that *a man* denotes the set of all those properties each of which holds of at least one individual with the man property (that is, at least one man). Formally, *a man* denotes $\bigcup\{I_x\colon p \in I_x\}$. Note that a property p is a member of an individual I_x iff $x \in p$, since p is a subset of U and I_x is the set of all the subsets of U which contain x as a member. Thus we might also write the denotation of *every man* above $\bigcap\{I_x\colon x \in p\}$, and analogously for *a man*.

In discussing these denotations we have referred to unbounded intersections and unions. As these operations will come up again, let us give a more formal definition of them:

DEFINITION 11. Given a set B, let K be a collection of subsets of B.

Then,

$$\text{a. } \bigcap K =_{\text{df}} \{x \in B: \quad \text{for all} \quad k \in K, x \in k\} \quad \text{and}$$
$$\text{b. } \bigcup K =_{\text{df}} \{x \in B: \quad \text{for some} \quad k \in K, x \in k\}.$$

Thus an object is in the intersection of a collection of sets just in case it is in each set over which the intersection is taken. And it is in the union of a collection of sets just in case it is in at least one of the sets over which the union is taken. Notice also the following useful notation. For K as above, we often write $\bigcap K$ as $\bigcap_{k \in K} k$ and $\bigcup K$ as $\bigcup_{k \in K} k$.

Consider now what the type for $\bar{N}$ should be on this view. It must include as elements all the individuals, as proper nouns are among the $\bar{N}$'s and they denote individuals. As noted these individuals are subsets of T_N, thus elements of $(T_N)^*$, the power set of T_N. Moreover we want $T_{\bar{N}}$ to be closed under complements and unbounded intersections and unions in order to provide denotations for negative $\bar{N}$'s such as *not a student* (= *no student*), *not every student*, etc. and for universally quantified $\bar{N}$'s like *every student* and existentially quantified $\bar{N}$'s like *a student*. Thus we want $T_{\bar{N}}$ not only to include all the individuals but also all the sets of properties obtainable from individuals by taking complements, and unbounded intersections and unions. We will see in a moment that the sets obtained in this way constitute *all* the sets of properties, that is, all the subsets of T_N. So on this approach we must take $T_{\bar{N}}$ to be the power set of T_N.

Before proving that any set of properties is in fact obtainable from the individuals by intersections, unions, and complements we note first that e.g. unions of two or more distinct individuals are not themselves individuals. For example, where x and y are distinct elements of U, $I_x \cup I_y$ will contain both $\{x\}$ and $\{y\}$ as members, and thus there can be no $z \in U$ such that every element of $I_x \cup I_y$ has z as a member. For one of x, y must be different from z, hence one of $\{x\}$, $\{y\}$ will fail to contain z as a member. By similar reasoning $I_x \cap I_y$ is not an individual, nor is $(I_x)'$. Hence taking intersections, unions, and complements of individuals yields new sets of properties (ones which are not possible proper noun denotations). What we want to show is that *any* set of properties can be built up from the individuals by taking intersections, unions, and complements.

Now if Q is a set of properties then Q is clearly identical to the union of its unit sets, i.e. $Q = \bigcup \{\{q\}: q \in Q\}$. So if each unit set $\{q\}$ can be built up from the individuals set theoretically then so can Q just by taking unions of the unit sets. We state the results for unit sets below as a theorem (proof at the end of this section).

THEOREM 1. For all $q \in T_N$ ($= U^*$), $\{q\} = \bigcap\{I_x \colon x \in q\} \bigcap \bigcap\{(I_x)' \colon x \notin q\}$.

In summary then, Montague's approach to this problem, which we shall refer to for the nonce as EFOL (Extended First Order Logic), consists in the following: The semantic primitives are two: U and 2, the latter being a boolean algebra and the type for P_0, the former being any non-empty set. The type for N is U^*, the type for $\bar{N}$ is $(T_N)^*$ ($= (U^*)^*$), and $T_{\bar{N}_{\mathrm{prop}}} = \{I_x \colon x \in U\}$.

Stated thus, this approach is precisely that taken in Keenan and Faltz (1978). EFOL suffers at least from two serious drawbacks however, one ontological and the other linguistic. Ontologically we may note that U is no longer the type for any category of English (or of L). No expressions denote elements of U. Yet denotations for common nouns, proper nouns, and complex noun phrases are all ultimately defined in terms of U. Thus the interpretations of many basic expressions in English are defined in terms of semantic entities which we cannot in principle refer to in English, whence our knowledge of these entities must be remote at best. U rather appears now as a kind of noumenal world of entities which 'supports' the phenomenological world of individuals. U then is an essential *mystery* on this approach and the ontology which comprises it is essentially mysterious. In the extension of this approach we propose below the mysterious U is eliminated completely, though proper nouns, full noun phrases, and common nouns otherwise preserve exactly the character they have on the mysterious approach.

Linguistically EFOL has to some extent thrown the baby out with the bathwater. It has achieved on the one hand a better correspondence between English forms and logical forms by interpreting elements of a same category, *John* and *every man*, as elements of a same type, $T_{\bar{N}}$. On the other hand, it formally treats lexically simple expressions, e.g. *John*, as semantically complex. Thus the interpretation of *John* is given as a function of something, namely an element of U, but in violation of our version of Compositionality in the Overview, *John* is not derived from anything which denotes this element of U. This dependency is made explicit in (extensional) versions of Montague Grammar in which *John* is translated into $(\lambda P)\,(P(j))$, itself interpreted as the set of properties which hold of the denotation of j.

On the approach we propose below there is no motivation for translating *John* into a syntactically complex expression in order to interpret it. All expressions are interpreted directly; the interpretation of *John* is simply an arbitrary element of the type for $\bar{N}_{\mathrm{prop}}$, and is not given as a function of the interpretation of any other expression.

Eliminating the Universe (!)

Eliminating U from the ontology of EFOL will necessitate alternate definitions for T_N and $T_{\bar{N}_{prop}}$ as these are directly defined in terms of U. Once this is done, the type for $\bar{N}$ is defined, as before, to be $(T_N)^*$. Our intent here is to eliminate U in such a way that these two types nonetheless have the same semantic properties they have in EFOL. Thus we will not alter the class of valid arguments in the system, but only simplify the ontology and improve the correspondence between logical forms and surface forms. On the other hand, once the alternate formulation is given, it will admit of some natural generalizations which will allow us to significantly enrich the class of valid arguments we can characterize. Moreover our intuitive understanding of the semantics of common nouns and hence of other types constructed from the type for common nouns will be enriched. That is, our semantics will point out semantic properties of common nouns which have not to our knowledge been previously noted.

Conceptually the elimination of U will proceed in three steps: First, and most fundamentally, an alternate characterization of T_N must be found. Then T_N will then be taken as a primitive instead of U. Next *individuals* (proper noun denotations), will be defined as subsets of T_N which satisfy certain conditions. Crucial here is that these conditions are stated solely in terms of the boolean structure of T_N and thus do not require any antecedently existing universe of discourse to 'support' them. Finally, $T_{\bar{N}}$ will be defined as before, namely as the power set of T_N regarded as a boolean algebra via (7).

Characterizing T_N

In EFOL T_N is, as we have seen, a power set boolean algebra. Now it turns out that power set algebras (we drop *boolean* where clear from context) are a special case of boolean algebras which are characterized by two additional properties they meet over and above those required of boolean algebras in general. Namely, they are *complete* and *atomic*. Below we define these notions, noting the important fact that they are defined solely in terms of the primitives of boolean algebra. Then T_N will be primitively taken as an arbitrary complete and atomic algebra. As such it will possess *exactly* the boolean structure of a power set algebra, but need not literally be the power set of some set.

Completeness of boolean algebras. Let $\langle S^*, \emptyset, S, \cap, \cup, ' \rangle$ be a power set algebra as defined in (7). Since S^* is a collection of sets, the subset relation, $\subseteq$, is defined on S^*. Note that the subset relation is definable solely in terms of the structure of the algebra. For example, for all $A, B \in S^*$, we may define $A \subseteq B$ iff $A \cap B = A$. The reader can check that $\subseteq$ so defined coincides exactly with the subset relation as standardly defined. Moreover for any boolean algebra a comparable boolean relation is defined as follows:

DEFINITION 12. Let $\beta = \langle B, 0, 1, \wedge, \vee, ' \rangle$ be an arbitrary boolean algebra. Then for all $x, y \in B$, $x \leqslant y$ iff $x \wedge y = x$.

Note that from Definition 12 it follows that the boolean relation, $\leqslant$, is the subset relation, $\leqslant$, in a power set algebra: since the meet operation in such an algebra is just set theoretic intersection, we have that for $A, B \in S^*$, $A \leqslant B$ iff $A \cap B = A$ by Definition 12, whence by the set theoretical equivalence noted above we infer that $A \leqslant B$ iff $A \subseteq B$. The reader may check that the following object language theorems concerning the boolean $\leqslant$ relation follow from the axioms of boolean algebra together with Definition 12 (Proofs at the end of this section.)

THEOREM 2. For all $x, y, z \in B$, B the domain of a boolean algebra,

- (a) $0 \leqslant x$ and $x \leqslant 1$
- (b) $x \leqslant x$ (Reflexivity)
- (c)   if $x \leqslant y$ and $y \leqslant x$ then $x = y$ (Antisymmetry)
- (d)   if $x \leqslant y$ and $y \leqslant z$ then $x \leqslant z$ (Transitivity)
- (e) $(x \wedge y) \leqslant x$ and $(x \wedge y) \leqslant y$
- (f) $x \leqslant (x \vee y)$ and $y \leqslant (x \vee y)$
- (g)   if $x \leqslant y$ and $x \leqslant z$ then $x \leqslant (y \wedge z)$
- (h)   if $x \leqslant z$ and $y \leqslant z$ then $(x \vee y) \leqslant z$
- (i) $x \leqslant y$ iff $(x \wedge y') = 0$
- (j) $x \leqslant y$ iff $(y \vee x) = y$.

Since the theorems above hold in all boolean alegbras, they hold in particular for power set algebras. For example, taking X and Y as elements of a power set algebra S^*, (e) guarantees that $(X \cap Y) \subseteq X$ and $(X \cap Y) \subseteq Y$. Similarly from (f) we have that $X \subseteq (X \cup Y)$ and $Y \subseteq (X \cup Y)$.

In an arbitrary algebra, the relation $\leqslant$ cannot be identified necessarily with any otherwise definable relation on the elements. However, by abuse of language, if $x \leqslant y$ (x and y elements of some arbitrary alegbra B), we may say that x is *contained in* y, or that y *contains* x, even though there is no true sense of containment involved. Another, perhaps less misleading way of describing this relation is to say that y *dominates* x.

Note that Theorems (b)–(d) above state that the boolean relation is a partial ordering relation. (a) says that the zero element of the algebra is a minimal element (provably unique) in this ordering and that the unit element is the maximal element (provably unique) in the ordering.[7] And Theorems (e) and (f) say that meets and joins behave in a regular way with respect to the ordering. Specifically, taking meets forms smaller (or at least not greater) elements than what you started with, and taking joins forms bigger elements. In fact somewhat more can be said here. Let us define:

DEFINITION 13. For B an arbitrary boolean algebra and D any subset of B,

> (a) a *lower bound* (1b) for D in B is an element $x \in B$ such that for all $d \in D$, $x \leqslant d$;
> (b) an *upper bound* (ub) for D in B is an element $x \in B$ such that for all $d \in D$, $d \leqslant x$.

It follows immediately from Theorem (2e) that for all elements x, y in an algebra B, $(x \wedge y)$ is a lower bound for $\{x, y\}$; and from Theorem (2f) it follows that $(x \vee y)$ is an upper bound for $\{x, y\}$. In fact, $(x \wedge y)$ is the largest of the lb's for $\{x, y\}$ and $(x \vee y)$ is the smallest of the ub's for $\{x, y\}$. Formally,

DEFINITION 14. For B an arbitrary boolean algebra and D any subset of B,

> (a) an element $x \in B$ is a *greatest lower bound* (glb) for D iff (i) x is a lb for D and (ii) for all $y \in B$, if y is a lb for D in B then $y \leqslant x$;
> (b) an element $x \in B$ is a *least upper bound* (lub) for D iff (i) x is an ub for D and (ii) for all ub's y for D, $x \leqslant y$.
> (c) if D has a glb it is denoted $\wedge D$; if it has a lub it is denoted $\vee D$. We often write $\wedge_{d \in D} d$ for $\wedge D$ and $\vee_{d \in D} d$ for $\vee D$.

Note that if both x and z are glb's for D then necessarily x is z. For by clause (i) in (a) above each of x and z is a lb for D, so by clause (ii) $x \leqslant z$ and $z \leqslant x$, thus by antisymmetry (Theorem 2c), $x = z$. Similarly if x and z are both lub's for D they must be identical. Thus if a subset of an algebra has a glb (lub) it is unique. The following theorem is then straightforward:

THEOREM 3. For x, y elements of an arbitrary algebra B, $(x \wedge y)$ is the glb for $\{x, y\}$ and $(x \vee y)$ is the lub for $\{x, y\}$.

Thus in any algebra certain subsets always have a glb and a lub, in particular those subsets of the form $\{x, y\}$. In fact all finite subsets of an algebra have a glb and a lub. Thus if $D = \{d_1, d_2, \ldots, d_n\}$ is a finite subset of B a straightforward induction proof shows that $(\ldots (d_1 \wedge d_2) \wedge \ldots \wedge d_n)$ is the glb for D. Replacing $\wedge$ by $\vee$ above we obtain a lub for D.

We might point out here two special cases of finite sets which might be confusing in this regard. Consider first the empty set, $\emptyset$. It is a finite subset of any algebra. The glb of $\emptyset$ is the unit element 1. It is trivially a lb since $1 \leqslant$ every element of $\emptyset$ is vacuously true. It is the glb since if y is a lb for $\emptyset$ then $y \leqslant 1$ since every element in the algebra is $\leqslant 1$ (Theorem 2a). Similar reasoning shows that the zero element is the lub for $\emptyset$.

Secondly, consider unit sets. From Theorem 2 above, choosing x and y to be the same element we have that the set $\{x, y\}$ is just $\{x\}$. Thus from the theorem we have that $(x \wedge x)$ is the glb for $\{x\}$ and $(x \vee x)$ is the lub for $\{x\}$. Note that the Idempotent Laws, $x = (x \wedge x)$ and $x = (x \vee x)$ are object language theorems of boolean algebra. Thus x is the glb for $\{x\}$ and x is also the lub for $\{x\}$.

However, while every finite subset of an algebra has a glb (lub) it is not necessarily the case that every infinite subset of an algebra does. If even the infinite subsets of an algebra have glb's and lub's that algebra is said to be complete. Formally,

DEFINITION 15. A boolean algebra B is *complete* iff for every subset D of B there is an element $x \in B$ such that x is a glb for D, and there is an element $y \in B$ such that y is a lub for D.

(We note without proof that if every subset D of B has a glb then every subset D has a lub, and conversely.)

Note that every finite algebra (i.e. one whose domain is finite) is complete since any subset of it must be finite, and from what we indicated earlier, every finite subset of an algebra has a glb and a lub. However not all infinite algebras are complete (see Mendelson (1970), p. 161 for examples). But all power set algebras, whether finite or infinite, are complete. Specifically let

$S*$, the domain of a power set algebra, be infinite and let K be any subset of $S*$. So each $k \in K$ is a set, i.e. an element of $S*$ and thus a subset of S. It is easily seen that $\bigcap K$ is a glb for K. Since $\bigcap K$ is the set of all the elements in S which are in each $k \in K$, $\bigcap K$ is clearly a subset of S and thus an element of $S*$. Moreover it is a lb for K, since for any $k \in K$, each element of $\bigcap K$ is in k, so $\bigcap K \in k$, for each $k \in K$; thus $\bigcap K$ is a lb for K. Now suppose that Y is a lb for K. So each $y \in Y$ is in each k in K. But $\bigcap K$ is the set of all the elements in each k in K, thus $y \in \bigcap K$. As y was arbitrary in Y, then $Y \subseteq \bigcap K$, and thus $\bigcap K$ is the greatest of the lb's for K. Analogous reasoning shows that $\bigcup K$ is the lub for K. Thus an arbitrary subset K of $S*$ has both a glb and a lub, so $S*$ is complete.

Atomicity of boolean algebras. Let us turn now to the second characteristic property of power set algebras, *atomicity*.

DEFINITION 16. For B an arbitrary boolean algebra,

   (a)   an element $x \in B$ is an *atom* iff (i) $x \neq 0$ and (ii) For all $y \in B$, if $y \leqslant x$ then either $y = 0$ or $y = x$.
   (b) B is *atomic* iff for all non-zero elements x in B there is an atom $y \in B$ such that $y \leqslant x$.

Some algebras have no atoms at all and thus are clearly not atomic. Others have atoms but still fail to be atomic since there are some elements which dominate no atom. Power set algebras however are always atomic. For let $S*$ be a power set algebra and let K be a non-zero element of $S*$. Then $K \neq \emptyset$, since $\emptyset$ is the zero element of $S*$, so K has at least one member, say k. Since K is a subset of S then $\{k\}$ is also a subset of S and thus an element of $S*$. And clearly $\{k\} \subseteq K$. Now we claim that $\{k\}$ is an atom. Clearly it is not $\emptyset$, satisfying clause (i) in Definition (16a). Now suppose that Y in $S*$ is a subset of $\{k\}$. If Y is not empty then the only member of Y is k, otherwise $Y \nsubseteq \{k\}$. Thus if Y is not empty then $Y = \{k\}$, so either Y is $\emptyset$ or $Y = \{k\}$, satisfying the second clause of Definition (16a). Thus the unit sets in a power set algebra are atoms, and for any non-empty element K of a power set algebra there is an atom $\{k\} \subseteq K$, so the power set algebra is atomic.

   The illustration of atoms in power set algebras should help to clarify the intuition behind the notion of an atom. Basically an atom is a smallest non-zero element of an algebra. Nothing in a boolean algebra is strictly smaller than an atom except the zero element. So, loosely, an atom is a non-trivial element of an algebra with no proper parts which are non-trivial. We note the following useful theorems regarding atoms in an algebra:

THEOREM 4. Let B an arbitrary algebra and b an atom in B. Then,

(a) For all $x \in B$, either $(b \wedge x) = 0$ or $(b \wedge x) = b$.
(b) For all $x \in B$, either $b \leqslant x$ or $b \leqslant x'$ but not both.
(c) For all $c \in B$, if c is an atom of B and $c \neq b$ then $(b \wedge c) = 0$.

As the concept of an atom will play some role in the sequel, it might be useful here to illustrate an atomic algebra whose elements are not sets and thus whose atoms are not unit sets.

THEOREM 5. Let X be a non-empty set and let $F_{2/X}$ be the set of all functions with domain X and range included in 2 (= $\{0, 1\}$). Then $\langle F_{2/X}, 0, 1, \wedge, \vee, ' \rangle$ is an atomic boolean algebra, where the zero element is that function in $F_{2/X}$ which maps each $x \in X$ onto the zero element of 2; the unit element is that function mapping each $x \in X$ onto the unit element in 2; and the meet, join, and complement operations are defined as follows: for all functions $f, g \in F_{2/X}$, and all $x \in X$,

(a) $(f \wedge g)(x) = (f(x) \wedge_2 g(x)$ and
(b) $(f \vee g)(x) = f(x) \vee_2 g(x)$ and
(c) $(f')(x) = (f(x))'_2$.

First let's understand the definition. The zero element in $F_{2/X}$, which we might have denoted $0_{F_{2/X}}$ were it not so cumbersome, is clearly a function from X into 2. It maps each $x \in X$ onto the zero element of 2 (namely 0). Omitting subscripts, as we have, we may write $0(x) = 0$, which looks confusing, since the '0' on the left of the equation refers to a function from X into 2, and the '0' on the right refers to an element of 2. We prefer to clear up this confusion verbally, as we have just done, rather than use the less confusing but more awkward notation $0_{F_{2/X}}(x) = 0_2$. Similarly the unit element of $F_{2/X}$ as defined is clearly a function from X into 2. So the unit and zero elements of the algebra are elements of the domain of the algebra as required.

Now consider the meet, join, and complement operations on $F_{2/X}$. To define a function from X into 2 we must state the value of that function at each x in the domain X of the function. If f and g are elements of $F_{2/X}$, namely functions from $X \to 2$, we define $(f \wedge g)$ to be that function in F_2/X whose value at any $x \in X$ is $f(x) \wedge_2 g(x)$. Thus $(f \wedge g)$ maps x onto the element of 2 obtained by forming $f(x)$, an element of 2, and $g(x)$, an element of 2, and then taking the meet of these two elements in the algebra 2. Similarly $(f \vee g)$ maps each x onto the element of 2 obtained by taking the join in 2 of $f(x)$ with $g(x)$. And finally f' is that function from X into 2 whose value at any x is the element of 2 formed by looking first at $f(x)$, an element of 2, and then taking the complement in 2 of that element.

Thus the meet and join operations as defined on F_2/X are binary functions mapping pairs of functions in F_2/X onto a third function in F_2/X. And $'$ as defined is a unary function from F_2/X into F_2/X.

Now let us sketch a proof that the algebra defined in Theorem 5 satisfies the axioms of boolean algebra. Note first that the zero and unit elements are distinct. To show that two functions are distinct it is sufficient to show that they have different values at at least one argument. Since X is taken to be non-empty let x be an element of X. Then $0(x) = 0_2$ and $1(x) = 1_2$. Thus the zero and unit functions have different values at x, since the zero and unit elements of 2 are distinct. Let us illustrate the proof that the other axioms hold with the example of the first distributive law. For f, g, h arbitrary elements of F_2/X we must show that $(f \wedge (g \vee h))$ is the same function as $((f \wedge g) \vee (f \vee h))$, that is we must show that they have the same value at every argument. Let x be arbitrary in X. Then,

$$
\begin{aligned}
(f \wedge (g \vee h))(x) &= f(x) \wedge (g \vee h)(x) && \text{Def of } \wedge \text{ in } F_2/X \\
&= f(x) \wedge (g(x) \vee h(x)) && \text{Def of } \vee \text{ in } F_2/X \\
&= (f(x) \wedge g(x)) \vee (f(x) \wedge h(x)) && \text{Distributivity in 2} \\
&= (f \wedge g)(x) \vee (f \wedge h)(x) && \text{Def of } \wedge \text{ in } F_2/X \\
&= ((f \wedge g) \vee (f \wedge h))(x) && \text{Def of } \vee \text{ in } F_2/X
\end{aligned}
$$

Thus $f \wedge (g \vee h)$ and $(f \wedge g) \vee (f \wedge h)$ take the same value at an arbitrary argument and hence are equal.

The other axioms are proven similarly. Thus F_2/X as defined is a boolean algebra.

Consider now the boolean $\leq$ relation on F_2/X. By definition we have that $f \leq g$ iff $(f \wedge g) = f$, all f, g in F_2/X. And note,

$$
\begin{aligned}
(f \wedge g) = f \quad &\text{iff for all } x \in X, (f \wedge g)(x) = f(x) && \text{Identity for functions} \\
&\text{iff for all } x \in X, f(x) \wedge g(x) = f(x), && \text{Def } \wedge \text{ in } F_2/X \\
&\text{iff for all } x \in X, f(x) \leq g(x) && \text{Def } \leq \text{ in 2}
\end{aligned}
$$

Thus $f \leq g$ in F_2/X iff for all $x \in X, f(x) \leq g(x)$ in 2.

Now let us consider the atoms of F_2/X. For $f \in F_2/X$ to be an atom it must be different from the zero function and whenever $g \leqslant f$ then either g is the zero function or g is f. We claim that for each $x \in X$, the functions f_x defined below are atoms of F_2/X.

DEFINITION 17. For all $y \in X$, $f_x(y) = 1_2$ if $y = x$ and $f_x(y) = 0_2$ if $y \neq x$.

Clearly f_x is not the zero function since it maps x onto 1_2 and the zero function maps all elements of X onto 0_2. Now suppose that $g \leqslant f_x$, so for all $y \in X$, $g(y) \leqslant f_x(y)$. For any y different from x, $g(y) = f_x(y) = 0_2$. (Otherwise $g(y) = 1_2$ and so $g \not\leqslant f$, contrary to the assumption). So g and f have identical values at all $y \neq x$. Now consider their values at x. If $g(x) = 0$ then g is the zero function in F_2/X. If $g(x) \neq 0$ then $g(x) = 1 = f_x(x)$, so g and f_x have the same values at all arguments, so $g = f_x$. Thus f_x is an atom.

We can now show that F_2/X is atomic. Let f be any nonzero element of F_2/X. Since f is nonzero, there must be at least one element x of X such that $f(x) = 1$. We now claim that the atom f_x is contained in f. For, if $y \neq x$, $f_x(y) = 0 \leqslant f(y)$ (by part (a) of Theorem 2); and $f_x(x) = 1 \leqslant f(x)$, since $f(x) = 1$ (by part (b) of Theorem 2). Thus, $f_x(y) \leqslant f(y)$ for every element y of X, whence $f_x \leqslant f$. This shows that F_2/X is atomic.

We might point out that the algebra F_2/X is also complete, and that in fact F_2/X is isomorphic to the power set algebra X^*.

Defining T_N Without a Universe

We have seen above that all power set algebras are both complete and atomic; and in EFOL we took T_N to be a power set algebra, U^*, and thus to be a complete and atomic algebra. Note now the following standard result:

THEOREM 6. A boolean alegbra B is complete and atomic iff B is isomorphic to a power set algebra.

For the import of this theorem to be clear let us consider first exactly what is meant by an isomorphism between two algebras. Intuitively an isomorphism is a way of saying that the two algebras have exactly the same structure. To give an example, suppose we define an algebra TF whose domain has two elements, the letter t and the letter f, where 't' is the unit element and 'f' the zero. Intuitively TF has the same structure as the algebra 2 we have taken as the type for formulas. It would be completely pointless for example to argue that TF is in any way better or worse than 2 as a type of P_0. The reason is that the only properties of Tp_0 used in the logic are its boolean ones. For example we make use of statements such as "the meet of the zero element of Tp_0 with the unit is the zero element". But all such statements hold in 2 iff they hold in TF. Hence the two algebras are equally good candidates for being the type for P_0. The only differences between them concern the identity of the objects in their domains, i.e. what it is that makes the letter t different from the number one. And these differences are irrelevant in determining which arguments are represented as valid in L.

It is perhaps even more obvious that the identity of the elements in U (and thus $U*$) is irrelevant to the logic, since U is just any non-empty set. All that is relevant for characterizing the valid arguments in L concerning $U*$ is its *structure* as a power set. E.g. it is relevant that it has a minimal (zero) and maximal (unit) element, that it has atoms, etc. But the actual identity of the elements of $U*$ is irrelevant. Thus we may take as a type for N any object which has the boolean structure of a power set algebra. And the theorem above states that the complete and atomic algebras are exactly the class of algebras having the structure of power set algebras. We conclude that the complete and atomic algebras are exactly the class of objects which may be appropriately taken as the type for N.

Note that this class properly includes the power set algebras. For example, it includes the algebra $F_{2/X}$, which is not a power set algebra: its elements are functions, not subsets of one set. However, $F_{2/X}$ is isomorphic to a power set algebra $(X*)$; that is, the algebraic structure of $F_{2/X}$ is identical to the algebraic structure of some power set algebra.

Let us sketch out the proof of Theorem 6. We begin with a formal definition of the notion *isomorphism*.

DEFINITION 18. For B and D domains of arbitrary boolean algebras,

(a) i is an *isomorphism* from B onto D iff i is a one-to-one function from B onto D such that for all $x, y \in B$,
   (1) $i(x \wedge y) = i(x) \wedge i(y)$ [i preserves meets]
   (2) $i(x \vee y) = i(x) \vee i(y)$ [i preserves joins]
   (3) $i(x') = (i(x))'$ [i preserves complements]

(b) B is isomorphic to D iff there exists an isomorphism from B onto D.

Note that in (1)–(3) above meets, joins, and complements on the left side of the equations refer to these operations in B since x and y are elements of

B. On the right they refer to the corresponding operations in D, since $i(x)$ and $i(y)$ are elements of D. Note further what it means to say, as we have in (1)–(3), that i preserves the boolean operations. It says that whenever an element z of B is related in some boolean way to others, say $z = (x \vee (y \wedge w))$ then $i(z)$ is related in exactly the same way to $i(x)$, $i(y)$, and $i(w)$. Thus no element z in B has any boolean property not possessed by $i(z)$ in D. So in terms of the boolean structure we cannot distinguish between B and D. The following theorems regarding isomorphisms then are unsurprising:

THEOREM 7. Let i be an isomorphism from B onto D. Then,

(a) $i(0_B) = 0_D$ and $i(1_B) = 1_D$.
(b) $x \leqslant_B y$ iff $i(x) \leqslant_D i(y)$.
(c) x is an atom of B iff $i(x)$ is an atom of D.
(d) i preserves unbounded meets and joins, i.e. For $K \subseteq B$, $i(\wedge K) = \wedge \{i(k): k \in K\}$ and $i(\vee K) = \vee \{i(k): k \in K\}$ where these equations are interpreted to mean that if the meet (join) on the left exists, (i.e. if K has a glb (lub) in B), then the meet (join) on the right exists and the equation holds.
(e) the function i^{-1} from D into B defined by $i^{-1}(d) = b$ iff $i(b) = d$ is an isomorphism from D onto B. Thus B is isomorphic to D iff D is isomorphic to B, and we write $B \simeq D$.

Let us now indicate the essential steps in the proof of Theorem 6. Going first from right to left, let B be isomorphic to a power set algebra S^*. By (e) above let f be an isomorphism from S^* onto B. Then $\{f(x): x$ an atom of $S^*\}$ is the set of atoms of B by (c) above. Now, if x is a nonzero element of B, then $f^{-1}(x)$ is a nonzero element of S^*, and so contains an atom, say $\{s\}$. But then $f(\{s\})$ is an atom of B (by Theorem 7c); call it b. Moreover, by (7b), $b \leqslant x$. Thus, every nonzero element of B contains an atom, and so B is atomic. To show B complete, let f be an isomorphism from B onto S^* and let K any subset of B. Then $\{f(k): k \in K\}$ is a subset of S^* and has a glb, say z. $f^{-1}(z)$ is the glb for K in B.

Going from left to right, the case of greater interest for us, let B be a complete and atomic algebra. We must show B to be isomorphic to a power set algebra.

Let A_B denote the set of atoms of B. Since B is atomic and 1_B is not the zero element there is at least one atom in B, so $A_B = \emptyset$. Thus $(A_B)^*$ is the domain of a power set algebra. We show that B is isomorphic to $(A_B)^*$.

Define a function f from B into $(A_B)^*$ as follows: For all $x \in B$, $f(x) =_{\mathrm{df}}$ $\{b \in A_B: b \leqslant x\}$. Clearly f is a function from B into $(A_B)^*$, and it is standard to show that f is one-to-one, onto, and that it preserves meets, joins, and complements.

Thus a complete and atomic algebra can always be thought of as the power set of its atoms (though the atoms of course need not be sets, as was illustrated for the algebra $F_{2/X}$ given earlier).

In view of Theorem 6 then we may take T_N to be simply an arbitrary complete and atomic algebra. It may or may not be a power set algebra but it is isomorphic to a power set algebra and thus possesses exactly the boolean structure of such algebras. Note that we have defined the type for N solely in terms of its boolean properties; thus we no longer need an antecedently existing set U in order to define T_N. Moreover defining individuals in terms of the boolean structure of T_N is now quite easy.

Defining Proper Noun Denotations Without U

In EFOL recall the individual generated by $x \in U$ was $\{K \subseteq U: x \in K\}$. Noting the triviality that $x \in K$ iff $\{x\} \subseteq K$ we may equivalently define I_x to be $\{K \subseteq U: \{x\} \subseteq K\}$. Note that $\{x\}$ is an element of U^* (= T_N on this view). In fact it is an atom. And the subset relation is just the boolean $\leqslant$ relation for power set algebras. So taking T_N as an arbitrary complete and atomic algebra we may give an equivalent (non-temporary) definition of *individual* as follows:

DEFINITION 10. For B any boolean algebra and b any atom of B, I_b, or *the individual generated by* b, $=_{\mathrm{df}} \{p \in B: b \leqslant p\}$. We denote by I_B the set $\{I_b: b$ an atom of $B\}$ and refer to its elements as *individuals*.

We may then define the type for proper nouns as I_{T_N}, the set of individuals on T_N. Thus we have defined individuals solely in terms of the boolean structure of T_N, the properties, eliminating all reference to U. These results are formally summarized below.

The Ontology and Some Basic Types for L: Summary

DEFINITION 19. An *ontology*, or set of *semantic primitives*, for L is a pair $\langle P, 2 \rangle$ where P is an arbitrary complete and atomic boolean algebra called *the (extensional) properties*, and 2 is the boolean algebra 2, called *truth values*.

DEFINITION 20. Relative to an ontology $\langle P, 2 \rangle$ we define the types for $P_0, N, \bar{N},$ and $\bar{N}_{\text{prop}}$ as follows:

(a) $T_{P_0} =_{\text{df}} 2$.
(b) $T_N =_{\text{df}} P$.
(c) $T_{\bar{N}} =_{\text{df}} P^*$, regarded as a power set boolean algebra.
(d) $T_{\bar{N}_{\text{prop}}} =_{\text{df}} I_P$, the set of individuals on P.

Discussion

In presenting our conception of an ontology and the types as defined in Definition 20, we have relied on the reader's awareness of the advantages of EFOL as a system of semantic representation for natural language and presented our system as one which preserves EFOL's nice properties but which is ontologically less objectionable and linguistically more in accordance with the Principle of Compositionality. But that mode of presentation suffers from at least one serious shortcoming: it fails to reflect the novelty and naturalness of the basic ontology. More specifically it does not provide any direct motivation for the ontology or the types in terms of representing valid arguments of English, and it fails to suggest that such an ontology would be naturally arrived at by direct reasoning concerning the pretheoretical judgments of semantic relatedness of English expressions.

Consequently we would like to ask the reader, now equipped with the necessary boolean apparatus, to reread Definitions 19 and 20 as though they were presented on page 1 of the *Semantics for L* section of this paper. A great many questions should arise concerning the naturalness and intuitive support for our ontology and types. Just what are the properties we take as primitive? Why should they form a boolean algebra much less a complete and atomic one? Are proper noun denotations really 'cognitively more complex' than common noun denotations as our types suggest? What specifically are the atoms of T_N? Can they be naturally expressed in English or are they just as mysterious as the elements of U were in EFOL? Below we answer these and some related questions.

(i) *Ontologically speaking just what are these properties which we take as primitive*? To be sure we cannot require of a primitive concept in a system that it be *definable*, otherwise it wouldn't be a primitive. But isn't it reasonable to have some intuitive idea what properties are in the same sense in which, when we give a semantics for the language of arithmetic, we have some idea what numbers are, or what points are in the language of Euclidean

geometry, or what sets are in the language of set theory? The basic query
here seems to us a natural one, at least it is a query which has occurred to
us more than once. Any sort of thorough answer to the query of course
would carry us much farther into epistemology and philosophy of science
and mathematics than we need to go in order to provide a semantics for a
fragment of English.

So here we shall just present several answers to this query which contrast,
we think favorably, our ontology with that of standard FOL which takes
a universe of discourse U as primitive rather than P.

First let us countenance the following 'snap' reaction to the contrasting
ontologies: "The standard ontology (U primitive) is natural, since elements
of U may be common concrete objects of everyday experience, like John,
Mary, etc. These are obviously fundamental elements in our cognition,
relevant to our survival, etc., so it is natural that more complex, abstract
things like properties should be understood in terms of them — say they
should be sets of them anyway."

Part of this reaction is at best a quibble of our choice of the word *property*.
We might have named T_N anything we liked. We call its elements properties
since they will be denotations of common nouns like *man, woman*, etc. and
traditional usage in philosophy and rhetoric sanctions that *man* determines
a property, the property of being a man. Of course other categories, such as
the category of verb phrases, also determine properties in this sense; and to
anticipate our development we might point out that in L, T_N will turn out
to be isomorphic to the type for P_1, as well as to the type for 'absolute'
adjectives, such as *male, female*, etc. which also traditionally determine
properties.

But it is decidedly not the case that elements of T_N in our system have
to be abstract objects. They can be any sort of objects we like. All that is
relevant about them is that they are a boolean set, that is a set with a specific
sort of boolean structure. The identity of the elements of T_N is irrelevant
to the use we make of T_N in the logic. Consider for example an algebra whose
two elements are Ronald Reagan and Francois Mitterand, taking Reagan
as the zero element and Mitterand as the unit. The values of the boolean
operations are uniquely determined on the zero and unit; the resulting
algebra is of course complete because it is finite, and it is atomic, Mitterand
being the only atom. (The algebra is of course isomorphic to 2.) So this
algebra is a possible choice of T_N, and its elements are clearly concrete
objects of everyday experience. One might of course think it strange usage
to call Reagan a property, in particular the zero property, of an algebra.

But in fact all that is strange is that we overtly identified the zero element of the algebra with something characterized by properties irrelevant to the algebra, e.g. being the President of the United States, being a former movie actor, etc. To see that this is what is peculiar about the usage, consider a comparable example from the language of arithmetic. Let us take as a model of arithmetic the standard set theoretical one in which the set of 'numbers' (the universe of discourse) is the set whose members are $\emptyset$, $\{\emptyset\}$, $\{\emptyset, \{\emptyset\}\}$, etc., and the numeral zero in the language of arithmetic is interpreted as $\emptyset$. One may or may not find this peculiar depending on mathematical habit. But consider a different but equally good model of arithmetic whose elements are the following sequences of letters: *r, rm, rmm*, etc. In this model zero names the letter *r*. It is peculiar to say that zero *is* the 18th letter of the English alphabet because we seem to be attributing to zero properties which are not arithmetical ones. The only arithmetically relevant property of zero in arithmetic is that it is the least element of the ordering of the universe of discourse. What those elements are is irrelevant. Any set which possesses the right kind of ordering (i.e. linear ordering, non-dense, least but no greatest element, etc.) can be the basis of a model of arithmetic. It is pointless to attempt to distinguish among them for the same reasons that it is pointless to distinguish between TF and 2 as models of sentence denotations in logic.

So far then two conclusions: one, elements of T_N are not necessarily more or less abstract than elements of U. Two, we have no business being concerned at all with the identity of elements in a mathematical structure. The only properties of relevance are those determined by the structure defined on the set.

But what about the brute force claim that individuals are somehow cognitively more basic than properties, so the latter should be defined in terms of the former, as in FOL but not in *L*? Let use note first the following mildly interesting result: In FOL T_N ($= T_{P_1}$) is defined to be the power set of U, which is itself the denotations for proper nouns and thus constitutes the set of individuals in FOL. In *L* of course individuals are defined in terms of properties, just the opposite from the direction of definition in FOL, but it is still the case that T_N is indistinguishable from the power set of the individuals in *L*. Thus,

THEOREM 8. P ($= T_N$) is isomorphic to $(I_p)^*$, the power set of the individuals on P. The function sending each $p \in P$ to the set of individuals it is a member of is an isomorphism.

Now, what can we make of the claim that individuals are somehow cognitively more basic than properties? What evidence could be brought to bear? One can imagine psycholinguistic tests that could be brought to bear, but we know of no solid results in this area. One suggestive piece of evidence would be if the records of child language acquisition clearly showed that children learned many proper names first and only later learned common nouns and verb phrases. Assuming they use the name meaningfully this would suggest that they have understood proper noun denotations before common noun ones, suggesting that in fact they do form their concepts of common noun denotations in terms of proper noun denotations. But the little evidence we have seen (see Bloom, 1973) while incomplete, strongly suggests the contrary. Early utterances include many property denoting expressions such as *cookie, baby, chair*, etc. and few if any expressions which are unequivocally individual denoting. The best candidate here is *Mommy* but even in the earliest stages of Bloom's corpora *Mommy* is used to refer to individuals other than the child's mother. Moreover the early utterances include frequent uses of 'determiners' such as *no* and *more* whose use clearly presupposes the ability to recognize an object as a member of a class.

There is moreover somewhat better documented, though still circumstantial, evidence of a purely linguistic sort supporting the primacy of property denoting phrases over individual denoting ones. Namely, in very many languages (Hebrew, Malagasy, commonly in American Indian languages, Bantu, etc.) the expressions which function as proper nouns are syntactically and morphologically derived from property denoting expressions. For example, Lakhota names familiar from American history are Sinte Gleska ('Spotted Tail'), Mahpiya Luta ('Red Cloud'), and Tatanka Iyotaka ('Sitting Bull'). Similarly consider Hebrew names *Aryeh* 'lion', *Dov* 'bear', *Zvi* 'male deer', etc. In Malagasy proper names are productively formed with a proper name particle and verb phrases, adjective phrases, and common nouns, translating literally into English as e.g. 'Mr. born on a lucky day', 'Mr. noble and yellow', etc., e.g. Ramanandraibe = Ra + manana + rai + be = 'Mr.' + has + father + big, 'Mr. has many children', etc. In fact historically many proper names in English are derived from common nouns: Smith, Butcher, Carpenter, etc. Last names, being the most recently innovated, are the most transparent in this regard of course, but dictionaries also give etymologies for first names. E.g. the first author is happy to report that Edward comes from Anglo Saxon *ead* 'riches' + *weard* 'guardian, protector'. Similarly Leonard < OHG Lewenhart = lewe 'lion' + hart 'strong' = 'strong as a lion'.

It seems extremely general moreover across languages that individual denoting phrases are formed from property denoting phrases, e.g. *this man* from *man*, etc., whereas the converse process is only sporadic (cf. gerrymander). This fact is curious on a view in which properties are thought of as defined in terms of individuals but is reasonable on the converse view, the one suggested by our ontology.

These considerations are of course speculative, but recognizing them as such, let us pursue a further speculation along these lines before returning to the hard core reality of boolean algebra. Namely, consider the following global scenario for the development of cognitive capacities in the child. Initially his visual perception of the world is unorganized – he falls, bumps into things, etc. He must learn to assess heights, depths, and distances. Little by little he learns to partition his visual field into increasingly refined classes – objects which move are distinguished from objects which don't, ones which make noises from ones which don't, later ones which bite from ones which don't, ones which are edible from ones which aren't, etc. It is only at a stage later than this that the child learns to discriminate one particular object to the exclusion of the others in the class to which that object belongs. Such discrimination is, relatively speaking, not of primary relevance. We do of course have some need to discriminate among the individual humans who affect our lives early, and we do assign them proper names. But few of us find it useful to discriminate among our pet goldfish and probably none of us has any serious sense of the identity of the potato we had for dinner tonight as opposed to the one we saved for tomorrow.

We recognize of course that our child development scenario is speculative and superificial, but it does have some plausability. It reasonably suggests that it is of primary survival value to discern properties of objects rather than their absolute identity. The man in a tree who perceives a tiger kill an antelope is more likely to survive if he learns from the experience that tigers kill things rather than if he merely learns that that tiger killed something. It would seem then that the burden of proof in the matter lies with those who want to claim that individuals are somehow cognitively primary.

Let us turn now to the matter of justifying the boolean nature of T_N (= P) and of defining individuals in terms of the boolean properties of P as we have done.

(ii) *Why should T_N be a boolean algebra?* We will show here that the boolean nature of T_N and the concomitant definition of $T_{\overline{N}_{\text{prop}}}$ follow naturally and directly from pretheoretical consideration of the valid arguments of English.

The ultimate basis for our reasoning here is that we intend T_N to provide denotations for English common noun phrases. These will include not only elements such as *man, student, woman*, etc. but ultimately more complex N's such as: *non-student, tall man, tallest student in the class, tall and handsome student, smart but not very hard-working student, woman who John knows, student taller than every teacher, student who is taller than some teacher, woman who John knows best, first man who landed on the moon, man who was the first President of the U.S.*, and even *individual who is Bill*. Thus we shall argue that to represent correctly the valid arguments into which such expressions enter they must take their denotations in a boolean set. We shall refer to their denotations non-committally as properties, and justify then that such properties should be elements of a complete atomic boolean algebra.

We shall furthermore accept the reasons given earlier for taking proper noun denotations as sets of properties (principally to allow that *John* and *every man* take their denotations in the same type). We shall refer non-committally to proper noun denotations as individuals. Obviously we do not assume for this discussion Definition 10 given earlier; indeed it is the reasonableness of such a definition we are trying to justify on pretheoretical grounds.

Taking individuals as sets of properties does of course provide a natural way to represent the idea that individuals 'have' or fail to have certain properties according as these sets contain or fail to contain these properties as members. All languages have basic ways of saying that an individual has or does not have a certain property. For example to state in English that the individual John has the vegetarian property we say simply *John is a vegetarian*. Thus we want such a sentence to come out true in some state of affairs just in case in that state of affairs the vegetarian-property is an element of the John-individual.

The example also illustrates that properties determine P_1 denotations. That is, given the interpretation of *vegetarian* the interpretation of the P_1 *be a vegetarian* (we ignore verb agreement as always) is obviously determined as the P_1 denotation which holds of an individual just in case that individual has the vegetarian property. Moreover if *vegetarian* and *Republican* are interpreted as different properties in some state of affairs then *be a vegetarian* and *be a Republican* must be interpreted as different P_1's in that state of affairs; conversely, if *be a vegetarian* and *be a Republican* are interpreted as different elements of T_{P_1} then *vegetarian* and *Republican* must be interpreted differently. Somewhat more generally if e is a (first order, extensional) P_1 then the property which e predicates of individuals is expressed by an N of the form *individual who e's*, e.g. *is singing* holds of John iff the property expressed by *individual who is singing* is a member of John. Note that *vegetarian* and *individual who is a vegetarian* are logical synonyms.

Since properties can be thus viewed either as the interpretations of N's or as objects determined by the interpretations of P_1's, we shall feel free, in our discussion of the nature of properties, to make use of both N's and P_1's in giving illustrations of pretheoretical judgments which must be represented by any logically adequate semantic system.

To show that T_N should possess a boolean structure let us begin by considering what property John should have in order for (8) to be true:

(8)   John is both a vegetarian and a Republican.

If *be a vegetarian* determines a property, say p, and *be a Republican* a property q, then clearly the property determined by the P_1 of (8) is dependent upon, that is, is some function of, p and q. Let us call that function M and denote the property determined by the P_1 of (8) by pMq. Then qMp will be the property determined by the P_1 of (9) below:

(9)   John is both a Republican and a vegetarian.

Clearly we are motivated to take M as a commutative function guaranteeing that pMq and qMp are the same element of T_N, for if we do then (8) will be true just in case (9) is, which is correct.

Notice now that p, q and pMq may all be different properties. But these properties cannot be randomly distributed among the individuals (the proper noun denotations). Specifically, since we are going to define individuals as sets of properties, we must guarantee that whenever an individual has both of p and q then it also has pMq and conversely. The direct motivation for this constraint on individuals is that (10) is logically equivalent to (9), that is, (10) entails (9) and conversely.

(10)   John is a vegetarian and John is a Republican

Thus we shall require that any $I \subseteq T_N$ which is a proper noun denotation satisfy the following condition:

(11)   For $I \subseteq T_N$, if $I \in T_{\overline{N}_{\text{prop}}}$ then for all $p, q \in T_N$,
$p \in I$ and $q \in I$ iff $(pMq) \in I$.

This says in effect that pMq is the property an individual has iff he has (or is) both p and q.

Note that there is further motivation for wanting to define the function M on T_N. Consider for example complex N's of the form *tall student*. Since *tall student* denotes a property, as does *student*, it is reasonable to interpret adjectives like *tall* as functions from properties into properties. Letting f be the tall-function, then, and letting s be the property which interprets *student,* $f(s)$ will be the property which interprets *tall student*. Similarly let g be the function which interprets the adjective *handsome*, so *handsome student* is interpreted by $g(s)$. Now what property should interpret *tall and handsome student*? Obviously enough an individual has that property iff he has both the *tall student* and the *handsome student* property. That is, [*tall and handsome*] *student* is interpreted by $f(s)Mg(s)$. Thus we are motivated to define M on T_N in order to provide denotations for N's expressed by combining simple N's with conjunctions of adjectives.

Next, in analogy to the above discussion, consider the property John must have in order for (12) to be true.

(12)   John is either a vegetarian or a Republican.

This too is a property which depends on both p and q (the vegetarian and Republican properties respectively), but of course the dependency is not in general the same as in (9). So we want another binary function, call it J, to be defined on T_N. Since (12) is logically equivalent to *John is either a Republican or a vegetarian* we are motivated to require that J also be commutative, i.e. that $pJq = qJp$, all elements p, q of T_N. And since p, q, and pJq may all be different properties, we shall impose the constraint below on what subsets of T_N may count as proper noun denotations:

(13)   If $I \subseteq T_N$ is an element of $T_{\bar{N}\,\mathrm{prop}}$
          then $(pJq) \in I$ iff either $p \in I$ or $q \in I$.

Thus pJq is the property an individual has iff he has at least one of the two properties p and q. As in the case for M, we are additionally motivated to define J on T_N to provide denotations for N's formed with disjunctions of adjectives. Thus correct entailments are predicted if we take *tall or handsome student* to denote $f(s)Jg(s)$ under the interpretation conventions given a moment ago for *tall* and *handsome*.

M and J are beginning to smell suspiciously like boolean meet and join functions; at least they are both binary functions and both commutative. Further it is easy to see that each should distribute with respect to the other. Specifically if we require of T_N that M and J distribute then we predict for example that (14a) will be logically equivalent to (14b) since the property determined by the P_1 in (14a) will be $pM(qJr)$ and that of (14b) will be $(pMq)J(pMr)$, and distributivity guarantees that these are the same elements of T_N.

(14) a. John is a vegetarian and either a Republican or a Democrat.
   b. John is either a vegetarian and a Republican or a vegetarian and a Democrat.

We leave it to the reader to construct an example showing that the second distributivity law should be satisfied by M and J (i.e. $pJ(qMr) = (pJq)M(pJr)$).

Another property that M and J share with boolean meets and joins respectively is *idempotency*. That is, in any boolean algebra, $(x \wedge x) = x$ and $(x \vee x) = x$. Similarly in T_N we have that $pMp = p$ and $pJp = p$, trivially, since e.g. pMp is the property an individual has just in case he has both p and p, that is, just in case he has p. Analogously for J.

Consider now the property John must have for (15) to be true:

(15)   John is not a vegetarian.

Clearly which property this is depends on which property the vegetarian property is. Let us denote it then Np, where *vegetarian* denotes p.

To see how p and Np are related note first that we want (16a) to be logically true and (16b) to be logically false.

(16) a. Either John is a vegetarian or John is not a vegetarian.
   b. John is a vegetarian and John is not a vegetarian.

These judgments tell us first that, since vegetarian is an arbitrarily selected element of T_N, we want p to be different from Np, for any property p. For suppose that p and Np were the same property, say q. Then either the John individual has q or he doesn't. If he does, then (16b) is true, contradicting our pretheoretical judgement that (16b) must be false. And if John doesn't have q, then (16a) must be false, contradicting our intuition that it is true. We conclude then that $p \neq Np$, for all p. This guarantees, note, that T_N must have at least two elements; for given that it is not empty (we want elements of N to have denotations after all) we have that for each element p of T_N there is a distinct element Np in T_N.

Further, for each $p \in T_N$, the distribution of p and Np in individuals is not random. Thus we judge (17a) to be logically equivalent to (17b); and similarly for (18a) and (18b).

(17) a. John is not a vegetarian.
      b. It is not the case that John is a vegetarian.
(18) a. John is a vegetarian.
      b. It is not the case that John is not a vegetarian.

These judgements will be guaranteed if we constrain the sets of properties which can interpret proper nouns to meet the condition given below:

(19)   If $I \subseteq T_N$ is an individual then for all $p \in T_N$,
         $p \in I$ iff $Np \notin I$.

Thus Np is the property an individual has iff he does not have p. Note that the condition $p \in I$ iff $Np \notin I$ is logically equivalent to either $p \in I$ or $Np \in I$ but not both. This latter rendition makes it immediate that (16a) is logically true and (16b) logically false.

Additional motivation for defining the N function on the type for common nouns comes directly from the common noun modifier *non-*. Interpreting *non-* as the function N we have for example that *non-student* is interpreted by $N(s)$ when *student* is interpreted by s. Thus by (19) an individual will have the student property iff he does not have the non-student property. This correctly guarantees for example that *John is a non-student* entails *it is not the case that John is a student*.

Unsurprisingly the function N we have described will turn out to satisfy the boolean axioms for complements. To see this consider what property John must have for (20) to be true.

(20)   John is either a vegetarian or not a vegetarian.

Intuitively the property must be one which all individuals have, since no matter what individual we think of *John* as denoting (20) is true, in fact logically true as it is judged to entail and be entailed by (16a) above. Let us then denote the property which all individuals have by 1_{T_N}, or simply 1 where clear from context. Arguably it is the denotation of the common noun *individual* (or *entity*, or *existent*).

Note however that we are already committed to representing the denotation of the P_1 in (20) by $pJ(Np)$. Thus, we want $pJ(Np) = 1$ to hold; moreover this holds no matter what property p is chosen. E.g. *be either a Republican or not a Republican* also holds of every individual. Thus $pJ(Np) = 1$ holds of all elements p in T_N. But this is just one of the complement laws which are required to be satisfied in any boolean algebra.

Analogously let us define 0_{T_N} to be the property an individual John has just in case (21) is true:

(21)   John is both a vegetarian and not a vegetarian.

Clearly this property is one that no individual has, since (21) is judged logically equivalent to (16b) and thus logically false. So we have that $pM(Np)$, our denotation for the P_1 in (21), must be 0; and since the choice of p was arbitrary, we have that $pM(Np) = 0$, all $p \in T_N$ satisfying the other axiom of complements.

Note further that $N(1) = 0$, since if 1 is in all individuals then $N(1)$ is in none by (19), and thus $N(1)$ is the property John has if (21) is true, that is, it is 0. And since for all $p \in T_N$, $p \neq Np$, we have that $1 \neq N(1) = 0$, so the axiom requiring that the unit and zero elements be distinct is satisfied.

For the remaining two axioms, $pM(1) = p$ and $pJ(0) = p$ it is sufficient to note for example that (22a) is logically equivalent to (22b):

(22) a. John is a Republican.
        b. John is a Republican and either a vegetarian or not a vegetarian.

The property expressed by the P_1 in (22b) is just $pM(1)$, so if $pM(1)$ is p the logical equivalence of (22a) and (22b) is correctly predicted. Interchanging *and* and *or* in (22b) yields of P_1 which determines the property $pJ(0)$; the equivalence of (22b), as modified, and (22a) shows that $pJ(0) = p$, thus satisfying the final axiom.

Thus we have shown that direct consideration of valid arguments from English supports the correctness of taking T_N as a boolean algebra and of taking individuals to be subsets of T_N satisfying conditions (11), (13), and (19). As the functions M, J and N were shown to satisfy the boolean axioms we shall henceforth refer to them by the ordinary boolean names, $\wedge$, $\vee$, and $'$ respectively.

Why Should T_N Be Complete and Atomic?

We have yet to justify that we want T_N to be a complete and atomic algebra. To see this, let us consider the $\leqslant$ relation we have defined on T_N.

By definition, for all elements p, q in T_N, $p \leqslant q$ iff $(p \wedge q) = p$. But just what does it mean to say $(p \wedge q) = p$? Given (11), (13), and (19), which constrain the sets of properties which can constitute individuals, we can show that one consequence of $(p \wedge q) = p$ is that the set of individuals with p is a subset of the set of individuals with q. For, suppose that $p \in I$. Then, since $p = p \wedge q$, we have that $p \vee q \in I$, and so by (11), $q \in I$. It will also turn out that the converse of this is true as shown below in Theorem 11.

The relation $\leqslant$ will naturally be used in the semantics of extensional adjectives. In particular, we want to draw the functions f which can interpret APs like *tall, female*, etc. from those functions f from T_N into T_N which meet the condition that for all $p \in T_N$, $f(p) \leqslant p$. Thus the tall student property $f(s)$ will be $\leqslant$ to the student property s, guaranteeing that any individual with the tall student property will have the student property, and hence guaranteeing that sentences like *all tall students are students* are logically true, which is correct. (Of course not all APs will be interpreted by functions which meet this condition, e.g. *alleged, fake*, etc.; but many natural classes of APs do meet this condition, in particular, all those which can be treated extensionally. Note that *alleged* is not extensional in the sense that if the same individuals are murderers as thieves, so *thief* and *murderer* have the same extension, it does not follow that the alleged thieves and the alleged murderers are the same individuals. Hence *alleged* cannot be represented as a *function* from property extensions into property extensions.) See Section B for further discussion.

Now, why do we want T_N to be a complete algebra? That is, why now do we want any set of properties to have a glb? The general answer is that if we place this requirement on T_N then we correctly characterize many valid arguments.

Specifically let p be the property which interprets *man taller than every woman*, and for each individual W with the woman property, let p_W be the property *man taller than W*. We claim that p is the glb for $\{p_W: W$ an individual with the woman property$\}$. Call this set K. That p is an lb for K is seen by the fact that pretheoretically (23a) below entails (23b):

(23)   a. John is a man taller than every woman and Mary is a woman.
       b. John is taller than Mary.

If (23a) is true then p is a member of the John individual. Since p is an lb for K then $p \leqslant p_{Mary}$, the property of being a man taller than Mary. Hence p_{Mary} is an element of the John individual since from what we said above, $p \leqslant p_{Mary}$ guarantees that the set of individuals with p is a subset of those with p_{Mary}. Thus, by taking p to be a lower bound of K, the entailment in (23) is predicted.

Now, why should p be a glb of K? Suppose that z is an lb for K and thus every individual with z also has p_W, for each individual W with the woman property. And suppose that John has z. Thus for every woman W, John is a man taller than W. Clearly then we can infer that John has the property expressed by *man taller than every woman*, namely p; thus an arbitrary lower bound z for K is contained in P, which is just to say that p is the glb for K.

Now, K can be arbitrarily large, depending on how many individuals with the woman property there are. We thus want P to provide glb's for arbitrary sets of properties in order to guarantee the existence of interpretations for property denoting phrases such as *man taller than every woman*.

Correspondingly we must impose a somewhat stronger 'meets condition' on individuals than (11). That is, suppose that for every woman W, John has the property of being a man taller than W. Then he must also have the property expressed by *man taller than every woman*. But the finite meets condition which (11) imposes on individuals is not strong enough to guarantee this. That is, there exist subsets I of certain algebras which satisfy the condition that $\{p, q\} \subseteq I$ iff $p \wedge q \in I$ but which do not satisfy the condition that $K \subseteq I$ iff $\wedge K \in I$, for K an arbitrary subset K of the algebra. Formally, then, we shall require:

(24)   *The Meets Condition*
       If $I \subseteq T_N$ is a proper noun denotation then for each $K \subseteq T_N$, $K \subseteq I$ iff $\wedge K \in I$.

We leave it to the reader to construct the analogous argument that every subset of T_N should have a lub. Specifically we want the property which interprets *man taller than some woman* to be the lub for the set K given above. And similarly we must constrain individuals to meet the stronger joins condition:

(25)   *The Joins Condition*
       If $I \subseteq T_N$ is a proper noun denotation then for all $K \subseteq T_N$, $K \cap I \neq \emptyset$ iff $\vee K \in I$.

We have then justified that T_N should be a complete algebra and that elements of $T_{\overline{N}\text{prop}}$ should be subsets of T_N satisfying the Meets, Joins, and Complement Conditions, the latter restated formally below:

(26)   *The Complements Condition*
       If $I \subseteq T_N$ is a proper noun denotation then for all $p \in T_N$, $p \in I$ iff $p' \notin I$.

These three conditions turn out, perhaps surprisingly, to fully characterize individuals as defined earlier. Recall that for each atom b in T_N, we took

I_b, or the individual generated by b, to be $\{p \in T_N: b \leqslant p\}$. Let us now define individuals as follows:

DEFINITION 21. For all $I \subseteq T_N$, I is an *individual* iff I satisfies the Meets, Joins, and Complement Conditions.

The theorem below says that the two definitions are equivalent:

THEOREM 9. Assume that T_N is a complete and atomic algebra. Then for $I \subseteq T_N$, I satisfies the Meets, Joins, and Complements Conditions iff there exists an atom $b \in T_N$ such that $I = I_b$.

The significance of this theorem is that the notion of an individual is conceptually independent of the notion of an atom. We have not yet for example justified that T_N should even have any atoms, much less be atomic. Suppose for example that we allowed T_N to be an atomless algebra (there are many such). Then Theorem 9 says that there would simply be no individuals on T_N. Thus one (but not the only) motivation for wanting T_N to have at least some atoms is that we want to provide denotations for proper nouns, and if there are no atoms there will be no such denotations. Hence the notions of an individual does not rely crucially on some 'mysterious' notion of an atom. (Moreover as we shall see below atoms are in any event not mysterious; many ordinary common nouns are naturally intended to be interpreted by atoms.) So let us sketch the crucial steps in the proof of Theorem 9.

Proof. Let I be a subset of T_N satisfying Meets, Joins, and Complement. Show there is an atom $b \in T_N$ such that $I = I_b$.

Since trivially $I \subseteq I$, we have by Meets that $\bigwedge I \in I$. We claim

(a) $\bigwedge I$ is an atom and (b) $I = I_b$, where b is the atom $\bigwedge I$.

(a) $\bigwedge I$ *is an atom*

We must show that $\bigwedge I \neq 0$ and that for all $p \in T_N$ if $p \leqslant \bigwedge I$ then either $p = 0$ or $p = \bigwedge I$.

Suppose that $\bigwedge I = 0$. Then $0 \in I$ and since $0 = 0 \wedge 1$ we have that $0 \wedge 1 \in I$, whence by the Meets Condition, $1 \in I$. But $1 = 0'$, so both 0 and $0'$ are in I, contradicting the Complements Condition. Hence $\bigwedge I \neq 0$.

Suppose now that $p \leqslant \bigwedge I$. Assume $p \neq 0$. We must show that $p = \bigwedge I$. Trivially either $p \in I$ or $p \notin I$. Suppose first that $p \in I$. Then $\bigwedge I \leqslant p$ since $\bigwedge I$ is an lb for I. Thus since $p \leqslant \bigwedge I$ by assumption and $\bigwedge I \leqslant p$, we have by antisymmetry of $\leqslant$ that $p = \bigwedge I$.

Suppose alternatively that $p \notin I$. Then by the Complement Condition $p' \in I$, so $\bigwedge I \leqslant p'$ since $\bigwedge I$ is an lb for I. But $p \leqslant \bigwedge I$, so by the transitivity of $\leqslant$, $p \leqslant p'$. Thus $(p \wedge p') = p$. But $(p \wedge p') = 0$, whence $p = 0$, contradicting the original assumption that $p \neq 0$. Thus $p \in I$, and by the above then $p = \bigwedge I$.

Thus for all $p \in T_N$, if $p \leqslant \bigwedge I$ then either $p = 0$ or $p = \bigwedge I$, whence $\bigwedge I$ is an atom.

(b) $I = I_{\bigwedge I}$.

Let $p \in I$. Then $\bigwedge I \leqslant p$ since $\bigwedge I$ an lb for I. Thus $p \in I_{\bigwedge I}$, the set of q such that $\bigwedge I \leqslant q$. So $I \subseteq I_{\bigwedge I}$. Let $p \in I_{\bigwedge I}$. Then $\bigwedge I \leqslant p$. Suppose that $p \notin I$. Then by the Complements Condition, $p' \in I$, so $\bigwedge I \leqslant p'$. But from $\bigwedge I \leqslant p$ and $\bigwedge I \leqslant p'$ we conclude that $\bigwedge I \leqslant (p \wedge p') = 0$, so $\bigwedge I = 0$, contradicting that $\bigwedge I$ is an atom, shown in (a) above. Hence $p \in I$, so $I_{\bigwedge I} \subseteq I$. Combining (i) and (ii) we infer that $I = I_{\bigwedge I}$.

This completes the first half of the theorem. The other direction, that each I_b satisfies the Meets, Joins, and Complement Conditions, is unsurprising and given at the end of this section.

Consider now the justification that T_N should have atoms, and moreover be atomic (every non-zero element of T_N should dominate an atom). We have seen above that a proper noun denotation I possesses at least one atom, namely $\bigwedge I$. And it is easy to see that it cannot have more than one atom. For if say b and d are distinct atoms in I then by Meets, $(b \wedge d) \in I$. But (Theorem 4c) the meet of distinct atoms is 0 and by the argument in (a) above, 0 cannot be an element of any I. Thus, each individual contains exactly one atom.

From this it is easy to show that an atom is a property which is contained in exactly one individual. For, let p be an atom, and suppose that p is contained in I_1 and I_2. By Theorem 9, $I_1 = I_{b_1}$ and $I_2 = I_{b_2}$, where b_1 and b_2 are atoms. Since I_1 contains the atoms p and b_1, we conclude that $p = b_1$, by what we have just shown above. Similarly, since I_2 contains the atoms p and b_2, we have $p = b_2$. But this means that $b_1 = b_2$, whence $I_1 = I_2$.

Conversely, if p is a property which is contained in exactly one individual, then we can show easily that p must be an atom, provided we assume that T_N is atomic. For, by Theorem 9 above, there is exactly one atom b such that $b \leqslant p$. Now, p must actually be equal to b. For, if $b \leqslant p$ but $p \neq b$, then $(p \wedge b') \neq 0$ (for, if $(p \wedge b') = 0$, then $p \leqslant b$ (Theorem 2i), whence $p = b$, by the antisymmetry of $\leqslant$). There must therefore be some atom c such that $c \leqslant (p \wedge b')$. But then $c \leqslant p$ (Theorem 2e and transitivity of $\leqslant$), so that

$p \in I_c$; and $c \neq b$ (since $c \leqslant b'$ (by Theorem 2e and transitivity of $\leqslant$), whence $c \wedge b = 0$ (by Theorem 4c)); if $c = b$, then $c \wedge b = 0$ implies that $c = b = 0$, which is impossible if c and b are atoms). Thus, p would be a member of the individual I_c as well as I_b, contradicting the assumption that p was a member of exactly one individual.

And we are motivated to require that T_N have such properties for several reasons. As mentioned, if T_N has no such properties then there are no individuals on T_N and thus proper nouns would have no denotations, i.e. they could not be interpreted. Moreover motivation for atoms is more directly supported by the existence of common noun phrases which are clearly intended to denote properties which just one individual has. Examples are: *tallest student, first man who set foot on the moon, man who was the first President of the U.S.*, etc. Note of course that such expressions may fail to denote atoms. Suppose for example that no one ever set foot on the moon. Then *first man who set foot on the moon* would denote a property which no individual had, namely 0. However it is clear that the intended use of such common noun phrases is that they denote properties which just one individual has, so we want T_N to provide such properties: otherwise they would *have* to denote 0, which is incorrect. Moreover some common nouns will of necessity denote atoms. For example, *individual who is John* is a property which John and no other individual has. Thus we want T_N to provide atoms, and atoms are not at all mysterious in the way that elements of U were in EFOL. Namely they are the intended denotations of many ordinary expressions in English such as *tallest student*, etc.

Moreover it also seems reasonable to require that T_N be atomic. That is, if *vegetarian* denotes a non-zero property then it is a property which some individual has. Interpret *John* as such an individual. Then *vegetarian who is John* is a property which only John has and is thus an atom. And it ought to be an atom less than or equal to the vegetarian property, since every individual who has the vegetarian-who-is-John property clearly has the vegetarian property. So any non-zero property should contain an atom.

This completes our informal justification that T_N should be a complete and atomic algebra and that individuals on T_N should be those subsets of T_N which satisfy the Meets, Joins, and Complements Conditions, which means that the individuals are just the I_b's defined earlier.

Further, our definitions guarantee that L satisfies a further adequacy criterion, namely, *extensionality*, in the sense of (27):

(27)   *Extensionality*: for all properties p and q, $p = q$ iff the set of individuals which contain p is the same as the set which contain q.

Our intent all along has been that L be an extensional logic in this sense, and we have informally used this assumption in reasoning about properties above. For example, we argued above that if the vegetarian property was not the zero property then it held of at least one individual. This assumes of our course that if two properties are different then they hold of different individuals. Our assumption of extensionality here is one of simplification. We first present a language L to represent properties of English in so far as they can be represented in an extensional system and then, in Part II, we shall extend the semantics of L to include properly non-extensional constructions. For the nonce then we want L to be extensional, and it is perhaps reasonable to prove that we have succeeded. The proof moreover is enlightening in a surprising way. It will show that the extensionality assumption is in a certain sense equivalent to the assumption of the atomicity of T_N. And this in turn suggests a novel approach to intensional logics, allowing these to be constructed without the cumbersome apparatus of possible worlds. To establish this let us first note the following standard result in boolean algebra:

THEOREM 10. Let B be a complete boolean algebra. Then B is atomic iff for all $p \in B$, $p = \bigvee A_p$ (where $A_p =_{\mathrm{df}} \{b \in B: b$ is an atom and $b \leqslant p\}$).

Proof. Assume first that B is not atomic. We show that there exists a $p \in B$ which is not identical to the join of the atoms it dominates. Since B is not atomic there exists a p which is non-zero and which dominates no atoms. So $A_p = \emptyset$ for that p, so $\bigvee A_p = 0$, thus $\bigvee A_p \neq p$, which was taken as not 0.

Assume now that B is atomic and let $p \in B$ be arbitrary. We show that $p = \bigvee A_p$. Since p is an upper bound for A_p we have that $\bigvee A_p \leqslant p$, since $\bigvee A_p$ is the least upper bound for A_p. We must show then that $p \leqslant \bigvee A_p$, whence by antisymmetry, $p = \bigvee A_p$.

Suppose $p \not\leqslant \bigvee A_p$. Then (Theorem 2i) $p \wedge (\bigvee A_p)' \neq 0$, and so since B is atomic, there is an atom $b \leqslant p \wedge (\bigvee A_p)'$, whence $b \leqslant p$ and $b \leqslant (\bigvee A_p)'$. So by a general law of boolean algebra $\bigvee A_p \leqslant b'$ (i.e. in all algebras we have $x \leqslant y$ iff $y' \leqslant x'$). But b is an atom $\leqslant p$, so $b \in A_p$, thus $b \leqslant \bigvee A_p$ which is an upper bound for A_p. Thus by transitivity of $\leqslant$, $b \leqslant b'$, so $b \wedge b' = b$. But $b \wedge b' = 0$, so $b = 0$, contradicting the assumption that b was an atom. Hence $p \leqslant \bigvee A_p$ proving the theorem.

Note crucially that if B in Theorem 10 is not atomic then it contains a property which is not identical to the join of its atoms. We may now prove that L is extensional. In fact we show something slightly more general:

THEOREM 11. For all $p, q \in T_N$, $p \leqslant q$ iff $\{I: p \in I\} \subseteq \{I: q \in I\}$.

Proof. Suppose $p \leqslant q$ and assume $p \in I$. Then $p = (p \wedge q) \in I$, whence by the Meets condition on I, $q \in I$. So $\{I: p \in I\} \subseteq \{I: q \in I\}$. Suppose now $\{I: p \in I\} \subseteq \{I: q \in I\}$. Assume contrary to what we want to show that $p \nleqslant q$. Then $p \wedge q' \neq 0$, whence there is an atom $b \leqslant p \wedge q'$, so $b \leqslant p$ and $b \leqslant q'$, so $p \in I_b$ and $q' \in I_b$, whence by the Complement condition on individuals, $q \notin I_b$. So $\{I: p \in I\} \nsubseteq \{I: q \in I\}$ contradicting the supposition. Thus $p \leqslant q$.

COROLLARY 1. L is *extensional*. Viz.: For all $p, q \in T_N$, $p = q$ iff $\{I: p \in I\}$ $= \{I: q \in I\}$.

Proof. $p = q$ iff $p \leqslant q$ and $q \leqslant p$ from which the corollary follows immediately.

Note that the proof of Theorem 11 crucially uses the fact that T_N is atomic. If T_N were not atomic then T_N would contain a $p \neq 0$ which dominated no atoms. Thus p and 0 would dominate the same atoms and thus be distinct properties in the same individuals, contradicting the corollary and thus the theorem. So given that T_N is taken to be a complete algebra we can see that the atomicity requirement on T_N is equivalent to Extensionality. And this fact suggests a novel approach to non-extensional logics: Namely, we simply relax the requirement that T_N be atomic. We may still require that it have atoms, and thus by the remark made earlier, it can have as many individuals as we like. But such a T_N would allow that distinct properties determine the same sets of individuals, and this is in fact realistic. Thus it seems reasonable that we predicate something different of John when we claim he is a doctor than when we claim he is a thief, even if it happens that the doctors and the thieves are 'accidentally' so to speak the same individuals. So in such a T_N *doctor* and *thief* could be interpreted as different properties but still be members of the same individuals. Thus we have an approach to non-extensional logics which does not invoke the more problematic and not fully satisfactory (see Part II) notion of possible worlds. We are currently pursuing this approach to intensional logic but are not yet confident enough of the details to include this presentation here.

Let us note finally that Theorem 11 has another useful corollary:

COROLLARY 2. For K any set of individuals there is exactly one property p_K which is in just the individuals in K.

Proof. By the Theorem 11 there cannot be two such properties so it suffices to show that there is at least one. Define $p_K =_{df} \vee \{b \in P: b$ is an atom and $I_b \in K\}$. Let I arbitrary in K. Then $I = I_b$ for some atom b, and since p_K is an upper bound for the set of those atoms, $b \leqslant p_K$, whence by Theorem 11 $p_K \in I_b = I$. Thus for all $I \in K, p_K \in I$.

Suppose next that $I \notin K$, say $I = I_{b_0}$, and that $p_K \in I_{b_0}$. Then, by the Joins condition, since $p_K = \vee I_b \in K$ b, we must have $b \in I_{b_0}$ for some b such that $I_b \in K$. But then I_{b_0} would contain two atoms (b and b_0; they cannot be equal since $I_b \in K$ and $I_{b_0} \notin K$), contradicting the discussion following Theorem 9.

The significance of Corollary 2 is that we can define an element of T_N just by specifying what individuals it is in, and we can specify that set of individuals in any way we like.

We return now to the definitions of the other basic types for L.

Defining T_{Det} (= $T_{\bar{N}/N}$)

Having taken T_N as a complete and atomic algebra P and $T_{\bar{N}}$ as its power set algebra P^*, we shall interpret elements of Det (= $\bar{N}/N$) as functions from P into P^*. We might take T_{Det} to be $F_{P^*/P}$, the entire set of functions from P into P^*. But should we? Are there not perhaps some constraints on what functions from properties into sets of properties can be interpretations of extensional English Dets?

On the face of it there would appear to be severe constraints. All the elements of Det in L are intuitively logical constants; that is, *every* for example cannot be randomly interpreted in T_{Det} no matter what set we take T_{Det} to be. There is only one function from P into P^* which can interpret *every*. It might seem then that we could simply define the interpretations of elements of Det and define T_{Det} to be the set of functions so defined. But this approach is both unfeasible and uninteresting. It is unfeasible since even in L we have some ways of forming complex Dets, namely by boolean combinations. E.g. *not all, some but not all*, etc. are syntactically complex elements of Det and their denotations are not the same as any of the lexically simple members of Det. More importantly we shall in the sequel extend Det so as to include expressions which are not logical constants. For example, possessives such as *John's* and *no student's* as they occur in e.g. *John's* *car was stolen, no student's car was stolen*, etc. will be analyzed as Dets. Anticipating somewhat, we would like to define T_{Det} so as to be large enough to provide denotations for these non-logical Dets. The issue then is whether the variety of non-logical Dets in English justifies taking T_{Det} as the entire set of functions from P into $P*$ or not. If not, we would like to give substantive constraints on the meanings of extensional English Dets. We shall in fact claim that such constraints can be given. We refer the reader to Keenan and Stavi (1981) for a detailed justification of this point, only giving the broad outlines of that investigation here.

Consider first however one apparent argument in support of taking T_{Det} to be $F_{P*/P}$. Namely, that set of functions is naturally regarded as a boolean algebra, called a *pointwise algebra*, and it is the case that the boolean operations in that algebra are the natural interpretations for boolean combinations of English Dets. Let us first define pointwise algebras and note a few of their basic properties.

DEFINITION 22. Let D be the domain of a boolean algebra and B any non-empty set. Then $\langle F_{D/B}, 0, 1, \wedge, \vee, ' \rangle$ is a boolean algebra, where:

(i) $F_{D/B}$ is the set of functions with domain B and range included in D, and for all $f, g \in F_{D/B}$ and all $x \in B$,

(ii) $0(x) = 0_D$ and $1(x) = 1_D$,

(iii) $(f \wedge g)(x) = f(x) \wedge_D g(x)$, $(f \vee g)(x) = f(x) \vee_D g(x)$ and $(f')(x) = (f(x))'_D$.

$F_{D/B}$ so defined is easily seen to be a boolean algebra; it is called the pointwise algebra from B into D. We note further that if D is a complete algebra then so is $F_{D/B}$. If K is any subset of $F_{D/B}$ then the function f_K which maps each x in B onto $\wedge \{k(x): k \in K\}$ is the glb for K; lub's are defined analogously. Moreover if D is atomic then so is $F_{D/B}$. For each atom $d \in D$ and each element $b \in B$, then function $f_{d,b}$ which sends b to d and all other elements of B to 0_D is an atom of $F_{D/B}$.

Thus we may regard $F_{P*/P}$ as a complete and atomic boolean algebra. And the operations so defined are in fact the natural interpretations of *and, or,* and *not* as applied to Dets. E.g. the pointwise definitions say that (*not all*) (*student*) denotes the same element of $P*$ as does *not* (*all student*). Similarly, (*some but* (*not all*)) (*student*) will be synonymous with ((*some student*) *but* ((*not all*) (*student*))), which seems correct, e.g. (28a) is clearly logically equivalent to (28b).

(28) a. Some but not all students attended the meeting.
      b. Some students but not all students attended the meeting.

We shall then want to define the boolean operations on T_{Det} pointwise. But this of course does not mean that $T_{Det} = F_{P*/P}$, it only means that T_{Det} is closed under the pointwise operations. That is, whenever f and g are in T_{Det}, then so are $f \wedge g$, $f \vee g$, and f' as well as 0 and 1, where these operations and elements are defined as in the pointwise algebra.

So in fact the natural definition of T_{Det} for Det as given is to take it as the boolean closure of the interpretations we need for the lexically simple Dets. That is, we take the functions we need to interpret the lexically simple Dets we have endowed *L* with, and add to that set all the functions we can obtain from them by adding 0 and 1 and taking all combinations of meets, joins, and complements. Let us formally define the operation of taking boolean closures, as this will prove a useful general way of defining types (it will be used again in the intensional logic in Part II). As we are only interested in complete algebras we just give the definition for that case.

DEFINITION 23. For B a complete algebra and K a subset of B, K is *completely B-closed* iff (i) 0, 1 $\in K$ and (ii) for all $b \in B$, if $b \in K$ then $b' \in K$, and (iii) for $G \subseteq B$, if $G \subseteq K$ then $\wedge G \in K$ and $\vee G \in K$.

DEFINITION 24. For B a complete algebra and $K \subseteq B$, B_K, or *the complete B closure of K*, $=_{df} \bigcap \{G \subseteq B \colon K \subseteq G$ and G is completely B-closed$\}$

THEOREM 12. For B a complete algebra, K a subset of B,

  (i) B_K is completely B-closed and
  (ii) B_K is the domain of a complete boolean algebra, where the 0 and 1 are the same as in B and meets, joins, and complements are the operations in B restricted to B_K. Moreover, if $G \subseteq B_K$ then the glb (lub) of G in B_K is identical to its glb (lub) in B.

The algebra B_K so defined is called the (complete) *subalgebra of B generated by K*, and K is called a set of *(complete) generators* for B_K.

Thus we might reasonably define T_{Det} to be the complete subalgebra of the pointwise algebra $F_{P*/P}$ generated by the denotations of the lexically simple Dets. And this approach is in fact adequate for *L*, but not for the extensions of *L* we shall propose. To account for the extensions of *L* we shall investigate briefly the properties which denotations of simple Dets have in common and then take the set of functions from P into $P*$ which have those properties as the generators for T_{Det}. Let us then consider first the denotations of the lexically simple Dets of L.

DEFINITION 25. *every* is that function from P into $P*$ such that for all $p \in P$, *every* $(p) = \bigcap \{I: p \in I\}$, I ranging over individuals.

In defining interpretations for L we shall require that *each*, *every* and *all* be interpreted by *every*. (So we treat *each*, *every* and *all* as logical synonyms here, ignoring the slightly subtle differences between them as they are not easily represented in a first order logic.) Thus *every student* will be interpreted as the value of the *every* function at the student property, namely the intersection of the individuals which have the student property. So *every student* denotes the set of properties which the individual students have in common.

DEFINITION 26. *a* is that element of $F_{P*/P}$ which sends each $p \in P$ to $\bigcup_{p \in I} I$.

We will interpret both *a* and *some* by *a*. So *a student* will denote the set of properties which at least one individual student has.

DEFINITION 27. *no* = $(a)'$

So *no student* then, by the pointwise definition of $'$, will denote the complement in $P*$ of *a student*, namely the set of properties which fail to be in any individual with the student property.

DEFINITION 28: *the* is that function which maps p onto I_p if p is an atom and onto $\emptyset$ otherwise.

Thus *the student* will denote the unique individual with the student property if there is exactly one individual with that property. Otherwise it will denote the empty set.

Note that of the lexically simple Dets in L, *no* is somewhat exceptional in that its denotation is naturally given as a boolean function of another simple Det, *a*. If we define T_{Det} to be the boolean closure of any set which includes *a* that set will then include *no*. So we need not guarantee that *no* has a denotation in T_{Det} by specifically including it among the generators; it is sufficient to include a. We might note in passing that it can be reasonably argued on the basis of pairs like *ever/never, one/none, either/neither*, etc. that *no* is bi-morphemic, consisting of a negative morpheme *n-* and a base *-o*. Historically this is correct, *no* being the preconsonantal form of Anglo-Saxon *nan* deriving ultimately from *ne* 'not' + *an* 'one'.

In any event, excluding **no** let us consider the properties that the other simple determiner denotations have in common. There turn out (Keenan and Stavi, 1981) to be two which are sufficient to provide a rich enough set of generators for English extensional Dets: that of being *increasing* and that of being *weakly conservative*. We define these notions below:

DEFINITION 29. For K a subset of a boolean algebra B,

    (i) K is *increasing* iff for all $x, y \in B$, if $x \leqslant y$ and $x \in K$ then $y \in K$;

    (ii) K is *decreasing* iff for all $x, y \in B$, if $x \leqslant y$ and $y \in K$ then $x \in K$.

    (iii) For all $f \in F_{B^*/B}$, f is *increasing* iff for all $x \in B$, $f(x)$ is increasing; f is *decreasing* iff for all $x \in B$, $f(x)$ is decreasing.

THEOREM 13.

    (i)   For B an arbitrary algebra,

        (a) $\emptyset$ and B are both increasing and decreasing subsets of B, and are the only subsets with this property

        (b) Arbitrary unions and intersections of increasing sets are increasing

    (ii)   An individual on B is an increasing subset of B (since if $p \in I$ and $p \leqslant q$ then $p = p \wedge q \in I$, so by Meets, $q \in I$).

From Theorem 13 it is immediate that the simple determiner denotations (except **no**) are increasing, as their values are always increasing subsets of P. Note further that many fairly simple non-logical Dets will also be interpreted by increasing functions. For example, consider *John's. John's car* will denote the individual with the car property which John 'has' if there is just one, otherwise it will denote the empty set. Thus the value of **John's** at p is either an individual or the empty set, in any event an increasing set, so **John's** is an increasing Det denotation.

The property of being *(weakly) conservative* is a somewhat less obvious one:

DEFINITION 30. For B a boolean algebra and $f \in F_{B^*/B}$,

(i) f is *weakly conservative* iff for all $x, y \in B$,
   if $x \in f(y)$ then $(x \wedge y) \in f(y)$

(ii) f is *conservative* iff for all $x, y \in B$, $x \in f(y)$
   iff $(x \wedge y) \in f(y)$.

Formally it is not hard to show that *every*, *a*, and **the** are weakly conservative. To see this intuitively suppose that p is a property which every student has. Then clearly every student has $p \wedge$ the student property, that is every student is both a p and a student. Similarly if some student is a p then some student is both a p and a student; ditto for the student. And if p is a property of John's car then so is $p \wedge$ the car-property, i.e. John's car is both a p and a car, so **John's** is weakly conservative. We might note that being *increasing* and *weakly conservative* are completely independent properties. For example, the function f defined by $f(x) = \{1_B\}$, all $x \in B$ is increasing but not weakly conservative; the function g defined by $g(x) = \{y \in B: y \leqslant x\}$ is weakly conservative but not increasing. On the other hand, note that if f is weakly conservative and increasing then f is conservative. For suppose $(x \wedge y) \in f(y)$. Then x must be in $f(y)$ since $(x \wedge y) \leqslant x$ and f is increasing. Thus in fact the simple Det denotations above are all conservative (and increasing).

In Keenan and Stavi (*op. cit.*) it is shown that if we define T_{Det} to be the subalgebra of $F_{P*/P}$ generated by the increasing and weakly conservative functions in that set we obtain a set large enough to provide denotations for an exceedingly large class of extensional Dets in English. We refer the reader to that work then for the empirical justification of the adequacy of the following definition:

DEFINITION 31. T_{Det} = the subalgebra of $F_{P*/P}$ generated by the set of increasing and weakly conservative functions in $F_{P*/P}$.

And we may note the following theorem:

THEOREM 14. $T_{\text{Det}} = \{f \in F_{P*/P}; f \text{ is conservative}\}$

We might also note that our definition of conservative coincides with that of *lives on its arguments* taken as the defining property of English Dets in Barwise and Cooper (1980). On our view, as pointed out above, it is a theorem that a determiner lives on its arguments. Note finally the following theorem:

THEOREM 15. For complete and atomic algebras P, T_{Det} is a (very) proper subset of $F_{P*/P}$. Specifically, where n is the number of atoms of P, the cardinality of $T_{Det} = 2^{(3^n)}$ and the cardinality of $F_{P*/P} = 2^{(4^n)}$.

For example, if P has only 2 atoms (and thus two individuals) there are $2^{3^2} = 2^9 = 512$ logically possible determiner denotations. But there are $2^{4^2} = 2^{16} = 65,536$ elements in $F_{P*/P}$. So even for very small P most functions from P into $P*$ are not possible extensional Det interpretations in English.

Defining the Types for the P_n's

We shall first define the type for P_1 ($= P_0/\bar{N}$) in terms of those for P_0 and $\bar{N}$; then we generalize the definition to yield, for each $n \geqslant 0$, a type for P_{n+1} in terms of those for P_n and $\bar{N}$. A final generalization allows us to construct types for any predicative hierarchy $\{C_n: n \geqslant 0\}$ once the type for C_0 has been given as a complete and atomic algebra. Note that T_{P_0} has already been given as the complete and atomic (ca-) algebra, 2.

As P_1's will be interpreted by functions from $T_{\bar{N}}$ ($= P*$) into T_{P_0} ($= 2$) we may wonder, in analogy to the query raised for T_{Det}, whether just any function from $P*$ into 2 is a possible interpretation for a first order extensional P_1 or not. If so, we will take the type for P_1 to be $F_{2/P*}$, the entire set of functions from $P*$ into 2. But if not, then being a first order extensional predicate imposes non-trivial conditions on what functions from $\bar{N}$ denotations into truth values may be their interpretations. And in fact, it is easy to see that this latter option is correct. Consider for example that (29a) entails (29b), and that (29b) and (29c) are judged logically equivalent.

(29)   a. John spoke.
         b. Either John or Mary spoke.
         c. Either John spoke or Mary spoke.

That (29a) entails (29b) says that *spoke* cannot be interpreted by a randomly selected element of $F_{2/P*}$. For if the spoke-function assigns the denotation of *John* value 1 then it must assign the denotation of *John or Mary* value 1, otherwise we could have a situation in which (29a) is true and (29b) false. Somewhat more formally, let *John* and *Mary* be interpreted by individuals I_x and I_y respectively. Then *John or Mary* is interpreted by $I_x \vee I_y$ ($= I_x \cup I_y$, since joins are unions in power set algebras, and I_x and I_y are elements of the power set algebra $P*$). Then the truth values of the sentences in (29) are represented as in (30) below, using f to represent the function from $P*$ into 2 which interprets *spoke*.

(30) a. $f(I_x)$ ('John spoke')
      b. $f(I_x \vee I_y)$ ('John or Mary spoke')
      c. $(f(I_x) \vee f(I_y))$ ('John spoke or Mary spoke')

To say then that (29a) entails (29b) is to say then that if f assigns value 1 to I_x then it must assign value 1 to $I_x \cup I_y$; thus f is not an arbitrary element of $F_2/P*$. Moreover the logical equivalence of (29b) and (29c) says that the truth value f associates with a join of individuals must be the same as the join (in the truth value algebra) of the ones it associates with each of the individuals consider separately. That is, (30b) and (30c) above must be identical elements of 2, otherwise there could be a situation in which one was true and the other false. We may say then that f preserves (finite) joins in the sense that it maps a join of $\overline{N}$ denotations onto the corresponding join in the truth value algebra. Note that the $\overline{N}$ denotations need not be individuals. For example (31a) is logically equivalent to (31b) and every student (as well as every teacher) denotes an intersection of individuals, a set which is not in general an individual.

(31) a. Either every student or every teacher spoke.
      b. Either every student spoke or every teacher spoke.

Let us formally define the concept of 'preserving joins' and then require that elements of T_{P_1} be functions which preserve joins.

DEFINITION 32. Let B and D be boolean algebras, and f a function in $F_{D/B}$. Then,

   (i) f preserves finite joins iff for all $x, y \in B, f(x \vee y) = f(x) \vee f(y)$,
   (ii) f preserves (arbitrary) joins iff for all $K \subseteq B$, if K has a lub in B then $\{f(k): k \in K\}$ has a lub in D and $f(\vee K) = \vee\{f(k): k \in K\}$.

To see that we want P_1 interpretations to preserve (arbitrary) joins consider first the glb's and lub's for arbitrary subsets K of 2:

(32)

K	$\wedge K$	$\vee K$
$\emptyset$	1	0
$\{0\}$	0	0
$\{1\}$	1	1
$\{0, 1\}$	0	1

Thus the join of a bunch of truth values is 1 iff 1 is one of the elements over which the join is taken; otherwise it is zero. And the meet of a bunch of truth values is 0 just in case 0 is one of those over which the meet is taken; otherwise the meet is 1. And to see that we want P_1 interpretations to preserve (arbitrary) joins consider that we want the truth value of (33a) below, expressed in (33b), to be identical to that expressed in (33c):

(33) a. A student spoke
      b. $f(\bigvee\{I\colon s \in I\})$ (*I* ranges over individuals, and *s* is the student property)
      c. $\bigvee\{f(I)\colon s \in I\}$

Now (33c) is 1 just in case one of the elements $f(I)$ is 1, that is, just in case there is an individual with the student property who spoke. Clearly we want the truth value which the spoke-function associates with the denotation of *a student*, represented directly in (33b), to be identical to the truth value represented in (33c). Otherwise for example (33b) might be 1 and (33c) 0, which would mean that *a student spoke* was true even though no individual student spoke, which is intuitively incorrect.

We shall require then that functions which can interpret P_1's of *L* be ones which preserve joins. An analogous argument shows that we also want these functions to preserve meets. Thus (34a) and (35a) are judged logically equivalent, so we want the truth values expressed in (34b) and (35b) to of necessity be the same:

(34) a. A student and a teacher spoke
      b. $f(\bigvee_{s \in I} I \wedge \bigvee_{t \in I} I)$
(35) a. A student spoke and a teacher spoke
      b. $f(\bigvee_{s \in I} I) \wedge f(\bigvee_{t \in I} I)$

Here of course '*f*' denotes the interpretation of *spoke*, '*s*' that of *student*, '*t*' that of *teacher*, $\bigvee_{s \in I} I$ $(= \bigcup\{I\colon s \in I\})$ that of *a student*, etc. Similarly we want the spoke-function to preserve arbitrary meets, as we want the truth value of (36a) below, expressed directly in (36b), to be the same as that in (36c).

(36) a. Every student spoke
      b. $f(\bigwedge_{s \in I} I)$
      c. $\bigwedge_{s \in I} f(I)$

(36c) of course is just a notational variant of $\wedge\{f(I): s \in I\}$, and a meet of a set of truth values is 1 iff each of the values in the set is 1. Thus *every student spoke* will be true in L iff each individual with the student property spoke, which is intuitively correct. If the spoke-function were not required to preserve infinite meets then the truth values denoted in (36b) and (36c) could be different, say (36b) is 1 and (36c) is 0. But then *spoke* would hold of the denotation of *every student* even though there was some individual I with the student property of which the spoke-function failed (since (36c) is a meet of a set of truth values and thus has value 0 iff 0 is in the set, that is, iff $f(I) = 0$ for some individual I with the student property). Formally then let us define:

DEFINITION 33. For B and D boolean algebras and f in $F_{D/B}$,

    (i) *f preserves finite meets* iff for all $x, y \in B$, $f(x \wedge y) = f(x) \wedge f(y)$.

    (ii) *f preserves (arbitrary) meets* iff for all $K \subseteq B$, if $\wedge K$ exists then $\wedge\{f(k): k \in K\}$ exists and $f(\wedge K) = \underset{k \in K}{\wedge} f(k)$.

And we shall require of elements in T_{P_1} that they preserve meets as well as joins. Finally note that we also want first order extensional P_1's to *preserve complements*; that is, the truth value which the spoke-function assigns to the complement of an $\bar{N}$ denotation should be the opposite (= complement) of the value it assigns to the $\bar{N}$ denotation itself. E.g. the denotation of *not (every student)* is the complement of that of *every student*, and we want the spoke-function to assign these sets opposite truth values as denotations. This. guarantees for example that (37a) and (37b) are logically equivalent.

(37) a. (not (every student)) spoke.
       b. not [(every student) spoke].

Formally then we may define:

DEFINITION 34. For B and D boolean algebras and $f \in F_{D/B}$, *f preserves complements* iff for all $x \in B$, $f(x') = f(x))'$

Of course the complement sign on the right hand side of the equation above refers to complements in D since $f(x)$ is an element of D; on the left it refers to complements in B.

    We want then to limit T_{P_1} to those functions from P^* into 2 which preserve meets, joins, and complements. These are just the (complete) homomorphisms from $P*$ into 2. Formally let us define:

DEFINITION 35. For B and D boolean algebras and $h \in F_{D/B'}$

    (i) h is a *homomorphism* from B into D iff h preserves finite meets, finite joins, and complements.

    (ii) h is a *complete homomorphism* from B into D iff h preserves arbitrary meets, arbitrary joins, and complements.

We may note without proof that if h is a function from B into D which preserves complements and finite meets then h also preserves finite joins and is thus a homomorphism. Similarly if h preserves complements and arbitrary meets then it also preserves arbitrary joins and is thus a complete homorphism. (Moreover the two previous claims may be modified by replacing everywhere 'meets' by 'joins' and 'joins' by 'meets' and remain true). Some further unsurprising properties of homomorphisms are given by:

THEOREM 16. For h a homomorphism from B into D,

    (i) $h(0_B) = 0_D$ and $h(1_B) = 1_D$.

    (ii) For all $x, y \in B$, if $x \leqslant_B y$ then $h(x) \leqslant_D h(y)$

We might note further that for B a finite algebra the homomorphisms from B into any algebra D are all complete, so the homomorphisms and the complete homomorphisms coincide. But for B an infinite algebra this need not be the case. In fact, for B an infinite complete and atomic (*ca*) algebra, there are very many homomorphisms which are not complete homomorphisms. In addition we may note that any isomorphism (see Definition 18) from B onto D is of course a homomorphism and provably a complete homomorphism.

We shall in general denote the set of complete homomorphisms from an algebra B into an algebra D by $H_{D/B}$. And we shall define the type for P_1 to be $H_{2/P*}$, the set of complete homomorphisms from $T_{\bar{N}}$ into T_{P_0}.

But if we define T_{P_1} to be $H_{2/P*}$ have we guaranteed that P_1 interpretations are in a one-to-one correspondence to the properties T_N? More generally, are the elements of $H_{2/P*}$ just the one place predicates of standard first order logic? To see that they are, consider that to define a P_1 in FOL we must state exactly what individuals they hold and fail of. And Theorem 17 below says that this is exactly how we define elements of $H_{2/P*}$.

THEOREM 17. (*The Justification Theorem*, JT). For P and B any complete and atomic algebras and f any function from I_P, the set of individuals on P, into B there is exactly one complete homomorphism h_f from P^* into B which agrees with f on the individuals, i.e. such that $h_f(I) = f(I)$, all individuals I.

The significance of the JT is that we can define a P_1 homomorphism just by stating its values on the individuals, and we may do that in any way we like. E.g. we may say, let h be that element of H_2/P^* which maps each individual I onto 1_B. We have explicitly stated what h does to the individuals, and the JT says that there is exactly one element of H_2/P^* which has a fixed set of values on the individuals. As JT is slightly more difficult to prove than other theorems we have presented up to now we give the proof in two steps, Lemma 1 and Lemma 2 below:

LEMMA 1 (*Uniqueness*). Let P, B be arbitrary ca-algebras and h and k complete homomorphisms from P^* into B such that for all individuals $I \in I_P$, $h(I) = k(I)$. Then $h = k$, that is, for all $Q \in P^*$, $h(Q) = k(Q)$.

Proof. Note first that for any $q \in P$, $h(\{q\}) = k(\{q\})$; since,

$$h(\{q\}) = h(\bigcap_{q \in I} I \cap \bigcap_{q \notin I} (I')) \qquad \text{Theorem 1}$$

$$= \bigwedge_{q \in I} h(I) \wedge \bigwedge_{q \notin I} h(I') \qquad h \text{ preserves meets}$$

$$= \bigwedge_{q \in I} h(I) \wedge \bigwedge_{q \notin I} (h(I))' \qquad h \text{ preserves complements}$$

$$= \bigwedge_{q \in I} k(I) \wedge \bigwedge_{q \notin I} (k(I))' \qquad \begin{array}{l} h(I) = k(I), \text{ all } I \text{ by} \\ \text{assumption} \end{array}$$

$$= k(\bigwedge_{q \in I} I \wedge \bigwedge_{q \notin I} (I')) \qquad \begin{array}{l} k \text{ preserves meets and} \\ \text{complements} \end{array}$$

$$= k(\{q\}) \qquad \text{Theorem 1}$$

Whence for any $Q \in P^*$,

$$h(Q) = h(\bigcup_{q \in Q} \{q\}) \qquad Q = \bigcup_{q \in Q} \{q\}$$

$$= \bigvee_{q \in Q} h(\{q\}) \qquad h \text{ preserves joins}$$

$$= \bigvee_{q \in Q} k(\{q\}) \qquad h(\{q\}) = k(\{q\}) \text{ by above}$$

$$= k(Q) \qquad k \text{ preserves joins}$$

Thus $h = k$.

Thus there cannot be two different complete homomorphisms from $P*$ into B with the same values on the individuals. Now let us show that any way of assigning values in B to the individuals extends to a complete homomorphism.

LEMMA 2 (*Existence*). For P, B arbitrary ca-algebras and f any function from I_P into B, there is a complete homomorphism h_f from $P*$ into B such that $h_f(I) = f(I)$, all individuals $I \in I_P$.
  Proof.

  (i) given f as above, define a *function* h_f from $P*$ into B by:
$$h_f(Q) = \bigvee_{q \in Q} (\bigwedge_{q \in I} f(I) \wedge \bigwedge_{q \notin I} (f(I))'), \text{ all } Q \in P*$$

h_f as defined is clearly a function from $P*$ into B. We must show that h_f is a complete homomorphism and that h_f extends f.

SUBLEMMA. For all *atoms* $b \in B$, define $p_b \in P$ by: $p_b \in I$ iff $b \leq f(I)$, all individuals I in I_P. Then, for all $Q \in P*$, and all atoms $b \in B$, $b \leq h_f(Q)$ iff $p_b \in Q$.[8]
  Proof. Let Q and b arbitrary as above. Then,

$b \leq h_f(Q)$ iff $b \leq \bigvee_{q \in Q} (\bigwedge_{q \in I} f(I) \wedge \bigwedge_{q \notin I} (f(I))')$ Def of h_f

  iff $\exists q \in Q, b \leq \bigwedge_{q \in I} f(I) \wedge \bigwedge_{q \notin I} (f(I))'$ b is an atom

  iff $\exists q \in Q, b \leq \bigwedge_{q \in I} f(I)$ and $b \leq \bigwedge_{q \notin I} (f(I))'$

  iff $\exists q \in Q, (\forall I) (q \in I \rightarrow b \leq f(I)$
      and $(\forall I) (q \notin I \rightarrow b \leq (f(I))'$

  iff $\exists q \in Q, (\forall I) (q \in I \rightarrow b \leq f(I))$
      and $(\forall I) (q \notin I \rightarrow b \notin f(I))$

  iff $\exists q \in Q, (\forall I) (q \in I \leftrightarrow b \leq f(I))$

  iff $\exists q \in Q, q = p_b$

  iff $p_b \in Q$.

  (ii) h_f extends f, i.e. $h_f(I) = f(I)$, all individuals I.

We show that for all I, $h_f(I)$ and $f(I)$ dominate the same atoms of B, whence they are the same element of B by, essentially, Theorem 11.
  For an arbitrary atom $b \in B$,

$$b \leqslant f(I) \quad \text{iff} \quad p_b \in I \qquad \text{Def of } p_b$$
$$\quad\quad\quad\quad \text{iff} \quad b \leqslant h_f(I) \qquad \text{Sublemma}$$

(iii) h_f *preserves complements.*

Let Q arbitrary in P^*, b an arbitrary atom in B. Then,

$$b \leqslant h_f(Q') \quad \text{iff } p_b \in Q' \qquad\qquad \text{Sublemma}$$
$$\text{iff } p_b \notin Q \qquad\qquad \text{Def of } '$$
$$\text{iff } b \nleqslant h_f(Q) \qquad\qquad \text{Sublemma}$$
$$\text{iff } b \leqslant (h_f(Q))' \qquad b \text{ is an atom.}$$

Thus $h_f(Q') = (h_f(Q))'$ since these two elements of B dominate the same atoms and B is complete and atomic.

(iv) h_f *preserves meets*

Let K an arbitrary subset of P^*, b an arbitrary atom $\in B$. Then,

$$b \leqslant h_f(\wedge K) \text{ iff } b \leqslant h_f(\bigcap K) \qquad \wedge = \bigcap \text{ in power set algebras}$$
$$\text{iff } p_b \in \bigcap K \qquad\qquad \text{Sublemma}$$
$$\text{iff } \forall k \in K, p_b \in k \qquad \text{Def of } \bigcap$$
$$\text{iff } \forall k \in K, b \leqslant h_f(k) \qquad \text{Sublemma}$$
$$\text{iff } b \text{ is a lb for } \{h_f(k) : k \in K\}, \quad \text{Def of lb}$$
$$\text{iff } b \leqslant \underset{k \in K}{\wedge} h_f(k) \qquad\qquad \text{Def of glb}$$

Thus $h_f(\wedge K) = \wedge_{k \in K} h_f(k)$ since these two elements of B dominate the same atoms and B is complete and atomic.

Since h_f preserves meets and complements it also provably preserves joins. Thus h_f is a complete homomorphism which extends f, proving the theorem.

Note that the JT does not require that B be the minimal algebra 2. It is sufficient that B is a *ca*-algebra. Thus we have as a special case of JT that an element of $T_{P_1} = H_2/P^*$ is defined by stating its values on the individuals in any way we like, which is just to say that T_{P_1} is the set of one place predicates of standard first other logic.

To see formally that the elements of T_{P_1} as defined correspond in a natural one-to-one way to elements of T_N, note that we may consider a complete homomorphism from P^* into 2 as a function which assigns a set of properties Q value 1 iff a fixed property p is a member of Q. Formally,

DEFINITION 36.

(i) For all $p \in P$ $(= T_N)$ define a function f_p from P^* into 2 by:
$f_p(Q) = 1$ if $p \in Q$ and $f_p(Q) = 0$ if $p \notin Q$
(ii) $F_P =_{df} \{f_p : p \in P\}$

THEOREM 18. $F_P = H_{2/P^*}$

Note that F_P and H_{2/P^*} are both subsets of F_{2/P^*}. The straightforward proof of Theorem 18 is sketched out at the end of this section.

Now, we want to regard T_{P_1} as a boolean algebra since we want to provide interpretations for boolean combinations of P_1's, e.g. (both) *sing and dance*, (either) *sing or dance, not sing*, etc. The definitions of the meet, join, and complement operations on T_{P_1} will have to be made with some care, as we must guarantee for example that our representation for (38a) does *not* entail that for (38b).

(38) a. Each student was either singing or dancing.
      b. Either each student was singing or each student was dancing.

Thus the interpretation of *sing or dance* cannot be handled pointwise on P^* since then the interpretation of *sing or dance* would map any set of properties, say the interpretation of *every student*, onto the join in the truth value algebra of the values obtained by applying each disjunction to that set. That is, (38a) and (38b) would be logically equivalent, which is incorrect. On the other hand, boolean combinations of P_1's do behave pointwise on *individuals*. Thus (39a) below is logically equivalent to (39b).

(39) a. John was either singing or dancing.
      b. Either John was singing or John was dancing.

Note further that in (38a), *sing or dance* does behave as a homomorphism. For *each student* will be interpreted as the meet (= intersection) of the individuals with the student-property, and the truth value which *sing or dance* associates with that meet is the one obtained by applying it to each of the individuals over which the meet was taken — obtaining a truth value in each case — and taking the meet of the resulting truth values. Thus *each student was singing or dancing* is true just in case for each individual I with the student property, I was singing or dancing, that is, I was singing or I was dancing. And given that we may define a P_1 homomorphism just by stating its values on the individuals, and that should be clearly done pointwise as per (39), we may then define the sing-or-dance homomorphism as that one whose value at an individual I is the join of the value of the sing-homomorphism at I with the dance-homomorphism at I. Formally:

DEFINITION 37. $T_{P_1} = H_2/P*$, regarded as a boolean algebra where $0, 1, \wedge,$ $\vee$, and $'$ are define *pointwise on the individuals* as follows:

  (i)   0 is that element of $H_2/P*$ which maps each individual I onto 0_2, the zero element of 2;

  (ii)   1 is that element of $H_2/P*$ which maps each I onto 1_2; and

  (iii)   for all $h, k \in H_2/P*$,

     (a) $(h \wedge k)$ is that element of $H_2/P*$ such that for all individuals I, $(h \wedge k)(I) = h(I) \wedge k(I)$;

     (b) $(h \vee k)$ is that element of $H_2/P*$ such that for all I, $(h \vee k)(I) = h(I) \vee k(I)$; and

     (c) (h') is that element of $H_2/P*$ such that for all I, $(h')(I) = (h(I))'$.

Of course the meet, join, and complement signs on the right of the equations in (iii) refer to these operations in 2, since $h(I)$ and $k(I)$ are elements of 2. By the JT $(h \wedge k)$, $(h \vee k)$, and h' above are well defined elements of $T_{P_1} = H_2/P*$ since there is exactly one element of $H_2/P*$ with a given set of values on the individuals and in each case we have stated what their values on the individuals are. Crucially, then, the boolean operations on T_{P_1} are not defined pointwise on $P*$ itself, but only on the subset of $P*$ consisting of the individuals. By the JT this is sufficient.

As the application of these definitions in particular cases can sometimes be tricky, let us first show that (40) below, our representation for (39a), is logically equivalent to (41), our representation for (39b).

(40)   John   (sing   or   dance)

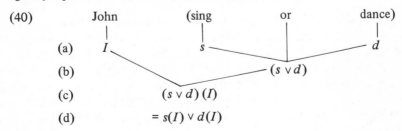

    (a) I s d

    (b) $(s \vee d)$

    (c) $(s \vee d)(I)$

    (d) $= s(I) \vee d(I)$

In line (a) we indicate that *John* is interpreted as some individual I; *sing* and *dance* as P_1 homomorphisms s and d respectively. In line (b) *sing or dance* is interpreted as the P_1 homomorphism $(s \vee d)$. In line (c) the truth value of the entire sentence is represented as $(s \vee d)(I)$, the value of $(s \vee d)$ at the individual I. Line (d) indicates that this value is the same as $s(I) \vee d(I)$, joins now of course taken in the truth value algebra. The equality is directly justified by our definition of v in the P_1 algebra — namely pointwise on *individuals*.

(41)

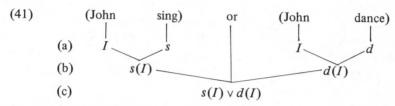

Here the interpretations of *John, sing*, and *dance* are as before, as indicated in line (a). Line (b) says that truth value of (*John sing*) is given by $s(I)$, the value of the sing homomorphism at the individual John; similarly $d(I)$ gives the value (*John dance*). And line (c) says that the value of (41) is the join of these two truth values. As line (c) here is identical to line (d) in (40) it is clear that (40) and (41) will be represented by the same truth value when their lexical components are interpreted the same. That is, (40) and (41) will be logically equivalent.

Consider now the trickier case of (42), our representation for (38a) and that of (43), our representation for (38b), which must turn out not to be logically equivalent.

(42)

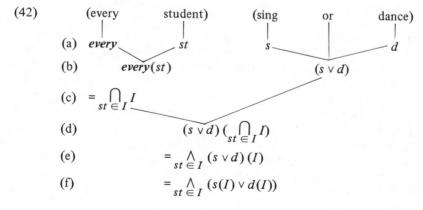

Here line (a) gives the interpretations of the lexical expressions in (42). Line (b) says that *every student* is the value of the every-function at the student property, and *sing or dance* is the join of the sing-homomorphism with the dance-homomorphism. Line (c) gives the value of *every student* as the intersection of the individuals with the student-property. Line (d) says that the truth value of (42) is the value of $(s \vee d)$ at this intersection. Line (e) is justified since $(s \vee d)$ is a homomorphism and thus maps an intersection of individuals onto the meet in the truth value algebra of the values obtained by applying $(s \vee d)$ to each of those individuals. Line (f) replaces $(s \vee d)\,(I)$ by $s(I) \vee d(I)$, which we may do by the definition of $\vee$ in join in P the P_1 algebra since the argument of $(s \vee d)$ is an individual. Note crucially that since $(s \vee d)$ is a homomorphism its value at $\bigcap_{st \in I} I$ is determined to be $\bigwedge_{st \in I} (s \vee d)\,(I)$. It would simply be false to say in general that its value at $\bigcap_{st \in I} I$ was e.g. $s(\bigcap_{st \in I} I) \vee d(\bigcap_{st \in I} I)$.

(43)   ((every student) sing) or ((every student) dance)

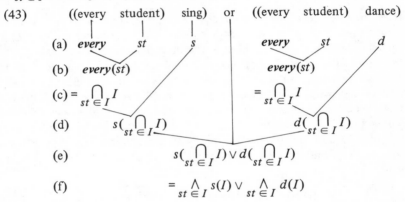

(a) *every*   *st*   *s*   *every*   *st*   *d*

(b) *every*(st)   *every*(st)

(c) $= \bigcap_{st \in I} I$ $= \bigcap_{st \in I} I$

(d) $s(\bigcap_{st \in I} I)$ $d(\bigcap_{st \in I} I)$

(e) $s(\bigcap_{st \in I} I) \vee d(\bigcap_{st \in I} I)$

(f) $= \bigwedge_{st \in I} s(I) \vee \bigwedge_{st \in I} d(I)$

The interpretation of the lines down to (d) is obvious. Line (d) merely says that *every student sing* is interpreted as the value of the sing homomorphism at the denotation of *every student*; and similarly for *every student dance*. And (e) says the truth value of (43) is expressed by the join of these two truth values. The equality of (e) with (f) follows from the fact that s and d are both homomorphisms and thus preserve meets. And it is obvious that line (f) here need not be the same truth value as that in line (f) of (42). For (f) in (43) to be 1 it must be the case that at least one of the truth values we take the join of is 1. That is, either *every student is singing* is true or *every student is dancing* is true. But line (f) in (42) can be 1 if some students are singing but not dancing and the others are dancing but not singing, since it only requires that of each individual with the student property, either he is singing or he is dancing. Thus (f) in (42) can be 1 in models where (f) in (43) is 0. Thus (42) and (43) are not logically equivalent on our semantics.

As a further exercise in this notation we invite the reader show the following: (*not* [(*every man*) *sing*]) is logically equivalent to ([*not* (*every man*)] *sing*), and neither is equivalent to [(*every man*) (*not sing*)] . ((*no man*) *sing*) is equivalent to ((*not* (*a man*)) *sing*); ((*some student*) (*sink and swim*)) is not equivalent to [(*some student*) *sink*] *and* [(*some student*) *swim*] .

Returning now to the definition of T_{P_1} note that we must prove that the boolean operations 0, 1, ∧, ∨, and ′ as defined actually satisfy the axioms of a boolean algebra. Let us in fact show more:

THEOREM 19. T_{P_1} as defined is a complete and atomic algebra.
   Proof sketch

(i) T_{P_1} is a boolean algebra.

We have already shown that 0 and 1 are well defined elements of $H_{2/P*}$ = T_{P_1} as are $(h \wedge k)$, $(h \vee k)$, and h' whenever h and k are in $H_{2/P*}$. To show that the operations as defined satisfy the axioms of a boolean algebra let us illustrate the proof that the complement law $(h \wedge h') = 0$ holds. We must show that $(h \wedge h')$ and 0 have the same values on all elements of $P*$. By the JT (uniqueness) it is sufficient to show that they have the same values on the individuals given that both $(h \wedge h')$ and 0 are complete homomorphisms from $P*$ into 2. Let I be an arbitrary individual. Then,

$$
\begin{aligned}
(h \wedge h')(I) &= h(I) \wedge (h')(I) && \text{pointwise def of } \wedge \text{ on individuals} \\
&= h(I) \wedge (h(I))' && \text{pointwise def of } ' \text{ on individuals} \\
&= 0_2 && \text{complement laws in 2} \\
&= 0(I) && \text{def 0 in } T_{P_1}
\end{aligned}
$$

As I was arbitrary, $(h \wedge h')(I) = 0(I)$ for all I, so by the JT $(h \wedge h') = 0$. The other axioms are proven analogously.

To show T_{P_1} complete, note first the following lemma:

LEMMA 1. For B any *ca*-algebra, h, k any elements of $H_{B/P*}$,

$$h \leqslant k \text{ iff for all individuals } I, h(I) \leqslant k(I).$$

Proof.

$$h \leqslant k \quad \text{iff} \quad h \wedge k = h \qquad\qquad\qquad \text{def of} \leqslant$$
$$ \quad \text{iff} \quad (\forall I)\,((h \wedge k)\,(I) = h(I)) \qquad \text{JT}$$
$$ \quad \text{iff} \quad (\forall I)\,((h(I) \wedge k(I)) = h(I)) \quad \text{pointwise def of} \wedge \text{ on individuals}$$
$$ \quad \text{iff} \quad (\forall I)\,(h(I) \leqslant k(I)) \qquad\qquad \text{def} \leqslant \text{ in } B$$

    (ii) T_{P_1} is complete

Let K be a subset of $H_2/P*$. Define h_K in $H_2/P*$ by $h_K (I) = \wedge \{k(I)\colon k \in K\}$, all individuals I. Since 2 is complete, $\{k(I)\colon k \in K\}$ has a glb in 2; by the JT h_K is a well-defined element of $H_2/P*$. It is routine to show that h_K is the glb for K. Similarly f_K defined by $f_K (I) = \vee \{k(I)\colon k \in K\}$ is the lub for K in T_{P_1}. Thus T_{P_1} is complete.

    (iii) T_{P_1} is atomic.

For all individuals I and all atoms $x \in 2$, define $f_{I,\,x}$ in $H_2/P*$ by $f_{I,\,x} (J) = x$ if $J = I$, $f_{I,\,x} (J) = 0$ if $J \neq I$. Each $f_{I,\,x}$ is easily shown to be an atom and any non-zero element of $H_2/P*$ is easily shown to dominate an atom. Thus T_{P_1} is atomic. Note that the only atom in 2 is the unit element. We have stated (iii) with slightly more generality than needed here for purposes of later generalization.

To conclude our discussion of T_{P_1} let us note:

THEOREM 20. T_N is isomorphic to T_{P_1}.

    Proof sketch. The function f from P ($= T_N$) into $H_2/P*$ ($= T_{P_1}$) which sends each $p \in P$ to f_p, defined in Definition 36, is easily seen to be an isomorphism from P onto $H_2/P*$.

Defining T_{P_n}, all n

Note that we want the P_1 (*kiss (John and Bill)*) to be interpreted as the same element of T_{P_1} as ((*kiss John*) *and* (*kiss Bill*)). This will guarantee for example that our representations for (44a) and (44b) will be logically equivalent:

    (44)   a. Mary kissed both John and Bill.
            b. Mary kissed John and kissed Bill.

Of course by the pointwise definition of meet in individuals in T_{P_1}, (44b) above will be logically equivalent to (44c) below:

    (44)   c. Mary kissed John and Mary kissed Bill.

So this semantics will correctly predict that (44a) and (44c) are logically equivalent. But to say that the P_1's in (44a, b) are the same elements of T_{P_1} is just to say that the interpretation of the P_2 *kiss* preserves meets. Similarly *(to) kiss either John or Bill* should be interpreted the same as *(to) kiss John or kiss Bill* whence it will follow that *Mary kissed either John or Bill* will be represented as logically equivalent to *Mary kissed John or Mary kissed Bill*, which is correct. So the kiss-function should preserve joins. Similarly *(to) kiss no student* should mean the same as *(to) not (kiss a student)*, so kiss preserves complements. Thus elements of T_{P_2} should be homomorphisms from $T_{\overline{N}} = P^*$ into T_{P_1}.

Moreover boolean combinations of P_2's are clearly interpreted pointwise on individuals. Thus *(to) both hug and kiss John* means the same as *(to) hug John and (to) kiss John*, etc. Thus we want T_{P_2} to be the set of complete homomorphisms from P^* into T_{P_1}, regarded as a boolean algebra where the operations are defined pointwise on the individuals. Since T_{P_1} is a ca-algebra the JT says that we may define elements of $H_{T_{P_1}/P^*}$ just by stating their values on the individuals. We immediately generalize this approach for n-place predicates as follows:

DEFINITION 38. For all $n \geqslant 0$, T_{P_n} is defined inductively as follows:

(i) $T_{P_0} = 2$.

(ii) $T_{P_{n+1}} = H_{T_{P_n}/P^*}$, regarded as a complete and atomic boolean algebra where the operations are defined pointwise on the individuals. That is, $0_{n+1}(I) = 0_n$, all individuals I; analogously for 1_{n+1}. And $(f \wedge_{n+1} g)(I) = f(I) \wedge_n g(I)$, all individuals I. Analogously for $\vee_{n+1}$ and $'_{n+1}$.

THEOREM 21. For all $n \geqslant 0$, T_{P_n} as above is a complete and atomic boolean algebra.

Proof sketch: by induction on n.

(i) for $n = 0$ we have that $T_{P_0} = 2$ is a *ca*-algebra.

(ii) Assume the theorem for n, show it for $n + 1$. Then T_{P_n} is a *ca*-algebra by the induction hypothesis, hence 0_{n+1}, and 1_{n+1} are well defined elements of $H_{T_{P_n}/P^*}$ by the JT, as are $(f \wedge_{n+1} g)$, $(f \vee_{n+1} g)$ and f'_{n+1} when f and g are in $T_{P_{n+1}}$. The proof that the boolean axioms are satisfied follows the paradigm illustrated for T_{P_1}. The atoms of $T_{P_{n+1}}$ map a single individual onto some atom of T_{P_n} and all other individuals onto 0_n. And the glb for a subset K of $T_{P_{n+1}}$ maps each individual onto the glb for $\{k(I): k \in K\}$ in T_{P_n}. Analogously for lub's.

We have then defined T_{P_n} for all (finite) n. We note as well the following two theorems (whose induction proofs are omitted):

THEOREM 22. (*Generalized Justification Theorem*: GJT). For all $n > 0$, if f is a function from $(I_P)^n$ into 2 then there is a unique complete homomorphism $h_f \in T_{P_n}$ such that for all individuals $I_1, I_2, \ldots, I_n$ ($\ldots ((h_f(I_1)) (I_2)) \ldots) (I_n) = f(I_1, I_2, \ldots, I_n)$.

For example, the GJT says that we may define an element of T_{P_2} merely by giving a function from pairs of individuals into 2. E.g. we may define *be* as that element of T_{P_2} such that for all individuals I_1, I_2 *be* $(I_1) (I_2) = 1$ if $I_1 = I_2$; otherwise *be* $(I_1) (I_2) = 0$.

Finally, let us note that in the same way that T_{P_1} is isomorphic to the power set of I_P, the set of individuals on P (= T_N), so T_{P_n} is isomorphic to the power set of $(I_P)^n$. For let K be an element of that power set. Then K is a set of n-tuples of individuals. Define by the GJT the element f_K in T_{P_n} by $((\ldots (f_K (I_1)) \ldots) (I_n) = 1$ iff $\langle I_1, I_2, \ldots, I_n \rangle \in K$. The function f from $((I_P)^n)^*$ into T_{P_n} which sends each K in $((I_P)^n)^*$ to f_K is the desired isomorphism. Thus:

THEOREM 23. For all $n \geqslant 0$, T_{P_n} is isomorphic to the power set of $(I_P)^n$. Theorem 23 says in effect that n-place predicates in L are semantically just sets of n-tuples of individuals, as they are in standard FOL.

Defining Types for Predicative Hierarchies in General

The method of constructing types for the P_n generalizes immediately to any predicative hierarchy (though in each case of course we must check that the definition is descriptively adequate, i.e. the right elements are in fact judged to behave as homomorphisms and operations on them are pretheoretically judged to behave pointwise on the individuals).

More specifically, let C be any category such that T_C is a complete and atomic algebra. Then the predicative hierarchy generated by C is defined inductively as follows: $C_0 = C$ and $C_{n+1} = C_n/\overline{N}$. Types for the C_n are defined inductively as follows:

(i) $T_{C_0} = T_C$ and

(ii) $T_{C_{n+1}} = H_{T_{C_n}/P^*}$, regarded as a complete and atomic algebra where the operations are defined pointwise on the individuals.

Thus the type for N_1 ($= N/\bar{N}$) is defined as the set of complete homomorphisms from $T_{\bar{N}} = P^*$ into T_{N_0} ($= T_N$), since T_N is a complete and atomic algebra. The adequacy and interest of this definition will be discussed in the extensions to L proposed shortly. For the nonce we may note that N_1 is an empty category of L, as are P_3, P_4, etc. Once we add a lambda operator to L however it will follow that whenever a category C is interpreted by a ca-algebra then for all n, C_n is non-empty.

    This completes the definition of the types for L. For convenience to the reader we present these definitions in toto below:

Summary Definition of the Types

DEFINITION 39. An *ontology*, or *set of semantic primitives*, for L is a pair $\langle P, 2 \rangle$ where P is a complete and atomic boolean algebra and 2 is the minimal boolean algebra

DEFINITION 40. Relative to an ontology $\langle P, 2 \rangle$ we define for each category C, T_C, or *the type for C*, as follows:

$T_N = P$,

$T_{\bar{N}} = P^*$, regarded as a power set boolean algebra,

$T_{\bar{N}_{\text{prop}}} = \{I: I$ is an individual on $P\}$, where I *is an individual on* P iff I is a subset of P such that

(i) for all $p \in P$, $p \in I$ iff $p' \notin I$ and

(ii) for all $K \subseteq p$, $\wedge K \in I$ iff $K \subseteq I$.

    Remark: individuals so defined provably satisfy the Joins Condition. We denote the set of individuals on P by I_P.

$T_{\bar{N}/N} = \{f \in F_{P^*/P}: f$ is conservative$\}$, regarded as a complete and atomic boolean algebra where the operations are defined pointwise on P.

T_P ($= T_{P_0}$) $= 2$

For C any of N, P, $\bar{N}$, or $\bar{N}/N$ we use C_0 to abbreviate C and C_{n+1} to abbreviate $C_n/\bar{N}$ and define inductively:

(i) $T_{C_0} = T_C$ and

(ii) $T_{C_{n+1}} = H_{T_{C_n}}/P*$, the set of complete homomorphism from $P*$ into T_{C_n}, regarded as a complete and atomic boolean algebra where the operations are defined pointwise on I_P.

For all categories C not mentioned above, $T_C = \emptyset$.

Defining Interpretations for L

An interpretation for L will be a function m from $L = \bigcup_{C \in \text{Cat}} C$ into $\bigcup_{C \in \text{Cat}} T_C$ which assigns to each expression e of L of category C some element of T_C in accordance with certain constraints on lexical expressions and constraints on derived expressions. Since the interpretation of a derived expression is uniquely determined once the interpretations of those it is derived from is given it will turn out that an interpretation m is uniquely determined by an interpretation M of the primitive expressions of L. Accordingly we shall first define a *lexical interpreting function M* and then extend M to a complete interpretation m. The domain of M will be the basic vocabulary V less the syncategorematic symbols *and, or,* and *not.* For convenience let us define:

DEFINITION 41. *Lex*, or *the lexicon of L,* $= V - \{e \in \text{PE}_V : e$ is syncategorematic$\}$, where e in PE_V is *syncategorematic* iff $e \notin C$ for any category C.

DEFINITION 42. A model μ of L is a triple $\langle P, 2, M \rangle$, where $\langle P, 2 \rangle$ is an ontology for L and M is a function from lex into $\bigcup_{C \in \text{Cat}} T_C$ which satisfies the following conditions:

(i)   For all $e \in \text{Lex}$ and all categories C, if $e \in C$ then $M(e) \in T_C$,

(ii)   *conditions on logical constants*

   (a) $M(individual) = M(existent) = 1_{T_N}$
   (b) $M(exist) = 1_{T_{P_1}}$
   (c) $M(be) = be$, that element of T_{P_2} such that for all individuals I_1, I_2 $(be(I_1))(I_2)$
   $$= \begin{cases} 1 & \text{if} \quad I_1 = I_2 \\ 0 & \text{if} \quad I_1 \neq I_2 \end{cases}$$
   (d) $M(every) = M(all) = M(each) = every$, that element of $T_{\bar{N}/N}$ which sends each $p \in T_N$ to $\bigcap_{p \in I} I$, where I ranges over individuals on P;

$M(a) = M(some) = a$, that element of $T_{\bar{N}/N}$ which maps each $p \in T_N$ onto $\bigcup_{p \in I} I$

$M(no) = a'$

$M(the)$ is that element of $T_{\bar{N}/N}$ which sends each $p \in T_N$ to $\emptyset$ if p is not an atom and to I_p, the individual generated by p, if p is an atom;

(iii)   *conditions on non-logical constants*

$M(bachelor) \leqslant M(man)$

$((M(kill)\,(I_1))\,(I_2) \leqslant (M(die))\,(I_1)$, all individuals I_1, I_2.

We may now extend M to an interpretation of L as follows:

DEFINITION 43. For all models $\langle P, 2, M \rangle$, *m is an interpretation of L relative to* $\langle P, 2, M \rangle$ iff m is a function from L into $\bigcup \{T_C \colon C \in \text{Cat}\}$ which satisfies the following conditions:

(i)   for all $e \in \text{Lex}$, $m(e) = M(e)$

(ii)   for all X, Y in CAT^n, if $e_1 \in X/Y$ and $e_2 \in Y_i$, $1 \leqslant i \leqslant n$, then
$m(\{e_1, e_2\}) = m(e_1)\,(m(e_2))$

(iii) for all categories C, if $e_1 \in C$ and $e_2 \in C$ then
$m(\{e_1, and, e_2\}) = m(e_1) \wedge m(e_2)$ and
$m(\{e_1, or, e_2\}) = m(e_1) \vee m(e_2)$ and
$m(\{not, e_1\}) = (m(e_1))'$.

DEFINITION 44. *m is an interpretation of L* iff for some model $\langle P, 2, M \rangle$, m is an interpretation of L relative to $\langle P, 2, M \rangle$.

In terms of interpretations we may now define the fundamental semantic relation, $\leqslant$, called *extensional inclusion*, (= *extensionally more informative than*) of which the classical entailment relation is but a special case.

DEFINITION 45. For all categories C, all $K \subseteq C$, and all $e \in C$, $K \leqslant e$ iff for all interpretations m of L, $\bigwedge_{k \in K} m(k) \leqslant m(e)$.

Notational remarks on Definition 45

(i)   if $K \leqslant e$ as per the above we say that K is (*extensionally*) included in e.

(ii)   if K is a unit set $\{e_1\}$, we write $e_1 \leqslant e$ rather than $\{e_1\} \leqslant e$.

(iii) if C in Definition 45 is the category P_0 and $K \leqslant e$ we say that K *entails* e and write $K \models e$.

Discussion of Definition 45 Note first that our definition of inclusion does in fact coincide with entailment when applied to sentences, i.e. elements of P_0. Thus if S is a sentence and K a set of sentences our definition says that K entails S iff $\wedge \{m(k): k \in K\} \leqslant m(S)$, for all interpretations m of L. Thus, given an arbitrary interpretation m, if all the sentences k in K are true in m, that is, $m(k) = 1$ for all $k \in K$, then $\wedge_{k \in K} m(k) = 1$ and thus $m(S)$ must be 1. Thus to say that K entails S is just to say that S is true whenever all the sentences in K are true. Of course if K is a unit set, say $\{T\}$, then $\wedge_{k \in K} m(k) = \wedge \{m(T)\} = m(T)$. Thus T entails S iff for all interpretations m, if $m(T) = 1$ then $m(S) = 1$.

But our definition of course is much more general than the classical one. It says that entailment among sentences is just the special case of boolean inclusion. So the definition applies equally well to any expressions interpreted as elements of a given boolean algebra. For example it follows on our semantics that (*sing and dance*) $\leqslant$ *sing, kiss John and Mary* $\leqslant$ *kiss John, some but not all* $\leqslant$ *some, sing* $\leqslant$ *sing or dance, John* $\leqslant$ *John or Mary*, etc. and in the various extensions of L that we propose *walk slowly* $\leqslant$ *walk, tall student* $\leqslant$ *student*, etc.

As an exercise in our semantics we invite the reader to verify that the sets of sentences in the a-examples below entail the corresponding b-sentence:

(45) a. John (kiss (no student))
          Mary (be (a student))
      b. John (not (kiss Mary))
(46) a. John ((hug and kiss)) ((some student) and (every teacher))),
          Mary (be (a teacher))
      b. John (hug Mary)
(47) a. (John or (every student)) spoke
          Mary (be (a student))
      b. (John or Mary) spoke
(48) a. ((not every) student) spoke
      b. (some student) (not spoke)

In standard logic a certain number of other semantic properties of expressions are defined in terms of entailment. These are of course definable in our system and, like extensional inclusion, apply to all categories, not just P_0. Some examples follow:

DEFINITION 46.   For all categories C, all $e_1, e_2 \in C$,
    e_1 is *logically equivalent* ($\equiv$) to e_2 iff $e_1 \leqslant e_2$ and $e_2 \leqslant e_1$.

For example, in the same way that (*John sang*) *and* (*Mary worked or Peter slept*) is logically equivalent to ((*John sang and Mary worked*) *or* (*John sang and Peter slept*) in standard FOL so here e.g. *John and* (*Mary or Peter*) is logically equivalent to (*John and Mary*) *or* (*John and Peter*).

DEFINITION 47. For all categories C and all $e \in C$, e is *logically 1* iff $\emptyset \leqslant e$.

It follows that for $e \in C$, e is logically 1 iff for all interpretations m, $m(e) = 1_{TC}$. If e is logically 1 and $e \in P_0$ we say that e is *logically true*.

DEFINITION 48. An expression e is *logically 0* iff (*not e*) is logically 1.

It follows that for $e \in C$, e is logically 0 iff for all m, $m(e) = 0_{TC}$. When e is logically 0 and $e \in P_0$ we say that e is *logically false*.
 The reader may verify that in *L*, *existent*, *exist*, and *every student be a student* are all logically 1. Their negations are all logically 0.

DEFINITION 49. An expression e is *logically trivial* iff e is logically 1 or e is logically 0. e is *synthetic* iff e is not logically trivial.

DEFINITION 50. For $K \subseteq C$ and $e \in C$, e is *independent of K* iff $K \nleqslant e$. K is *independent* iff for all $k \in K$, k is independent of $K - \{k\}$.

Advantages of the Generalized Entailment Relation

It is perhaps reasonable to query here just what the advantage of generalizing the classical entailment relation is. Our purpose is only to show that in the same way that the meanings of *and*, *or*, and *not* are not specific to sentence meanings so entailment is not specific to sentence meanings. It is in essence just the boolean inclusion relation. Thus we have a direct way of expressing the intuitively felt relation between e.g. *walk slowly* and *walk, sing and dance* and *sing*, etc. We feel however that the generalizations we have offered will have further utility. We suggest below a few possibilities for further thought, though none will be explored here in any detail.
 First, it is often taken as a truism of sorts that extensional inclusion is the converse of intensional inclusion. Loosely, we may say that e_1 is intensionally included in e_2 if the meaning of e_1 is 'part of' the meaning of e_2, i.e. if we know what e_2 means then necessarily we know what e_1 means. But

the claim that the two inclusion relations are converses can easily be shown to be false, though many simple cases appear to support it. For example *walk* is intensionally included in *walk slowly*, and indeed *walk slowly* is extensionally included in *walk*. Similarly *sing* is intensionally included in *sing and dance* while *sing and dance* is extensionally included in *sing*. But it is also true that *sing* is intensionally included in *sing or dance* but not true that *sing or dance* is extensionally included in *sing*. Similarly, anticipating the addition of adjectives to L, it will turn out that *a tall student* is extensionally included in *a student* and intuitively *a student* is intensionally included in *a tall student*. But by parity of reasoning *every student* is intensionally included in *every tall student*, but the converse does not obtain as regards extensional inclusion. In fact, *every student* is extensionally included in *every tall student* (the set of properties which all students have in common is a subset of those which the tall students have in common).

Second, and potentially much farther reaching, it seems to us likely that the use of the boolean $\leqslant$ relation in all categories will be useful in formulating properly natural deductive systems — that is, systems which formalize logical reasoning in ordinary language. Consider for example the following crudely stated first approximations to rules of inference on ordinary language (we use d, d_1, d_2, etc. as variables ranging over P_1 and n, n_1, n_2, etc. as variables ranging over $\overline{N}$):

(49)   From a P_0 of the form $(n_1 d)$ infer $(n_2 d)$ if $n_1 \leqslant n_2$.

Thus from *Both John and Mary are linguists* we may infer *Mary is a linguist* since *John and Mary* $\leqslant$ *Mary*; and from *no student sang* we may infer *no tall student sang* since (see Section B) *no student* $\leqslant$ *no tall student*. Note that (49) is a sound rule since d is interpreted by a homomorphism and for any homomorphism h we have $h(x) \leqslant h(y)$ if $x \leqslant y$. So in fact for $d \in P_k$, any $k \geqslant 1$, we have that for all interpretations m, $m(dn_1) = m(d)$ $(m(n_1)) \leqslant m(d) (m(n_2)) = m(dn_2)$ when $m(n_1) \leqslant m(n_2)$. But (49) only licenses inferring one sentence from another by replacing n_1 by n_2, $n_1 \leqslant n_2$, when n_1 is the *subject* of the sentence. (We may define n_1 to be the *subject of* of $S \in P_0$ iff $S = (n_1 d)$ for some $d \in P_1$). If non-subjects are replaced the inference in L is not generally valid. Thus (50a) below does not entail (50b):

(50) a. No student kissed both John and Mary
      b. ⊭ No student kissed John

Of course, *kiss (John and Mary)* $\leqslant$ *kiss John*, but whether $(n_1$ *(kiss (John and Mary)))* $(n_1$ *kiss John)* or not depends on whether n_1 is logically *increasing*, *decreasing*, or *neither*. Formally,

DEFINITION 51. For $n_1 \in \bar{N}$, n_1 is (logically) *increasing* iff for all interpretations m, $m(n_1)$ is increasing; n_1 is (logically) *decreasing* iff for all m, $m(n_1)$ is decreasing.

We may then posit, as first approximations, (51) and (52) as rules of inference:

(51)   From a P_0 (nd_1) infer (nd_2) if $d_1 \leqslant d_2$ and n is increasing.
(52)   From a P_0 (nd_1) infer (nd_2) if $d_2 \leqslant d_1$ and n is decreasing.

Thus by (51) we may infer *every student is either singing or dancing* from *every student is singing*, since *sing* $\leqslant$ *sing or dance*. And by (52) we may infer *no student is singing* from *no student is either singing or dancing*.

Space will not permit deeper consideration of the suggested rules of inference above. We should only note that much more needs to be said concerning the formulation of the proof language in expressions which are shown to bear the $\leqslant$ relation to each other. Nonetheless the examples are suggestive enough, we think, to justify a certain optimism concerning the general use of $\leqslant$ in representing everyday reasoning in natural language.

A Concluding Remark on Comparative Ontologies

It appears that an ontology for L, a pair $\langle P, 2 \rangle$, is somewhat more complex than the corresponding ontology $\langle U, 2 \rangle$ for standard first order logic in that both our primitives are required to be boolean algebras whereas in the standard case only 2 is required to possess a boolean structure, U being an arbitrary non-empty set. In fact, however, this judgment of relative complexity is somewhat spurious. We claim for example that the standard ontology is actually more complex than ours, as it requires the existence of two rather different primitives, one a boolean algebra, the other not; whereas our approach is simpler since it requires the existence of two rather similar primitives, complete and atomic boolean algebras in both cases.

To see that our claim is something more than a quibble over words, consider that we may easily omit 2 as a primitive, limiting our primitives thus to $P = T_N$. To do this we simply define T_{P_0} to be the set whose elements are just the zero and unit of P, the boolean operations just being those of P restricted to $\{0_P, 1_P\}$. There will be no change in the arguments represented as valid or the sentences represented as logically true since the 'new' T_{P_0} is isomorphic to the old one. And now our ontology seems clearly simpler than that of standard FOL since we have only one primitive and FOL has two, neither of which can be reduced to the other.

Whether we want in fact to simplify our ontology in this way however raises a host of non-trivial questions concerning the nature of 'truth values' and their relation to common noun denotations. Notice that we did not justify 2 as the type for P_0 in the informal way in which we justified the other types; we simply carried it over from standard FOL without change. Can we in fact justify 2 as the type for P_0? More specifically, what properties of T_{P_0} have we used in our semantics, and are they sufficient to justify that T_{P_0} should be the minimal algebra 2?

We have used the fact that T_{P_0} is a boolean algebra in order to correctly interpret conjunctions, disjunctions, and negations of sentences. Moreover we have used the fact that T_{P_0} is complete and atomic in defining the types for the other P_n's, in particular the P_1's. If T_{P_0} were not both complete and atomic the Justification Theorem would not apply and we could not define P_1 interpretations merely by giving their values on the individuals, so the logic would not be a first order extensional one.

But can we justify that T_{P_0} should specifically be the algebra 2 rather than an arbitrary complete and atomic algebra? The answer is no. No further properties of T_{P_0} have been assumed in our treatment. Hence we should take T_{P_0} to merely be an arbitrary ca-algebra. And relaxing our requirement that T_{P_0} be specifically the algebra 2 no changes in which arguments are determined to be valid ensues. So the weaker ontology is as adequate as the one we took; by Occam's Razor, it should be chosen.

It is worth noting however that being a ca-algebra does impose cardinality constraints on the choice of T_{P_0}. Such algebras as we have seen are isomorphic to, and hence of the same cardinality as, power set algebras, whence they must have 2^k elements for some cardinal k. So we cannot use a three valued, or a five valued logic, or even an 0 valued logic, as they are not cardinality 2^k for any cardinal k.

It is also worth noting that standard approaches to intensional logic take T_{P_0} as $F_{2/W}$, the set of functions from an arbitrary non-empty set W of 'possible worlds' into 2. As this set is isomorphic to W^* and W is arbitrary this amounts to taking T_{P_0} as an arbitrary complete and atomic algebra, by Theorem 6.

Proofs of the Theorems

Here we sketch out those proofs which were not given explicitly in the text.

Our first proof is that of:

THEOREM 1. For all $q \in T_N$ $(= U^*)$, $\{q\} = \bigcap\{I_x : x \in q\} \cap \bigcap\{(I_x)' : x \notin q\}$.

By Temporary Definition 10, if $x \in q$, then $q \in I_x$. Thus, $q \in \bigcap\{I_x : x \in q\}$. Again by Temporary Definition 10, if $x \notin q$, then $q \notin I_x$, whence $q \in (I_x)'$. Thus, $q \in \bigcap\{(I_x)' : x \notin q\}$. We conclude that $q \in \bigcap\{I_x : x \in q\} \cap \bigcap\{(I_x)' : x \notin q\}$, which is to say that $\{q\} \subseteq \bigcap\{I_x : x \in q\} \cap \bigcap\{(I_x)' : x \notin q\}$.

To prove the reverse inclusion, let r be an arbitrary member of U^* such that r is an element of $\bigcap\{I_x : x \in q\} \cap \bigcap\{(I_x)' : x \notin q\}$. Thus, $r \in \bigcap\{I_x : x \in q\}$ and also $r \in \bigcap\{(I_x)' : x \notin q\}$.

Now, let I_{x_1} be an arbitrary individual (as defined in Temporary Definition 10). Either $x_1 \in q$ or else $x_1 \notin q$ (but not both).

If $x_1 \in q$, then $q \in I_{x_1}$, whence $r \in I_{x_1}$. If $x_1 \notin q$, then $r \in (I_{x_1})'$, whence $r \notin I_{x_1}$. In other words, the individuals which contain r as a member are precisely those which contain q as a member. By Temporary Definition 10, the individual I_{x_1} contains r as a member iff $x_1 \in r$. Thus, we conclude that the elements of r are precisely the elements of q; that is, $r = q$. Since r was an arbitrary member of $\bigcap\{I_x : x \in q\} \cap \bigcap\{(I_x)' : x \notin q\}$, this proves this set is included in $\{q\}$.

Next, we have the following theorem about the $\leqslant$ relation in any boolean algebra:

THEOREM 2. For all x, y, $z \in B$, B the domain of a boolean algebra,

    (a) $0 \leqslant x$ and $x \leqslant 1$
    (b) $x \leqslant x$ (Reflexivity)
    (c) if $x \leqslant y$ and $y \leqslant x$ then $x = y$ (Antisymmetry)
    (d) if $x \leqslant y$ and $y \leqslant z$ then $x \leqslant z$ (Transitivity)
    (e) $(x \wedge y) \leqslant x$ and $(x \wedge y) \leqslant y$
    (f) $x \leqslant (x \vee y)$ and $y \leqslant (x \vee y)$
    (g) if $x \leqslant y$ and $x \leqslant z$ then $x \leqslant (y \wedge z)$
    (h) if $x \leqslant z$ and $y \leqslant z$ then $(x \vee y) \leqslant z$
    (i) $x \leqslant y$ iff $(x \wedge y') = 0$
    (j) $x \leqslant y$ iff $(y \vee x) = y$

(a) $0 \wedge x = (x \wedge x') \wedge x$ (Complement Law)
$ = (x \wedge x) \wedge x'$ (Commutative and Associative Law)
$ = x \wedge x'$ (Idempotent Law)
$ = 0$ (Complement Law)

Note: this proof makes use of two laws which are not part of Definition 9, namely:

Associative Law: for all x, y, $z \in B$, B the domain of a boolean algebra,

$$x \wedge (y \wedge z) = (x \wedge y) \wedge z \quad \text{and}$$
$$x \vee (y \vee z) = (x \vee y) \vee z$$

Idempotent Law: for all $x \in B$, B the domain of a boolean algebra,

$$(x \wedge x) = x \quad \text{and}$$
$$(x \vee x) = x$$

These can be proved from the axioms in Definition 9. We omit the proofs here, but the interested reader can find them in Mendelson (1970), pp. 52–58.

The fact that $x \leqslant 1$ follows directly from Definition 12 and the Law of the unit (Definition 9(e)).

(b)   This follows directly from Definition 12 and the Idempotent Law.

(c) $x \leqslant y$ implies $x \wedge y = x$, and $y \leqslant x$ implies $y \wedge x = y$.

By the Commutative Law, $y \wedge x = x \wedge y$. Thus $y = y \wedge x = x \wedge y = x$.

We omit the proofs of the remaining parts, which are equally mechanical (if somewhat longer, in a few cases). However, the following additional lemma should be noted, since it comes in handy in many situations:

Complement Flip Law: For all x, $y \in B$, B the domain of a boolean algebra,
if $x \leqslant y$ then $y' \leqslant x'$.

For, if $x \leqslant y$, we have $x \wedge y = x$ (Definition 12), whence $x' = x' \vee y'$ (De-Morgan Law), so $y' \leqslant x'$ by part (j) of Theorem 2. Here we have made use of:

DeMorgan Laws: For all $x, y \in B$, B the domain of a boolean algebra,

$$(x \wedge y)' = x' \vee y' \quad \text{and}$$
$$(x \vee y)' = x' \wedge y'.$$

Again, these can be proved directly from the axioms in Definition 9.

THEOREM 3. For x, y elements of an arbitrary algebra B, $(x \wedge y)$ is the glb for $\{x, y\}$ and $(x \vee y)$ is the lub for $\{x, y\}$.

By Theorem 2(e), $(x \wedge y)$ is a lower bound for $\{x, y\}$. If z is a lower bound for $\{x, y\}$, then $z \leqslant x \wedge y$ by Theorem 2(g). Thus, $(x \wedge y)$ is the glb for $\{x, y\}$. The proof that $(x \vee y)$ is the lub for $\{x, y\}$ is similar.

THEOREM 4. Let B be an arbitrary algebra and b be an atom in B. Then

  (a) For all $x \in B$, either $(b \wedge x) = 0$ or $(b \wedge x) = b$.
  (b) For all $x \in B$, either $b \leqslant x$ or $b \leqslant x'$ but not both.
  (c) For all $c \in B$, if c is an atom of B and $c \neq b$ then $(b \wedge c) = 0$.

   (a) Since $b \wedge x \leqslant b$ (by Theorem 2(e)), this follows directly from Definition 16(a).
   (b) If $b \leqslant x$ and $b \leqslant x'$, then $b \leqslant x \wedge x'$ (Theorem 2(g)), whence $b \leqslant 0$ (Complement Law), and hence (since $0 \leqslant b$ by Theorem 2(a)) $b = 0$, contradicting Definition 16(a). If $b \not\leqslant x$, then $b \wedge x \neq b$, whence $b \wedge x = 0$ by (a). But then $b \leqslant x'$ by Theorem 2(i) (since $x'' = x$).
   (c) If b and c are both atoms and $b \wedge c \neq 0$, then $b \wedge c = b$ (by (a)) and also $b \wedge c = c$ (by (a)), so $b = c$.

   The proof of Theorem 5 is sketched in the text, as is the proof of Theorem 6. However, we give here the details of the proof that any complete atomic algebra B is isomorphic to the power set $(A_B)^*$, where A_B is the set of atoms of B. Recall that a function $f: B \rightarrow (A_B)^*$ is defined by setting $f(x) = \{b \in A_B : b \leqslant x\}$ for each $x \in B$. We show that f is an isomorphism.
   First, f is one-to-one. For let $x, y \in B$ with $x \neq y$. By Theorem 2(c), we cannot have both $x \leqslant y$ and $y \leqslant x$. Say $x \not\leqslant y$. Then $x \wedge y' \neq 0$ (by Theorem 2(i)). If b is an atom such that $b \leqslant x \wedge y'$, then $b \leqslant x$ (whence $b \in f(x)$) and $b \leqslant y'$, so that (Theorem 4(b)) $b \not\leqslant y$ (whence $b \notin f(y)$). Thus $f(x) \neq f(y)$.
   Next, f is onto. For, let $K \in (A_B)^*$ be arbitrary. Define $x = \bigcup K$; we show that $f(x) = K$.

If $b \in K$, then $b \leqslant \bigcup K = x$, so $b \in f(x)$. Thus, $K \subseteq f(x)$.

If $b \in f(x)$, then $b \leqslant x = \bigcup K$. Now, we must have $b \in K$; for otherwise, $b = b \wedge x = b \wedge (\bigcup K) = \bigcup_{b_0 \in K} \{b \wedge b_0\} = 0$ by Theorem 4(c), contradicting the fact that b is an atom. Thus, $f(x) \subseteq K$, whence $f(x) = K$.

We have shown that f is a one-to-one mapping of B onto $(A_B)^*$. We now show that f preserves meets, joins, and complements.

For x, $y \in B$, we have $b \in f(x \wedge y)$ iff $b \leqslant x \wedge y$ iff $b \leqslant x$ and $b \leqslant y$ (Theorem 2(e) and 2(g)) iff $b \in f(x) \cap f(y)$. Thus, f preserves meets. The proof that f preserves joins is similar. Finally, $b \in f(x')$ iff $b \leqslant x'$ iff $b \nleqslant x$ (Theorem 4(b)) iff $b \notin f(x)$ iff $b \in (f(x))'$, so f preserves complements. This shows that f is an isomorphism.

THEOREM 7. Let i be an isomorphism from B onto D. Then,

(a) $i(0_B) = 0_D$ and $i(1_B) = 1_D$.
(b) $x \leqslant_B y$ iff $i(x) \leqslant_D i(y)$.
(c) x is an atom of B iff $i(x)$ is an atom of D.
(d) i preserves unbounded meets and joins, i.e. for $K \subseteq B$, $i(\wedge K) = \wedge\{i(k): k \in K\}$ and $i(\vee K) = \vee\{i(k): k \in K\}$ where these equations are interpreted to mean that if the meet (join) on the left exists, (i.e. if K has a glb (lub) in B), then the meet (join) on the right exists and the equation holds.
(e) the function i^{-1} from D into B defined by $i^{-1}(d) = b$ iff $i(b) = d$ is an isomorphism from D onto B.

(a) Given any $x \in B$, since $0_B = x \wedge x'$, we have $i(0_B) = i(x \wedge x') = i(x) \wedge i(x') = i(x) \wedge (i(x))' = 0_D$. The proof that $i(1_B) = 1_D$ is similar.

Next we skip to

(e) Since $i: B \to D$ is one-to-one and onto, i^{-1} is a well-defined function from D into B which is also one-to-one and onto. Now, i^{-1} preserves meets, for, given w, $z \in D$, there exist unique x, $y \in B$ such that $i(x) = w$ and $i(y) = z$. Then $i^{-1}(w \wedge z) = i^{-1}(i(x) \wedge i(y)) = i^{-1}(i(x \wedge y)) = x \wedge y = i^{-1}(w) \wedge i^{-1}(z)$. Similarly, i^{-1} preserves joins and complements.

Now back to:

(b) If $x \leqslant_B y$, then $x \wedge y = x$, whence $i(x) \wedge i(y) = i(x \wedge y) = i(x)$, so that $i(x) \leqslant_D i(y)$. If $i(x) \leqslant_D i(y)$, then by what we have just proved, $i^{-1}(i(x)) \leqslant_B i^{-1}(i(y))$, that is, $x \leqslant_B y$.

(c) Let x be an atom of B. Then $i(x) \neq 0_D$, for otherwise $i^{-1}(i(x)) = x = 0_B$. Moreover, if $z \leqslant i(x)$, then let $y = i^{-1}(z)$. By part (b), $y \leqslant x$, whence

$y = 0$ or $y = x$. Since $z = i(y)$, this means that $z = 0$ or $z = i(x)$. Thus, $i(x)$ is an atom.

If $x \in$ *is arbitrary and* $i(x)$ is an atom, then, by what we have just proved, $x = i^{-1}(i(x))$ is an atom.

(d) Let us use the notation $i(K) = \{i(k): k \in K\}$. If $\wedge K$ exists, then by part (b) $i(\wedge K)$ is a lower bound for $i(K)$. If $z \in D$ is a lower bound for $i(K)$, then, again by part (b), $i^{-1}(z)$ is a lower bound for K, whence $i^{-1}(z) \leqslant \wedge K$. But this means that $z = i(i^{-1}(z)) \leqslant i(\wedge K)$. Thus, $i(\wedge K)$ is the glb of $i(K)$. Similarly $i(\vee K)$ is the lub of $i(K)$.

We need not prove Theorem 8, since that theorem is just a special case of Theorem 6.

Half of Theorem 9 is proved in the text. Here we give the other half. Namely, we prove that if $b \in T_N$ is an atom, then I_b satisfies the Meets, Joins, and Complement Conditions.

Given $K \subseteq T_N$. If $K \subseteq I_b$, then b is a lower bound for K, whence $b \leqslant \wedge K$, that is, $\wedge K \in I_b$. Conversely, if $\wedge K \in I_b$, then $b \leqslant \wedge K$, whence b is a lower bound for K, so that $K \subseteq I_b$. Thus, I_b satisfies the Meets Condition.

If $K \cap I_b \neq \emptyset$, then there is at least one $k \in K$ such that $b \leqslant k$. Thus, $b \leqslant \vee K$, whence $\vee K \in I_b$. Conversely, if $\vee K \in I_b$, that is if $b \leqslant \vee K$, then $b = b \wedge (\vee K) = \vee_{k \in K} (b \wedge k)$; since $b \neq 0$ and $b \wedge k = b$ or 0, we must have $b \wedge k = b$ for at least one $k \in K$. This k is an element of $K \cap I_b$. Thus, I_b satisfies the Joins Condition.

Finally, $p \in I_b$ iff $b \leqslant p$ iff $b \not\leqslant p'$ iff $p' \notin I_b$, so I_b satisfies the Complements Condition.

Theorems 10 and 11 are proved in the text. Theorem 12 is straightforward and left to the reader to check. The reader should see Keenan and Stavi (1981) for Theorems 13, 14, and 15.

The reader can easily check that the proof given above for Theorem 7(a) and the first part of the proof given for Theorem 7(b) constitute proofs of the two parts of Theorem 16.

Theorem 17 is proved in the text.

We have next:

THEOREM 18. $F_P = H_{2/P*}$

F_P and $H_{2/P*}$ are both subsets of $F_{2/P*}$. We prove the theorem by proving the two inclusions $F_P \subseteq H_{2/P*}$ and $H_{2/P*} \subseteq F_P$.

To prove the first inclusion, we need only prove that an arbitrary f_p is a homomorphism.

To show that f_p preserves meets, let $\{Q_\alpha\}$ be a (possibly infinite) set of subsets of P. Then $f_p(\bigcap_\alpha Q_\alpha) = 1$ iff $p \in \bigcap_\alpha Q_\alpha$ iff $\forall_\alpha\ p \in Q_\alpha$ iff $\forall_\alpha f_p(Q_\alpha) = 1$ iff $\wedge_\alpha f_p(Q_\alpha) = 1$. Thus $f_p(\bigcap_\alpha Q_\alpha) = \wedge_\alpha f_p(Q_\alpha)$. The proofs that f_p preserves joins and complements are equally straightforward.

To prove the second inclusion, given any $h \in H_{2/P^*}$, we must show that $h = f_{p_h}$ for some $p_h \in P$. Define p_h by the condition that $p_h \in I$ iff $h(I) = 1$, for any individual I; by Corollary 2 to Theorem 11, this is a proper definition of a unique element of P. Now, $h = f_{p_h}$; for, by the first part of the proof, f_{p_h} is a homomorphism, and by the definition of p_h, h and f_{p_h} take the same values on the individuals ($f_{p_h}(I) = 1$ iff $p_h \in I$ iff $h(I) = 1$), so the Justification Theorem can be applied.

Sketches for the proofs of Theorems 19, 20, 21, and 23 are given in the text; we leave it to the reader to fill in the details. We omit the proof of Theorem 22, which is a straightforward induction.

NOTES

[1] Treating PP's this way leads to many cases of multiple analysis. Thus, the English sentence *John found Mary in the garden* can be analyzed either as (i):

    (i)   John ((find Mary) (in the garden))

in which *in the garden* functions as a member of category P_1/P_1, or as (ii):

    (ii)   John ((find (in the garden)) (Mary))

in which *in the garden* functions as a P_2/P_2. In general, we will claim that these multiple possibilities are welcome; see Section I.B3.

[2] For example, we might define $\mathrm{PE}_V = \bigcup_{0 \,\leqslant\, n \,\leqslant\, \omega} V_n$, where V_n are defined inductively for all natural numbers n as follows:

    (i) $V_0 =_{df} V$ and (ii) $V_{n+1} =_{df} V_n \cup (V_n)^*$.

[3] But recall that there is no linear order among constituents of expressions in L, whereas such order does exist for constituents of English phrases. Thus, order is one respect in which the L-representation of an English expression is not isomorphic to that expression.

[4] It is easy to show that any boolean algebra whose domain has exactly two elements must be isomorphic to 2 (see below, Definition 18, for a discussion of the notion of isomorphism). Briefly, by condition (a) of Definition 18, if B has exactly two elements, these elements must be the zero and the unit. It is then relatively straightforward to prove, on the basis of the remaining conditions, that the meet, join, and complement operations applied to various combinations of these two elements must agree with the corresponding truth functions.

[5] The *intersection* of the sets X and Y is the set of all those elements which are members of both X and Y. The *union* of the sets X and Y is the set of all those elements each

of which is a member either of X or of Y (or both). If X is a subset of S, the *complement* of X relative to S is the set of all those elements of S which are not elements of X.

In general, we assume that the reader is familiar with these set-theoretic operations and with their properties.

[6] This development is not usually followed in standard presentations of FOL, which only allow *and, or*, and *not* to combine with formulas. However, the boolean character of U^* does allow the direct interpretation of boolean combinations of P_1's even in FOL, and so we thought to mention it here, anticipating the general approach we will be following in defining the semantic system for L.

[7] Suppose that $m \in B$ is a least element with respect to the ordering $\leqslant$. Then $m \leqslant 0$. But, by Theorem 2a, $0 \leqslant m$, whence $m = 0$, by Theorem 2c. The proof that 1 is the only maximal element is done analogously.

[8] Note that an atom b in an algebra is $\leqslant$ join of elements iff it is $\leqslant$ one of the elements over which the join is taken. Formally, for b an atom in B, $K \subseteq B$, $b \leqslant \vee K$ iff for some $k \in K$, $b \leqslant k$.

PART I: THE EXTENSIONAL LOGIC

B. *Extending the Core Language*

In this section we present a variety of ways in which the syntax of L can be enriched so as to represent a significantly larger fragment of English. Broadly speaking L is enriched in two sorts of ways: We add new lexical items in heretofore empty categories, and we add new operators forming derived expressions in new ways.

Among the lexical additions we enrich L to include new Modifiers and new Predicatives. Among the Modifiers we now have expressions like *tall, female*, etc. of category N/N or Adjective Phrase; and secondly we add a variety of Predicate Modifiers (of category P_n/P_n, for each $n \geqslant 1$) such as *here, in the garden*, etc. Among the Predicatives we add a variety of expressions which combine with full NP's to form expressions in already existing (non-empty) categories. These include 'transitive' common nouns like *friend (of)*, *colleague (of)*, etc., 'transitive' adjective phrases like *fond (of)*, *jealous (of)*, etc., ditransitive verb phrases such as *give, show*, etc., and Prepositions such as *in, on*, etc.

Of the new ways of forming derived expressions from simpler ones we add: (1) the *'s* which forms Determiners from full NP's; (2) some valency affecting operators such as Passive which forms P_n's from P_{n+1}'s; and (3) several variable binding operators, ones which form relative clauses and reflexives in addition a generalized lambda operator.

1. MODIFIERS

In general an expression will be called a *modifier* if its category is C/C for some category C, and the category C/C itself will be called a *modifier category*. So modifiers form C's from C's, for various choices of C. There are no modifiers in the core language L, but in the extensions of L proposed below we add expressions to the category N/N or Adjective Phrase and we add expressions to the category P_n/P_n or Predicate Modifiers.

Adjective Phrases

The category N/N of *Adjective Phrases* (APs) is a new category in our logical

118

language L whose expressions are intended to represent attributive adjectives in English, as well as certain complex expressions, such as relative clauses, which function as attributive-adjective-like modifiers. The lexical members of this category will ultimately consist of the full range of English adjectives which can be used attributively, such as *tall, female, skillful, good, fake, alleged*, etc., although we shall see that rather many of these are properly intensional, and hence will not be able to be dealt with by means of the constructions to be presented in this section.

Syntactically, APs combine with Ns (common noun phrases) to form expressions which themselves are Ns. Thus, for example, the lexical AP *tall* can be combined with the N *student* to form the expression *tall student*. Semantically, it is reasonable that the (extensional) denotation of this expression should be a property, just as the denotation of *student* is. Syntactically, *tall student* should be combinable with determiners to form noun phrases such as *every tall student, a tall student, no tall student*, or *the tall student*. We therefore regard the expression *tall student* as a N, and take *tall* to be of category N/N.

Since AP (= N/N) is a slash category, the denotation of an AP will be some function from T_N into T_N, that is, from P into P. The type T_{AP} of the category AP will therefore be some subset of the set $F_{P/P}$ of all such functions. In order to determine which subset of $F_{P/P}$ should be taken to be T_{AP}, we must examine the adjectives more closely. Traditionally, as well as in the recent logical literature, a variety of subclasses of adjectives are distinguished on intuitive semantic grounds. We shall begin by discussing several such classes informally to see what properties we want the functions which interpret them to have. We will then define a number of subcategories for the major category AP of our logical language which will correspond to certain of the subclasses of English adjectives we will have discussed. Each of these subcategories will have its own subset of $F_{P/P}$ as it type; the type for the major category AP will then be the union of the types for all the subcategories.

Let us first consider the *scalar adjectives*. Very roughly and intuitively, the semantics of such adjectives involves the notion that an individual which has the property denoted by an N which is composed of such an adjective and another N is at the extreme of some imagined scale of values. Examples of scalar adjectives are adjectives denoting size, such as *large, tall, short, wide*; many value-judgment adjectives, such as *good, bad, smart, beautiful*; and manner adjectives, such as *rapid, slow, clumsy, skillful*; the manner adjectives perhaps all have a value judgment component.

Scalar adjectives can compare: *taller than, smarter than, more beautiful than*; there are also equality comparison forms which these adjectives enter into, such as *as tall as*, as well as negative comparative forms like *less tall than*. Scalar adjectives also have intensive forms: *very tall, very good*, etc.

An important logical property of scalar adjectives which we will have occasion to refer to in a number of different contexts is the property of being *restrictive*. This means that an individual which, for example, has the property denoted by *tall student*, necessarily has the property denoted by *student*. We can give a general definition of the notion of being restrictive by considering the function $f: P \to P$ which would interpret a restrictive adjective. To say that f is restrictive simply means that, for any property p, if an arbitrary individual has the property $f(p)$, then that individual must have the property p. Examining the statement of Theorem 11 of Section A, we see that the notion of restrictiveness can be defined very simply as follows:

DEFINITION 1. Let $f \in F_{P/P}$ be arbitrary. Then f is *restricting* iff for each $p \in P, f(p) \leqslant p$.

Theorem 11 then guarantees us that for f restricting, any individual with $f(p)$ is of necessity an individual with p.

It will be noticed that the simplicity of Definition 1 is made possible by the fact that P is a boolean algebra, and hence has a relation $\leqslant$ defined on it. It will be useful later to have a more general notion of restricting function. As modifiers are always interpreted as functions from a boolean algebra into itself, we may define the notion of restrictiveness for any such function exactly as we did for functions from P into P, as follows:

DEFINITION 2. Let B be a boolean algebra, and let $f \in F_{B/B}$ be arbitrary. Then f is *restricting* iff for each $x \in B, f(x) \leqslant x$.

Since scalar adjectives are restricting, it is clear that if a scalar adjective is to be interpreted by a function from P into P, then that function must be a restricting function, in the sense of Definition 1. But *can* scalar adjectives be interpreted by functions from P into P? In many cases, and perhaps in most cases, the answer is *no*. To see this, suppose that the adjective *severe* were to be interpreted as a function from P into P. Then, in any model in which, say, *parent* and *teacher* happened to be interpreted as the same (extensional) property (which means that, in that model, the parents and the teachers were the same individuals), the expressions *severe parent* and *severe teacher* would be interpreted as the same property. But this is cleary false. If, for example, the individual John is the only parent and also the only teacher, we certainly want to allow for the possibility that John might be a severe parent but a lax teacher. Thus, even though *parent* and *teacher* are interpreted as the same property, *severe parent* and *severe teacher* should not have to be. We conclude that the interpretation of *severe* cannot be a function from P into P. Analogous arguments can be constructed for most scalar adjectives.

Let us say that an adjective is *transparent* if it can be represented as a function from P into P. What we have just said can then be rephrased by saying that most scalar adjectives are not transparent. This means that such adjectives cannot be represented in our logical system as it has been developed so far. In fact, the nontransparency of most scalar adjectives is one serious motivation for extending our logic to an intensional one. When we do so, we will see that scalar adjectives can be represented, and that the functions which interpret them are restricting, but in the more general sense of Definition 2.

It may be the case that the best analysis would have *all* scalar adjectives nontransparent. However, it seems to us that adjectives of physical size like *tall, short, wide, narrow*, etc. are actually transparent scalar adjectives. For example, in a model in which the doctors and the teachers are the same individuals, if John is a tall doctor, it seems necessarily the case that John is a tall teacher, and vice versa. This is clear if we think of the process of determining whether a given individual I has the *tall doctor* property as one of comparing the height of I with the heights of all the individuals which have the *doctor* property and seeing if the height of I is in some sense substantially greater than the average height of these individuals. If such a process is followed, then whether an individual has the *tall doctor* property or not depends on a physical property of the set of individuals which have the *doctor* property. Thus, if *doctor* and *teacher* happened to be interpreted as the same extensional property, then this process of checking an individual for the *tall doctor* property would necessarily lead to the same answer as checking that individual for the *tall teacher* property. But this means that the interpretation of *tall* depends only on the extensional denotation of the N with which it is combined; that is, *tall* can be interpreted as a function from P into P. In other words, *tall* is transparent.

On the other hand, objections have been cited to this argument. For example, it might be argued that in a model in which the jockeys and the basketball players were the same individuals, a given individual could be a short basketball player but not a short jockey. While our judgments here are not certain, our feeling is that there is a confusion here between the idea of being a tall jockey and of being tall *for* a jockey. In a model in which there are neither jockeys nor basketball players (so the sets of individuals which have the properties which interpret *jockey* and *basketball player* are trivially the same), an individual could surely be tall for a jockey but not tall for a basketball player. It also seems reasonable that we would want to say of an individual in some world that he was a tall jockey but not tall for a jockey (that is, he is well within the height limits we expect jockeys to have, but he is still taller than most jockeys, and hence a tall jockey). Thus, being a tall jockey and being tall for a jockey are perhaps independent properties. If this is so, it seems reasonable to regard *tall* as transparent, that is, as having an extensionally definable interpretation.

Another argument that *tall* is transparent, as opposed to most scalar adjectives like, say *smart*, is provided by the transparency of the APs created by their comparative forms. Namely, if John is a taller doctor than Bill, and if John and Bill are both lawyers as well as doctors, then John is a taller lawyer than Bill. However, if John is a smarter doctor than Bill, and if John and Bill are both lawyers as well as doctors, we cannot necessarily conclude that John is a smarter lawyer than Bill.

For these reasons, we tentatively propose that the category AP in our extensional language does contain lexical items like *tall*, *wide*, etc. Since these are all restricting adjectives, we enrich SF_L, the subcategorization features for L, to include the feature r (for *restricting*); then, the above lexical items are all in the subcategory AP_r. Moreover, let us specify that the type for this subcategory be the set of all restricting functions from P into P:

DEFINITION 3: $T_{AP_r} = \{f \in F_{P/P} : f \text{ is restricting}\}$

The next subclass of adjectives we want to discuss are the *intersecting adjectives*. Roughly, these are the adjectives which by themselves determine a property independent of the N with which they are combined. Among the adjectives usually regarded as intersecting are *male* and *female*; nationality adjectives, such as *Albanian, Ugandan*, etc.; color adjectives, such as *blue, aquamarine*, etc.; shape adjectives, such as *square, rectangular*, etc.; and certain social class adjectives like *Republican, Communist*, etc. In addition, all relative clauses fall into this subclass; but we will discuss these much later.

The sense in which an intersecting adjective determines a property can be described as follows. If Dana is a female student and if Dana is also an athlete, then Dana is a female athlete. More generally, what *female* attributes to Dana in the formula *Dana is a female e* is independent of the choice of the common noun *e*. This is in striking contrast to the scalar adjectives: if Dana is both a jockey and a basketball player and if Dana is a tall jockey, it is not necessarily the case that Dana is a tall basketball player.

Another way of describing the intersecting character of an adjective like *female* is to note that, for example, to be a female student means exactly the same as to be a female existent (individual) and also a student. Thus, the set of individuals who are female students is the intersection of the set of individuals who are students with the set of individuals who are female existents, hence the term *intersecting adjective*. Alternatively, we can say that the property which interprets *female student* is the meet (in P) of the property which interprets *student* with the property which interprets *female existent*. Viewed this way, it is easy to give a characterization of the kind of function which is needed to interpret an intersecting adjective:

DEFINITION 4. Let $f \in F_{P/P}$ be arbitrary. Then f is *intersecting* iff for each $p \in P$, $f(p) = p \wedge f(1)$.

(Of course, the symbol *1* refers to the unit element in P; recall that *existent* is a logical constant which is always interpreted as 1.)

As in the case of the notion *restricting*, the above definition for the notion *intersection* can be generalized to the case of a function from any boolean algebra B into itself. We give the general definition, which will be applicable to other modifiers.

DEFINITION 5. Let B be a boolean algebra and let $f \in F_{B/B}$ be arbitrary. Then f is *intersecting* iff for each $x \in B$, $f(x) = x \wedge f(1)$.

(Here, *1* is the unit element in B.)

The following theorem is immediate:

THEOREM 1. For B a boolean algebra and $f \in F_{B/B}$, if f is intersecting then f is restricting.

Proof. Let f as above be intersecting. We must show that for all $b \in B$, $f(b) \leqslant b$. Since f is intersecting we know that $f(b) = b \wedge f(1)$. By Theorem 2e, Section A we have that $(b \wedge x) \leqslant b$, x any element of the algebra. Thus $f(b) \leqslant b$, so f is restricting.

We may now add intersecting APs to our language as follows: The feature i (for intersection) is added to SF_L and expressions like *male, female, Albanian*, etc. are added to the basic vocabulary and assigned by lexical rule to the subcategory AP. We specify that the type for this subcategory be the set of all intersecting functions from P into P:

DEFINITION 6. $T_{AP \atop i} = \{f \in F_{P/P}: f \text{ is intersecting}\}$.

We will have more to say about the scalar and the intersecting adjectives, but first we want to briefly consider two other classes of adjectives.

In Montague (1973) it was pointed out that there exist adjectives which are not restricting. Among these is the class of *negative adjectives*, which includes *fake, bogus, phony*, and perhaps *ungrammatical, false*. That these adjectives are not restricting is seen by noting that, for example, a fake gun need not be a gun. That these adjectives are negative is seen by noting that a fake gun *cannot* be a gun, or at least, it cannot be a real gun. Similarly, an ungrammatical sentence is, possibly, not a sentence, nor is a false theorem a theorem.

We are tempted to say that a negative adjective should be interpreted by a function f which is required to satisfy the condition that $f(p) \leqslant p'$ for all properties p. This would guarantee that, say, an individual which had the property which interprets *fake doctor* would also have the complement of the property which interprets *doctor*, so that that individual would not have the doctor property.

However, closer examination shows that the functions which interpret negative adjectives cannot be transparent; that is, a negative adjective cannot be interpreted by a function from P into P. For example, suppose that in some model *gun* and *diamond* are both interpreted as 0 (that is, no individual has the gun property and no individual has the diamond property). If *fake* were interpreted by a transparent function, then, since *gun* and *diamond* have the same (extensional) interpretation, it would be the case that *fake gun* and *fake diamond* would be interpreted by the same property. But this is clearly counter to what we want. There might be, for example, no fake guns but many fake diamonds in the model under consideration, even if there are no real guns and no real diamonds. Whether an individual has the fake gun property or not simply has nothing to do with whether there are any individuals with the (real) gun property or not. For this reason, *fake* (and the other negative adjectives) will be interpreted by a properly intensional, that is, non-transparent, function.

There is another class of nonrestricting adjectives, which we term *conjectural adjectives*. These are adjectives whose semantic effect is to indicate that the individual is merely considered, hypothesized, or conjectured, etc. to have the property denoted by the N with which it is combined. Examples of such adjectives are *ostensible, alleged, apparent, possible, likely*. These adjectives are not restricting, since, for example, an alleged thief is not necessarily a thief. However, they are also not negative, since an alleged thief is not necessarily a non-thief.

Like the negative adjectives, the conjectural adjectives are not transparent. Thus, in a model in which *thief* and *murderer* are interpreted as the same (extensional) property, so that the thieves and the murderers are the same individuals, it still does not follow that the alleged thieves and the alleged murderers are the same individuals.

It seems clear, however, that there is a semantic connection between any given conjectural adjective and some 'sentence operator'. Thus, a possible millionnaire is a person for whom it is the case that it is possible that he/she is a millionnaire; an alleged thief is a person who has been alleged to be a thief.

When we come to discuss our intensional language, negative adjectives and conjectural adjectives will be members of subcategories AP_n and AP_c, respectively, with appropriately defined types. For now, we do not discuss these adjectives any further.

Returning to the extensional language, we see that we have added a new major category AP, with two subcategories, namely AP_r and AP_i. Actually, since all transparent adjectives appear to be restricting, we do not need to define a subcategory AP_r for the extensional language; we can simply regard the non-intersecting adjectives as members of AP, and define the type of AP as being the set of all restricting functions from P into P. Of course, in the intensional language, there will be many members of AP that are not restricting, as we have seen, so that AP_r will be a proper subcategory.

We have also given the type for our two subcategories. With what we have done so far, we can show, for example, that *John kissed a tall student* entails that *John kissed a student*. To do so, we first calculate the interpretation of *John kissed a tall student* in our system, as follows:

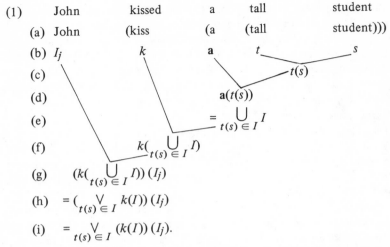

(1)   John   kissed   a   tall   student

(a) John   (kiss   (a   (tall   student)))

(b) I_j k   a   t.   s

(c) $t(s)$

(d) $a(t(s))$

(e) $= \bigcup_{t(s) \,\in\, I} I$

(f) $k(\bigcup_{t(s) \,\in\, I} I))$

(g) $(k(\bigcup_{t(s) \,\in\, I} I))\,(I_j)$

(h) $= (\bigvee_{t(s) \,\in\, I} k(I))\,(I_j)$

(i) $= \bigvee_{t(s) \,\in\, I} (k(I))\,(I_j).$

We leave it to the reader to provide the justification of each step. A similar analysis of *John kissed a student*, which we represent in our language by the formula *John (kiss (a student))*, shows that this is interpreted as

$$\bigvee_{s \,\in\, I} (k(I))\,(I_j).$$

To show that *John (kiss (a (tall student)))* entails *John (kiss (a student))*, we have to show that in any model in which

$$\bigvee_{t(s) \,\in\, I} (k(I))\,(I_j) = 1,$$

it is necessarily the case that

$$\bigvee_{s \,\in\, I} (k(I))\,(I_j) = 1.$$

Suppose, then, that the first of these two equations is true in some model. Then it is the case that there exists an individual I which contains the property $t(s)$ such that $(k(I))\,(I_j) = 1$. Now, since *tall* is a member of the category AP, t is a restricting function, so we conclude that $t(s) \leqslant s$. Since I is an individual, we can apply Theorem 13(ii) of Section A to conclude that $s \in I$. Thus, we have shown that there is an individual I containing the property s such that $(k(I))\,(I_j) = 1$. But this is just the condition necessary and sufficient for the second equation above to hold. That is, whenever the first equation holds for some model, the second one must hold also, which proves the entailment.

The reverse entailment, of course, is false. The reader may easily construct a model in which *John (kiss (a student))* is true but *John (kiss (a (tall student)))* is false (for example, take a model in which there are exactly two students, say, Betty and Sally, with only Betty being a tall student, and with John kissing Sally but not Betty). The statements in (2) and (3) below can also be shown to hold based on what we have done so far; the reader is invited to prove these statements as an exercise.

(2)   *John (kiss (every student))* entails *John (kiss (every (tall student)))*,

but the reverse entailment does not hold.

(3)   *(Mary (be (an (Albanian doctor))))* and *(Mary (be (a lawyer)))* entails *Mary (be (an (Albanian lawyer)))*.

If the only adjective phrases we needed to deal with consisted of single lexical adjectives which occurred only in combination with Ns to form Ns, this would complete our study of them, at least as far as the extensional language is concerned. However, if our language is to have anything like the richness of real English, we have to consider complex APs, as well as APs occurring in situations other than combined with Ns. We proceed to consider several extensions along these two lines now.

We begin by noting that adjectives can combine with the syncategorematic expressions *and, or,* and *not* to form complex APs. This is particularly clear in the case of scalar adjectives: *a tall and heavy student, a tall or heavy student, a tall but not heavy student.* In the case of intersecting adjectives, conjunctions are typically odd: *?a male and Communist student*, while disjunctions are often acceptable: *a Communist or Socialist student.* Moreover, *not* can often combine with an intersecting adjective in the special form *non-: a non-Communist student.* We also note that combinations of a scalar with an intersecting adjective tend to be odd: *?a tall and Communist student, ?a tall or Communist student.* However, it is important to keep in mind that all of the odd combinations involving adjectives and the syncategorematic expressions are nevertheless easily interpretable. Our approach here will be to allow all such combinations to be formed and interpreted. We will then have something to say concerning the oddness of some of the combinations.

To allow for the construction of these combinations, we need only declare that AP is a boolean category. (Non-restricting adjectives strongly resist combining with *and, or,* and *not*; we will discuss this later.) To provide for interpretations of boolean combinations of adjectives, we have to define operations on the set T_{AP} which will turn that set into a boolean algebra. The proper way to do this will become clear by considering the meanings of Ns which contain boolean combinations of adjectives.

It is clear, for example, that an individual which has the property which interprets *tall and heavy student* must have the property which interprets *tall student* and also the property which interprets *heavy student*. Moreover, the converse holds also: if an individual has the properties which interpret *tall student* and *heavy student* respectively. then we certainly would want that individual to have the property which interprets *tall and heavy student*. By virtue of this, we would like to make the following definition:

DEFINITION 7. Let $f, g \in T_{AP}$ be arbitrary. Then $f \wedge g$ is defined by setting $(f \wedge g)(p) = f(p) \wedge g(p)$ for each $p \in P$.

It is clear that by this definition $f \wedge g$ is a function from P into P. However, in order to be a member of T_{AP}, it is also necessary that $f \wedge g$ be restricting, that is, that $(f \wedge g)(p) \leqslant p$ for all p. But $(f \wedge g)(p) = f(p) \wedge g(p) \leqslant f(p)$. Since $f(p) \leqslant p$ (since f is restricting), we conclude that $(f \wedge g)(p) \leqslant p$, whence the function $(f \wedge g)$ is restricting.

We leave it to the reader to formulate the arguments which motivate the following definition for the operation $\vee$ in T_{AP}:

DEFINITION 8. Let $f, g \in T_{AP}$ be arbitrary. Then $f \vee g$ is defined by setting $(f \vee g)(p) = f(p) \vee g(p)$ for each $p \in P$.

The argument that $f \vee g$ is restricting is slightly different. Since $f(p) \leqslant p$ and $g(p) \leqslant p$ (since f and g are restricting), we have that $f(p) \vee g(p) \leqslant p$, by Theorem (2h) of Section A, and hence $(f \vee g)(p) \leqslant p$.

We have yet to define an operation $'$ in T_{AP}. On the basis of the two definitions above, it might seem that the appropriate definition would be that f' is defined by the equation $f'(p) = (f(p))'$. However, f' defined this way would not be restricting. This is most easily seen by assuming that P is a power set algebra, so that 'properties' are sets and $\leqslant$ is the subset relation. Then, if $f(p)$ is a proper subset of p, $(f(p))'$ would contain all the elements of p', together with those elements of p which are not in $f(p)$; this is clearly not a subset of p. More generally, for any algebra P, if $f(p) \leqslant p$, then $p' \leqslant (f(p))'$, by Theorem (2k) of Section A. Thus, we cannot have $(f(p))' \leqslant p$ in general, since this would mean that $p' \leqslant p$, that is, that $p' \wedge p = p'$, whence $p' = 0$, or $p = 1$.

The way out is easily seen by examining the meaning of a phrase like (*not tall*) *student* (say, as in *a heavy but not tall student*). An individual has the property denoted by this N if and only if that individual has the student property, but does not have the tall student property. The correct definition is therefore the following:

DEFINITION 9. Let $f \in T_{A}P$ be arbitrary. Then f' is defined by setting $f'(p) = p \wedge (f(p))'$ for each $p \in P$.

It is clear by Theorem 2e of Section A that f' defined this way is restricting.

Now, it happens that under the operations $\wedge$, $\vee$, and $'$ defined above, $T_{A}P$ is a boolean algebra. While not completely obvious, this fact is easy to prove. We leave the proof to the reader, noting here only the following. The zero element of $T_{A}P$ is the function which maps every property onto the zero property; we may write this as $0(p) = 0$ for every $p \in P$, if we understand the first 0 to refer to the zero element of the type for restricting adjectives, and the second 0 to refer to the zero property. And, the unit element of $T_{A}P$ is the function which maps each property into itself; that is, $1(p) = p$. Readers not wishing to bother proving that $T_{A}P$ is a boolean algebra may note that this fact follows from the more general theorem to be discussed momentarily.

We saw earlier that the notion of a restricting function could be defined whenever we were dealing with functions from any boolean algebra into itself. The definitions we have just given for operations in $T_{A}P$ can also be given in the general case. The following theorem summarizes the situation:

THEOREM 2. Let $R_{B/B} = \{f \in F_{B/B} : f \text{ is restricting}\}$, where B is an arbitrary boolean algebra. Then $R_{B/B}$ is a boolean algebra under the operations $\wedge$, $\vee$, and $'$ defined as follows:

  (a) For $f, g \in R_{B/B}$ arbitrary, $f \wedge g$ is defined by setting $(f \wedge g)(b) = f(b) \wedge g(b)$ for each $b \in B$.
  (b) For $f, g \in R_{B/B}$ arbitrary, $f \vee g$ is defined by setting $(f \vee g)(b) = f(b) \vee g(b)$ for each $b \in B$.
  (c) For $f \in R_{B/B}$ arbitrary, f' is defined by setting $f'(b) = b \wedge (f(b))'$ for each $b \in B$.

Moreover, if B is a complete algebra, then $R_{B/B}$ is complete, and if B is atomic, then $R_{B/B}$ is atomic.

See the end of this section for proofs of theorems not given in the body of the texts.

DEFINITION 10. If B is a boolean algebra, then the algebra $R_{B/B}$ is called the *restricting algebra on B*.

Thus, we can summarize what we have done so far by saying that the type for restricting (transparent) adjective phrases shall be the restricting algebra on P.

Turning now to the intersecting adjectives, we note that by Theorem 1 T_{A_iP} is a subset of T_{A_rP}. However, we can say more. Suppose that f and g are two intersecting functions from P into P. Since f and g are restricting functions from P into P, we can apply Definition 7 and form the restricting function $f \wedge g$. An easy argument shows that $f \wedge g$ is itself intersecting. (Namely, $(f \wedge g)(p) = f(p) \wedge g(p) = (p \wedge f(1)) \wedge (p \wedge g(1)) = p \wedge f(1) \wedge g(1)) = p \wedge (f \wedge g)(1))$. In other words, starting inside the (proper) subset T_{A_iP} of T_{A_rP}, we stay inside this subset whenever we operate with $\wedge$. This is described by saying that T_{A_iP} is *closed under the operation* $\wedge$. The importance of this is that the operation $\wedge$, which we have defined on the larger set T_{A_rP}, can be viewed as an operation on the smaller set T_{A_iP} as well.

It turns out that T_{A_iP} is closed under the operations $\vee$ and $'$ as well. Since the operations $\wedge$, $\vee$, and $'$, satisfy the axioms of boolean algebra (since T_{A_rP} is a boolean algebra), we can conclude immediately that T_{A_iP} is a boolean algebra under these operations which it 'inherits' by being a subset of T_{A_rP}. This situation is described by saying that T_{A_iP} is a *subalgebra* of T_{A_rP}.

Again, what we have here is a special case of a more general situation:

THEOREM 3. Let $I_{B/B} = \{f \in R_{B/B} : f$ is intersecting$\}$, where B is an arbitrary boolean algebra. Then $I_{B/B}$ is a subalgebra of $R_{B/B}$. Moreover, if B is complete, then $I_{B/B}$ is complete, and if B is atomic, then $I_{B/B}$ is atomic.

DEFINITION 11. If B is a boolean algebra, then the algebra $I_{B/B}$ is called the *intersecting algebra on B*.

If we examine the definition of the notion of intersecting function, it is clear that such a function f is completely defined once we specify the value of $f(1)$. This means that it is possible to define a mapping of P into T_{A_iP} by associating to the property p that intersecting function f such that $f(1) = p$. We then have the following important theorem:

THEOREM 4. Let the function $u: P \to T_{A_iP}$ be defined as follows: given $p \in P$, $u(p)$ is that function from P into P such that for each $q \in P$, $(u(p))(q) = q \wedge p$. Then u is an isomorphism of P onto T_{A_iP}.

Among other things, this theorem tells us that an intersecting adjective determines a property; in fact, the intersecting adjective function f determines the property $f(1)$. Thus, for example, the adjective *Albanian* determines the property associated with the common noun phrase *Albanian existent*.

The fact that an intersecting adjective determines a property correlates with the fact that intersecting adjectives appear to be more common-noun-like than scalar adjectives. Thus, intersecting adjectives can often be used as common nouns: *two males, an Albanian, every Communist, no square*, etc. Similarly, intersection adjectives, like common nouns, are negatable by *non-:* *non-Albanian* (cf. *non-student*).

As in the case of our earlier definitions and theorems, Theorem 4 can be generalized to a statement that any boolean algebra B is isomorphic to $I_{B/B}$; the formal statement and proof will be found in the section at the end of this chapter.

We pointed out earlier that intersecting adjectives sound odd when conjoined with *and* although they combine acceptably with *or* and with *not* (usually in the form *non-*). The following theorem sheds some light on this:

THEOREM 5. Let $f, g \in T_{AP}$ be arbitrary. The, for each $p \in P$, $(f \wedge g)(p) = f(g(p)) = g(f(p))$.

This theorem tells us that, for example, the common noun phrase (*male and Communist*) *student* has the same interpretation as the phrase *male* (*Communist student*). The oddity of the phrase *male and Communist student* can be perhaps explained by saying that this phrase is always passed over in favor of the equivalent phrase *male Communist student*, which is at least shorter, and possibly easier to process. Since boolean combinations of intersection adjectives involving *or* and *not* cannot be paraphrased this way, they, unlike combinations involving *and*, are used in real English, and do not sound odd.

Unfortunately, an approach such as this cannot be used to explain the oddity of combining an intersecting and a (nonintersecting) restricting adjective with *and*, as in the phrase *tall and Communist student*. In particular, (*tall and Communist*) *student* and *tall* (*Communist student*) are not necessarily equivalent. For, an individual which has the property which interprets *tall* (*Communist student*) need only be tall relative to the Communist students in the relevant model; he/she need not be tall with respect to *all* the students. However, as we have seen, an individual which has the property which interprets (*tall and Communist*) *student* does have the property which interprets *tall student*, so such an individual has to be tall with respect to all students in the model, not just the Communist ones. Since an individual could easily be tall with respect to the Communist students in a model but not with respect to all students (if, say, all the Communist students were rather short), the *tall (Communist student)* property could hold of individuals for which the *(tall and Communist) student* does not hold.

However, the situation may not be hopeless. For, it appears that in real English there is a phrase whose logical interpretation is in fact representable as *(tall and Communist) student* in our logical language, namely the phrase *tall, Communist student* (not to be confused with the phrase *tall Communist student*, which appears to be representable as *tall (Communist student)*). Thus, there is actually nothing odd at all about the logical phrase *(tall and Communist) student*; it is simply a fact about real English that comma intonation is the method that is used to conjoin adjectives rather than the word *and*. Unfortunately, the oddness of *tall or Communist student* remains unexplained. (The phrase *tall but not Communist student* sounds a bit less odd to us.)

Let us turn now to some other considerations concerning adjectives. We noted earlier that scalar adjectives like *tall* can compare (*a taller man than Bill*) and have intensive forms (*a very tall man*). However, the situation is different for intersecting adjectives; phrases like *a more Albanian student than Bill* or *a very Albanian student* seem uninterpretable unless we read into *Albanian* a content richer than the usual meaning of Albanian as simply an indication of nationality-membership. We can gain some understanding of this from what we have developed so far. First, let us note the following theorem, which follows almost immediately from Theorem 5:

THEOREM 6. Let $f \in T_{A_i P}$ be arbitrary. Then, for each $p \in P$, $f(f(p)) = f(p)$.

In fact, if we make the following definition:

DEFINITION 12. Let X be an arbitrary set, and let $f: X \to X$ be an arbitrary function. Then, for each nonnegative integer n, define $f^n: X \to X$ as follows:

    (a) $f^0(x) = x$, for each $x \in X$;
    (b) $f^{n+1}(x) = f(f^n(x))$ for each $x \in X$,

then, by a simple inductive argument, we can show the following:

THEOREM 7. Let $f \in T_{A_i P}$ be arbitrary. Then, for any positive integer n, $f^n = f$.

But if f is any restricting (not necessarily intersecting) adjective function, then the best we can say is the following:

THEOREM 8. Let $f \in T_{\underset{r}{A}P}$ be arbitrary. Then, if n and m are nonnegative integers with $n > m$, then $f^n \leqslant f^m$.

(Note that, since $T_{\underset{r}{A}P}$ is a boolean algebra, the relation $\leqslant$ is defined between members of it. The fact that f^n is a restricting adjective function if f is follows directly from the definitions.)

If the restricting adjective function f is not intersecting, it may be the case that $f^{n+1} < f^n$ for every nonnegative integer n. A simple example of this is the following. Let P be the power set of the positive integers, so that an element of P is a set of positive integers. Let f be defined as follows: if $p \in P$ is any nonempty set of positive integers, then $f(p)$ is the set obtained by removing from p the smallest integer. We also set $f(\emptyset) = \emptyset$. It is obvious that f is a restricting function. Moreover, applying f successively to the unit element 1 of P (where, of course, 1 is actually the set $\{1, 2, 3, \ldots \}$), we find that $f^n(1) = \{n + 1, n + 2, \ldots \}$. In particular, for every nonnegative integer n, $f^{n+1}(1)$ is a proper subset of $f^n(1)$. Thus $f^{n+1} \neq f^n$ for each n, whence $f^{n+1} < f^n$ for each n.

Now, suppose that the restricting adjective function f interprets *tall* is some model. If p is the property which interprets *student*, then *tall student* is, of course, interpreted as $f(p)$. Now, $f^2(p) = f(f(p))$ is thus the interpretation of *tall (tall student)*; so an individual has the property $f^2(p)$ iff that individual is tall with respect to the tall students. Let us tentatively propose that this is just what is meant by the phrase *very tall student*. Formally, *very* will be a member of the category $A_{\underset{r}{}}P/A_{\underset{r}{}}P$. Moreover, it will be a logical constant: in any model, *very* will be interpreted as the function *very*: $T_{\underset{r}{A}P} \to T_{\underset{r}{A}P}$ defined by setting *very*$(f) = f^2$. Let us consider some facets of this proposal.

First of all, *very* is a member of the category $A_{\underset{r}{}}P/A_{\underset{r}{}}P$, which is a category of modifiers, being of the form X/X; we might call this category the category of *ad-adjectives*. Thus, the English phrase *very tall student* is represented in our logical language as (*very tall*) *student*, where *very tall* is an adjective phrase.

Next, we anticipate a later discussion and note that modifiers are typically restricting. In the case of the adjectives, we have seen that the two largest groups of adjectives, namely, the scalar adjectives and the intersecting adjectives, are restricting, whereas the nonrestricting adjectives fall into a number

of rather small groups each definable by a highly particular semantic characterization. Accepting the idea that modifiers are typically restricting, we
would prefer that *very* be restricting. But, with the suggested proposal, this
is indeed the case, as follows directly from Theorem 8.

Finally, under this proposal, we would have that, for any *intersecting*
adjective function f, $very(f) = f$, by Theorem 7. What this means is that in
our logical language, *very Albanian* will be a well-formed AP, but that it will
be interpreted the same as *Albanian* in all models. We can then explain the
necessary reinterpretation of *Albanian* in the English phrase *very Albanian*
as follows. Since *very* is logically redundant if *Albanian* is given its usually
interpretation as an intersecting adjective, the presence of *very* constitutes
a pragmatic invitation to reinterpret *Albanian* in such a way that *very* is no
longer redundant, that is, as a nonintersecting, scalar adjective. This is in
fact just what happens: *Albanian* is reinterpreted as denoting not mere
nationality-membership, but rather the scalar quality of possessing the
characteristics associated with that membership. As a general principle we
may say that logically redundant elements when present in an expression
constitute a pragmatic invitation to reinterpret the expression that element is
combined with. We will see other examples of this from time to time.

Comparative Adjectives

Turning next to the matter of comparative expressions, we note that the
semantics of such expressions clearly involves the idea of comparing degrees
of possession of some quality along a scale. We defer a precise statement of
the syntax and semantics of comparatives; here we make some preliminary
investigations into the matter of scalarity.

Theorem 8 provides us with a way of defining a discrete scale for restricting adjectives. Namely, it follows from that theorem that if I is an individual,
p is a property, and f is a restricting adjective function, then either there is
a unique largest integer n such that I has the property $f^n(p)$ but not the
property $f^{n+1}(p)$, or else I has the property $f^n(p)$ for all positive integers
n. In the former case, we may say that I has the property $f(p)$ *to degree n*;
in the latter case, we would say that I has the property f *to countable degree*
(or, *to degree aleph-null*). Now, it is clear that if the individual which interprets *John* has the *tall student* property to a degree strictly greater than the
individual which interprets *Bill*, then, in that model, we would want *John
is a taller student than Bill* to be interpreted as true. Unfortunately, this
procedure cannot be made definitional for the comparative, since we would

not want the converse to hold. For example, John and Bill might both be short students, making them both tall students to degree zero, and yet one of them might be taller than the other. In general, two individuals might have the *tall student* property to the same degree and still differ in height.

A more promising approach emerges if we recall that the atoms of P represent the properties of being particular individuals. Thus, if a is an atom of P, there is a unique individual I_a such that a is a member of the set I_a but of no other individual (see Section A, Theorem 9), so that a can be regarded as the property of being I_a. If a and b are distinct atoms, then I_a and I_b are distinct individuals.

Now, consider the property $a \vee b$. Since $a \leqslant a \vee b$, I_a must contain the property $a \vee b$; and similarly, I_b contains the property $a \vee b$. However, no other individual contains $a \vee b$. For, suppose that the individual I contains $a \vee b$. We know that $I = I_c$ for some atom c. Thus, $c \leqslant a \vee b$, which we may rewrite $c = c \wedge (a \vee b) = (c \wedge a) \vee (c \wedge b)$. If a, b, and c are three distinct atoms, then by Theorem 4c of Section A $c \wedge a = c \wedge b = 0$, whence $c = 0$, a contradiction to the fact that c is an atom. We conclude that I_a and I_b are exactly those individuals which contain the property $a \vee b$.

Suppose now that f is the restricting adjective function interpreting a scalar adjective such as *tall*. We can apply f to the property $a \vee b$; since f is restricting, there are four possible results:

(5) (1) $f(a \vee b) = a \vee b$
     (2) $f(a \vee b) = a$
     (3) $f(a \vee b) = b$
     (4) $f(a \vee b) = 0.$

To interpret these possibilities, recall that if p is the property of being, say, a student, then $f(p)$ is the property of being a tall student, that is, of being substantially taller than the average height for the set of individuals with the student property. Following the same line of thought, we can say that $f(a \vee b)$ represents the property of being taller than the average height for the set of individuals with the property $a \vee b$, that is, for the set $\{I_a, I_b\}$. But, if $f(a \vee b) = a$, only I_a has this property; that is, I_a is the unique individual which is taller than the average height of I_a and I_b. Clearly, we may identify this situation as the case of I_a being taller than I_b. Similarly, $f(a \vee b) = b$ may be identified with the situation that I_b is taller than I_a.

There remain the other two possibilities. It seems reasonable to view $f(a \vee b) = 0$ as representing the situation in which I_a and I_b are sufficiently similar in height so that neither can be said to be substantially taller than their average. On the other hand, the case in which $f(a \vee b) = a \vee b$ seems uninterpretable; to be consistent with the discussion so far, we would have to say that $f(a \vee b) = a \vee b$ means that both I_a and I_b are substantially taller than their average, a situation which ought to be impossible. One way to deal with this is simply to require that any function f which interprets a lexical scalar adjective shall be *strictly restricting* in the following sense:

DEFINITION 13. $f \in F_{P/P}$ is *strictly restricting* iff f is restricting and for all $p \in P$, if $p \neq 0$ then $f(p) \neq p$.

Thinking of such an f as the interpretation of *tall*, and defining an individual I_a to be *taller than* an individual I_b iff $f(a \vee b) = a$, Definition 13 guarantees that of any two individuals either one is taller than the other or they have approximately the same height (the case where $f(a \vee b) = 0$). It also guarantees that no individual is taller than himself, since if I_a were taller than I_a then $f(a \vee a)$ would be a, which is impossible since $(a \vee a) = a$ by idempotency and $f(a) = 0$ since f is strictly restricting.

However the constraint on the interpretation of scalar APs given in Definition 13 is not adequate to guarantee an empirically correct definition of e.g. *taller than* since it does not imply that that relation on individuals is transitive. For example, a strictly restricting function f might behave as follows on distinct atoms a, b, and c: $f(a \vee b) = a$ (I_a is taller than I_b); $f(b \vee c) = b$ (I_b is taller than I_c); and $f(a \vee c) = c$ (I_c is taller than I_a). So let us further require that functions which can interpret scalar APs be *transitive*:

DEFINITION 14. $f \in F_{P/P}$ is *transitive* iff for all atoms a, b, $c \in P$, if $f(a \vee b) = a$ and $f(b \vee c) = b$ then $f(a \vee c) = a$.

Now our informal definition of *taller than* above does determine a transitive relation on the individuals (or atoms). But still more is needed. We want to define more than a binary relation *is taller than* on the set of all individuals; we want to define the sorts of relations expressed by *is a taller student than*. Informally, then, let us define for any property p, I_a is a taller p than I_b iff $a \leq p$ and $b \leq p$ and $f(a \vee b) = a$, where f interprets *tall*. Thus *John is a taller student than Bill* holds just in case both John and Bill are students and John is taller than Bill. Note that *John is taller than Bill* is now logically equivalent to *John is a taller individual than Bill*. Note further that this approach has treated *taller . . . than* as a discontinuous operator, syntactically speaking.

We may informally define a non-discontinuous operator *taller than* as follows: I_a is a p taller than I_b iff $a \leqslant p$ and $f(a \vee b) = a$, where f interprets *tall*. Thus *John is a taller student than Bill* does not imply that Bill is a student.

A final problem remains: *taller . . . than* is a transitive relation on individuals, given that *tall* is interpreted by a transitive strictly restricting function from P into P, but we have not guaranteed that this relation is respected by the interpretation of *tall*. We must guarantee for example that John is a tall student whenever John is taller than Bill, John is a student, and Bill is a tall student. This we do by requiring that the functions which may interpret scalar APs are *order consistent*:

DEFINITION 15. A strictly restricting function $f \in F_{P/P}$ is *order consistent* iff for all $p \in P$ and all atoms a, b satisfying $a \leqslant p$ and $b \leqslant p$,

    (i) if $f(a \vee b) = a$ and $b \leqslant f(p)$ then $a \leqslant f(p)$ and
    (ii) if $f(a \vee b) = 0$ then $a \leqslant f(p)$ iff $b \leqslant f(p)$.

Requiring that scalar APs like *tall* be interpreted by strictly restricting, transitive, order consistent functions and interpreting comparatives and superlatives as suggested above yields, we believe, a semantic analysis of these constructions which enables us to represent many of their entailment properties. It is however open to at least two objections. The first, and least serious to our minds, is that the constraints on the interpretations of *tall* are motivated by the desire to make the semantics of comparative forms empirically correct rather than by direct consideration of arguments involving the non-comparative form.

This objection is simply not correct. For example, the conjunction of the sentences in (5a) below entails on our semantics (5b) and the proof (left as an exercise for the reader) crucially requires that *tall* be interpreted by an order consistent function.

(5)   a. John is a tall student, Bill is student but not a tall one,
           John is a jockey, Bill is a tall jockey
    b. John is a tall jockey

As none of the sentences in (5) use anything other than the bare adjective *tall* we may conclude that our semantics for such APs would be inadequate if we omitted the order consistency requirement.

Similarly the transitivity condition on *tall* is needed to guarantee entailments between sentences none of which mention the comparative form. For example, the conjunction of the sentences in (6a) below entails (6b) in virtue of the transitivity condition on *tall*.

(6)   a. John and Bill are the only students, John is a tall student and
         Bill isn't, Bill and Sam are the only socialists, Bill is a tall socialist
         and Sam isn't, John and Sam are the only vegetarians,
      b. John is a tall vegetarian and Sam isn't.

Finally, the strict restricting condition guarantees the validity of sentences like those in (7). (The judgments are admittedly less compelling than in (5) and (6) above but still we feel more right than wrong.)

(7)   a. Not all students are tall students.
      b. If John is a tall student then there is a student different from
         John who is not a tall student.

A second objection to our approach is that the three conditions we have imposed on the interpretations of scalar APs would all follow automatically on an approach in which the semantics of these APs was primitively taken to involve comparison of individuals on a scale. That amounts to taking the interpretation of *taller than* as basic, as in Bartsch (1976), and defining the semantics for *tall* in terms of it. Whatever its elegance when worked out in detail, however, we object to this approach on the grounds that it violates the Compositionality condition. Namely, in English and in all languages with which we are familiar, the comparative forms of APs are given as a function of the non-comparative one — they contain it as a discernable part, whence the interpretation of *tall-er than* should be given in terms of the interpretation of *tall*, as we have done, and not conversely.

A second objection to defining non-comparative in terms of comparative forms, one which we find suggestive even though it is not worked out in enough detail to be convincing, is the following. The semantics for comparatives of non-transparent APs suggests that only (at most) the transitivity requirement should hold, but that strict restrictiveness and order consistency should not be required. If this is so then the three conditions are in fact (partially) independent since some APs satisfy all of them while others only satisfy transitivity.

Examples supporting these claims are, first, that John can be a skillful surgeon (or a good driver or a famous jockey) even if he is the only one, whence the interpretations of *skillful, good* and *famous* need not be strictly restrictive. And second, if John and Bill are both doctors and both drivers and John is a more skillful doctor than Bill it clearly does not follow that he is a more skillful driver than Bill, whence order consistency would appear to fail for *skillful*.

Predicate Adjectives

Given the semantics for (non-comparative) APs above and the semantics for one place predicates (P_1's) of Section A, we consider now the semantics of P_1's formed from AP's, such as *be happy, seem bored, look disgusting, feel sticky, taste lousy, sound horrible*, etc. Each of these involves a lexical item which can be combined with an AP to yield a P_1. Of the various lexical items appearing in these examples, only *be* can be treated in an extensional system. For example, even if *happy* and *healthy* are interpreted as the same function from P into P, it will not follow that *seem happy* and *seem healthy* should be interpreted as the same P_1 function. An individual can seem (look, appear) happy without seeming healthy, regardless of whether in fact all the happy e's are exactly the healthy e's, for each common noun phrase e.

To treat *be* as it occurs in an expression like *be happy*, we first recall that in the core language L there is already an expression *be* of category $P_2 = P_1/\bar{N}$. This earlier *be* is a logical constant; its interpretation is given in Definition 42 of Section A. Clearly, the *be* of *be happy* should likewise be a logical constant, but this *be* is of category P_1/AP. In our earlier treatment (Keenan and Faltz, 1978), these two *be*'s were treated as distinct, and, in fact, unrelated lexical items (denoted be_1 and be_2), but, given the general system of category names defined in Section A, we are not forced to do this here. Rather, we can (and do) propose that there is a lexical item *be* of category $\langle P_1, P_1 \rangle / \langle \bar{N}, AP \rangle$. This simply means that *be* can be grammatically combined either with an expression of category $\bar{N}$ or else with an expression of category AP; in either case, the resulting expression is of category P_1.

Next, to define the interpretation of *be*, we note the general principle for interpreting an expression of category $\langle X_1, X_2 \rangle / \langle Y_1, Y_2 \rangle$. Namely, if e is an expression of this category, then $M(e)$ is a function from $T_{Y_1} \cup T_{Y_2}$ into $T_{X_1} \cup T_{X_2}$ which has the property that, when $M(e)$ is applied to an element of T_{Y_1}, the result is an element of T_{X_1}, and when $M(e)$ is applied to an element of T_{Y_2}, the result is an element of T_{X_2}. If f is such a function, then f is equivalent to a pair $\langle f_1, f_2 \rangle$, where $f_1: T_{Y_1} \to T_{X_1}$ and $f_2: T_{Y_2} \to$

T_{X_2}. For, given f, we can define f_1 by setting $f_1(z) = f(z)$ if $z \in T_{Y_1}$; and similarly, we can set $f_2(z) = f(z)$ if $z \in T_{Y_2}$. Conversely, if we have two functions $f_1 : T_{Y_1} \to T_{X_1}$ and $f_2 : T_{Y_2} \to T_{X_2}$, where T_{Y_1} and T_{Y_2} are disjoint, then the function f defined by setting $f(z) = f_1(z)$ if $z \in T_{Y_1}$ and $f(z) = f_2(z)$ if $z \in T_{Y_2}$ is a function from $T_{Y_1} \cup T_{Y_2}$ into $T_{X_1} \cup T_{X_2}$ with the property given above.

In the matter of the interpretation of the logical constant *be*, we must therefore define the function $(M(be))_1 : P^* \to T_{P_1}$ (which interprets *be* when it is combined with a noun phrase) and the function $(M(be))_2 : T_{AP} \to T_{P_1}$ (which interprets *be* when it is combined with an adjective phrase). Now, for $(M(be))_1$, we just take the function already defined earlier, when *be* was introduced as a logical constant of category P_2 in the core language (Definition 42 of Section A). For $(M(be))_2$, we make the following definition:

DEFINITION 16. For any $f \in T_{AP}$, $(M(be))_2(f)$ is that complete homomorphism from P^* into 2 such that, for any individual I, $((M(be))_2(f))(I) = 1$ iff $\bigvee\limits_{p \in P} f(p) \in I$.

We may rephrase this definition by saying that $(M(be))_2(f)$ is the verb phrase homomorphism which is associated with the property $\bigvee_{p \in P} f(p)$, in the sense of Definition 36 and Theorem 18 of Section A.

To see what this definition means, note first that by the joins condition for individuals, an individual I has the property $\bigvee_{p \in P} f(p)$ iff I has the property $f(p)$, for some property p. Suppose, then, that f interprets *tall*, so that $(M(be))(f)$ is the interpretation of the verb phrase *be tall*. By this definition an individual I has the property associated with *be tall* just in case, for some property p, I is tall for the set of individuals which have the property p. In particular, it does not necessarily follow from the truth of *John (be tall)* that John is a tall existent (in contrast to, say, the system of Montague, 1970, where this does follow). This accords with our pretheoretical intuitions, according to which, for example, we would want *John is tiny* to be true in a model in which *John is a tiny elephant* is true, even if *John is a tiny existent* is not true.

Let us examine the consequences of our definition a bit closer. In the case of intersecting AP's, the following theorem shows that our definition leads to a reasonable result:

THEOREM 9. If $f \in F_{P/P}$ is intersecting then $\bigvee\limits_{p \in P} f(p) = f(1)$.

What this says for example is that the property associated with the P_1 *be male* is the same as the property determined by the intersecting AP *male* (see Theorem 4 above and the discussion following it). Thus for intersecting AP's like *male* (*Albanian*, etc.) *John is male* is logically equivalent to *John is a male existent*, clearly a desired result.

The case of scalar adjectives does not work out quite as well. In real English, a sentence like *John is tall* is interpreted to mean, approximately, *John is a tall e*, where *e* denotes some N which defines a set of individuals whose tallness provides a standard with respect to which John's tallness is measured. Since *John* is typically the name of a man, and since tallness is a property which is often saliently predicated of men, *John is tall* is reasonably likely to be interpreted to mean *John is a tall man*, in the absence of other contextual factors. However, if it is known that John is a jockey, and if the context of the utterance makes this fact salient, then *John is tall* would probably be interpreted to mean that John is a tall jockey. In any case, the context supplies a specific set of individuals (of which John is a member) whose tallness is the standard of measurement.

However, we have not at this time provided for a method by means of which such a contextually defined distinguished set of individuals (or, equivalently, a contextually defined property) can be represented in our system. It is for this reason that we have settled on the definition given above, according to which *John is tall* is true just in case for some property *p* John is tall for the set of individuals which have the property *p*. But if we assume that the scalarity of *tall* is reasonably represented in some manner (for example, by imposing the conditions of strict restrictiveness, transitivity, and order-consistency discussed earlier on the function which interprets *tall*) our definition leads to the unpleasant conclusion that *John is tall* is true just in case there is an individual who is shorter than John. (For, if there is such an individual, say, Bill, then John is tall relative to the set consisting just of the individuals John and Bill. The converse is obvious.) For now we leave things as they are, contenting ourselves with the remark that the representation of contextually determined elements seems to be necessary for any fully adequate treatment of predicate adjective phrases.

With this we end our discussion of adjective phrases in our extensional system. In the next section we will see how much of what we have done here can be extended immediately to the case of other modifiers.

Proofs of Theorems from This Section

The first theorem we have to prove is the following:

THEOREM 2. Let $R_{B/B} = \{f \in F_{B/B} : f \text{ is restricting}\}$, where B is an arbitrary boolean algebra. Then $R_{B/B}$ is a boolean algebra under the operations $\wedge$, $\vee$, and $'$ defined as follows:

(a) For $f, g \in R_{B/B}$ arbitrary, $f \wedge g$ is defined by setting $(f \wedge g)(b) = f(b) \wedge g(b)$ for each $b \in B$.

(b) For $f, g \in R_{B/B}$ arbitrary, $f \vee g$ is defined by setting $(f \vee g)(b) = f(b) \vee g(b)$ for each $b \in B$.

(c) For $f \in R_{B/B}$ arbitrary, f' is defined by setting $f'(b) = b \wedge (f(b))'$ for each $b \in B$.

Moreover, if B is a complete algebra, then $R_{B/B}$ is complete, and if B is atomic, then $R_{B/B}$ is atomic.

We note that since $T_{A,P} = R_{P/P}$, it follows from this theorem that $T_{A,P}$ is a complete atomic boolean algebra.

We first have to show that $f \wedge g$, $f \vee g$, and f' as defined above are actually members of $R_{B/B}$. However, the proofs of these statements are essentially identical to the corresponding proofs for $T_{A,P}$, which were given explicitly in the text. We leave it to the reader to verify that this is indeed the case.

To prove that $R_{B/B}$ is a boolean algebra, we have to verify that the axioms of a boolean algebra are satisfied (see Definition 9 of Section A). As in the case of previous proofs of this sort, we will only prove some of these axioms explicitly, leaving the others for the reader.

The commutativity axioms follow obviously from the fact that the operations in B satisfy these axioms. The distributivity axioms likewise follow in a straightforward way from the definitions. For example, to prove that the first distributivity axiom holds in $R_{B/B}$, let f, g, and h be arbitrary members of $R_{B/B}$, and let b be an arbitrary element of B. Then,

$$
\begin{aligned}
(f \wedge (g \vee h))(b) &= f(b) \wedge (g \vee h)(b) && \text{(definition of } \wedge \text{ in } R_{B/B}) \\
&= f(b) \wedge (g(b) \vee h(b)) && \text{(definition of } \vee \text{ in } R_{B/B}) \\
&= (f(b) \wedge g(b)) \vee (f(b) \wedge h(b)) && \text{(distributive axiom in } B) \\
&= (f \wedge g)(b) \vee (f \wedge h)(b) && \text{(definition of } \wedge \text{ in } R_{B/B}) \\
&= ((f \wedge g) \vee (f \wedge h))(b) && \text{(definition of } \vee \text{ in } R_{B/B})
\end{aligned}
$$

Now, since $(f \wedge (g \vee h)) (b) = ((f \wedge g) \vee (f \wedge h)) (b)$ for every b in B, we conclude that $f \wedge (g \vee h) = (f \wedge g) \vee (f \wedge h)$.

The remaining axioms involve the distinguished elements 0 and 1. We define 0 as that element of $R_{B/B}$ such that $0(b) = 0$ for each element b of B (where, of course, the second 0 refers to the zero element of B). Note that, since $0 \leqslant b$ for every $b \in B$ by Theorem 2 of Section A, the function 0 thus defined is indeed restricting (that is, it is a member of $R_{B/B}$).

We can now show that the first complement axiom in the definition of a boolean algebra is satisfied by $R_{B/B}$. Let f be an arbitrary member of $R_{B/B}$, and let b be an arbitrary element of B. Then:

$$
\begin{aligned}
(f \wedge f') (b) &= f(b) \wedge f'(b) && \text{(definition of } \wedge \text{ in } R_{B/B}) \\
&= f(b) \wedge (b \wedge (f(b))') && \text{(definition of ' in } R_{B/B}) \\
&= b \wedge (f(b) \wedge (f(b))') && \text{(commutative and associative laws in } B) \\
&= b \wedge 0_B && \text{(complement axiom in } B) \\
&= 0_B && \text{(Theorem 2a, c of Section A applied to } B) \\
&= 0(b) && \text{(definition of 0 in } R_{B/B}).
\end{aligned}
$$

Since $(f \wedge f') (b) = 0(b)$ for each $b \in B$, we conclude that $f \wedge f' = 0$.

Next, we define 1 as that element of $R_{B/B}$ such that $1(b) = b$ for each element of b of B. That 1 thus defined is in fact restricting (that is, an element of $R_{B/B}$) follows from the fact that $b \leqslant b$ (Theorem 2b of Section A). With this definition, we prove that the second complement axiom of the definition of a boolean algebra is satisfied by $R_{B/B}$ by letting $f \in R_{B/B}$ and $b \in B$ be arbitrary elements and noting that:

$$
\begin{aligned}
(f \vee f') (b) &= f(b) \vee f'(b) && \text{(definition of } \vee \text{ in } R_{B/B}) \\
&= f(b) \vee (b \wedge (f(b))') && \text{(definition of ' in } R_{B/B}) \\
&= (f(b) \vee b) \wedge (f(b) \vee (f(b))') && \text{(distributivity in } B) \\
&= (f(b) \vee b) \wedge 1_B && \text{(complement axiom in } B) \\
&= f(b) \vee b && \text{(axiom } e \text{ in } B) \\
&= b && \text{(} f \text{ is restricting, that is, } f(b) \leqslant b) \\
&= 1(b)
\end{aligned}
$$

Since $(f \vee f') (b) = 1(b)$ for each $b \in B$, we conclude that $f \vee f' = 1$.

The proofs of the remaining axioms are similar, and are left to the reader.

Now, let us suppose that B is a complete algebra. To show that $R_{B/B}$ is complete, we must show that every subset K of $R_{B/B}$ has a glb and a lub. In order to do this, it is convenient to have the following lemma, which allows us to operate easily with the relation $\leqslant$ in $R_{B/B}$, where B is any boolean algebra.

LEMMA. Let B be a boolean algebra, and let $f, g \in R_{B/B}$ be arbitrary. Then, $f \leqslant g$ iff for each $b \in B$, $f(b) \leqslant g(b)$.

For, suppose first that $f \leqslant g$. This means that $f \wedge g = f$, so that, for each $b \in B$, $f(b) = (f \wedge g)(b) = f(b) \wedge g(b)$ (the last equality by the definition of $\wedge$ in $R_{B/B}$), so that $f(b) \leqslant g(b)$ for each $b \in B$.

Conversely, if for each $b \in B$ we have $f(b) \leqslant g(b)$, this means that, for each $b \in B$, $f(b) = f(b) \wedge g(b) = (f \wedge g)(b)$, whence $f = f \wedge g$, that is, $f \leqslant g$. This proves the lemma.

Now, assume that B is complete, and let $K \subseteq R_{B/B}$ be an arbitrary subset. For each $b \in B$, define $f(b) = \bigwedge \{k(b): k \in K\}$. Then $f(b)$ is well defined (because B is complete), and is a function from B into B. Moreover, since $k(b) \leqslant b$ for each k in K, it follows that $f(b) \leqslant b$. Thus, f is a restricting function, that is, a member of $R_{B/B}$. We show that f is the glb of K.

Let $k \in K$ be arbitrary. For each $b \in B$, $f(b) = \bigwedge\{k(b): k \in K\} \leqslant k(b)$, so by the lemma, $f \leqslant k$. Since this holds for each element k of K, we conclude that f is a lower bound for K.

Next, suppose that y is a lower bound for K. Let $b \in B$ be arbitrary. Since $y \leqslant k$ for every $k \in K$, we have $y(b) \leqslant k(b)$ for every $k \in K$, by the lemma. But, by the definition of f, we conclude that we must have $y(b) \leqslant f(b)$. Since this holds for arbitrary b, we have, again by the lemma, that $y \leqslant f$, that is, f is the greatest lower bound.

The definition and proofs for least upper bounds are dual to the ones for greatest lower bounds; we leave it to the reader to formulate them.

Finally, assume that B is atomic. We will show that $R_{B/B}$ is atomic.

First, what are the atoms of $R_{B/B}$? For each $b \in B$ where $b \neq 0_B$ and each atom $a \leqslant b$, let us define the function f_{ab} as follows: for each $c \in B$, $f_{ab}(c) = 0_B$ if $c \neq b$, and $f_{ab}(b) = a$. Then, since $f_{ab}(c) = 0_B \leqslant c$ (for the case that $c \neq b$), and $f_{ab}(b) = a \leqslant b$, f_{ab} is a restricting function from B into B, that is, an element of $R_{B/B}$. Moreover, f_{ab} is an atom. First, $f_{ab} \neq 0$ since $f_{ab}(b) \neq 0_B$. Second if $g \leqslant f_{ab}$, then (by the lemma) $g(c) \leqslant f_{ab}(c) = 0_B$ if $c \neq b$, whence $g(c) = 0_B$ if $c \neq b$. Also, $g(b) \leqslant f_{ab}(b) = a$, whence, since a is an atom, $g(b) = 0_B$ or $g(b) = a$. In the first case, $g = 0$, and in the second, $g = f_{ab}$. Thus, f_{ab} satisfies the definition of an atom. We leave it to the reader to show that any atom of $R_{B/B}$ must be of the form f_{ab}, a fact we do not need in the current proof.

To show that $R_{B/B}$ is atomic, let $f \in R_{B/B}$ be arbitrary, with $f \neq 0$. We show that there exists an atom a of B and an element b of B, with $a \leqslant b$, such that $f_{ab} \leqslant f$.

Since $f \neq 0$, there must exist at least one element of B, say, b, such that $f(b) \neq 0_B$. Since f is restricting, we have $f(b) \leqslant b$, whence we also have that $b \neq 0_B$. Since B is atomic, there must exist at least one atom, say, a, such that $a \leqslant f(b)$. Then, we also have that $a \leqslant b$, so that f_{ab} is well defined for the elements a and b we have just chosen. Now, it is the case that $f_{ab} \leqslant f$. For, if $c \neq b$, then $f_{ab}(c) = 0_B \leqslant f(c)$, no matter what $f(c)$ actually is. And, $f_{ab}(b) = a \leqslant f(b)$, by the way a was chosen. Thus, by the lemma, $f_{ab} \leqslant f$, whence $R_{B/B}$ is atomic. This completes the proof of the theorem.

Our next theorem is the following:

THEOREM 3. Let $I_{B/B} = \{f \in R_{B/B}: f$ is intersecting$\}$, where B is an arbitrary boolean algebra. Then $I_{B/B}$ is a subalgebra of $R_{B/B}$. Moreover, if B is complete, then $I_{B/B}$ is complete, and if B is atomic, then $I_{B/B}$ is atomic.

The fact that $I_{B/B}$ is a subalgebra of $R_{B/B}$ will follow if we can show that $I_{B/B}$ is closed under the operations $\wedge$, $\vee$, and $'$ defined in $R_{B/B}$, and if $I_{B/B}$ contains the elements 0 and 1 of $R_{B/B}$; for then the axioms of a boolean algebra must be fulfilled in $I_{B/B}$, since they are fulfilled in $R_{B/B}$.

Suppose that f and g are elements of $I_{B/B}$. Then, for $b \in B$ arbitrary we have:

$$
\begin{aligned}
(f \wedge g)(b) &= f(b) \wedge g(b) && \text{(definition of } \wedge \text{ in } R_{B/B}) \\
&= (b \wedge f(1)) \wedge (b \wedge g(1)) && (f \text{ and } g \text{ are intersecting)} \\
&= (b \wedge b) \wedge (f(1) \wedge g(1)) && \text{(commutative and associative laws} \\
& && \text{in } R_{B/B}) \\
&= b \wedge (f(1) \wedge g(1)) && \text{(idempotent law in } R_{B/B}) \\
&= b \wedge (f \wedge g)(1) && \text{(definition of } \wedge \text{ in } R_{B/B})
\end{aligned}
$$

which shows that $f \wedge g$ is intersecting. We also have:

$$
\begin{aligned}
(f \vee g)(b) &= f(b) \vee g(b) && \text{(definition of } \vee \text{ in } R_{B/B}) \\
&= (b \wedge f(1)) \vee (b \wedge g(1)) && (f \text{ and } g \text{ are intersecting)} \\
&= b \wedge (f(1) \vee g(1)) && \text{(distributive law in } R_{B/B}) \\
&= b \wedge (f \vee g)(1) && \text{(definition of } \vee \text{ in } R_{B/B})
\end{aligned}
$$

which shows that $f \vee g$ is also intersecting.

To show that $I_{B/B}$ is closed under $'$, let f be an element of $I_{B/B}$. Then, for $b \in B$ arbitrary, we have:

$$
\begin{aligned}
f'(b) &= b \wedge (f(b))' && \text{(definition of $'$ in $R_{B/B}$)} \\
&= b \wedge (b \wedge f(1))' && \text{(f is intersecting)} \\
&= b \wedge (b' \vee (f(1))') && \text{(DeMorgan law in $R_{B/B}$)} \\
&= (b \wedge b') \vee (b \wedge (f(1))') && \text{(distributive law in $R_{B/B}$)} \\
&= b \wedge (f(1))' && \text{(since $b \wedge b' = 0$)} \\
&= b \wedge (1 \wedge (f(1))') && \text{(since $(f(1))' = 1 \wedge (f(1))'$}) \\
&= b \wedge f'(1) && \text{(definition of $'$, in $R_{B/B}$)}
\end{aligned}
$$

showing that f' is intersecting.

Finally, for any $b \in B$, $0(b) = 0_B = b \wedge 0_B = b \wedge 0(1)$, and $1(b) = b = b \wedge 1 = b \wedge 1(1)$, so that 0 and 1 are intersecting. This completes the proof that $I_{B/B}$ is a subalgebra of $R_{B/B}$.

If B is complete or atomic, it will follow directly from Theorem 4$'$, proven below, that $I_{B/B}$ is complete or atomic, since $I_{B/B}$ is, in fact, isomorphic to B. The reader may easily verify that nothing in the proof of Theorem 4$'$ makes use of the fact that $I_{B/B}$ is complete or atomic if B is.

However, before proceeding to that proof, it is instructive to examine directly what is going on in $I_{B/B}$. As far as completeness is concerned, we can verify directly that if $K \subseteq I_{B/B}$, then $\wedge K$ and $\vee K$, which are well defined elements of $R_{B/B}$ (since $R_{B/B}$ is complete), are elements of $I_{B/B}$. To show this, let b be an arbitrary element of B. Then, first of all, we have that $(\wedge K)(b) = \wedge_{f \in K} f(b) = \wedge_{f \in K} (b \wedge f(1)) = b \wedge [\wedge_{f \in K} f(1)] = b \wedge (\wedge K)(1)$, where we have used the definition of $\wedge K$ as given in the proof of Theorem 2, together with the fact that the elements of K are intersecting. Of course, the equation $(\wedge K)(b) = b \wedge (\wedge K)(1)$ shows that K is intersecting.

Similarly, we have $(\vee K)(b) = \vee_{f \in K} f(b) = \vee_{f \in K} (b \wedge f(1)) = b [\vee_{f \in K} f(1)] = b \wedge (\vee K)(1)$, so that $(\vee K)$ is intersecting.

The matter of atomicity is more interesting. By Theorem 2 above if B is atomic, so is $R_{B/B}$. However, it is easy to show that none of the functions f_{ab}, which were defined in the proof of Theorem 2 and shown there to be the atoms of $R_{B/B}$, are elements of $I_{B/B}$. Thus, the atoms of $I_{B/B}$ must be certain elements which are *not* atoms when viewed as elements of $R_{B/B}$. From the statement of Theorem 4$'$ below, it follows that the atoms of $I_{B/B}$ must be exactly those functions f_a defined as follows: if a is an atom of B, then, for arbitrary $b \in B$, $f_a(b) = b \wedge a$. Alternatively, the reader may supply the entirely straightforward direct proof that the functions f_a so defined are indeed atoms in $I_{B/B}$, and that for any $f \in I_{B/B}$, $f \neq 0$, there exists some f_a such that $f_a \leqslant f$. This completes the proof and discussion of Theorem 3.

Rather than proving Theorem 4 of the text, we prove the following slightly more general theorem:

THEOREM 4'. Let B be a boolean algebra, and let the function $u : B \rightarrow F_{B/B}$ be defined as follows: given $b \in B$, $u(b)$ is that function from B into B such that for each $c \in B$, $(u(b))(c) = c \wedge b$. Then u is an isomorphism of B onto $I_{B/B}$.

First of all, note that $(u(b))(1) = 1 \wedge b = b$, so that $(u(b))(c) = c \wedge (u(b))(1)$, whence $u(b)$ is intersecting. Thus, we may regard u as a function from B into $I_{B/B}$.

Next, suppose that $b_1 \neq b_2$. Then, $(u(b_1))(1) = b_1 \neq b_2 = (u(b_2))(1)$, so that $u(b_1)$ and $u(b_2)$ are distinct functions from B into B; that is $u(b_1) \neq u(b_2)$. This proves that u is one-to-one.

Suppose next that f is an arbitrary element of $I_{B/B}$. Since $f(1)$ is an element of B, it makes sense to consider $u(f(1))$. But $(u(f(1))(c) = c \wedge f(1) = f(c)$ (since f is intersecting), whence $u(f(1)) = f$. Since f was arbitrary, this shows that u is onto.

We have shown that u, regarded as a function from B into $I_{B/B}$, is one-to-one and onto. The proof will be complete if we can show that u is a homomorphism. We show that u preserves meets and complements.

Let b_1 and b_2 be arbitrary elements of B. For any $c \in B$, we have:

$$
\begin{aligned}
(u(b_1 \wedge b_2))(c) &= c \wedge (b_1 \wedge b_2) && \text{(definition of } u) \\
&= (c \wedge c) \wedge (b_1 \wedge b_2) && \text{(idempotent law in } B) \\
&= (c \wedge b_1) \wedge (c \wedge b_2) && \text{(commutative and associative} \\
& && \text{laws in } B) \\
&= (u(b_1))(c) \wedge (u(b_2))(c) && \text{(definition of } u) \\
&= (u(b_1) \wedge u(b_2))(c) && \text{(definition of } \wedge \text{ in } I_{B/B})
\end{aligned}
$$

Since this holds for arbitrary $c \in B$, we conclude that $u(b_1 \wedge b_2) = u(b_1) \wedge u(b_2)$, that is, u preserves meets.

Finally, let b be an arbitrary element of B. For any $c \in B$, we have:

$$
\begin{aligned}
(u(b'))\,(c) \; &= c \wedge b' && \text{(definition of } u\text{)} \\
&= (c \wedge b') \vee (c \wedge c') && \text{(since } c \wedge c' = 0\text{)} \\
&= c \wedge (b' \vee c') && \text{(distributive law in } B\text{)} \\
&= c \wedge (b \wedge c)' && \text{(Demorgan law in } B\text{)} \\
&= c \wedge ((u(b))\,(c))' && \text{(definition of } u\text{)} \\
&= (u(b))'\,(c) && \text{(definition of } ' \text{ in } I_{B/B}\text{)}
\end{aligned}
$$

Since this holds for arbitrary $c \in B$, we conclude that $u(b') = (u(b))'$, that is, u preserves complements. Thus, u is a homomorphism, and, since it is a one-to-one mapping of B onto $I_{B/B}$, it is an isomorphism of B onto $I_{B/B}$. This completes the proof.

Let us note that in the part of the above proof in which we showed that u is onto, we proved the equation $u(f(1)) = f$, which, together with the fact that u is one-to-one, shows explicitly that the intersecting adjective function f determines the property $f(1)$.

Again, rather than proving Theorem 5 of the text, we prove the slightly more general:

THEOREM 5′. Let B be a boolean algebra and let $f, g \in I_{B/B}$ be arbitrary. Then, for each $b \in B$, $(f \wedge g)\,(b) = f(g(b)) = g(f(b))$.

For, we have

$$
\begin{aligned}
(f \wedge g)\,(b) \; &= f(b) \wedge g(b) && \text{(definition of } \wedge \text{ in } I_{B/B}\text{)} \\
&= (b \wedge f(1)) \wedge (b \wedge g(1)) && (f \text{ and } g \text{ are intersecting)} \\
&= (b \wedge f(1)) \wedge g(1) && \text{(commutative, idempotent, and} \\
&&& \text{associative laws in } B\text{)}
\end{aligned}
$$

And we also have

$$
\begin{aligned}
g(f(b)) \; &= f(b) \wedge g(1) && (g \text{ is intersecting)} \\
&= (b \wedge f(1)) \wedge g(1) && (f \text{ is intersecting)}
\end{aligned}
$$

Thus, $(f \wedge g)\,(b)$ is equal to $g(f(b))$, since they are both equal to $(b \wedge f(1)) \wedge g(1)$. The proof that $f(g(b))$ is also equal to $(b \wedge f(1)) \wedge g(1)$ is similar, and left to the reader.

We now prove a slightly generalized version of Theorem 7, from which Theorem 6 follows immediately as a special case.

THEOREM 7'. Let B be a boolean algebra and let $f \in I_{B/B}$ be arbitrary. Then, for any positive integer n, $f^n = f$.

The proof is by induction on n. Clearly, the statement $f^n = f$ is true for the case that $n = 1$. Assume, then, that it is true for $n = k$.

Letting $b \in B$ be arbitrary, we have that

$$
\begin{aligned}
f^{k+1}(b) &= f(f^k(b)) &&\text{(part (b) of Definition 12)}\\
&= f(f(b)) &&\text{(inductive assumption)}\\
&= f(b) \wedge f(1) &&\text{(f is intersecting)}\\
&= (b \wedge f(1)) \wedge f(1) &&\text{(f is intersecting)}\\
&= b \wedge f(1) &&\text{(associative and idempotent laws in B)}\\
&= f(b) &&\text{(f is intersecting)}
\end{aligned}
$$

which proves the theorem.

We similarly generalize Theorem 8 as:

THEOREM 8'. Let B be a boolean algebra and let $f \in R_{B/B}$ be arbitrary. Then, if n and m are nonnegative integers with $n \geqslant m$, then $f^n \leqslant f^m$.

We prove this by induction on the set of integers greater than m; we will make continual use of the lemma of Theorem 2 above.

For the case $n = m + 1$, we have, for each $b \in B$,

$$
\begin{aligned}
f^{m+1} &= f(f^m(b)) &&\text{(part (b) of Definition 12)}\\
&\leqslant f^m(b) &&\text{(f is restricting)}
\end{aligned}
$$

whence $f^{m+1} \leqslant f^m$, by the lemma.

Next, we assume that the statement of the theorem is true for $n = m + k$. For $n = m + k + 1$, we have, for each $b \in B$,

$$
\begin{aligned}
f^{m+k+1}(b) &= f(f^{m+k}(b)) &&\text{(part (b) of Definition 12)}\\
&\leqslant f^{m+k}(b) &&\text{(f is restricting)}\\
&\leqslant f^m(b) &&\text{(inductive assumption).}
\end{aligned}
$$

Whence $f^{m+k+1} \leqslant f^m$, by the lemma. This proves the theorem.

The final theorem of this section shows that the property associated with a predicate intersecting adjective is just the property determined by that adjective, in the sense of Theorem 4. Again, we give a slightly more general theorem than the one stated in the text:

THEOREM 9′. Let B be a complete boolean algebra and let $f \in I_{B/B}$ be arbitrary. Then $\bigvee_{b \in B} f(b) = f(1)$.

We have that

$$\bigvee_{b \in B} f(b) \quad\quad = \bigvee_{b \in B} (b \wedge f(1)) \quad\quad (f \text{ is intersecting})$$
$$= \left(\bigvee_{b \in B} b\right) \wedge f(1) \quad\quad (\text{infinite distributive law in } B)$$
$$= 1 \wedge f(1) \quad\quad (\text{since } 1 = \text{lub } (B))$$
$$= f(1) \quad\quad (\text{since } f(1) = 1)$$

This concludes the proofs for this section.

2. PREDICATE MODIFIERS

We come next to the category of predicate modifiers, which we shall abbreviate as PM. Much of the work carried out in the previous section for the APs will carry over to the case of the PMs, as well as to other modifiers.

By a predicate modifier we mean, to begin with, any expression of category P_n/P_n, for some nonnegative integer n. For the first part of our discussion, the reader may wish to think of predicate modifiers as simply being of the category P_1/P_1 although the more general approach will ultimately be taken. Thus, predicate modifiers include all expressions normally thought of in any sense as adverbial.

Now, relatively few such are lexical expressions. In the discussions to follow, we will be most concerned with prepositional phrases, such as *in a garden, with John*, etc., and with adverbs derived from adjectives, such as *skillfully, allegedly*, etc. Prepositional phrases are formed by combining an expression of category $\bar{N}$ with a (mostly lexical) expression of a new category which we call, of course, prepositions (abbreviated Prep); and adverbs like *skillfully* are formed by combining an adjective with the logical constant *ly*. Following our general program, since, clearly, Prep = PM/$\bar{N}$, we will want to interpret a preposition as a function from $T_{\bar{N}}$ into T_{PM}; and, similarly, the interpretation of *ly* will be some function from T_{AP} into T_{PM}. Thus we find it necessary to discuss PMs before taking up the discussion of prepositions or of other adverb-formers, even though most of our examples will involve such elements, since we need to know what T_{PM} is in order to study functions which have T_{PM} as their range. As it turns out, however, in addition to the more common complex PMs, there will be a small number of lexical PMs, such as the logical constants *somewhere* and *everywhere*, as well as certain other lexical expressions such as *here, there*, etc.

As in the case of the APs, PMs can be subdivided into a number of distinct groups. We now consider some of these groups.

Recall that many common scalar adjectives, such as *skillful*, as well as nonrestricting adjectives, such as *fake* or *alleged*, are properly intensional; that is, they cannot be interpreted as functions from N extensions into N extensions. We called those APs which *can* be so interpreted *transparent*. Similarly, let us say that a PM is *transparent* if it can be defined as a function on the set of possible extensional interpretations of the predicate with which it is combined.

Now, in the case of PMs, it appears that a striking majority of them are nontransparent. Let us examine a few representative cases.

Manner adverbs such as *skillfully* or *slowly* are nontransparent. For, suppose that in a given model those individuals who are singing are exactly those individuals who are dancing. Then, *sing* and *dance* will be interpreted as the same (extensional) P_1 homomorphism, in that model. Now, we certainly would not want to conclude that those individuals who are singing slowly are exactly the same as those individuals who are dancing slowly. However, if *slowly* were interpreted transparently, this unfortunate conclusion would follow, since the function which interprets *slowly* would be applied to the same argument in order to produce the interpretations of *sing slowly* and of *dance slowly*.

Similarly, comitative phrases such as *with Fred* are nontransparent. If, for example, the individuals who are working are exactly those individuals who are talking, then *work* and *talk* would be interpreted as the same P_1 homomorphism. But we would not want to conclude that those individuals who are working with Fred are exactly the same as those individuals who are talking with Fred; obviously, one could be working with Fred but only talking with John, who is sitting on the sidelines. Thus, *with Fred* had better not be interpreted as a function which takes as argument the extensional interpretation of *work* or of *talk*, for if it were, *work with Fred* and *talk with Fred* would have the same interpretation.

Benefactive phrases are not transparent. If those who are buying a present are exactly those who are whistling a tune, it will not follow that those who are buying a present for Mary are those who are whistling a tune for Mary.

Directional phrases are not transparent. If those who are driving a taxi are exactly those who are spitting, it will not follow that those who are driving a taxi through the store window are exactly those who are spitting through the store window.

Instrumental phrases are not transparent. If those who are eating a pickle are exactly those who are killing a snake, it will not follow that those who are eating a pickle with a fork are exactly those who are killing a snake with a fork.

Subject-matter phrases are not transparent. If those who are lecturing are exactly those who are thinking, it will not follow that those who are lecturing about the Common Market are exactly those who are thinking about the Common Market.

Finally, source and goal expressions are not transparent. If those who are talking are exactly those who are waving, it will not follow that those who are talking to Bill are exactly those who are waving to Bill. Similarly, if those who are running are exactly those who are stealing an apple, it does not follow that those who are running from the police are exactly those who are stealing an apple from the police. (But see the discussion below on argument-oriented PMs.)

There is, however, an important class of predicate modifiers which do seem to be transparent. These are the stative locatives, such as *in the park, under a table*, etc. If, say, in some model, the individuals who are singing are exactly those who are dancing, we *can* conclude that those who are singing in the park are exactly those who are dancing in the park.

As a matter of fact, in the case of these stative locatives, we can say something more precise. Namely, the sentence *John is singing in the park* is true if and only if *John is singing* and *John exists* (= *is*) *in the park* are both simultaneously true. Suppose that *sing* is interpreted as the P_1 homomorphism f, and that *in the park* is interpreted as the function g. Then *sing in the park* will be interpreted as the P_1 homomorphism $g(f)$, while *exist in the park* is interpreted as $g(1)$ (since the logical constant *exist* is interpreted as 1 in every model). But by what we have just said, this means that $g(f) = f \wedge g(1)$. If we examine Definition 5 of the previous section, we see that g is just an intersecting function, that is, a member of $I_{T_{P_1}/T_{P_1}}$. At this point, therefore, we might be tempted to say that for the extensional language the category PM consists just of stative locatives, that $PM = P_1/P_1$, and that $T_{PM} = I_{T_{P_1}/T_{P_1}}$. While we will see shortly that such an approach is not sufficient for our purposes, it is instructive to see how much can be done just with this, based on what we have developed so far.

First, by Theorem 1 of the previous section, we can conclude that stative locatives are restricting. However, we can easily verify that all of the adverbial phrases we have been discussing are restricting. Thus, for example, from the truth of *John is working skillfully* we can surely conclude that *John is working* must be true. Similarly, if *Fred is spitting into the tub* is true, it must be true that *Fred is spitting*. In fact, predicate modifiers which are *not* restricting are rare. We will see examples of such occasionally (including the transparent formula-modifier *false*, discussed later in this section). In general, however, PMs support the notion suggested in the previous section on the basis of the APs that modifiers generally are typically restricting.

Next, since T_{P_1} is a complete atomic boolean algebra (by, essentially, Theorem 19 of Section A), we conclude by Theorem 3 of the previous section that $I_{T_{P_1}/T_{P_1}}$ is a complete atomic boolean algebra. Let us see what relevance this has to our system.

The fact that $I_{T_{P_1}/T_{P_1}}$ is a boolean algebra allows us to regard the stative locatives as a boolean category, something we certainly want to do, inasmuch as they can be combined with *and, or,* and *not* in ordinary English: *John is singing in the garden and/or in the park, John is singing in the garden but not in the park.* The boolean operations on $I_{T_{P_1}/T_{P_1}}$, calculated as in Definition 37 of the previous section, allow such combinations to be interpreted if the interpretations of the constituent parts are known. For example, if the P_1 homomorphism f interprets *sing*, and if the functions g_1 and g_2 interpret *in the garden* and *in the park* respectively, then it follows from that definition that, say, *sing in the garden and in the park* is interpreted by $(g_1 \wedge g_2)(f) = g_1(f) \wedge g_2(f)$, which is the interpretation of the P_1 *sing in the garden and sing in the park*. A similar statement can be made for the combination with *or*. Finally, it follows from that definition that *sing not (in the garden)* is interpreted as $g'_1(f) = f \wedge (g_1(f))'$, that is, as *sing and not (sing in the garden)*. These interpretations accord with our intuitions.

But here too what we have just said about stative locatives holds for all (restricting) adverbials. For example, we would certainly want the P_1 *sing* ((*with Mary*) *and* (*about peace*)) to have the same interpretation as (*sing with Mary*) *and* (*sing about peace*) (and similarly with *or* replacing *and*). We will still be able to achieve this if we assume that the intensional type of P_1 is some boolean algebra B; for then the interpretations of the adverbials will be in $R_{B/B}$, which is a boolean algebra, by Theorem 2 of the previous section. Of course, B cannot be the set T_{P_1} that we have defined for our (extensional) core language; we will have to wait until we consider enlarging our system to an intensional one before we learn what B should be.

Returning to the stative locatives, we note next that $I_{T_{P_1}/T_{P_1}}$ is complete. The usefulness of this will be easier to appreciate after we discuss the prepositions. However, we can anticipate a bit and note that a phrase such as *in a park* will be interpreted as the join of functions each of which could be thought of as the interpretation of a phrase like *in e*, where e is an $\overline{N}$ whose interpretation ranges over all the parks. The completeness of $I_{T_{P_1}/T_{P_1}}$ allows this procedure to be well defined even in the case that there is an infinite number of parks. Similar considerations hold for other quantifiers.

Again, it appears that completeness is relevant to the analysis of all (restricting) adverbials, not just to the stative locatives. Thus, for example, the interpretation of a phrase such as *about a number* (as in, say, *John argued about a number*) will be the join of functions each of which can be thought of as the interpretation of a phrase like *about e*, where e is an $\overline{N}$ whose interpretation ranges over all the numbers. If the interpretations of these adverbials lie in a complete algebra, then this join will be well-defined. This will be the case if the the intensional type of P_1 is a complete algebra B; for then the adverbial interpretations will lie in $R_{B/B}$, which, by Theorem 2 of the previous section, is complete.

Turning to the matter of atomicity, and again restricting our attention just to the stative locatives, we recall from the proof and the discussion of Theorem 3 of the previous section that $I_{T_{P_1}/T_{P_1}}$ is atomic because it is in fact isomorphic to T_{P_1}, by Theorem 4' of the previous section. By the construction used in the proof of this latter theorem it is clear that $g \in I_{T_{P_1}/T_{P_1}}$ is an atom if and only if $g(1)$ is an atom in T_{P_1}. But an atom of T_{P_1} is simply a homomorphism which takes the value 1 on exactly one individual, as shown in the proof of Theorem 19, Section A. Thus, the stative-locative interpretation function g is an atom just in case the P_1 homomorphism $g(1)$ takes the value 1 on exactly one individual. But, as we saw earlier, $g(1)$ is the interpretation of the P_1 formed by combining the stative locative which g interprets together with *exist*. Thus, we may say that atomic locations are those defined by individuals, in the sense that a particular individual is at that location but no other individual is. Thus, a typical atomic location could be described as being 'where John is'. Our system therefore has a rather Leibnitzian, or, perhaps, Einsteinian flavor: space does not exist absolutely, independent of the individuals which populate it. Rather, space is defined by, or arises from, those individuals.

This being the case, it is interesting to reexamine the interpretations of boolean combinations of stative locatives. Suppose, for example, that *in the garden* and *in the park* are two such expressions, interpreted by g_1 and g_2 respectively. Then, as we have seen, *in the garden and in the park* is interpreted by $g_1 \wedge g_2$. Now, it follows directly from the definition of intersecting that $g_1 \wedge g_2 \neq 0$ if and only if $(g_1 \wedge g_2)(1) = g_1(1) \wedge g_1(1) \neq 0$. But this is true if and only if there exists at least one individual for which $g_1(1)$ and $g_2(1)$ both take the value 1. In other words, $g_1 \wedge g_2 \neq 0$ if and only if *in the garden* and *in the park* share at least one atomic location; intuitively, this would mean that the spaces referred to by *in the garden* and by *in the park* overlap. Moreover, a formula like *John* (*sing* ((*in the garden*) *and* (*in the park*))) would be true just in case that (a) *John sing* is true, *and* (b) John's location is to be found in the overlap of these spaces. If the spaces do not overlap at all, then $g_1 \wedge g_2 = 0$, whence $(g_1 \wedge g_2)(f) = 0$ for any P_1 homomorphism f; in this case, such a formula would automatically be false.

Now, if we recall that our formulas are intended to be tenseless, then this is intuitively correct. In real English, if *in the garden* and *in the park* refer to totally disjoint (i.e. nonoverlapping) areas, then a sentence like *John is singing in the garden and in the park* is understood to refer to at least two occasions of singing, one in the garden and one in the park, which take place at different times.

Following this train of thought, it seems not unreasonable to define the interpretation of the logical constant *everywhere* as meaning something like 'at every atomic location', which we can formally define as the meet of all the atoms in $I_{T_{P_1}/T_{P_1}}$. However, except for the case of the boolean algebra with exactly one atom, this meet is always 0. Thus, as far as our extensional system is concerned, *everywhere* is always interpreted as 0. While this does not seem particularly insightful, it does at least capture the fact that, for example, in order for a sentence such as *John sang everywhere* to be true, it is necessary that more than one occasion of singing has to be involved (assuming that the world in which this sentence is supposed to apply offers more than one possible location). It also has the merit of indicating rather clearly the direction we will have to go in in order to represent the meaning of *everywhere* in a fully adequate way: we will have to provide for the representation of different occasions of an event-type (such as *sing*).

Similarly, if we imagine that the logical constant *somewhere* means something like 'at an atomic location', then we would define its interpretation in any model as being the join of all the atoms in $I_{T_{P_1}/T_{P_1}}$; but this join is always 1. Thus in our system, *somewhere* is logically redundant; e.g. *John*

sing and *John sing somewhere* are logically equivalent. Again, some fundamentally non-trivial extension of our system would be needed in order to
adequately represent the meaning of *somewhere*.

Finally, we would want to define *nowhere* as always being interpreted to
be equivalent to 'at no atomic location', Thus, in any model, *nowhere* is
interpreted as the intersection of the complements of all the atoms in
$I_{T_{P_1}/T_{P_1}}$ (or equivalently, as the complement of the join of all the atoms in
$I_{T_{P_1}/T_{P_1}}$). However, since the join of all the atoms in an atomic algebra is
1, this means that *nowhere* is interpreted always as 0. Thus, *John sings
nowhere* is logically false in our system, since, essentially, if this sentence
were true, then it would have to be true that John exists nowhere; but John
exists at the atomic location which he himself defines. This is different
from the usual interpretation of a P_1 like *sings nowhere* in real English,
which is, rather, equivalent to *not (sing somewhere)*. In this interpretation,
since *sing somewhere* and *sing* are logically equivalent, *John sings nowhere*
would be equivalent to *John doesn't sing*. We could, of course, define the
interpretation of the logical constant *nowhere* in our system in such a way
that when applied to the interpretation of a $P_1 e$, the resultant P_1 would be
equivalent to *not (e somewhere)*, but such an interpretation would not be
a member of $I_{T_{P_1}/T_{P_1}}$.

While we are on the subject of atoms, we might point out that the lexical
stative locative expressions *here* and *there* seem to refer to atomic locations,
though, of course, which ones depend on context. In our system, therefore,
it seems reasonable to require simply that these expressions be interpreted
as atoms. Thus, in a sense, *here* and *there* are locational proper nouns. A more
adequate treatment would require a theory of context.

The notion of atom is potentially available in the more general context
of adverbials. By Theorem 2 of the previous section, if the algebra B which
is the (intensional) type for P_1 is atomic, then $R_{B/B}$ is atomic. Thus, if
the type for adverbials turns out to be all of $R_{B/B}$, then the atoms of this
algebra could appear as the interpretations of certain adverbial expressions.
However, inasmuch as the definition of these atoms depend on the atoms
of the as yet undefined algebra B, we will not attempt a discussion of them
here.

Let us return now to the general question of classifying the subtypes of
adverbial expressions. In the case of the restrictive APs, we found that there
were essentially two subtypes of interest: intersecting APs, and scalar APs.
However, the situation for adverbial expressions is much more complicated.
In particular, not all nonintersecting restricting adverbials are scalar.

To be sure, there are scalar adverbials, the clearest examples of which are the manner adverbs, such as *skillfully, slowly*, etc. Note that such adverbs compare; we can say *John drives more skillfully than Bill*. We can also combine such adverbs with *very*: *Fred works very slowly*. An adequate representation of these adverbs should account for their scalarity. In principle, the discussion of scalarity of APs in the previous section is applicable here too. However, since that discussion centered around the notion of a relation defined on the atoms of the algebra which interprets the modified expression, and since the scalar adverbs are nontransparent, we cannot reasonably discuss their scalarity until we can define the notion of an intensional atom of a P_1, that is, until we define the atomic algebra B which will be the intensional type for the category P_1.

However, we can make one generalization here. Recall that in the previous section, *very* was put into the category AP_r/AP_r, and interpreted as a logical constant: in any model, *very* is interpreted as the function **very**, defined by **very** $(f) = f^2$, for each f in its domain. But we surely want to be able to combine *very* with adverbs as well, as we saw above. We can achieve this as follows. We will enter *very* into the category $\langle AP_r, PM\rangle/\langle AP_r, PM\rangle$; and we will interpret it again as the function **very** defined by means of the same equation as above, but now with a larger domain: f can be either the interpretation of an AP_r or the interpretation of a PM.

As in the case of intersecting APs, *very* is logically redundant when combined with any expression whose interpretation f satisfies the equation $f^2 = f$. For convenience, let us call such expressions *idempotent*. Formally:

DEFINITION 17. Let e be a modifier (that is, an expression of category X/X, for some X). Then e is *idempotent* iff, for any model, the function f which interprets it satisfies $f^2 = f$.

In the case of APs, we saw that intersecting expressions were necessarily idempotent; this is the content of Theorem 6 of the previous section. In the case of adverbials, the same theorem shows that stative locatives are necessarily idempotent. However, they may not be the only ones. For example, assuming that, say, ((*sing* (*about peace*)) (*about peace*)) is a well-formed P_1, we would certainly want it to be logically equivalent to *sing* (*about peace*). Similar statements can be made for the other types of adverbials mentioned above, with the exception of the manner adverbials, which are, as we have seen, clearly scalar, and hence nonidempotent. Thus adverbials provide examples of nontransparent idempotent modifiers. Theorem $7'$ of the previous section is not immediately applicable to these. At this point we leave open the question of whether the idempotency of these expressions should automatically follow as a consequence of other properties they must be required to have, or whether they should be specifically subcategorized as being idempotent (by means of a feature).

We now wish to consider a classification of PMs along a rather different line. In so doing, we will have to abandon the idea that PMs should be regarded syntactically as P_1 modifiers. We begin our discussion again with the case of stative locatives, whose properties can be represented within the framework of an extensional system.

We noted earlier that a stative locative such as *in the park* appears to behave as an intersecting P_1 modifier. Our example was the formula *John (sing (in the park))*, which is true in a model just in case *John sing* and *John (exist (in the park))* are both true. In this case, the PM *in the park* is combined with a lexical P_1 *sing*. However, when a stative locative is combined with a P_1 consisting of a transitive verb together with an object $\overline{N}$, the logical facts are often different.

Consider, for example, the real English sentence *John hit Mary in the park*. If this is true, then certainly we can conclude that *John hit Mary* is true. Moreover, if by 'hit' the speaker's intention is to refer to, say, an act of slapping or punching, in which a part of John's body comes into violent contact with a part of Mary's body, then we can conclude that *John was in the park* is true. So far, then, this sentence seems to be working the same as a sentence like *John sang in the park*.

However, we can note immediately that there is something else which can be concluded from *John hit Mary in the park*, namely the truth of *Mary was in the park*. This suggests the possibility that *John hit Mary in the park* might be logically equivalent to the *three* sentences: *John hit Mary, John was in the park, Mary was in the park*.

But this is not true. The reason is that *hit* might not refer to an event in which a part of John's body comes into violent contact with a part of Mary's body. The sentence *John hit Mary* could be used to indicate that a rock thrown by John came into violent contact with a part of Mary's body, or that a bullet shot from a gun by John came into violent contact with a part of Mary's body. Now, if *John hit Mary in the park* is uttered with such an event in mind, then, while it is true that *Mary was in the park* can be concluded, we cannot conclude the truth of *John was in the park*. Taking the various senses of 'hit' into consideration, then, it seems to us that the sentence *John hit Mary in the park* is logically equivalent to the *two* sentences *John hit Mary* and *Mary was in the park*.

Now, we would like our system to be able to represent this sort of fact. Letting g represent the function which interprets *in the park* and letting f be the P_1 homomorphism which interprets *hit Mary*, it cannot be the case that g is an intersecting function with f in its domain, for, if it were, then *hit Mary in the park* would be interpreted (by $g(f)$) as logically equivalent to *hit Mary and exist in the park*, as we have seen. We therefore have to abandon either the notion that g is an intersecting function, or the notion that the interpretation of *John hit Mary in the park* involved g taking f as an argument. If we were to take the former course and retain the idea that *hit Mary in the park* is interpreted as $g(f)$, then we are faced with the following problem. Suppose in some model the individuals who hit Mary are exactly those individuals who sing. Then *sing* and *hit Mary* have the same interpretation f. But this would mean that *sing in the park* and *hit Mary in the park* would have the same interpretation, whence, again, *hit Mary in the park* would be equivalent to *hit Mary and exist in the park* in this model (since *hit Mary* is equivalent to *sing* in this model, and *sing in the park* is equivalent to *sing and exist in the park*). Thus, we are forced to abandon the idea that *hit Mary in the park* is interpreted as $g(f)$. But this means that we must abandon the idea that, in this case, *in the park* combines with the P_1 *hit Mary*.

To deal with this situation, we will do the following. We retain the idea that *in the park* can be a P_1 modifier, and, as such, is interpreted by an intersecting function. However, we also allow *in the park* to be a P_2 modifier. This means that it can combine with *hit* to create the expression *hit in the park*; and, moreover, this latter expression is itself a P_2. To form the representation in our language of the English sentence *John hit Mary in the park*, this P_2 is combined first with the $\bar{N}$ *Mary* and then with the $\bar{N}$ *John*. We thus wind up with the expression; *John ((hit (in the park)) Mary)*.

What we have done, of course, is allow *in the park* to be a member of the category $\langle P_1, P_2 \rangle / \langle P_1, P_2 \rangle$. As such, it will be interpreted by a function $g: T_{P_1} \cup T_{P_2} \to T_{P_1} \cup T_{P_2}$ such that if $f \in T_{P_1}$ then $g(f) \in T_{P_1}$, and if $h \in T_{P_2}$ then $g(h) \in T_{P_2}$. In order to insure that the logical properties described earlier for P_1s like *sing in the park* are correctly represented, the restriction of g to T_{P_1} must be required to be an intersecting function. However, to insure that the logical properties of *hit Mary in the park* are properly represented, a further condition must be imposed on g. Clearly, if I_j and I_m are the individuals which interpret *John* and *Mary* respectively, and if h is the P_2 homomorphism which interprets *hit*, then we want the equation

(8) $((g\,(h))\,(I_m))\,(I_j) = (h\,(I_m))\,(I_j) \wedge (g\,(1))\,(I_m)$

to hold. Note that on the right hand side of this equation, '1' refers to the unit element of the P_1 (*not* the P_2) algebra, that is, to the interpretation of *exist*. Thus, this equation says exactly that *John hit Mary in the park* has the same truth value as *John hit Mary and Mary exist in the park*.

We have just seen that there is motivation for regarding stative locatives as P_2 modifiers as well as P_1 modifiers. We will see shortly that similar motivation exists in the case of a substantial number of other PM types. We therefore propose to generalize the definition of the category PM along the lines suggested above for stative locatives. However, rather than setting PM = $\langle P_1, P_2 \rangle / \langle P_1, P_2 \rangle$, we will make use of the fact that we have a category P_n of n-place predicates defined for any nonnegative n, and say that a PM is an expression which can be a P_n modifier for any $n \geqslant 1$. Thus, we have:

DEFINITION 18. PM = $\langle P_1, \ldots, P_n, \ldots \rangle / \langle P_1, \ldots, P_n, \ldots \rangle$.

For convenience, we will abbreviate this as PM = $\langle P_n / P_n \rangle$.

In the case of the stative locatives, we saw that an interpreting function must be intersecting when restricted to T_{P_1}, and that such a function must also satisfy Equation (8). We will be interested in imposing similar conditions on other classes of PMs. We therefore make the following definitions.

DEFINITION 19. Let S be a set of categories. Then $F_{\langle S \rangle / \langle S \rangle}$ is the set of those functions f from $\bigcup_{c \in S} T_c$ into itself such that, for each $c \in S$, if $x \in T_c$, then $f(x) \in T_c$.

Thus, $F_{\langle S \rangle / \langle S \rangle}$ is the set of all functions which are possible candidates for membership in $T_{\langle S \rangle / \langle S \rangle}$.

DEFINITION 20. The function $g \in F_{\langle P_n / P_n \rangle}$, is *argument-oriented of degree n* iff, for each $f \in T_{P_n}$ and for each set of n individuals $I_1, \ldots, I_n$ the following equation holds:

$$(g(f))\,(I_n) \ldots (I_1) = f(I_n) \ldots (I_1) \wedge g(1)\,(I_n)$$

where, on the right hand side, '1' refers to the unit element of T_{P_1}.

The reader will note that it follows directly from the definitions that g is argument-oriented of degree 1 iff the restriction of g to T_{P_1} is intersecting.

DEFINITION 21. The function $g \in T_{\langle P_n/P_n \rangle}$ is *argument-oriented* iff it is argument-oriented of degree n for every $n \geqslant 1$.

We can now say that, by our earlier discussion, the function which interprets a stative locative must be required to be argument-oriented.

Now, we noted earlier that, when viewed merely as P_1 modifiers, stative locatives formed a boolean category whose type was a complete atomic boolean algebra. Moreover, we pointed out that the category of PMs in general should be regarded as boolean, and that there was motivation for hoping that T_{PM} might be at least complete. Having defined the category PM not as that of P_1 modifiers, but rather as in Definition 21, we must reexamine the matter of a boolean structure for T_{PM}. It is clear that T_{PM} must be a subset of $F_{\langle P_n/P_n \rangle}$. However, the definitions and theorems of the last section do not apply directly, since the elements of $F_{\langle P_n/P_n \rangle}$ are not functions from a single boolean algebra into itself. Nevertheless, the essentials can be carried over, as will be seen in the proofs of the theorems we are about to give. As before, we present this material in a slightly more general form than is needed just for the PMs. We begin with two definitions which supersede Definition 19 above.

DEFINITION 22. Let S be a set of sets. A function $f: \bigcup S \to \bigcup S$ is a *proper function* iff, for each $X \in S$, if $x \in X$, then $f(x) \in X$.

DEFINITION 23. Let S be a set of sets. Then $PF_{S/S} = \{f: f \in F_{\bigcup S/\bigcup S}$ and f is a proper function$\}$.

DEFINITION 24. Let A be a set of boolean algebras and let $f \in PF_{A/A}$. Then f is *restricting* iff $f(x) \leqslant x$ for each x in the domain of f.

Note that by Definition 22, $f(x)$ and x in this definition are members of the same boolean algebra, so that it makes sense to ask whether or not $f(x) \leqslant x$ is satisfied.

DEFINITION 25. Let A be a set of boolean algebras. Then $PR_{A/A} = \{f: f \in PF_{A/A}$ and f is restricting$\}$.

We can now state the following theorem:

THEOREM 10. Let A be a non-empty set of disjoint boolean algebras. Then $PR_{A/A}$ is a boolean algebra under the operations $\wedge$, $\vee$, and $'$ defined as follows:

(a) Let $g_1, g_2 \in \mathrm{PR}_{A/A}$. Then, for each $x \in \bigcup A$,
$(g_1 \wedge g_2)(x) = g_1(x) \wedge g_2(x)$.

(b) Let $g_1, g_2 \in \mathrm{PR}_{A/A}$. Then, for each $x \in \bigcup A$,
$(g_1 \vee g_2)(x) = g_1(x) \vee g_2(x)$.

(c) Let $g \in \mathrm{PR}_{A/A}$. Then, for each $x \in \bigcup A$,
$g'(x) = (g(x))' \wedge x$.

Moreover, if each algebra in A is complete, then $\mathrm{PR}_{A/A}$ is complete, and if each algebra in A is atomic, then $\mathrm{PR}_{A/A}$ is atomic.

Since, even in the intensional system, almost all PMs are restricting, we will restrict our attention to the algebra $\mathrm{PR}_{A/A}$. If $A = \{T_{P_n}: n \geqslant 1\}$, then we will use the obvious notation $\mathrm{PR}_{\langle P_n/P_n \rangle}$ for the algebra of restricting functions in $F_{\langle P_n/P_n \rangle}$. The following theorem is easy but important:

THEOREM 11. If $g \in F_{\langle P_n/P_n \rangle}$ is argument-oriented, then g is restricting.

Let us denote the set of argument-oriented functions in $F_{\langle P_n/P_n \rangle}$ by $\mathrm{AO}_{\langle P_n/P_n \rangle}$. Then, Theorem 11 says that $\mathrm{AO}_{\langle P_n/P_n \rangle} \subseteq \mathrm{PR}_{\langle P_n/P_n \rangle}$. However, we can say more:

THEOREM 12. $\mathrm{AO}_{\langle P_n/P_n \rangle}$ is a complete subalgebra of $\mathrm{PR}_{\langle P_n/P_n \rangle}$. Moreover, $\mathrm{AO}_{\langle P_n/P_n \rangle}$ is atomic.

In fact, it is still the case that an atomic argument-oriented function is defined by a single individual. Thus, our earlier discussion concerning *somewhere, everywhere, nowhere, here,* and *there,* as well as the interpretation of boolean combinations of stative locatives, carries over essentially unchanged. Precisely, we can say the following:

THEOREM 13. Let $h: T_{P_1} \rightarrow \mathrm{AO}_{\langle P_n/P_n \rangle}$ be defined as follows: for each $g \in T_{P_1}$, and for each $f \in T_{P_n}$, $(h(g))(f)$ is that element of T_{P_n} such that, for individuals $I_1, \ldots, I_n, ((h(g))(f))(I_n) \ldots (I_1) = f(I_n) \ldots (I_1) \wedge g(I_n)$. Then h is an isomorphism of T_{P_1} onto $\mathrm{AO}_{\langle P_n/P_n \rangle}$.

Let us explicitly take note of the fact that by regarding stative locatives as members of the category $\langle P_n/P_n \rangle$ rather than P_1/P_1, we are automatically allowing more than one way to combine a given stative locative with an n-place predicate (if $n \geqslant 1$) and various noun phrases. For example, a stative locative can be combined with a P_2 and two $\bar{N}$s in two ways. Either the stative locative combines first with P_2 to create a compound P_2 which is then combined with the $\bar{N}$s, as in:

(9)   John ((call (in Boston)) Bill)

or else the P_2 combines with its object $\bar{N}$ to create a P_1 which is then combined with the stative locative, as in:

(10)   John ((call Bill) (in Boston)).

In general, we want to have both possibilities at our disposal. However, while certain English sentences appear to be genuinely ambiguous, such as *John called Bill in Boston* (which may be interpreted either as in (9) or as in (10)), many English sentences seem to allow only one of the possible interpretations. Thus, we have already seen that *John hit Mary in the garden* requires that Mary be in the garden; similar facts hold for *John saw/shot/washed/heard Mary in the garden*. On the other hand, if the transitive verb is properly intensional, the locative phrase apparently never applies to the object. Thus, *John criticized Mary in the garden* definitely requires that John be in the garden, but puts no demands on Mary. In addition, certain verbs denoting the creation of their objects require that the locative apply to the subject: if *John sang a song in the garden* is true, then surely John was in the garden.

We will not attempt to represent facts such as these formally in our system. One way to do so, of course, would be to restrict the syntax of our language (say, by appropriate features) so that, for example, an expression like *John ((criticize (in the garden)) Mary)* could not be constructed. However, such a method of subcategorization of transitive verbs would become rather complex, for a reason we shall see shortly. Another possible line of attack might be to change the interpretation of stative locative expressions in such a way as to become sensitive to the transitive verb with which it is combined. For now, we prefer to leave the matter open.

This almost completes our discussion of the extensional members of the category $\langle P_n/P_n \rangle$. However, before proceeding to other categories, let us consider the notion of argument-orientation as it may apply to other PMs. Facts similar to the ones we have seen in connection with stative locatives will provide further justification for taking the category PM to be $\langle P_n/P_n \rangle$.

Consider source PMs, which we identify here as prepositional phrases containing the preposition *from*. A phrase like *from the bus* denotes the beginning point of a trajectory of motion executed by some entity, or else the beginning point of a trajectory describing the progress or effect of the action of some entity. The entity in question may be the one denoted by the subject or the object $\bar{N}$, and, in some cases, there is ambiguity.

An example of an ambiguous case is the sentence *John grabbed the child from the bus*. On one reading, perhaps the more common one, John is, say, on the platform outside the bus, and the child is initially on the bus. John then grabs the child, causing it to move through a trajectory whose initial point is on/at the bus and whose final point is, presumably, near John. On the other reading, John is on the bus, the child is, say, on the platform, and John grabs the child and brings it into the bus with him. In this reading, the phrase *from the bus* denotes the initial point of the trajectory of action performed by John.

An ambiguity of this sort can be handled if we assume that the phrase *from the bus* is a member of the category $\langle P_n/P_n \rangle$ (rather than, say, just P_1/P_1), and if we further assume that this phrase is, in some sense, argument oriented. The following two sentences can then be constructed in our language:

(11)   John ((grab (from the bus)) (the child))
(12)   John ((grab (the child)) (from the bus))

In (11), *from the bus* is construed as a P_2 modifier. Since the phrase is argument-oriented, its denotation will involve the denotation of the argument of the phrase which it forms, namely, the argument of *grab (from the bus)*. But the argument of this phrase is *the child*. Thus, in (11), the source phrase denotes the initial point of the trajectory performed by the child. This, then, corresponds to the first of the two readings of the English sentence *John grabbed the child from the bus*.

In (12), *from the bus* is construed as a P_1 modifier. Again, since the phrase is argument-oriented, its denotation will involve the denotation of the argument of the phrase which it forms, but this time, it forms the P_1 (*grab (the child)*) (*from the bus*). Since the argument of this P_1 is *John*, the source phrase denotes the initial point of the trajectory performed by John. This corresponds to the second of the two readings of *John grabbed the child from the bus*.

As in the case of the stative locatives, the facts depend on the transitive verb involved. For example, if the verb is one of perception, a source phrase refers unambiguously to the subject. Thus, in the sentences

$$(13) \quad \text{John} \quad \left\{ \begin{array}{l} \text{saw} \\ \text{watched} \\ \text{spied on} \\ \text{studied} \\ \text{observed} \\ \text{touched} \end{array} \right\} \quad \text{Mary from the garden}$$

John is in the garden, and the source phrase refers to the conceived trajectory of John's perception. On the other hand, in the sentences

$$(14) \quad \text{John} \quad \left\{ \begin{array}{l} \text{knocked} \\ \text{threw} \end{array} \right\} \quad \text{Mary from the roof}$$

the source phrase seems to refer unambiguously to the trajectory of motion executed by the denotation of the object, that is, by Mary. Sentences like

$$(15) \quad \text{John} \quad \left\{ \begin{array}{l} \text{shot} \\ \text{pelted} \end{array} \right\} \quad \text{Mary from the roof}$$

seem to us ambiguous, with either John on the roof shooting or pelting Mary, or with Mary initially on the roof and falling off as a result of being shot or pelted.

Incidentally, if we compare these facts with the facts concerning stative locatives, we note a difficulty in handling the matter by means of subcategorization of the transitive verbs. Namely, particular transitive verbs do not behave the same with respect to stative locatives as they do with respect to source phrases. In particular, stative locatives with transitive verbs of perception (like *see, observe*) apply to the object, whereas, as we have just seen, source phrases with the same verbs apply to the subject. Thus, we cannot simply subcategorize these verbs either to insure that a PM combines with them before they are combined with an object, or to insure conversely that they combine with an object before a PM is combined with them. Of course, if the PMs themselves are subcategorized, then such a subcategorization of transitive verbs becomes possible, with the same verb being subcategorized to respond differently to PMs of different subtypes.

Having accepted the idea that source phrases are argument-oriented members of category $\langle P_n/P_n \rangle$, let us reexamine the issue of their extensionality or proper intensionality. We must be careful, in examining this issue, not to confuse the use of a particular source phrase as a P_1 modifier with the use of the same phrase as a P_2 modifier. With this taken into consideration, it seems to us that source phrases are extensional.

Suppose, for example, that those individuals who see Mary at a particular instant are exactly those individuals who spy on Karg at that instant. Then, surely, the individuals who see Mary from the control tower are exactly those who spy on Karg from the control tower. For, those who see Mary from the control tower are just those individuals who see Mary and who are in the control tower; and similarly, those who spy on Karg from the control tower are just those who spy on Karg and who are in the control tower. Thus, since the Mary-seers and the Karg-spiers are the same individuals in this world, the same set of individuals is obtained when either of these sets is intersected with the set of those individuals in the control tower. Note that a source phrase when used with the transitive verbs *see* and *spy on* refers to the subject in both cases.

Next, suppose that at a certain instant the verbs *throw* and *kick* have the same interpretation. This means that if individual I_1 is throwing individual I_2 at that instant, then I_1 is also kicking I_2 at that instant, and conversely. It seems that, given this, if I_1 is throwing I_2 from the roof, then I_1 must (since he is kicking I_2) also be kicking I_2 from the roof, and conversely. In both cases, *from the roof* denotes the initial point of the trajectory through which I_2 moves. Note that a source phrase when used with the transitive verbs *throw* and *kick* refers to the object to both cases.

This being the case, we can include source phrases in our system at the extensional level. They will be categorized as argument-oriented members of the category $\langle P_n/P_n \rangle$, just as the stative locatives were. They will differ from the stative locatives in that the transitive verbs with which they can function as P_2 modifiers will not be the same as the transitive verbs with which the stative locatives can.

However, this approach leads to a difficulty of a different sort, which we can see by examining Definitions 20 and 21. If we interpret *from the garden* as an extensional, argument-oriented PM, then *John ((see Mary) (from the garden))* turns out to be equivalent to *(John (see Mary)) and (John (exist (from the garden)))*. The difficulty resides, of course, in the second conjunct *John (exist (from the garden))*. On the one hand, it is not clear that we would want to allow such a sentence to be constructed. On the other hand, if we do allow its construction, it is not particularly clear that it is a viable representation of the semantics involved. One approach we could take would be to require (say, by a meaning postulate) that *from the garden* and *in the garden* be logically equivalent; surely, *John saw Mary from the garden* is at least logically equivalent to *John saw Mary and John was in the garden*, even if these two are not completely synonymous. Alternatively, there might be some way of representing the meaning of *from the garden* so that, in this case, *John* (*exist* (*in the garden*)) is at least entailed.

But the situation is worse in other cases. Consider, say, *John* ((*throw* (*from the roof*)) *Mary*). By our definitions earlier, this would be equivalent to (*John* (*throw Mary*)) *and* (*Mary* (*exist* (*from the roof*))). Here it is not even clear that we want to say that *Mary* (*exist* (*from the roof*)) entails *Mary* (*exist* (*on the roof*)), although the latter sentence must surely have been true at a moment just prior to the instant at which John threw Mary off the roof.

What we want, of course, is for a sentence such as *Mary* (*exist* (*from the roof*)) to represent, in our language, the situation of the roof being the initial point of a trajectory executed by Mary (either by virtue of her actually moving along that trajectory, or at least by her performing some action which follows that trajectory, in some sense). It seems to us not unreasonable that a single interpretation such as this might be adequate both for *John* ((*throw* (*from the roof*)) *Mary*) and for *Mary* ((*see Sally*) (*from the garden*)), say. If so, then it is perfectly reasonable to include source phrases in our extensional system as argument-oriented members of $\langle P_n/P_n \rangle$. But even if there are difficulties with the idea of source phrases being extensional, the facts we have been looking at here suggest strongly that they should definitely be regarded as argument-oriented modifiers capable of being combined with P_2s as well as with P_1s.

Certain other classes of PMs besides the stative locatives and the source phrases exhibit facts which suggest that they should be viewed as argument-oriented modifiers which can be combined with P_2s as well as with P_1s. For example, in the sentence *John saw Bill with Mary*, the most usual interpretation involves the idea that Bill is with Mary. However, in the sentence *John saw the show with Mary*, the interpretation is that John is with Mary. These facts can be accounted for by regarding *with Mary* as an argument-oriented PM. Then, the representation of *John saw Bill with Mary* in our system will be *John* ((*see* (*with Mary*)) *Bill*) which will be logically equivalent to (*John* (*see Bill*)) *and* (*Bill* (*exist* (*with Mary*))). On the other hand, *John saw the show with Mary* will be represented as *John* ((*see* (*the show*)) (*with Mary*)), which is logically equivalent to (*John* (*see* (*the show*)) *and* (*John* (*exist* (*with Mary*))). However, we will not pursue the analysis of these PMs here. Nor will we further examine other classes of PMs.

Before leaving the PMs, let us reexamine our analysis of the source phrases from a somewhat different point of view. We recall that source phrases were seen to refer to the initial point of a trajectory executed either by the subject or by the object. However, those instances in which the source phrase involves the object seem typically to be sentences containing a causative verb of motion. Now, it is not out of the question that such verbs should be analyzed as consisting, in some sense, of a verb *cause* combined with an (intransitive) verb of motion; thus, for example, *John threw Mary from the roof* might be represented as *John ((cause (by throwing)) (Mary (from the roof)))*, roughly. Note that in this structure *from the roof* involves the subject of the sentence of which it is most immediately a member.

This being the case, let us suppose, for the moment, that source phrases *always* refer to the initial point of the trajectory executed by the subject, but never by any other argument of an *n*-place predicate. Then our analysis suggested above is incorrect: source phrases are not argument-oriented members of the category $\langle P_n/P_n \rangle$. A simple way to handle them would be just to regard source phrases as intersecting members of P_1/P_1. Then, source phrases would be restricted to combine only with P_1s (so that a transitive verb would have to combine with its object first before the source phrase could apply to it), and they would necessarily involve the subject.

However, suppose that reasons are found for wanting source phrases to be able to combine with P_2s as well as with P_1s. If so, a different approach would be required. To see how this could be handled, let us make the following definitions:

DEFINITION 26. The function $g \in F_{\langle P_n/P_n \rangle}$ is *subject-oriented of degree n* iff, for each $f \in T_{P_n}$ and for each set of n individuals $I_1, \ldots, I_n$, the following equation holds:

$$(g(f))(I_n)\ldots(I_1) = f(I_n)\ldots(I_1) \wedge g(1)(I_1)$$

where, on the right hand side, '1' refers to the unit element of T_{P_1}.

Note that g is subject-oriented of degree 1 iff the restriction of g to T_{P_1} is intersecting.

DEFINITION 27. The function $g \in F_{\langle P_n/P_n \rangle}$ is *subject-oriented* iff it is subject-oriented of degree n for every $n \geqslant 1$.

Theorems similar to the ones given earlier for argument-oriented functions can also be given for subject-oriented functions. Thus, we have:

THEOREM 14. If $g \in F_{\langle P_n/P_n \rangle}$ is subject-oriented, then g is restricting.

If we let $SO_{\langle P_n/P_n \rangle}$ denote the set of subject-oriented functions in $F_{\langle P_n/P_n \rangle}$, then we have:

THEOREM 15. $SO_{\langle P_n/P_n \rangle}$ is a complete subalgebra of $PR_{\langle P_n/P_n \rangle}$. Moreover, $SO_{\langle P_n/P_n \rangle}$ is atomic.

And, more precisely:

THEOREM 16. Let $h: T_{P_1} \rightarrow SO_{\langle P_n/P_n \rangle}$ be defined as follows: for each $g \in T_{P_1}$, and for each $f \in T_{P_n}$, $(h(g))(f)$ is that element of T_{P_n} such that, for individuals $I_1, \ldots, I_n$, $((h(g))(f))(I_n) \ldots (I_1) = f(I_n) \ldots (I_1) \wedge g(I_1)$. Then h is an isomorphism of T_{P_1} onto $SO_{\langle P_n/P_n \rangle}$.

Now, even if we permit source phrases to be members of the category $\langle P_n/P_n \rangle$, so that they can modify n-place predicates for all $n \geqslant 1$, they will still involve the subject if we require that their interpretations be subject-oriented functions. Thus, suppose we form the sentence

(16)   John ((see (from the garden)) Mary)

By the equation in Definition 26, this sentence will be logically equivalent to

(17)   (John (see Mary)) and (John (exist (from the garden)))

which is what we want. Of course, (16) will also be equivalent to

(18)   John ((see Mary) (from the garden))

The duplication illustrated by (16) and (18) is an undesirable feature of this approach, unless reasons can be found for wanting to distinguish between these two structures. Except for this point, it is an adequate analysis of source phrases to assign them to the category $\langle P_n/P_n \rangle$ and to require that they be interpreted by subject-oriented functions, provided, as we said earlier, that causative verbs of motion are broken down into a cause component and a separate intransitive motion verb component (or are optionally broken down in this way, as in the case of verbs like *grab, shoot, pelt*, etc.; see (11) and (15) above).

It is reasonable here to wonder whether we have any reason for wanting exclusively subject oriented source phrases to ever combine with P_2s to form complex P_2s. One such reason is given by the interaction of such P_2s with *Passive*. We refer the reader here to the later section on *Valency Affecting Operators* noting only the broad outlines of our analysis here. If

p is a P_2 interpretation then its passive, *pass* (p), is a P_1 denotation which holds of an individual x iff for some individual y, $(p\ (x))\ (y)$ holds. Now if the predicate of *Mary was seen from the garden* is analyzed as the passive of the complex P_2 *see from the garden*, it will hold of Mary just in case (*see from the garden*) (*Mary*) holds of some individual y. And this will, correctly, entail that y, the individual who saw Mary, was in the garden. But if *from the garden* could only be analyzed as a modifier of the P_1 *was seen* (= {pass, see}) then *Mary was seen from the garden* would, incorrectly, entail that Mary was in the garden.

Even if the analysis of source phrases as subject-oriented does not turn out to be the best approach we shall still need the concept of subject-orientation to represent the semantics of agentive *by*-phrases in passives. Specifically *by Mary* in *John was kissed by Mary* is subject oriented in that semantically it predicates something of the subject argument of the P_2 *kiss*: it says that that argument is identical to Mary. A formal semantics for agentive *by* is given in our later section on *Passives*.

This completes our presentation of the predicate modifiers in the extensional system. Before closing this section, we make two additional comments.

First, at least some PMs should probably be viewed as members of the category $\langle N, P_n\rangle/\langle N, P_n\rangle$ (or even of $\langle N_m, P_n\rangle/\langle N_m, P_n\rangle$ (see the later section on *transitive common noun phrases*)), in order to be able to form expressions like *man in the garden*. Such an expression would be an N, interpreted by the property which is contained in exactly those individuals each of which both contains the property which interprets *man* and is mapped onto 1 by the interpretation of *exist in the garden*. (Loosely, an individual has the property which interprets *man in the garden* iff that individual is a man and is in the garden.) We omit a formal statement of this here.

Secondly, we note that our account above does not provide for the possibility of expressions of the category P_0/P_0. Clearly, there are such expressions, which we are going to want in our system, such as *possible, necessary*, etc. However, the vast majority of them are properly intensional, and so we defer detailed discussion until we develop our intensional system. At the extensional level, we note here that since T_{P_0} has only two elements, namely 0 and 1, there are only four functions which are available as extensional interpretations of expressions of category P_0/P_0. These functions are f_0, f_1, f_t, and f_f, defined by:

(18) $f_0\ (0) = f_0\ (1) = 0$
(19) $f_1\ (0) = f_1\ (1) = 1$

(20) $f_t(0) = 0, f_t(1) = 1$
(21) $f_f(0) = 1, f_f(1) = 0$

It seems reasonable to include the lexical expressions *true* and *false* in our extensional language as members of the category P_0/P_0. These will be logical constants: we require that in any model, *true* be interpreted as the function f_t defined in (20), and *false* be interpreted as f_f defined in (21). Thus, if e is any formula in our language, then *true e* (which can be thought of as representing the English sentence *it is true that e*) will be a formula whose truth value in any model is the same as the truth value of e. Similary, *false e* (representing *it is false that e*) will be a formula whose truth value in any model is the opposite of the truth value of e.

Proofs of Theorems from This Section

Our first theorem is:

THEOREM 10. Let A be a non-empty set of disjoint boolean algebras. Then $PR_{A/A}$ is a boolean algebra under the operations $\wedge$, $\vee$, and $'$ defined as follows:

(a) Let $g_1, g_2 \in PR_{A/A}$. Then, for each $x \in \bigcup A$,
   $(g_1 \wedge g_2)(x) = g_1(x) \wedge g_2(x)$.
(b) Let $g_1, g_2 \in PR_{A/A}$. Then, for each $x \in \bigcup A$,
   $(g_1 \vee g_2)(x) = g_1(x) \vee g_2(x)$.
(c) Let $g \in PR_{A/A}$. Then, for each $x \in \bigcup A$,
   $g'(x) = (g(x))' \wedge x$.

Moreover, if each algebra in A is complete, then $PR_{A/A}$ is complete, and if each algebra in A is atomic, then $PR_{A/A}$ is atomic.

This theorem is an extension of Theorem 2 of the previous section on APs. To prove it, our general method is to consider the restrictions of functions in $PR_{A/A}$ to the algebras which comprise the collection A and to apply that earlier theorem.

   We first show that $g_1 \wedge g_2$ as defined in (a) is a member of $PR_{A/A}$. Clearly, $g_1 \wedge g_2$ is a function from $\bigcup A$ into $\bigcup A$; we have to show that it is a proper function, and that it is restricting.

   To show that it is a proper function, choose $x \in \bigcup A$ arbitrary. Then, for one algebra $B \in A$, $x \in B$. Since g_1 and g_2 are proper functions, $g_1(x)$ and

$g_2(x)$ are members of B, whence so is $g_1(x) \wedge g_2(x)$, since B is a boolean algebra. Thus, if $x \in B$, then $(g_1 \wedge g_2)(x) \in B$, so $g_1 \wedge g_2$ is a proper function.

To show that this function is restricting, let B be an arbitrary member of A. Since g_1 and g_2 are restricting functions, their restrictions to B are restricting functions from B into itself; that is, the restrictions of g_1 and g_2 are members of $R_{B/B}$. By Theorem 2, the restriction of $g_1 \wedge g_2$ to B is a member of $R_{B/B}$; thus, for any $x \in B$, $(g_1 \wedge g_2)(x) \leqslant x$ in B. Since any x in the domain of $g_1 \wedge g_2$ is an element of one B, this proves that $g_1 \wedge g_2$ is restricting as a function from $\bigcup A$ into $\bigcup A$.

The proofs that $g_1 \vee g_2$ as defined in (b) and g' as defined in (c) are members of $\mathrm{PR}_{A/A}$ are similar and will be omitted.

The fact that the axioms of a boolean algebra are satisfied by the operations in $\mathrm{PR}_{A/A}$ follow from the fact that these axioms are satisfied by the restrictions of the functions in $\mathrm{PR}_{A/A}$ to individual algebras in A. For example, to prove that $g_1 \wedge (g_2 \vee g_3) = (g_1 \wedge g_2) \vee (g_1 \wedge g_3)$ for arbitrary g_1, g_2, and $g_3 \in \mathrm{PR}_{A/A}$, we have to show that $(g_1 \wedge (g_2 \vee g_3))(x) = ((g_1 \wedge g_2) \vee (g_1 \wedge g_3))(x)$ for each $x \in \bigcup A$. However, for one boolean algebra $B \in A$, $x \in B$, whence this equation holds, since the restrictions of g_1, g_2, and g_3 to B are members of $R_{B/B}$, and, by Theorem 2, $R_{B/B}$ is a boolean algebra.

By this approach, we see immediately that the zero element in $\mathrm{PR}_{A/A}$ is the function 0: $\bigcup A \to \bigcup A$ such that $0(x) = 0_B$ for each $x \in \bigcup A$, where B is the boolean algebra in the collection A which contains x. Similarly, the unit element of $\mathrm{PR}_{A/A}$ is the function 1: $\bigcup A \to \bigcup A$ such that $1(x) = x$ for each $x \in A$. It is clear that, for a given $B \in A$, the restrictions of 0 and 1 to B are just the zero and unit elements of $R_{B/B}$, so that the axioms which involve 0 and 1 must be satisfied in $\mathrm{PR}_{A/A}$, since these axioms are satisfied in each $R_{B/B}$, by an argument parallel to the one given above for the distributive axiom.

Let us next note that the proof of the lemma of Theorem 2 carries over unchanged to $\mathrm{PR}_{A/A}$. We can conclude from this that if $g_1, g_2 \in \mathrm{PR}_{A/A}$, then $g_1 \leqslant g_2$ iff this relation holds for the restrictions of g_1 and g_2 to B, for each $B \in A$.

Suppose now that every B in A is a complete algebra. Let $K \subseteq \mathrm{PR}_{A/A}$ be an arbitrary subset. For each $x \in \bigcup A$, define $g(x) = \bigwedge \{k(x) : k \in K\}$. Comparing this with the definition in the comparable part of the proof of Theorem 2, we see that the restriction of g to B (for each $B \in A$) is just the glb of the restrictions of the elements of K to B, viewed as members of $R_{B/B}$. In particular, g is well defined. It is obvious that g is a proper function; and the proof that g is restricting is exactly the same as in that previous theorem.

Thus, $g \in \mathrm{PR}_{A/A}$. Moreover, since the lemma of the section applies to $\mathrm{PR}_{A/A}$, the proof that $g = \mathrm{glb}\ K$ here is exactly the same as the proof in the earlier theorem. Thus, arbitrary subsets of $\mathrm{PR}_{A/A}$ have greatest lower bounds, and, dually, least upper bounds, so that $\mathrm{PR}_{A/A}$ is complete.

Finally, suppose that each B in A is atomic. For each $B_1 \in A$, for each atom $a \in B_1$, and for each $b \in B_1$ such that $a \leqslant b$, define $g_{ab}; \bigcup A \to \bigcup A$ as follows. Let $x \in \bigcup A$. If $x \in B_2$, where $B_2 \neq B_1$, then $g_{ab}\ (x) = 0_{B_2}$. If $x \in B_1$, then, if $x \neq b$, $g_{ab}\ (x) = 0_{B_1}$; and $g_{ab}\ (b) = a$. It is obvious that g_{ab} is a proper and restricting function, that is, a member of $\mathrm{PR}_{A/A}$. Moreover, the restriction of g_{ab} to any other algebra in the collection A is the zero of its restricting algebra. Again, since the lemma is valid for $\mathrm{PR}_{A/A}$, the proof that f_{ab} is an atom, given in the proof of Theorem 2, carries over intact to yield that g_{ab} is an atom in $\mathrm{PR}_{A/A}$. Similarly, we can prove that $\mathrm{PR}_{A/A}$ is atomic: let $g \in \mathrm{PR}_{A/A}$, with $g \neq 0$. Then for some $x \in \bigcup A$, $g\ (x) \neq 0_B$, where B is the algebra containing x. Since g is restricting, $g\ (x) \leqslant x$, whence $x \neq 0_B$, and since B is atomic, there is an atom $a \in B$ such that $a \leqslant x$. Thus, g_{ax} is well defined for the elements a and x we have just chosen. But, $g_{ax} \leqslant g$, exactly as in the proof of the earlier theorem. This completes the proof.

Our next theorem concerns the argument-oriented elements of $\mathrm{PR}_{\langle P_n/P_n \rangle}$.

THEOREM 12. $\mathrm{AO}_{\langle P_n/P_n \rangle}$ is a complete subalgebra of $\mathrm{PR}_{\langle P_n/P_n \rangle}$. Moreover, $\mathrm{AO}_{\langle P_n/P_n \rangle}$ is atomic.

The fact that $\mathrm{AO}_{\langle P_n/P_n \rangle}$ is a subalgebra of $\mathrm{PR}_{\langle P_n/P_n \rangle}$ will follow if we can show that it is closed under the operations $\wedge$, $\vee$, and $'$, and that $\mathrm{AO}_{\langle P_n/P_n \rangle}$ contains the elements 0 and 1 of $\mathrm{PR}_{\langle P_n/P_n \rangle}$.

Suppose that g_1 and g_2 are argument-oriented of degree n. Let $f \in T_{P_n}$ be arbitrary, and let $I_1, \ldots, I_n$ be n arbitrary individuals. Then we have:

$$((g_1 \wedge g_2)\ (f))\ (I_n) \ldots (I_1) = (g_1\ (f) \wedge g_2\ (f))\ (I_n) \ldots (I_1)$$
$$= (g_1\ (f)\ (I_n) \wedge g_2\ (f)\ (I_n))\ (I_{n-1}) \ldots (I_1)$$

where the first equality follows from the definition of $\wedge$ in $\mathrm{PR}_{\langle P_n/P_n \rangle}$, and the second equality follows from the definition of $\wedge$ in T_{P_n}. Iterating the procedure which gave us this second equality, we get finally:

$$((g_1 \wedge g_2)\ (f))\ (I_n) \ldots (I_1) =$$
$$= (g_1\ (f))\ (I_n) \ldots (I_1) \wedge (g_2\ (f))\ (I_n) \ldots (I_1)$$
$$= [f\ (I_n) \ldots (I_1) \wedge g_1\ (1)\ (I_n)] \wedge [f\ (I_n) \ldots (I_1) \wedge g_2\ (1)\ (I_n)]$$
$$= f\ (I_n) \ldots (I_1) \wedge [g_1\ (1)\ (I_n) \wedge g_2\ (1)\ (I_n)]$$
$$= f\ (I_n) \ldots (I_1) \wedge (g_1 \wedge g_2)\ (1)\ (I_n).$$

Using the fact that g_1 and g_2 are argument-oriented of degree n in the second equality, the commutative, associative and idempotent laws in the third equality, and the definition of $\wedge$ in $PR_{\langle P_n/P_n \rangle}$ in the fourth equality. But the fourth equality shows that $g_1 \wedge g_2$ is argument-oriented of degree n. If g_1 and g_2 are argument-oriented of all positive degrees, then so is $g_1 \wedge g_2$.

The proof that $g_1 \vee g_2$ is argument-oriented of degree n if g_1 and g_2 are is exactly parallel as regards the equation:

$$((g_1 \vee g_2)(f)(I_n) \ldots (I_1) =$$
$$= [f(I_n) \ldots (I_1) \wedge g_1(1)(I_n)] \vee [f(I_n) \ldots (I_1) \wedge g_2(1)(I_n)].$$

The next step is to use the distributive law, and then the definition of $\vee$ in $PR_{\langle P_n/P_n \rangle}$ to get:

$$\begin{aligned}((g_1 \vee g_2)(f))(I_n) \ldots (I_1) \quad &= f(I_n) \ldots (I_1) \wedge [g_1(1)(I_n) \vee g_2(1)(I_n)] \\ &= f(I_n) \ldots (I_1) \wedge (g_1 \vee g_2)(1)(I_n)\end{aligned}$$

which shows that $g_1 \vee g_2$ is argument-oriented of degree n. Again, if g_1 and g_2 are argument-oriented of all positive degrees, then so is $g_1 \vee g_2$.

Finally, suppose that g is argument-oriented of degree n. We have first that

$$\begin{aligned}(g'(f))(I_n) \ldots (I_1) \quad &= ((g(f))' \wedge f)(I_n) \ldots (I_1) \\ &= [((g(f))(I_n))' \wedge f(I_n)](I_{n-1}) \ldots (I_1)\end{aligned}$$

where the first equality follows from the definition of $'$ in $PR_{\langle P_n/P_n \rangle}$, and the second equality follows from the definitions of $\wedge$ and of $'$ in T_{P_n}. Iterating the procedure which gave us the second equality, we get eventually:

$$\begin{aligned}(g'(f))(I_n) \ldots (I_1) \quad &= ((g(f))(I_n) \ldots (I_1))' \wedge f(I_n) \ldots (I_1) \\ &= (f(I_n) \ldots (I_1) \wedge g(1)(I_n))' \wedge f(I_n) \ldots (I_1) \\ &= [(f(I_n) \ldots (I_1))' \vee (g(1)(I_n))'] \wedge f(I_n) \ldots (I_1) \\ &= 0 \vee [f(I_n) \ldots (I_1) \wedge (g(1)(I_n))'] \\ &= f(I_n) \ldots (I_1) \wedge (g(1))'(I_n) \\ &= f(I_n) \ldots (I_1) \wedge g'(1)(I_n)\end{aligned}$$

where the second equality follows from the fact that g is argument-oriented of degree n, the third follows from the deMorgan laws, the fourth from the distributive law (together with $x \wedge x' = 0$), the fifth from the definition of $'$ in T_{P_1} (together with $0 \vee x = x$), and the sixth from the definition of $'$ in

$PR_{\langle P_n/P_n\rangle}$, since $g'(1) = (g(1))' \wedge 1 = (g(1))'$. But the last equality shows that g' is argument-oriented of degree n. Therefore, if g is argument-oriented of all positive degrees, so is g'.

This shows that $AO_{\langle P_n/P_n\rangle}$ is closed under $\wedge$, $\vee$, and $'$. Let us now check that 0 and 1 are members of $AO_{\langle P_n/P_n\rangle}$. First, we have, on the one hand, $0 \, (f) \, (I_n) \ldots (I_1) = 0 \, (I_n) \ldots (I_1) = 0$, and on the other hand, $f \, (I_n) \ldots (I_1) \wedge 0 \, (1) \, (I_n) = f \, (I_n) \ldots (I_1) \wedge 0 \, (I_n) = f \, (I_n) \ldots (I_1) \wedge 0 = 0$. (We leave it to the reader to supply the justifications for the equalities.) Thus, $0 \, (f) \, (I_n) \ldots (I_1) = f \, (I_n) \ldots (I_1) \wedge 0 \, (1) \, (I_n)$, so 0 is argument-oriented of degree n. Since n is arbitrary, 0 is argument-oriented.

Secondly, $1 \, (f) \, (I_n) \ldots (I_1) = f \, (I_n) \ldots (I_1)$. On the other hand, $f \, (I_n) \ldots (I_1) \wedge 1 \, (1) \, (I_n) = f \, (I_n) \ldots (I_1) \wedge 1 \, (I_n) = f \, (I_n) \ldots (I_1) \wedge 1 = f \, (I_n) \ldots (I_1)$. Thus, $1 \, (f) \, (I_n) \ldots (I_1) = f \, (I_n) \ldots (I_1) \wedge 1 \, (1) \, (I_n)$, so 1 is argument-oriented of degree n. Since n is arbitrary, 1 is argument-oriented.

Thus, $AO_{\langle P_n/P_n\rangle}$ is a subalgebra of $PR_{\langle P_n/P_n\rangle}$. The fact that it is complete and atomic will follow from Theorem 13, to be proved below, since T_{P_1} is a complete and atomic algebra. Alternatively, these facts can be verified directly for $AO_{\langle P_n/P_n\rangle}$. For example, if $K \subseteq AO_{\langle P_n/P_n\rangle}$ is an arbitrary subset, then, since K is a subset of $PR_{\langle P_n/P_n\rangle}$, and since the latter is complete, by Theorem 10 above, $\wedge K$ and $\vee K$ are well defined. It is a straightforward matter to show directly that these are argument-oriented; we leave this to the reader.

As to atomicity, the situation here is similar to what we saw in the last section concerning $I_{B/B}$ for the case that B is atomic. Just as the atoms of $R_{B/B}$ are not elements of $I_{B/B}$, yet $I_{B/B}$ contains elements which are atoms in it but not in $R_{B/B}$, so the atoms of $PR_{\langle P_n/P_n\rangle}$ are not elements of $AO_{\langle P_n/P_n\rangle}$, yet this subalgebra contains elements which are atoms in it but not in $PR_{\langle P_n/P_n\rangle}$. It is clear from the construction in Theorem 13, to be proved shortly, that the atoms of $AO_{\langle P_n/P_n\rangle}$ are just those argument-oriented functions g such that $g \, (1_{T_{P_1}})$ is true for exactly one individual only. Incidentally, it is almost obvious from the definition of argument-orientation, and essentially proved as part of Theorem 13 (where it is shown that h is one-to-one and onto), that an argument-oriented function is completely determined by its value on $1_{T_{P_1}}$. Without further delay, let us proceed to:

THEOREM 13. Let $h: T_{P_1} \to AO_{\langle P_n/P_n\rangle}$ be defined as follows: for each $g \in T_{P_1}$, and for each $f \in T_{P_n}$, $(h \, (g)) \, (f)$ is that element of T_{P_n} such that, for individuals $I_1, \ldots, I_n$, $((h \, (g)) \, (f)) \, (I_n) \ldots (I_1) = f \, (I_n) \ldots (I_1) \wedge g \, (I_n)$. Then h is an isomorphism of T_{P_1} onto $AO_{\langle P_n/P_n\rangle}$.

Let g be an arbitrary member of T_{P_1}. We show first that $h(g)$ is indeed an argument-oriented function. (That it is a proper function from $\bigcup_n T_{P_n}$ into itself is obvious.) Applying $h(g)$ to the unit element of T_{P_1} and letting I be an arbitrary individual, we have, using the definition of h, as well as the properties of the unit of T_{P_1}, that $((h(g))(1)(I) = 1(I) \wedge g(I) = 1 \wedge g(I) = g(I)$. Since this is true for an arbitrary individual I, we have shown that $(h(g))(1) = g$. Substituting this in the equation which defines h, we get $((h(g))(f)(I_n) \ldots (I_1) = f(I_n) \ldots (I_1) \wedge (h(g))(1)(I_n)$, which shows that $h(g)$ is argument-oriented of degree n. Since n was arbitrary, $h(g)$ is argument-oriented.

Next, we show that h is a homomorphism by showing that it preserves meets and complements.

To show that h preserves meets, let g_1 and g_2 be arbitrary elements of T_{P_1}. If $f \in T_{P_n}$ and $I_1, \ldots, I_n$ are arbitrary individuals, then we have:

$$h(g_1 \wedge g_2)(f)(I_n) \ldots (I_1) = f(I_n) \ldots (I_1) \wedge (g_1 \wedge g_2)(I_n)$$
$$= f(I_n) \ldots (I_1) \wedge g_1(I_n) \wedge g_2(I_n)$$
$$= [f(I_n) \ldots (I_1) \wedge g_1(I_n)] \wedge [f(I_n) \ldots (I_1) \wedge g_2(I_n)]$$
$$= h(g_1)(f)(I_n) \ldots (I_1) \wedge h(g_2)(f)(I_n) \ldots (I_1)$$

where the first equality follows from the definition of h, the second by the definition of $\wedge$ in T_{P_1}, the third by the commutative, associative, and idempotent laws, and the fourth by the definition of h. But the fourth equality shows that h preserves meets.

To show that h preserves complements, let g be an arbitrary element of T_{P_1}. Again, if $f \in T_{P_n}$ and $I_1, \ldots, I_n$ are arbitrary individuals, we have:

$$h(g')(f)(I_n) \ldots (I_1) = f(I_n) \ldots (I_1) \wedge g'(I_n)$$
$$= f(I_n) \ldots (I_1) \wedge (g(I_n))'$$
$$= [f(I_n) \ldots (I_1) \wedge (f(I_n) \ldots (I_1))']$$
$$\vee [f(I_n) \ldots (I_1) \wedge (g(I_n))']$$
$$= f(I_n) \ldots (I_1) \wedge [(f(I_n) \ldots (I_1))' \vee (g(I_n))']$$
$$= f(I_n) \ldots (I_1) \wedge [f(I_n) \ldots (I_1) \wedge g(I_n)]'$$
$$= f(I_n) \ldots (I_1) \wedge [h(g)(f)(I_n) \ldots (I_1)]'$$
$$= (h(g))'(f)(I_n) \ldots (I_1)$$

where the first equality follows from the definition of h, the second from the definition of $'$ in T_{P_1}, the third from $x \wedge x' = 0$ and $0 \vee x = x$, the fourth from the distributive law, the fifth from DeMorgan's law, the sixth from the definition of h, and the seventh from the definition of $'$ in $AO_{\langle P_n/P_n \rangle}$. But the seventh equality shows that h preserves complements. Since h preserves meets and complements, h is a homomorphism.

To show that h is an isomorphism, we must show that h is one-to-one, and that h is onto.

To show that h is one-to-one, suppose that $g_1, g_2 \in T_{P_1}$, and that $g_1 \neq g_2$. Then, since a P_1 homomorphism is determined by its values on the individuals, there must be some individual, say I, such that $g_1(I) \neq g_2(I)$. Then, letting 1 be the unit of T_{P_1}, we have, from the definitions, that $h(g_1)(1)(I) = 1(I) \wedge g_1(I) = 1 \wedge g_1(I) = g_1(I)$, and similarly $h(g_2)(1)(I) = g_2(I)$. Thus, $h(g_1)(1)(I) \neq h(g_2)(1)(I)$, whence $h(g_1)(1) \neq h(g_2)(1)$, whence $h(g_1) \neq h(g_2)$, so that h is indeed one-to-one.

To show that h is onto, let k be an arbitrary member of $AO_{\langle P_n/P_n \rangle}$. Set $g = k(1_{T_{P_1}})$. Then $g \in T_{P_1}$, and we have, for arbitrary $f \in T_{P_n}$ and individuals $I_1, \ldots, I_n$:

$$
\begin{aligned}
(h(g))(f)(I_n) \ldots (I_1) \quad &= f(I_n) \ldots (I_1) \wedge g(I_n) \\
&= f(I_n) \ldots (I_1) \wedge k(1)(I_n) \\
&= (k(f))(I_n) \ldots (I_1)
\end{aligned}
$$

where the first equality follows from the definition of h, the second from the definition of g (here, '1' means the unit of T_{P_1}, of course), and the third from the fact that k is argument-oriented. But the third equality shows that $h(g) = k$. This shows that h is onto, and completes the proof of Theorem 13.

The remaining theorems of this section are 14, 15, and 16. It will be noticed that these theorems are exactly parallel to Theorems 10, 12 and 13, with the notion of subject-orientation replacing that of argument-orientation. We leave it to the reader to convince himself that the proofs given above for Theorems 10, 12, and 13 are transformed into proofs for Theorems 14–16 simply by replacing the appropriate occurrences of the symbol I_n by I_1.

3. PREDICATIVES

Syntactically we use the cover term *predicative* (*Pred* for short) to refer to categories of expressions which combine with $\bar{N}$s to form derived expressions. In the Intensional Logic in Part II the category $\bar{N}$ is generalized to that of Argument Category and Preds are expressions which combine with Arguments. New Argument categories will include $\bar{S}$ (= sentence complements), $\bar{P}_1$ (= infinitival nominals).

The new Preds we treat here are: 'transitive' common nouns (*friend of,* etc.), 'transitive' adjective phrases (*fond of*, etc.), ditransitive verb phrases, and prepositions. The construction of the types for these new categories follows the pattern established for the Preds considered in Section A (the $n \geqslant 0$ place predicates): in each case the new category is of the form $C/\bar{N}$, where T_C is a complete and atomic boolean algebra. The type for the category then may be represented as the set of complete homomorphisms from $T_{\bar{N}}$ into T_C, exactly as was done for the type for P_{n+1} ($= P_n/\bar{N}$). The empirical adequacy of defining the new types in this way is justified in the appropriate subsections below. Here we merely underline that a nice advantage of our system is that the types for (first order) predicatives in general are an immediate generalization of the basic cases of Preds considered in Section A. The generalization is significant in that the new categories seem syntactically fairly diverse. We turn now to a detailed consideration of the new categories.

Preliminary Remarks on Case Marking

We have so far ignored the fact that the n-place Preds of L impose case on their arguments. E.g. P_1s normally take their argument in the nominative (*nom*), P_2s in the accusative (*acc*), etc. As such case marking is largely only overt on pronominal forms, items we do not explicitly consider here, our logical structures have so far not differed appreciably from surface forms in these respects. But many of the new Preds we add to L take less trivial case marking, and while we shall by and large ignore it in our representations we do want to indicate how we might incorporate a case marking notation into our system and what the semantic motivation for this might be.

In keeping with the generalizations of Keenan (1979) we note that commonly across languages, expressions interpreted as functions on $\bar{N}$ denotations impose case on their ($\bar{N}$) arguments (and moreover may show agreement with these arguments). We shall then treat the case markers that a particular Pred imposes on its arguments as part of the representation of that Pred. Thus, technically, our representation for the English verb *sleep* would be $\underset{nom}{sleep}$, assigned by lexical rule to the category $\underset{nom}{P_1}$ ($= \underset{nom}{P_0}/\bar{N}$), itself a subcategory of P_1 (by a subcategory rule). Similarly $\underset{nom\ acc}{kiss}$ would be an element of $\underset{\langle nom\ acc \rangle}{P_2}$ ($= \underset{nom\ acc}{P_1}/\bar{N}$), a subcategory of P_2. And more generally, for a any n-tuple of case markers and c a case marker, $\underset{\langle d,\ c \rangle}{P_{n+1}}$ ($= \underset{d}{P_n}/\underset{c}{\bar{N}}$) is a subcategory of P_{n+1}, and its elements are represented as $\underset{\langle d,\ c \rangle}{e}$. Note then that using this notation, a given n-place Pred subcategorized by $c_1, \ldots, c_n$ imposes the case marker c_n on its argument to yield an n-1 place Pred subcategorized for $c_1, \ldots, c_{n-1}$. For example, treating the indirect object *to* as a case marker (as we will) a plausible tree structure for *John handed the book to Bill* would be:

(22)

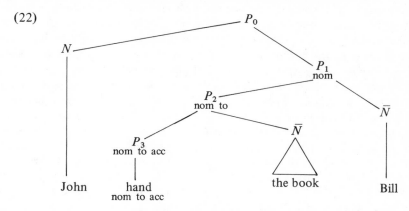

Note that the tree structure in (22) uniquely determines that *Bill* will be case marked *to*, since *Bill* is the argument of the P_2 *hand the book* which is marked as imposing *to* on its argument.

To simplify the case marking notation (in the few cases where we shall use it at all) we shall adopt the following conventions: (1) the argument of a P_1 will be understood as nominative unless marked otherwise; (2) argument of any *n*-place Pred other than P_1 will be understood as accusative unless marked otherwise; (3) when informally representing expressions in our language by strings of words, overtly indicated case markers will be given in parentheses next to the $\bar{N}$ they are imposed on. Thus our linear informal representation of (22) above is simply *John hand the book (to) Bill*. The finite set CM of case markers for English will include a variety of abstract elements such as *nom, acc, to, of*, and (homophones of) most lexically simple prepositions.

What about the types for the new subcategories of *n*-place Pred we have introduced above? Given that $P_{n\langle c_1, \ldots, c_n \rangle}$ is a subcategory of P_n we know that its type must be a subset of T_{P_n}. If the case marking is semantically irrelevant we could take $T_{P_n\langle c_1, \ldots, c_n \rangle} = T_{P_n}$ as previously defined. But by the remarks on the *Overview* if case marking is semantically irrelevant we have no motivation for including that notation in our logical structures at all.

There appear to be, however, several sorts of semantic motivation for including case marking at a level of logical form. For one thing, there appear to be *n*-place Preds which are semantically distinct but which differ formally only with respect to the case marker they impose on their argument. Consider for example the semantic differences between *call* ($= call_{nom\ acc}$) and *call for* ($= call_{nom\ for}$), or *ask* and *ask for*. The items taking their arguments with *for* are non-transparent on their argument, whereas the accusative ones appear to be transparent. Thus in a situation in which the only doctor is the President of the bank, *John asked a doctor to attend to the sick* must have the same truth value as *John asked the President of the bank to attend to the sick*. But *John asked for a doctor to attend to the sick* can be true in such a situation even though *John asked for the President of the bank to attend to the sick* is false.

Moreover, calling all case markers other than *non* and *acc obliques* (*obl*), it seems likely, following Anderson (1971), that there will exist regularities in the interpretations of P_2's which differ only with regard to whether their argument is *acc* or *obl*. Thus the difference between *shoot* and *shoot at* is, very roughly, that the object of *shoot at* is less wholly affected by the action than when it is the object of *shoot*. Similarly with *plow* vs. *plow in*, etc. We might be inclined to represent these regularities by imposing a general constraint on the lexical interpreting function M such that $M \left(_{\langle nom \; acc \rangle} e \right)$ $\leqslant M \left(_{\langle nom \; obl \rangle} e \right)$. This would guarantee for example that if John plowed the field then he plowed in the field. While this generalization is doubtless too gross, it seems right enough as a first approximation to support the claim that items which differ regularly in case marking differ regularly in semantic interpretation, and hence we want case marking represented at a level of semantic interpretation. Moreover E. Moravscik (1978) has shown that such semantic differences extend to a rather wide range of languages (see also Keenan, 1979, for further discussion) and in those which are more heavily case marked than English in a traditional sense these differences show up in the choice of case marker.

Another sort of motivation for including case marking in our logical structures concerns dependencies between case marking and selectional restrictions. For example consider that intransitive *run* implies that its subject, if an individual, *moves* more or less autonomously. We might build in this restriction by requiring that for all individuals x, M (*run*) $(x) \leqslant M$ (*move*) (x). Then, given that locative PP's such as *through the woods, across the mountain*, etc. are restricting, we infer that *John ran across the mountain* entails *John ran*, which entails *John moved*. However, *the telephone lines run across the mountain* does not entail *the telephone lines run* or *the telephone lines move*. So we clearly want telephone lines to be among the possible arguments of the interpretation of *run across the mountains* but not of that of *run*. One prima facie way to capture these facts is to say that in addition to the P_1 *run* we have a P_2, *run* which is a member of $P_2 \atop _{nom \; across}$. We are then free to state its selectional restrictions as we like. Furthermore, since *across* is (at least homophonously) both a case marker and a preposition, we have two logical forms for *John ran across Mary* according as *run across* is a P_2 taking *Mary* as its argument, or *run* is a P_1 combined with the Predicate Modifier *across Mary*. The latter case would get the interpretation in which *across Mary* specifies the path of John's movement (imagine John a dwarf and Mary a giant). The former interpretation could be constrained so that transitive *run across* plus human object means something like *meet*. In any event we have two logical forms for *John ran across Mary* and may thus in principle represent the (admittedly somewhat forced) ambiguity in the English sentence.

However, as indicated at the beginning of this section, we are not concerned in this monograph to represent the semantic properties of case marking and in consequence shall not generally employ the case marking notation introduced above. It will however be (we think) perspicuous to use that notation for certain of the Preds we discuss below which impose oblique case markers, and it is important to realize that the notation we use there can be given as a quite general extension of the notation used in the core language L and that its semantic motivation extends beyond the few examples in which we use it. We turn now to the specific extensions of L represented by the new classes of predicatives mentioned in the introduction to this section.

Transitive Common Noun Phrases

We want to enrich L so as to generate structures for $\bar{N}$'s such as *a friend of every senator, the father of John or Bill, no friend or colleague of the chairman of the department*, etc. We may do this very simply by adding *friend* (*of*), *father* (*of*), etc. to the basic vocabulary V and assigning them the category $N/\bar{N}$ (more exactly, $N/\bar{N}_{\text{of}}$, but we shall usually omit the case marker *of*). Then the rules of functional application plus the lexical rules we already have will generate expressions like that in (23a) below with the structure given in (23b).

(23) a. a friend of every senator

b.

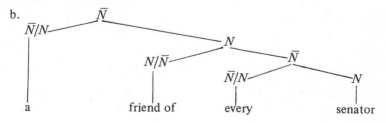

Using the Predicative Hierarchy notation developed earlier we may abbreviate the category of *friend (of)*, etc. as N_1. More explicitly, PH_N or the predicative Hierarchy generated by N, is the set of categories N_n, where N_0 'abbreviates' N, and N_{n+1} abbreviates $N_n/\bar{N}$. (The Predicative Hierarchy generated by P recall is the set of categories P_n, where $P_0 = P$ and $P_{n+1} = P_n/\bar{N}$).

The types we associate with these new (non-empty) categories is given inductively by: $T_{N_0} = T_N$, a primitive of the model, and $T_{N_{n+1}} = HT_{Nn}/T\bar{N}$, the set of complete homomorphisms from $T_{\bar{N}}$ into T_{N_n}, regarded as a complete and atomic boolean algebra where the operations are defined pointwise on the individuals. So elements of T_{N_1} are c-homomorphisms from full NP denotations into common noun denotations. This choice of type of course makes a variety of predictions concerning semantic equivalence of English expressions. It means for example that the *friend of John or Bill* property is the same as the *friend of John or friend of Bill* property. Thus Harry is a friend of John or Bill iff he is a friend of John or a friend of Bill, a correct prediction. Similarly since *friend of* preserves arbitrary meets we have that the *friend of every senator* property is the same as the meet of the *friend of x* property taken over all individuals x with the senator property. Whence it follows that Mary is a friend of every senator iff for every senator, Mary is a friend of his, again a correct prediction. And finally, since *friend of* preserves complements it follows that *friend of no senator* expresses the same property as *non-[friend of a senator]*, whence Mary is a friend of no senator iff she fails to have the *friend of a senator* property.

Notice that a different set of correct predictions follows from taking T_{N_1} as an algebra defined pointwise on the individuals. This means, recall, that where f and g are elements of T_{N_1} and x is an individual, $(f \wedge g)(x) = f(x) \wedge g(x)$, and $(f \vee g)(x) = f(x) \vee g(x)$, and $(f')(x) = (f(x))'$. Thus for x an individual, it follows that John has the *friend or colleague of Bill* property iff he has the *friend of Bill* property or the *colleague of Bill* property, which is correct. Of course these equalities fail in general if x is a set of properties which is not an individual. Thus the property expressed by *friend or colleague of every senator* is the property an individual has iff for every senator he is a friend of x or a colleague of x. But the property expressed by *friend of every senator or colleague of every senator* is one an individual has iff either he is a friend of every senator or a colleague of every senator. Similarly consider the two non-equivalent logical structures presented below. They differ with respect to the scope of *non-*, according as it has combined directly with the N_1 *friend* to form a derived N_1 (the complement of *friend* in the N_1 algebra) as in (24), or according as it has combined with the N_0 *friend of every senator*, as in (25). Arguably each structure expresses one way of understanding an expression like *(a) non-friend of every senator* so the (admittedly somewhat forced) ambiguity of this expression is represented in our system.

(24)   (non-friend) of every senator

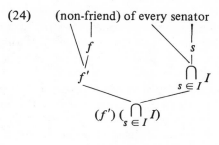

$$= \bigwedge_{s \in I} (f')(I) \qquad \text{since } f' \text{ is a homomorphism}$$
$$= \text{'for every senator, (a) non-friend of his'}$$

(25)   non-friend of every senator

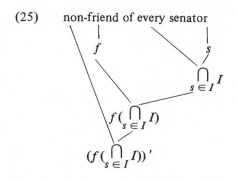

$$= (\bigwedge_{s \in I} f(I))' \qquad \text{since } f \text{ is a homomorphism}$$
$$= (\bigvee_{s \in I} (f(I))') \qquad \text{de Morgan laws}$$
$$= (\bigvee_{s \in I} (f')(I)) \qquad \text{pointwise definition of }'$$
$$= \text{'for some senator, (a) non-friend of his'}$$

Note that while the ambiguity in the scope of non- may seem somewhat artificial, there is a similar scope ambiguity with regard to nominal modifiers which we can capture in a similar way.

Modifiers of n-place Common Nouns

We have been treating the adjective phrases as the category N_0/N_0. But given now the nominal hierarchy of N_n we have defined it is easy to extend the domain of APs to be modifiers of N_n's in general. On this analysis then the lexical APs would be entered into the category $\langle N_n/N_n \rangle$ $(= \langle N_0, N_1, \ldots \rangle$ / $\langle N_0, N_1, \ldots \rangle$. And the type for that category would be the set of proper functions from T_{N_n} into T_{N_n} (so if p is in T_{N_n} then $f(p)$ is in T_{N_n}) which are restricting (for all n and all p in T_{N_n}, $f(p) \leqslant p$). The set of such f's is a restricting algebra as per Theorem 10.

While this extension of T_{AP} is algebraically both easy and natural, is there any motivation from the valid arguments of English for such an extension? It appears that there is. Thus consider the classically noted ambiguity in expressions like *an old friend of John, a good friend of John*, etc. On the one hand the first expression might denote properties which an individual has iff he is a long-time friend of John; and on the other hand the expression might denote properties of individuals who are friends of John and old (either absolutely or perhaps just relative to friends of John). In any case the ambiguity seems naturally representable as a function of the scope of old, good, etc. And on the proposed extension such expressions have two logical structures which differ in just this way:

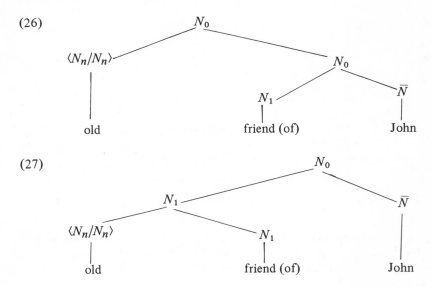

(26)

(27)

Moreover, in the absence of further restrictions on T_{N_n/N_n}, these two structures are not logically equivalent. The first one is any property g which $\leqslant$ *friend of John*. In the second what we know is that *old friend* is a N_1 semantically $\leqslant$ *friend*, whence (*old friend*) (*of*) *John* is $\leqslant$ *friend of John*. But since *old friend* can be any element of T_{N_1} less than or equal to *friend*, its value on John need not be g above, that is, it need not be the same as the value of *old* on the *friend of John* property. So this analysis says that if an individual has either of the properties denoted by (26) and (27) then he has the *friend of John* property, which seems correct. On the other hand, an individual can have either of the properties (26) and (27) without having the other, which also seems correct.

This analysis also yields some interesting predictions concerning the scope of *old* relative to quantified NPs. Thus if John is an (*old friend*) (*of*) *every senator*, then for every individual x with the senator property, John is a long-time friend of his. On the other hand, if John has the *old* (*friend* (*of*) *every senator*) property then John is merely a friend of every senator and is old (either relative to individuals generally or if old in this usage is 'merely' restricting, relative to the friends of every senator). And while these inter-pretations are slightly forced, they seem more right than wrong, and thus support the correctness of the extended analysis of APs.

Some Relations Between Nominals and Predicates

We have defined then two Predicative hierarchies, that generated by T_{P_0} and that generated by T_{N_0}. These hierarchies are not independent. In fact we have already shown that T_{P_1} is isomorphic to T_{N_0}, and it should not be surprising (we prove this below) that for every $n \geqslant 0$, $T_{P_{n+1}}$ is isomorphic to T_{N_n}. This isomorphism has considerable linguistic interest. For one thing it tells us as a special case that T_{N_1}, the type for the 'transitive' common noun phrases, is isomorphic to T_{P_2}, the transitive verb phrases, thereby justifying formally our pretheoretical intuition that *father* (*of*), *friend* (*of*), etc. should be called *transitive* even though they only take one argument.

More interestingly, however, accepting that there is a general correspon-dence between surface form and logical form, we can now (once we prove the theorem) justify that we should expect the internal structure of N_1's to be similar to that for P_2's, since semantically the types for these two sets are highly similar, in fact isomorphic. And much recent work in linguistics, beginning perhaps with Chomsky (1973), has pointed out several such syn-tactic similarities between the internal structures of 'noun phrases' and that of 'verb phrases', e.g. *destroy the city/destruction (of) the city*, etc. While we do not represent abstract nominals like *destruction* in our extensional language, we can extend the core language by some nominalizing functions which derive *n*-place nominals from *n*+1 place predicates. In fact, the agent nominalizer *er* (*swim → swim+er*) will be interpreted as the *natural isomorphism* (defined below) from TP_{n+1} into TN_n, for each $n \geqslant 0$. From this fact alone then the logical equivalences of the a-/b- sentences below follow:

> (28) a. John swims
>   b. John is a swim+er
> (29) a. John employs Bill
>   b. John is an employ+er (of) Bill
> (30) a. John contributes money (to) the church
>   b. John is a contribute+er (of) money (to) the church

Let us first prove the existence of the natural isomorphism referred to above and then show how the equivalences follow.

THEOREM 17. The function g defined below is, for all $n \geqslant 0$, an isomorphism from TP_{n+1} onto TN_n:

> g is a function from $\bigcup_{n \geqslant 0} TP_{n+1}$ into $\bigcup_{n \geqslant 0} TN_n$ defined recursively as follows:
> a. for $n = 0$ and all $h \in TP_{n+1}$, $g(h)$ is that element of TN_0 such that for all individuals I, $g(h) \in I$ iff $h(I) = 1$;
> b. for $n > 0$ and $h \in TP_{n+1}$, $g(h)$ is that element of TN_n such that for all individuals I, $(g(h))(I) = g(h(I))$.

Remarks on Theorem 17:

(1) In clause (a) we define a property, $g(h)$, by stating what individuals it is in. By corollary a to Theorem 11, Section A this does define a property.

(2) We call g in clause (a) *natural* because it picks out, for each one place predicate h, the property which h asserts of its argument. Recall from Section A that each such h is an f_p for some property p, where f_p is that P_1 homomorphism mapping a set of properties Q onto 1 iff $p \in Q$ (and onto 0 otherwise). To say that $g(h)$ is the property h asserts of its argument is just to say that $f_{g(h)} = h$. By Definition 36 (Section A) of $f_{g(h)}$ we have that $f_{g(h)}(I) = 1$ iff $g(h) \in I$, I any individual, and by the definition of g, this latter

condition obtains iff $h(I) = 1$. Thus $f_{g(h)}$ and h assign the same values to the individuals, and by the Justification Theorem they assign the same values to every set of properties Q. Thus $f_{g(h)} = h$.

(3) This last fact basically tells us that g, restricted to T_{P_1}, is an isomorphism from T_{P_1} onto T_{N_0}. For recall from Theorem 20, Section A, that the function f from T_{N_0} into T_{P_1} which sends each property p onto f_p, is an isomorphism. Hence its inverse f^{-1} is an isomorphism from T_{P_1} into T_{N_0}; in fact $g = f^{-1}$. From the definition of inverse we have for all h in T_{P_1} $f^{-1}(h) = p$ iff $f(p) = h$. In particular $f^{-1}(h) = g(h)$ iff $f(g(h)) = h$, and $f(g(h))$ is simply $f_{g(h)}$. So the latter equation holds by the end of remark 2. Since h was arbitrary, we have that $f^{-1} = g$, so g restricted to T_{P_1} is an isomorphism onto T_{N_0}.

(4) The semantic relations expressed by g and f above seem so simple and natural that we might reasonably expect a natural language to have ways of expressing these relations. Specifically for g, it appears (by and large) that the nominalizer -*er* transforms many P_1's into N_0's in such a way that p in P_1 holds of an individual iff that individual has the property expressed by p+*er*. E.g. John swims iff John has the property expressed by *swimmer* (= *swim+er*).

What about f? Given a common noun phrase such as *doctor*, English and indeed all languages have a regular way to assert that an individual, say John, has that property. English does it with the 'is a' construction. That is, on the semantics we have given *be* and *a* it follows that (*be* (*a doctor*)) holds of John iff the property which interprets *doctor* is a member of the individual which interprets *John*. Since *be* and *a* are both logical constants, we may conclude that English has a regular way of converting common nouns into P_1's. Many languages of course would perform this conversion more directly. At a decent guess only half the world's languages would use an overt copula (*be*) to express *John is a doctor*, and still fewer would use an indefinite article.

(5) Consider now clause (b) of the definition of g. The simplest and most relevant case is for $n = 1$. Then h is a member of T_{P_2}, a transitive verb phrase denotation, and $g(h)$ is a member of T_{N_1}, a transitive common noun denotation. Further, for any individual x, $h(x)$ is a member of T_{P_1}, a one place predicate denotation, and $(g(h))(x)$ is a property in T_{N_0}. The definition says that that property is just the one which $h(x)$ asserts of its argument. So for example taking h as the interpretation of *employ* and interpreting *er* now as the isomorphism g, we have that *employ+er* is that N_1 which maps an individual, say Bill, onto the property (*employ+er* (*of*)

Bill) which the P_1 *employ Bill* asserts of its argument. Thus it follows that John employs Bill is true iff John has the 'employer of Bill' property, that is, iff John is an employer of Bill. This result is particularly nice and provides serious justification for our treatment of N_1's and P_2's, since the naive semantics for *employer*, treating it as a property in T_{N_0} which an individual has iff he employs someone, is not sufficient to guarantee that he is an employer of Bill iff he employs Bill. Something further on that approach would have to be said about how 'PP's' like *of Bill* combine with N_0's to form further N_0's. But on our treatment nothing else of that sort need be said. It is sufficient to define the types for the relevant *n*-place Preds as we have done, and interpret *er* as g in Theorem 17, namely as the generalized isomorphism from $T_{P_{n+1}}$ into T_{N_n} all $n \geqslant 0$.

Proof of Theorem 17.

By induction on n; the case for $n = 0$ has already been proven in Remark 3 above, so for arbitrary n, assume the theorem holds for all $m < n$. We show it holds for n. By the induction hypothesis we have that for all $m < n$, g is an isomorphism from $T_{P_{m+1}}$ into T_{N_m}. We must show g to be an isomorphism from $T_{P_{n+1}}$ into T_{N_n}.

    (i) *g is a homomorphism*

    (a) *g preserves complements.*

We must show that for all h in $T_{P_{n+1}}$ $g(h') = (g(h))'$, that is, that these two homomorphisms have the same value at every individual x. (Note that for all P_{n+1} homomorphisms k, $g(k)$ is a homomorphism in T_{N_n} by clause (b) since the Justification Theorem tells us that we can define homomorphisms in T_{N_n} by stating their values on the individuals in any way we like). So in particular $g(h')$ is in T_{N_n}. Now,

$$
\begin{aligned}
(g(h'))(x) &= g(h'(x)) && \text{by definition of } g, \\
&= g((h(x)')) && \text{definition of ' in } T_{P_{n+1}} \\
&= (g(h(x)))' && h(x) \text{ is in } T_{P_n} \text{ so } g \text{ is an isomorphism by} \\
& && \text{the induction hypothesis} \\
&= (g(h))(x))' && \text{definition of } g \\
&= (g(h))'(x) && \text{definition of ' in } T_{N_n}
\end{aligned}
$$

    (b) *g preserves meets*; that is $g(h \wedge f) = g(h) \wedge g(f)$, all h, f in $T_{P_{n+1}}$. The proof parallels that in (a) and is left as an exercise for the reader.

    (ii) *g is one-to-one.*

Let h, f in $T_{P_{n+1}}$ such that $h \neq f$. Then for some individual x, $h(x) \neq f(x)$ (otherwise by the Justification Theorem $h = f$). So $g(h(x)) \neq g(f(x))$ since

$h(x)$ and $f(x)$ are in T_{P_n} and by the induction hypothesis g is an isomorphism on T_{P_n}. But by the definition of g, $g(h(x)) = (g(h))\,(x)$, and $g(f(x)) = (g(f))\,(x)$. So $(g(h)\,(x) \neq (g(f))\,(x)$, so $g(h) \neq g(f)$.

(iii) *g is onto*.

For k arbitrary in T_{N_n} define h in $T_{P_{n+1}}$ such that for all individuals x, $h\,(x) = g^{-1}\,(k\,(x))$. By the Justification Theorem this is a well definition, given that $k\,(x)$ is in $T_{N_{n-1}}$ and g is an isomorphism from T_{P_n} into $T_{N_{n-1}}$, so g^{-1} is an isomorphism from $T_{N_{n-1}}$ onto T_{P_n}. Then $g\,(h) = k$, since: for x an arbitrary individual,

$$
\begin{aligned}
(g\,(h))\,(x) \quad & = g\,(h\,(x)) && \text{definition of } g \\
& = g\,(g^{-1}\,(k\,(x))) && \text{definition of } h \\
& = k\,(x) && \text{definition of inverse.}
\end{aligned}
$$

Formally then we may extend L as follows. Add *er* to the basic vocabulary V, and by lexical rule assign *er* to the category N_n/P_{n+1}, which abbreviates $\langle N_0, N_1, \ldots \rangle \,/\, \langle P_1, P_2, \ldots \rangle$. The type for that category can (for the nonce) be taken as the entire set of proper functions whose domain is the union of the types for P_{n+1} and whose range is included in the union of the types for N_n, $n \geqslant 0$. Finally, constrain the lexical interpreting function M such that $M\,(er)$ is the natural isomorphism g defined in Theorem 17.

Subcategories of N_n

Finally, to conclude our discussion of the *n*-place nominals, we should consider whether these categories present any natural subcategories. They will in fact present many such, but few that we can represent within the confines of our system.

First let us consider one subcategory we can represent. The N_1's we have considered are all semantically arbitrary binary relations on the set of individuals (isomorphic to P_2). However certain of them, such as (biological) *father (of)*, and *mother (of)* should be constrained to be interpreted by relations which are (set theoretically speaking) functional. That is, at most one individual can have the property expressed by *father of John* (on the literal, biological sense of *father*). On the other hand we probably do not want to require that *father (of)* be a total function. Even for human individuals it does not seem a logical truth that every man has a father. Hence we shall require that expressions like *father (of)* take their denotations in a proper subset of T_{N_1}; those functions which are such that for every individual x, $f(x)$ is either the 0 element of T_{N_0} of $f(x)$ is an atom in T_{N_0}. That is, either no individual has the property $f(x)$ or exactly one does. And syntactically we may add the feature pf (for partial function) to SF_L and take the type of $N_1 \atop pf$ to be those functions T_{N_1} as previously defined which meet the conditions given above.

On the other hand, a great many apparent N_1's in English do not determine properties of individuals at all but rather are objects of some more abstract sort. Some examples would be: (the) *edge of the plate, corner of the table, sex of the President, temperature of the patient, acceleration of the vehicle, height of the teacher*, etc. None of these expressions naturally occur in or make sense in contexts like 'John is a   ' which is, as we have seen, the normal way in English to assert that an individual has a certain property. So such expressions seem not to denote properties of individuals. Moreover if they did, we would be forced to say that e.g. the sex of the President, the temperature of the room, etc. could denote individuals, and thus perhaps even be things like John, or you, or me, etc. This seems ontologically dubious at best. Most likely then the ontology of our model would have to be enriched before proper denotations of such expressions could be provided. So we skirt this problem by not adding such expressions to L.

Notice further than many 'abstract' N_1's in English will determine not properties of individuals but properties of the social roles or statuses they occupy and hence not be transparent (extensional). For example, if the President and the Commander of the Army are the same individual it will not follow that *the duties of the President* and *the duties of the Commander of the Army* are the same objects (whatever they are). It will follow however that the sex of the President and the sex of the Commander are the same object, so transparency is a logical feature which cross classifies with 'abstract'.

Transitive Adjective Phrases

There are a variety of lexically simple items in English which appear to combine with full NPs to form adjective phrases. Many such items, like the most common lexical N_1's, impose the case marker *of* on their NP arguments. Examples would be *fond of, jealous of, envious of, weary of, afraid of, proud of*, etc. as they occur in expressions like *a teacher fond of every student, a soldier weary of the battle*, etc. In addition there are many items of a syntactically similar sort which give the appearance of being derived from verbs and which impose other case markers on their arguments. Examples would be *infatuated with, bored with, fed up with*, even *in love with*, as well as *interested in, visible from, addicted to*, etc. We shall treat such items here as lexically primitive as we have no conviction that they can be verbally derived in a regular way, that is, in such a way that their interpretation can be given as a function of that of the verb they are derived from. (And note that in many cases, such as *fed up with, bored with*, there is in fact no obvious verbal source).

As very little is known either syntactically or semantically about such transitive adjectives, we shall only attempt a preliminary analysis here, one that can serve as a basis for a more detailed analysis.

As regards their syntax, let us define A_0 as an abbreviation for N_0/N_0, the adjective phrases already studied. Then, as before, A_{n+1} will be the category $A_n/\bar{N}$. Extend L then by adding *fond of* etc. to the basic vocabulary V, and by lexical rule put them in the category A_1 $(= A_0/\bar{N} = (N_0/N_0)/\bar{N})$. This then defines another Predicative hierarchy. As with the N_1's there appear to be no lexical members of A_n for $n > 1$, but again when the variable binding rules are introduced all such categories will have members.

Semantically we may define the type for A_{n+1} in the expected way. That is, since T_{A_0} itself is a complete and atomic boolean algebra, we may define, for all $n > 0$, $T_{A_{n+1}}$ to be the predicative algebra from $T_{\bar{N}}$ into T_{A_n}. This claims then that the A_1's are homomorphisms. This predicts that *teacher fond of John or Mary = teacher fond of John or fond of Mary = teacher fond of John or teacher fond of Mary*. And since a join of properties is in an individual iff at least one ·of the properties over which we take the join is in it, we have that Bill is a teacher fond of John or Mary iff Bill is a teacher fond of John or Bill is a teacher fond of Mary, which seems basically correct. Similarly if Bill is a teacher fond of no student then Bill must be a teacher such that for each individual x with the student property, Bill is not (fond of x). And this seems correct.

Moreover having taken A_n as boolean, for each $n \geqslant 0$, we can form expressions such as *both fond of and jealous of, either bored with or interested in*, etc. The pointwise definition of meets, joins, and complements in T_{A_n} predicts, correctly, that Mary is a teacher either bored with or interested in John iff Mary is a teacher bored with John or interested in John.

Notice finally that on the definitions of T_{A_n} as given, interpretations of *fond of John* etc. are merely required to be restricting functions from properties to properties, not necessarily intersecting ones. Consequently we expect that they should accept modification by *very*, which is correct as *Mary is a teacher very fond of John, very proud of every student*, etc. are sensible. But notice that this analysis predicts that Mary could be a teacher fond of John without being an individual fond of John. It is sufficient that relative to teachers she is fond of John. If very many people other than teachers are much fonder of John than she is then she might fail to be an individual fond of John. And while this is slightly forced, it seems more right than wrong.

Moreover this analysis together with the natural extension of the domain of *very* makes some interesting predictions concerning scope ambiguities analogous to those discussed earlier for *non-*. First, extend *very* as follows: *very* is now assigned the category $\langle A_n/A_n \rangle$ $(= \langle A_0, A_1, \ldots \rangle / \langle A_0, A_1, \ldots \rangle)$. For all f in T_{A_0}, the value of M (*very*) is given as before. And for all f in T_{A_n}, any $n > 0$, we merely constraint M (*very*) so that M (*very*) $(f) \leqslant f$. This guarantees then that (*very fond*) *of John* $\leqslant$ *fond of John*, as is *very* (*fond of John*); but the two A_0's need not be interpreted as the same element of T_{A_0}. And this difference seems (delicately) to show up when the argument of *fond of* is not an individual denoting expression. Thus to say that Mary is (*very fond*) of every student is to say that for each individual x with the student property, Mary is very fond of x. But to say that Mary is *very* (*fond of every student*) merely says that she has the fond of every student property to a great extent. That guarantees that she is fond of each student, but not necessarily that she is very fond of each student. Thus she might be fond of every student to a great extent even if there was say one of the 100 students in question that she was merely fond of but not very fond of.

Ditransitive Verb Phrases (P₃'s)

We shall be primarily concerned in this section to enrich L by including lexical predicates like *give, show*, and *hand* which combine with three $\bar{N}$'s to form a sentence. It might appear that there is little to say here since we may simply assign them the category P_3 $(= P_2/\bar{N})$ by lexical rule and interpret them freely in T_{P_3} which is already defined as the set of complete homomorphisms from $T_{\bar{N}}$ into T_{P_2}. However using the case marking notation developed earlier there are at least two plausible subcategories of P_3 to which such predicates might be assigned: P_3 and P_3 . These assignments yield different structural analysis of *John handed the book* (*to*) *Bill*, as follows:

(31)

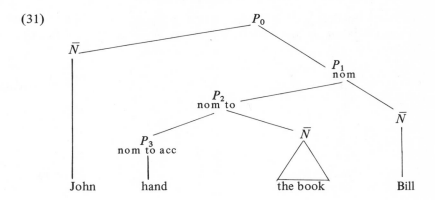

(32)

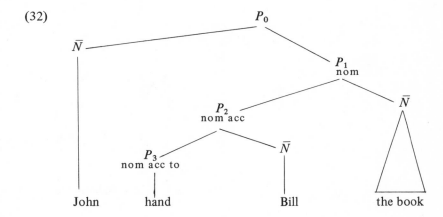

On the analysis in (31), henceforth the Patient analysis, the 'Patient' NP forms a logical constituent with the P_3, and the Recipient is the argument of the derived P_2 *hand the book*. On the analysis in (32), henceforth the Recipient analysis, it is the 'Recipient' which forms a constituent with the P_3 and the Patient NP is the argument of the derived P_2 *hand (to) Bill*.

Of these two analyses we prefer the Patient analysis in (31) since the two analyses make different predictions concerning the relative scope of the Patient and Recipient NP's and it is the Patient analysis which makes the correct predictions.

On the Patient analysis the Recipient $\bar{N}$ will have wide scope over the Patient $\bar{N}$, whereas just the opposite scope assignment will prevail on the

Recipient Analysis. (33) below is the semantic tree of *John handed a book to every student* on the Patient analysis. (*x* and *y* range over individuals of course):

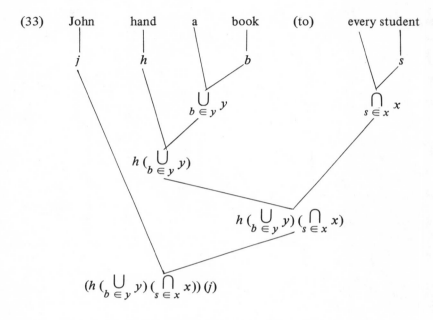

$$= ((\underset{s \in x}{\wedge} h (\underset{b \in y}{\cup} y)) (x)) (j) \qquad h (\underset{b \in y}{\cup} y) \text{ is a homomorphism}$$

$$= (\underset{s \in x}{\wedge} \underset{b \in y}{\vee} (h (y)) (x)) (j) \qquad h \text{ is a homomorphism}$$

$$= \underset{s \in x}{\wedge} \underset{b \in y}{\vee} ((h (y)) (x)) (j)) \qquad \text{pointwise definition of } \wedge \text{ and } \vee$$

= 1 iff for every individual *x* with the student property there is an individual *y* with the book property such that *j* (= John) gave *x* to *y*

Clearly then on this analysis *every student* has wide scope over *a book*, the preferred reading of the sentence. On the other hand, on the Recipient analysis illustrated below we find that *a book* was wide scope over *every student*, which is not correct.

(34)

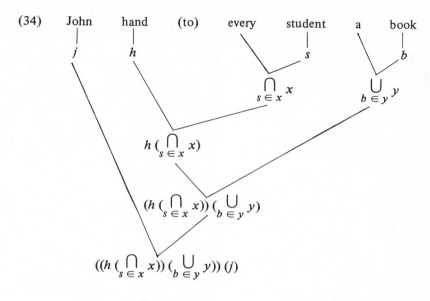

$$= (_{b \in y} \bigvee (h (_{s \in x} \bigcap x)) (y)) (j) \qquad h (_{s \in x} \bigcap x) \text{ is a homomorphism}$$

$$= (_{b \in y} \bigvee (_{s \in x} \bigwedge ((h (x)) (y)) (j))) \qquad h \text{ is a homomorphism}$$

= 1 iff for some individual y with the book property it is the case that for every individual x with the student property, John gave y to x

We add then *give, show, hand,* etc. to the category $P_{3 \text{ nom to acc}}$ and henceforth drop the case marking notation.

Since the type for P_3 consists of homomorphisms we then correctly predict that e.g. *John handed a book and a pen to Mary* is logically equivalent to *John handed a book and handed a pen to Mary,* which is correct. And since the elements of T_{P_3} are defined pointwise on individuals we correctly predict that the sentences in (35) below are all logically equivalent.

(35) a. John showed and gave the book to Mary.
     b. John showed the book and gave the book to Mary.
     c. John showed the book to Mary and gave the book to Mary.
     d. John showed the book to Mary and John gave the book to Mary.

Finally, with only some abuse we may enrich the subcategories of P_3 to include, for each $c \in \{in, on, under, next\ to, \ldots\}$ the subcategory $P_3 {}_{\text{nom } c\text{ acc}}$. The types for such categories will be P_3 homomorphisms h which meet the additional subcategory condition that for all individuals x, y, z $h(x)(y)(z) \leqslant be(c(y))(x)$. So assigning *put* to the subcategory $P_3 {}_{\text{nom on acc}}$ we guarantee that *John puts the book on the table* entails *the book is on the table*. This seems reasonable given that we have not in our semantics associated activity predicates with time intervals. A more adequate semantics with such an association would have to guarantee that a certain time relation held between the time of putting and the time of being on the table.

Prepositions and Predicate Modifier Hierarchies

In this section we provide a syntactic and semantic analysis of English prepositions such as *in, at, by, with, from, next to, near*, etc. which is compatible with our earlier treatment of Predicate Modifiers (PM's). We show in particular that the two types of PM's discussed earlier, subject oriented and argument oriented, are the generators of two Predicative Hierarchies, PM_n: $n \geqslant 0$ and PM_n: $n \geqslant 0$. The two classes of PM's discussed earlier are the PM_0's in their hierarchy, and prepositions are PM_1's, combining with $\bar{N}$'s to form PM_0's. In the concluding portion of this section we generalize the treatment of prepositions to allow them to combine directly with P_n's to form P_{n+1}'s.

We assume in what follows, though it plays little direct role in our analysis, that English prepositions occur in a variety of homophones. Thus in a richer treatment than we propose here we should need to distinguish three *with*'s, a *with_com* to represent the comitative use in *John left with Mary*, a *with_inst* to represent the instrumental use in *John dug a hole with a spoon*, and a *with_man* to represent the manner use in *John greeted Mary with joy*. It is only the instrumental use of *with* that we intend to represent here (and that only in the intensional logic). Similarly it is only the agentive use of *by*, as in *the University forbids cheating by students, John was kissed by Mary*, etc. that we intend to represent here. A fuller treatment would include as well a *by_loc* as in *John sat down by the window*, etc. Further, since the only structures using agentive *by* in a natural way which we represent in our system are passives we defer its semantics to the following section on passives.

Prepositions as Formers of Predicate Modifiers

Syntactically we treat prepositions as expressions which combine with $\bar{N}$'s such as *the garden* to form PM's such as *in the garden*. Recall from our earlier treatment that PM was formally the category $\langle P_n/P_n \rangle$, itself an abbreviation for $\langle P_1, P_2, \ldots \rangle / \langle P_1, P_2, \ldots \rangle$. Moreover we distinguished two subcategories of PM's according as they were subject oriented or argument oriented. Formally we add the features *subj* and *arg* to the logical subcategorization features of L thereby determining two subcategories of PM, which we will usually abbreviate PM_{subj} and PM_{arg}. These features also determine two subcategories of preposition: $\text{PM}_{subj}/\bar{N}$ and $\text{PM}_{arg}/\bar{N}$, which we commonly abbreviate simply as Prep_{subj} and Prep_{arg} respectively. We now enrich L to include *by* (and in the intensional logic of Part II *with*) in the former category and the locative prepositions *in, at, next to, under*, etc. in the latter category. On this syntactic analysis (36a) below is generated with the structure shown in (36b) (in which we have not, somewhat exceptionally, used all the abbreviations noted above).

(36) a. John sing in the garden

b.

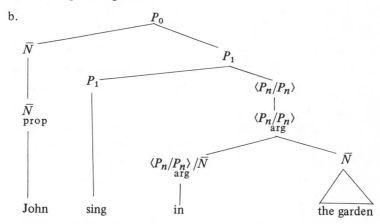

Semantically, argument oriented Preps will be interpreted by functions from $\bar{N}$ denotations into argument oriented PM denotations; analogously for subject oriented Preps. Moreover Prep interpretations are not just random functions in these sets, they behave homomorphically on their $\bar{N}$ arguments. Thus we want the PM *in (New York or Chicago)* to be interpreted by the same function as *in New York or in Chicago* in order to guarantee for example that (37a, b) below are logically equivalent.

(37) a. John is singing in (New York or Chicago)
b. John is singing (in New York or in Chicago)

This amounts to saying that the interpretation of *in* must preserve joins. Similarly, replacing *or* by *and* in the above example we infer that we want the interpretation of *in* to preserve meets. Finally the equivalence of (38a,c) below is shown if the interpretation of *in* preserves complements:

(38) a. John is singing in (New York and not Chicago)
      b. John is singing (in New York and in (not Chicago))
      c. John is singing (in New York and not (in Chicago))

Note that the types for subject and argument oriented PM's, given earlier as $SO_{\langle P_n/P_n \rangle}$ and $AO_{\langle P_n/P_n \rangle}$ in Definitions 26 and 20 respectively are both complete and atomic boolean algebras isomorphic to the type for P_1 (Theorems 13 and 16). It thus makes sense to represent subject and argument oriented Preps as homomorphisms whose values are determined by their values on the individuals as per the Justification Theorem of Section A. And of course we want Prep denotations to lie in a boolean algebra in order to directly interpret booleanly complex elements of Prep, as *either in or near, near but not in*, etc. as they occur in sentences like *John is singing near but not in Chicago*. Formally then we define:

DEFINITION 27. $T_{\text{Prep}_{\text{subj}}} = HT_{\text{PM}}/T_{\bar{N}_{\text{subj}}}$ regarded as a complete and atomic boolean algebra where the operations are defined pointwise on the individuals.

Replacing *subj* by *arg* in the above definition we obtain that for $T_{\text{Prep}_{\text{arg}}}$. Using Definition 27 (and our previous definitions) we can show in (39) below that *John is singing near but not in some bar* will be interpreted to mean *for some bar, John is near it and John is not in it and John is singing*. (x and y range over individuals of course.)

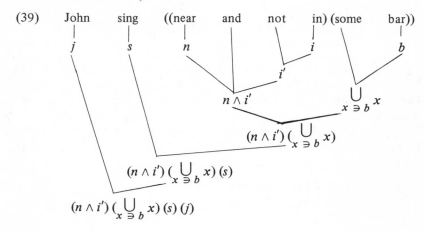

$$= (_x \bigvee_{\supseteq b} (n \wedge i')(x))(s)(j) \quad (n \wedge i') \text{ in } T\underset{\text{arg}}{_{\text{Prep}}} \text{ is a homomorphism}$$

$$= (_x \bigvee_{\supseteq b} (n \wedge i')(x)(s))(j) \quad \text{pointwise definition of } \vee \text{ in } T\underset{\text{arg}}{_{\text{PM}}}$$

$$= _x \bigvee_{\supseteq b} ((n \wedge i')(x)(s)(j)) \quad \text{pointwise definition of } \vee \text{ in } T_{P_1}$$

$$= _x \bigvee_{\supseteq b} (n(x) \wedge (i(x))')(x)(j) \quad \text{ptwise definition of } \wedge \text{ and } ' \text{ in } T\underset{\text{arg}}{_{\text{Prep}}}$$

$$= _x \bigvee_{\supseteq b} (n(x)(s) \wedge (i(x))'(s))(j) \quad \text{ptwise definition of } \wedge \text{ in } T\underset{\text{arg}}{_{\text{PM}}}$$

$$= _x \bigvee_{\supseteq b} ((n(x)(s) \wedge (s \wedge (i(x)(s))'))(j) \quad \text{definition } ' \text{ in } T\underset{\text{arg}}{_{\text{PM}}}$$

$$= _x \bigvee_{\supseteq b} (n(x)(s)(j) \wedge s(j) \wedge (i(x)(s)(j))') \quad \text{ptwise definition of } \wedge \text{ and } '$$
$$\text{in } T_{P_1}$$

$$= _x \bigvee_{\supseteq b} (n(x)(s)(j) \wedge s(j) \wedge (s(j) \wedge i(x)(1)(j))') \quad \text{definition } T\underset{\text{arg}}{_{\text{PM}}}$$

$$= _x \bigvee_{\supseteq b} (n(x)(s)(j) \wedge s(j) \wedge ((s(j))' \vee (i(x)(1)(j))')) \quad \text{de Morgan laws}$$

$$= _x \bigvee_{\supseteq b} (n(x)(s)(j) \wedge s(j) \wedge (i(x)(1)(j))' \quad \text{distributivity and laws for}$$
$$\text{zero elements}$$

$$= _x \bigvee_{\supseteq b} s(j) \wedge n(x)(1)(j) \wedge s(j) \wedge (i(x)(1)(j))' \quad \text{definition } T\underset{\text{arg}}{_{\text{PM}}}$$

$$= _x \bigvee_{\supseteq b} n(x)(1)(j) \wedge (i(x)(1)(j))' \wedge s(j) \quad \text{idempotency, commutativity}$$
$$\text{and associativity}$$

$= 1$ iff for some individual x with the bar property, John exist near x and it is not the case that John exist in x and John sing

Let us now properly generalize the treatment of prepositions so far given. First we have, for $\alpha \in \{\text{subj}, \text{arg}\}$; that $\underset{\alpha}{\text{Prep}}$ is just the second element of the Predicative Hierarchy defined by PM. Explicitly, from the general definition of Predicative Hierarchy in Section A, we have that $PM_0 = PM$ as previously defined, and $PM_{n+1} = PM_n/\bar{N}$. Choosing $\alpha = arg$ for illustrative purposes, the types for the elements of the argument oriented Predicative Hierarchy are given in Definition 28:

DEFINITION 28.

(a) $T\underset{\text{arg}}{_{\text{PM}_0}} = AO_{\langle P_n/P_n \rangle}$ (as per Definition 20)

(b) $T\underset{\text{arg}}{_{\text{PM}_{n+1}}} = H_{T\underset{\text{arg}}{_{\text{PM}_n}}/T\bar{N}}$, regarded as a complete atomic algebra, the operations being defined pointwise on the individuals.

The corresponding subject oriented Predicative Hierarchy is defined as in Definition 28 replacing *arg* everywhere by *subj*.

Note then that for $\alpha \in \{subj, arg\}$ the category we have been referring to as $\underset{\alpha}{Prep}$ is just PM_1. Moreover the linguistic intuition that prepositions are 'transitive' is justified as it is straightforward to prove that the type for $\underset{\alpha}{Prep}$, $\alpha \in \{subj, arg\}$, is isomorphic to the type for P_2. Formally,

THEOREM 18. For $\alpha \in \{subj, arg\}$; $T_{\underset{\alpha}{PM}_n}$ is isomorphic to $T_{P_{n+1}}$.

Proof sketch. To show that T_{P_2} is isomorphic to $T_{\underset{subj}{PM}_1}$ ($= T_{\underset{subj}{Prep}}$) define a function k from T_{P_2} into $T_{\underset{subj}{Prep}}$ ($= T_{\langle P_n/P_n\rangle/\bar{N}}$) as follows: For all $p \in T_{P_2}$, $k(p)$ is that homomorphism in $T_{\underset{subj}{Prep}}$ such that for all individuals I, $(k(p))(I) = h(p(I))$, where h is the isomorphism from T_{P_1} into $T_{\underset{subj}{PM}_0}$ ($= SO_{\langle P_n/P_n\rangle}$) defined in Theorem 16. Prove that k is an isomorphism.

To conclude this subsection let us note that we have so far been motivated to define four Predicative Hierarchies, those associated with n-place predicates, n-place common nouns, n-place common noun modifiers, and n-place predicate modifiers. This corresponds rather well to the linguistic intuition in current generative grammar that nominal, predicate, adjective, and preposition are the fundamental grammatical categories. Of note however is that the elementary expressions in PM_0 will not be bare prepositions combining with P_n's to form P_n's, but rather will be expressions like *here* and *there* (and perhaps expressions like *Eastwards, leftwards, bogwards*, etc. if lexically simple). We may note that bare Preps do sometimes seem to combine with P_n's to form P_n's as illustrated in (40) below:

(40) a. John *sleeps in* on Saturdays
      b. The project *fell through*
      c. John *talked on (and on)*.

The meaning of the 'prepositions' in these constructions seems however only idiosyncratically related to their use as PM_1's, so we prefer to treat such derived P_1's as *sleep in* (= sleep late), etc. as independent basic expressions related idiosyncratically by constraints on the lexical interpreting function M to the P_1's they are apparently derived from.

Prepositions as Verbal Extensors

The analysis of prepositions given above can be extended in several directions. One which is of some interest is a usage common in many languages such as Latin and Kinyarwanda (and other Bantu languages) in which prepositions appear to combine with P_n's to form P_{n+1}'s. Thus for a Latin P_2 such as *ferre* 'to carry' we may form P_3's such as *trans+ferre* 'to carry across', *in+ferre* 'to carry into', *ex+ferre* (= *efferre*) 'to carry from', etc.

Extending the syntax and semantics of Preps to accommodate this usage is quite easy in our system. First, for $\alpha \in \{$subj, arg$\}$, Prep_α would be the category $\langle P_n/P_n, P_{n+1} \rangle / \langle \bar{N}, P_n \rangle$. Functions in the corresponding type would be ones which, restricted to $T_{\bar{N}}$ behaved as the appropriate sort of PM_1's as already defined. The value of such a function f at a P_n denotation is given in (41) below, where f is assumed to be argument oriented for simplicity of presentation:

. (41) $f(p)$ is that element of $T_{P_{n+1}}$ such that for all individuals I_1, $I_2, \ldots, I_{n+1}$, $(f(p))(I_1) \ldots (I_{n+1}) = (f(I_1)(p))(I_2) \ldots (I_{n+1})$.

This definition guarantees for example that (42a, b) below are logically equivalent:

(42) a. John (slept (in the bed))
      b. John ((slept in) (the bed))

In (42b) the Prep *in* has combined with the P_1 *slept* to form a P_2 *slept in*.

Admittedly the motivation in English for assigning a structure like (42b) to *John slept in the bed* is not massive. But, as is well known (see Keenan and Faltz, 1978 for further discussion) some motivation does exist. Namely, while P_2's in English have passive forms, e.g. *was kissed* formed as the passive of the P_2 *kiss* (see the next section for an extensive discussion of passives), P_1's do not form passives in English, e.g. **was slept* from *sleep*. But (43) below appears to instantiate a passive form corresponding to the P_2 in (42b). Thus in order to generate (43) we are motivated to assign *sleep in* the category P_2.

(43)   The bed was slept in.

This completes our analysis of prepositions. Unless noted otherwise we only assume the PM analysis in the subsequent sections. We turn now to the treatment of Valency Affecting Operations, most specifically *Passives*.

4. VALENCY AFFECTING OPERATIONS

Languages present quite a variety of operations which derive predicates from predicates by modifying in some way their valency, that is, the number and arrangement of their arguments. In the last section for example we saw that some languages derive P_{n+1}'s from P_n's by adjoining a 'preposition' to the P_n. Another, even more common *valency increasing* operation is causative formation: many languages can form a P_2 translatable as *cause to cry* by affixing the P_1 which translates *cry*.

Equally languages may derive predicates from predicates by rearranging in various ways the argument structure of the predicate without increasing or decreasing the number of arguments. Arguably many Bantu languages for example can derive a P_3 which we might represent as *give-to* from a P_3 represented as *give*. The roughly stated semantic relation between the two predicates is given by: $(give\text{-}to)\ (x)\ (y)\ (z) = (give)\ (y)\ (x)\ (z)$. Some linguists in fact would argue that the relation between *give Mary the book* and *give the book* (*to*) *Mary* instantiates such an operation, although neither of the P_3's appears to be derived from the other in any morphological way.

Finally, languages present many valency decreasing operations. For example many languages (e.g. Uto–Aztecan) would derive the intransitive form of *sew* as in *John is sewing* from a transitive form, as in *John is sewing a shirt*. Again English shows no derivational morphology verb form in these cases. Another example: many languages derive reflexive and reciprocal P_1's (in the simplest cases) from P_2's by affixing the P_2's. E.g. we may form *self-hit* or *each other hit* from the P_2 *hit*.

It is a matter of considerable linguistic interest to characterize the possible valency affecting operations which natural languages may present. In this section we shall be principally concerned with one of these operations, Passive.

Passives

Our account of Passive is presented in three major parts. First, we present a generalized syntax and semantics for a Passive operator which derives P_n's from P_{n+1}'s. Second, we present a syntax and semantics for agent phrases (e.g. *by Mary* in *John was kissed by Mary*). These are generated as independently existing Predicate Modifiers in which a non-subject noun phrase semantically binds the subject argument. To our knowledge this treatment of agent phrases is novel and is the only one in the literature which explicitly treats agent phrases as 'semantic subjects' but not 'syntactic subjects'. Finally, we conclude with some curiosities regarding the logical nature of Passives and their relation to actually occurring passives in natural languages. This includes a generalization of the Passive operator to all the Predicative Hierarchies we have discussed so far.

A Generalized Passive Operator

In Keenan (1981), an extensive cross language study of passives, it is supported that the most widespread type of passive structure is that illustrated in (44b) below:

(44) a. John kissed Mary
      b. Mary was kissed
      c. Some individual kissed Mary

The meaning of (44b), at least up to logical equivalence, is given in (44c).

Clearly the main predicate of (44b) is a P_1 and, it would appear, equally clearly that that P_1 is a syntactic/morphological function of the P_2 *kiss*. We shall refer to the P_1 *was kissed* in (44b) as a *passive* predicate. Keenan (*op. cit.*) shows that the general form of such predicates across languages is given by (45) below:

(45) $\{(\text{Aux}), f(p_2)\}$:

Here p_2 is an expression of category P_2 and f is a strictly morphological function. That is, $f(p_2)$ differs from p_2 in strictly morphological ways — affixing or internal vowel change. Thus a passive P_1 may consist optionally, depending on the language, of an auxiliary verb together with a strict morphological function of a P_2. Let us refer to passives of the form in (45) as *canonical passives*. We shall first extend L to include canonical passives and then further extend L to include various non-canonical passives, specifically ones in which the predicate passivized is not a P_2 and ones in which an agent phrase is present.

DEFINITION 29. *Canonical Passives*

> a. *Syntax*: add the single symbol *pass* to the basic vocabulary V and assign it by lexical rule to the category P_1/P_2
> b. *Semantics*: $M\,(pass)$ is that function from T_{P_2} into T_{P_1} such that for all $p \in T_{P_2}$ and all individuals x, $M\,(pass)\,(p)\,(x) = (p\,(x))\,(\bigvee y)$, where y ranges over all individuals

Thus (44b) is represented in L as (46a) below, and its logical equivalence to (44c) is shown in (46b).

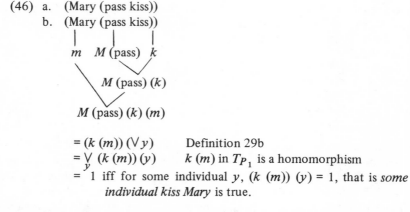

$$(46)\quad \text{a.}\quad (\text{Mary (pass kiss))}$$
$$\text{b.}\quad (\text{Mary (pass kiss))}$$

$$M\,(pass)\,(k)\,(m)$$

$$
\begin{aligned}
&= (k\,(m))\,(\bigvee y) &&\text{Definition 29b}\\
&= \bigvee_{y}\,(k\,(m))\,(y) &&k\,(m) \text{ in } T_{P_1} \text{ is a homomorphism}\\
&= 1 \text{ iff for some individual } y,\,(k\,(m))\,(y) = 1, \text{ that is } some\\
&\quad individual\ kiss\ Mary \text{ is true.}
\end{aligned}
$$

Note further that where j is the individual which interprets *John* we have immediately that $(k\,(m))\,(j) \leqslant \bigvee_{y}\,(k\,(m))\,(y)$ since $(k\,(m))\,(j)$ is one of the elements over which the join on the right is taken; more specifically, that join is an upper bound for a certain set, of which $(k\,(m))\,(j)$ is an element, and each element of the set is thus $\leqslant$ to that upper bound. Thus we have (for later reference):

THEOREM 19. (*John (kiss Mary)*) entails (*Mary (pass kiss)*)

Thus our representations for (44a) correctly entails that for (44b).

Before generalizing Definition 29 to a more adequate view of Passive we shall point out a few of its non-obvious features, ones which contrast favorably our treatment with certain other treatments in the linguistic literature. We consider specifically sentence level views of Passive and other predicate level views, referring the reader to Keenan (1980) for a more extended discussion of the contrast, especially as regards syntactic properties of passives.

Sentence Level Views

Many modern linguistic approaches to Passive have attempted to treat it as a relation between sentences (or clauses), not one between predicates as on our approach. For English, Passive would be the relation which held between (47a) and (47b) below, the latter being in various ways depending on the theory derived from the former:

(47)   a. $NP_1 \ V \ NP_2$
       b. NP_2 be V+en

We shall not examine these views in any detail, but do wish to point out that no sentence level derivational view of Passive can be made to satisfy the Fregean condition that the interpretation of the derived structure is given as a function of that from which it is derived. The reason is simple enough: basically there is no regular semantic relation between sentences of the form (47a, b). In particular sentences of form (47a) do not in general entail the corresponding sentence of form (47b). For example (48a) below not only fails to entail (48b), it is actually logically equivalent to its negation, as illustrated in (49).

(48)   a. No individual kissed Mary
       b. Mary was kissed

(49)   (no individual) (kiss Mary)

$$k \, (m) \, ((a') \, (1))$$

$= k \, (m) \, ((a \, (1)) \,')$	pointwise definition of $'$ in T_{Det}
$= (k \, (m) \, (a \, (1))) \,'$	$k \, (m)$ in T_{P_2} is a homomorphism
$= (k \, (m) \, (\bigcup_{y \ni 1} y)) \,'$	Definition of $M \, (a)$
$= (\text{pass} \, (k) \, (m)) \,'$	Definition 29 noting that all individuals y have 1
$= 1$ iff $(Mary \, (pass \, kiss))$ is false	

Note that in the above example we have represented the interpretation of logical constants c by the symbol c itself rather than M (c), a practice we shall continue.

Further since each of the sentences in (50) below can be true if (48a) is it follows that none of them entail the passive (48b).

(50) $\left\{\begin{array}{l}\text{No student}\\\text{At most two students}\\\text{Neither John nor Fred}\\\text{Fewer than three students}\\\text{No student's father}\end{array}\right\}$ kissed Mary

Clearly then active sentences do not in general entail their agentless passives, though of course some do as illustrated in Theorem 19. Furthermore the entailment failure cannot be localized to the decreasing character of the subject $\bar{N}$ of the active. For example the sentences in (51a) below, with a proper noun subject, fail to entail their corresponding passives in (51b).

(51) a. John kissed $\left\{\begin{array}{l}\text{exactly two students}\\\text{between five and ten students}\\\text{at most two students}\\\text{no student}\\\text{Mary but not Sue}\end{array}\right\}$

   b. $\left\{\begin{array}{l}\text{Exactly two students}\\\text{Between five and ten students}\\\text{At most two students}\\\text{No student}\\\text{Mary but not Sue}\end{array}\right\}$ were/was kissed

Nor would matters improve for the sentence level view of Passive if agentless passives were to be derived from corresponding actives whose subject was *some individual*. In the first place, if we replace *John* by *some individual* in (51a) the resulting active still does not in general entail the corresponding agentless passive in (51b). And in the second place, such actives would differ semantically from their passives with regard to judgments of relative scope as between the subject *some individual* and a quantified noun phrase object. Thus consider that (52a) below is most naturally interpreted as a paraphrase of (52b), though at least for some speakers it also has a less favored reading expressed in (52c). However the agentless passive in (52d) has only the less favored reading of (52c). It is not ambiguous. We exhibit its interpretation in (53).

(52) a. Some individual kissed every student
     b. For some individual x every student y is such that x kissed y
     c. Every student y is such that for some individual x, x kissed y
     d. Every student was kissed

(53)   (every student) (pass kiss)

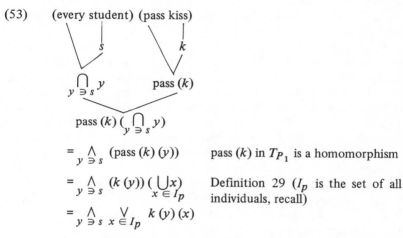

$$= \bigwedge_{y \ni s} (\text{pass } (k) \, (y)) \qquad \text{pass } (k) \text{ in } T_{P_1} \text{ is a homomorphism}$$

$$= \bigwedge_{y \ni s} (k \, (y)) \, (\bigcup_{x \in I_p} x) \qquad \text{Definition 29 } (I_p \text{ is the set of all individuals, recall})$$

$$= \bigwedge_{y \ni s} \bigvee_{x \in I_p} k \, (y) \, (x)$$

$= 1$ iff for every individual y with the student property there is an individual x such that x kiss y.

These examples show clearly that for given choices of NP_1 and NP_2 there is no regular entailment relation between (47a), $NP_1 \ V \ NP_2$, and its passive (47b), NP_2 be V+en. Whether such an entailment relation obtains depends in part, as we have shown, on how the NP's are interpreted.

In short, if we derive passive sentences from active ones we cannot give the interpretation of the derived structure as a function of the interpretation of the one it is derived from. This condition is of course satisfied if we derive passive predicates from active ones, as we have done in Definition 29. It appears then that the only regular semantic relation between actives and passives is the relation between their predicates. Given that relation, and the independently motivated semantics for quantified $\bar{N}$'s, the correct entailment relations between active and passive sentences are predicted.

In addition to satisfying the Fregean condition, predicate level views of Passive have other more specifically semantic advantages. Here we present just one. Namely, since *pass* is a function on P_2 denotations we may, in a more refined treatment than given in Definition 29, make its value depend on the semantic nature of the P_2 denotation it applies to. For example, in the intensional logic of Part II, P_n denotations are distinguished according as they are *transparent* on their arguments, and this semantic difference is preserved under Passive. That is, *pass* (p) must lie in the transparent P_1 denotations if p is a transparent P_2 denotation; but *pass* (p) is not so constrained if p is not a transparent P_2 denotation. See Part II for the definition of transparency.

Similarly we would like to distinguish among P_2 denotations ones which express an activity which affects their argument and ones which do not have that property. Call the former *activity* P_2 denotations. If p is an activity P_2 denotation then *pass* (p) is given as in Definition 29. But if p is not an activity P_2 denotation, it appears that we should require stronger truth conditions for *pass* (p) (x). Thinking of p as a denotation of, say, *respect*, or *admire*, or even *hate*, for *John was respected* to be true we want to require something like 'Most individuals who know John respect him', and not merely that some individual respected him. Though we don't know how to state precisely these truth conditions, nor do we attempt to represent in L the difference between activity and non-activity predicates, the point that the Passive operator behaves differently according to the semantic properties of its argument seems valid.

Predicate Level Views

Several recent treatments of Passive, notably Bach (1980), Bresnan (1978), Dowty (1978) and Thomason (1976) broadly agree with the treatment of canonical passives in Definition 29 though they differ in formalism. (Our treatment differs in more serious ways from theirs with regard to the treatment of agent phrases and the generalization of Passive to P_n's as well as to nominals.) Some of these treatments however (Dowty's and Bresnan's) would syntactically limit the P_2's which could form passives to lexical ones (elements of the basic vocabulary V in our notation).

This limitation cannot be motivated semantically, whatever its syntactic merits. We cannot tell by looking at an element of T_{P_n} whether it is the interpretation of a lexical or a syntactically complex expression. Obviously in some state of affairs it is possible that x is hugging y iff x is both hugging and kissing y, so in that state *hug* and *hug and kiss* would be interpreted as the same element of T_{P_2}. More generally it seems that we want to constraint the lexical interpreting function so that certain complex P_n's are always interpreted as (approximately) the same as certain lexical ones, e.g. *hop* and *jump up and down on one foot*, *brew* and *make beer*, *rewrite* and *write again*, *decapitate* and *remove the head of*, etc.

Furthermore there are many cases where we want *pass* to apply to complex P_2's since otherwise we obtain incorrect semantic interpretations. Consider for example P_2's consisting of a P_2 and a subject oriented PM (Predicate Modifier). The clearest example which we can represent in L is that of agentive *by* phrases which we treat in the next subsection. Another clear case which can be treated in the intensional logic is that of instrumental PM's, italicized in (54) below.

(54) a. John opened the can *with a stick*
      b. John tickled Bobby *with a feather*
      c. John whittled *with a knife*

The sentences in (54) entail, and are perhaps logically equivalent to, the corresponding ones in (55).

(55) a. John used a stick to open the can
      b. John used a feather to tickle Bobby
      c. John used a knife to whittle

To guarantee these entailment we want to constrain the interpretation of instrumental *with* and *use*. One approach would only put instrumental PM's in the category P_1/P_1, so *with* would be of category $(P_1/P_1)/\bar{N}$. Then we could (informally) constrain the lexical interpreting function M as follows:

(56)   For all individuals x and y and all $p \in T_{P_1}$,
        $M\,(with)\,(x)\,(p)\,(y) \leqslant M\,(use)\,(x)\,(to\ p)\,(y)$

(see Part II for the interpretation of *to p* as the individual generated by p.) This approach however leads to wrong predictions concerning passives. Thus the passive in (57a) would have to be analyzed as in (57b), wrongly predicting the entailment (57c).

(57) a. The can was opened with a stick

b.

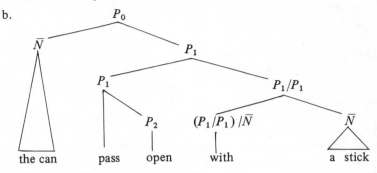

c. The can used a stick to be opened

A correct approach here is achieved if we let *with* combine with $\bar{N}$'s to form subject oriented PM's and constrain its interpretation as follows:

(58)   For all individuals $x, y_1, \ldots, y_n$ and all $p \in T_{P_n}$,
$$M \; (with) \; (x) \; (p) \; (y_1) \; \ldots \; (y_n) \leqslant M \; (use) \; (x) \; (to \; p) \; (y_1) \; \ldots \; (y_n)$$

Since *with a stick* may now combine with P_2's to form P_2's we may represent (57a) in L by (59a) below in which the complex P_2 *open with a stick* is under the scope of *pass*. From Definition 29 then (59a) will be equivalent to our representation for (59b) which essentially by (58) above will entail (59c).

(59) a. (the can) (pass (open with a stick))
      b. For some individual y, (open with a stick) (the can) $(y) = 1$
      c. For some individual y, y use a stick to open the can

Thus a correct interpretation of the *can was opened with a stick* is obtained if we allow *pass* to operate on syntactically complex P_2's such as *open with a stick*.

A similar argument can be given for source locatives. Recall from our first treatment of PM's that source locatives predicate of the subject argument of perception P_n's. Thus each of (60a, b) below entails (60c).

(60) a. John gazed from the mountain top
      b. John watched Mary from the mountain top
      c. John was on the mountain top

Assuming we could distinguish perception elements of T_{P_n} from others we could then constrain M such that M (*from*) lay in $T_{\text{Prep}}^{\text{subj}}$ and satisfied (61) below:

(61)   For all individuals $x, y_1, \ldots, y_n$ and all $p \in T_{P_n}^{+ \text{ perception}}$,

M (*from*) (x) (p) $(y_1) \ldots (y_n) = p$ (y_1) $(\ldots (y_n)) \wedge$
M (*at*) (x) (1) (y_n)

This would guarantee then that *John saw Mary from the house* entailed that *John was at the house*. Then the passive in (62a) below can be generated as in (62b), correctly entailing that some individual who saw Mary was at the house, as per (62c)

(62)   a. Mary was seen from the house
       b. (Mary (pass (see from the house)))

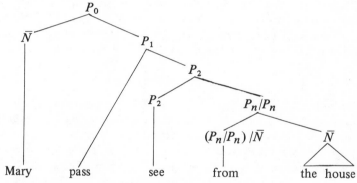

       c. M ((Mary (pass (see from the house)))) = 1 iff
          for some individual y, M ((see from the house) (Mary)) $(y) = 1$
          iff for some y, M (see Mary) $(y) \wedge M$ ((at (the house)) (exist)) (y)
          = 1

Once again then allowing complex P_2's such as *see from the house* be under the scope of *pass* permits us to represent a correct entailment. Conversely, if source locatives could only apply to P_1's then (62a) would have to be generated as (63a) below, which would incorrectly entail (63b).

(63)   a. (Mary ((pass see) (from the house)))
       b. Mary was seen and Mary was at the house

In fairness we should note that the prima facie motivation for treating Passive as purely lexical is that the distinctive passive morphology in English only shows up on the verb, not elsewhere in complex P_2's. (Such morphology does appear to show up elsewhere in both Turkish and Malagasy passives however. See Keenan (1980) for examples.) Moreover our syntactic analysis of passives as (pass e), for $e \in P_2$, does not explicitly assign any morphology to e. For us then, that morphology assignment rule would have to be stated so as to apply to syntactically complex e's. This in fact is unproblematic. We give an appropriate definition below, assuming that past participle forms of lexical P_2's are simply listed.

DEFINITION 30. (pass e) = be + en (e), where en (e) =

    (a)   the past participle of e if e is in V (i.e. lexical)
    (b)   (en (e_1), c, en (e_2)) if $e = (e_1, c, e_2)$ for $c \in \{and, or\}$
    (c)   (en (e_1), g) if $e = (e_1, g)$ for $g \in \text{PM} \cup \{not\}$.

Thus en (see from the house) = (en (see), (from the house)) by clause (c) above, which equals (seen, from the house) by clause (a). Essentially then the past participle forms of complex P_2's is given recursively as a function of what they are formed from; that for lexical P_2's is given ad hocly.

Generalizing Passive

Definition 29 is insufficiently general in several respects. For example in many languages, such as Latin, Turkish, Shona, etc. we may derive P_0's (sentences) from P_1's using the same verbal morphology as used to derive passive P_1's from P_2's. Thus from the P_2 *amat* 'love (3rd person singular)' we form *amatur* '(3sg) is loved' in the same way as from the P_1 *currit* '(3sg) runs' we form the P_0 *curritur* 'running is being done'. The obvious generalization here is that *pass* should be allowed to combine with P_{n+1}'s to form P_n's for all values of n. Thus:

DEFINITION 31. *Generalized Passive*

    a. *Syntax*: *pass* is assigned by lexical rule to the category $\langle P_n/P_{n+1} \rangle$, the category of expressions which combine with P_{n+1}'s to form P_n's, all $n \geqslant 0$;
    b. *Semantics*: M (*pass*) is that function from $\bigcup_{n \geqslant 0} T_{P_{n+1}}$ into $\bigcup_{n \geqslant 0} T_{P_n}$ such that for all $n \geqslant 0$. all $p \in T_{P_{n+1}}$, and all individuals $x_1, x_2, \ldots, x_n$,
$$M \text{ (pass) } (p) (x_1) \ldots (x_n) = p (x_n) (x_1) \ldots (x_{n-1}) (\bigcup_{y \in I_p} y).$$

From Definition 31 we may generate Latin *curritur* as in (64a) with the semantics indicated in (64b).

(64) a.

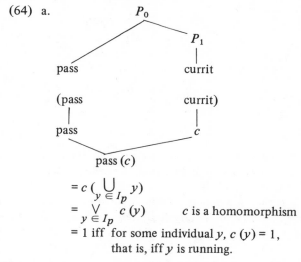

$$= c \left(\bigcup_{y \in I_p} y \right)$$
$$= \bigvee_{y \in I_p} c(y) \qquad c \text{ is a homomorphism}$$
$$= 1 \text{ iff for some individual } y, c(y) = 1,$$
$$\text{that is, iff } y \text{ is running.}$$

The existence of subjectless passives like (63a), traditionally called *impersonal*, provides further evidence for not restricting *pass* to lexical P_n's. It is completely natural for example to combine *currit* 'runs' with a PM such as *in the garden* and (impersonally) passivize the resulting complex P_1 yielding a P_0 meaning roughly *running in the garden is being done*.

A more interesting case for our purposes concerns impersonal passives formed from P_2's in combination with a $\bar{N}$. Such complex P_1's are naturally formed in Latin in cases where the P_2 (somewhat) exceptionally takes its argument in the dative rather than the accusative case. Compare:

(65) a.

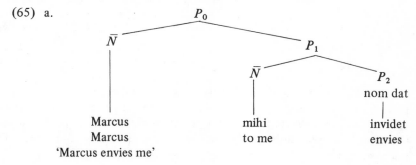

b.

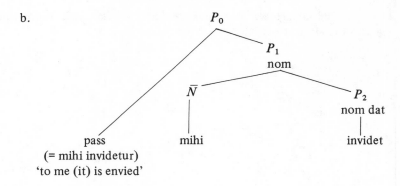

(= mihi invidetur)
'to me (it) is envied'

We have used here the case marking notation developed earlier. Note that the structure of (65b) is essentially that of (64a), *curritur*, except that the P_1 passivized is syntactically complex.

Of further interest is that dative object taking P_2's in Latin such as *envy, persuade, obey*, etc. also allow, in literary Latin (Horace) personal passives. Thus we may form (66a) below (where the subject pronoun would normally be omitted), generated in our grammar straightforwardly as in (66b).

(66) a. (Ego)   invideor
         1sg   am envied (1sg)
         nom
         'I am envied'

b.

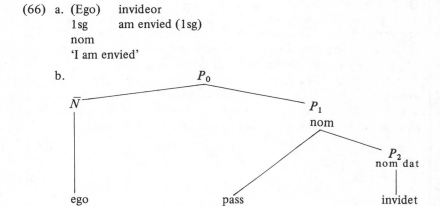

Note that both sentence level and (lexical) predicate level treatments of Passive have difficulty generating both of (65a) and (66a) since it would appear that we need to derive two structures from a single one. On our approach however both passives are naturally generated and uniformly interpreted.

Passives on P_3's in many languages (and perhaps even English) provide additional motivation for generalizing Passive as we have done. In languages like Malagasy and Kinyarwanda either non-subject argument of a P_3 may be the subject of a corresponding passive, using the same verbal morphology in both cases. Thus we can say, as we can in English in a restricted class of cases, either *Mary was given the book* or *The book was given (to) Mary*. Using English structures these two passives could be generated as in (67b, c), where (67a) gives the active for comparison.

(67) a.

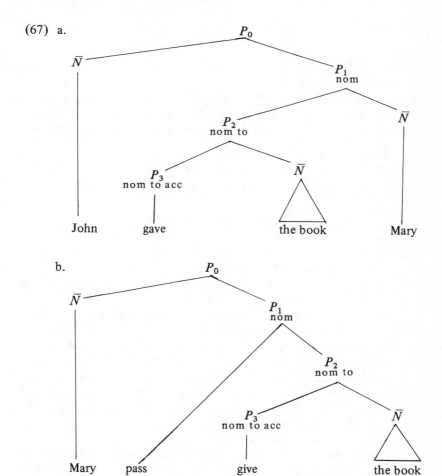

c.

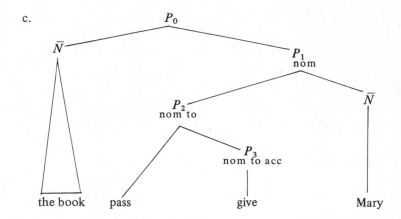

Note that in (67b) it is the P_2 *give the book* which is passivized and thus has no argument. In (67c) it is the P_3 *give* which is passivized and thus has no argument; the P_2 (*pass give*) does have an argument, marked with *to*.

Agent Phrases

By agent phrases we mean expressions like *by Mary* in (68).

(68)   John was was kissed by Mary

Traditionally we say of such sentences that *John* is the syntactic subject but not the semantic subject, whereas *Mary* is the semantic subject but not the syntactic subject. It is this intuition that we embody explicitly in our treatment of agent phrases.

First, just what sort of a non-subject is *Mary* in (68)? Clearly it forms a constituent with *by* which independently exists as a preposition in English (*He sent it by air mail, sat down by the window*, etc.). Superficially then *by Mary* appears to be a 'prepositional phrase', that is, a Predicate Modifier in our terminology. Moreover this similarity is quite general. As Keenan (1980) supports, commonly across languages agent phrases are presented like independently existing adverbials or oblique case noun phrases. Most commonly they resemble instrumentals, locatives, or genitives. Formally then we shall treat agent phrases as PM's.

Additional support for this treatment is that agent phrase are sometimes construed overtly as adverbials rather than as Prep + $\bar{N}$ combinations. Thus

(69a, b) are paraphrases showing that *universally* is understood synonymously with *by everyone*.

(69) a. The proposal was rejected by everyone
      b. The proposal was universally rejected

Semantically, how can we say that *by Mary* determines the 'semantic subject' in (68)? Note first that it is the 'semantic subject' of *kiss*, not of *was kissed*. Since *by Mary* predicates something (identity with Mary) of the subject argument of the denotation of *kiss* it appears that we want to treat *by Mary* semantically as a subject oriented PM, and *by* as a subject oriented preposition (PM_1). Thus we want $M(by)$, the interpretation of *by*, to satisfy (70) below, as per Definition 26:

(70)   For all individuals $x, y_1, \ldots, y_n$ and all $p \in T_{P_n}$,
        $M(by)(x)(p)(y_1) \ldots (y_n) = p(y_1) \ldots (y_n) \wedge$
        $M(by)(x)(1)(y_n)$

To define $M(by)$ the following is sufficient:

DEFINITION 32. $M(by)$ is that element of T_{Prep} such that for all individuals x, $M(by)(x)(1_{P_1}) = M(be)(x)$.   subj

It follows then that $M(by)(x)(1_{P_1})$ holds of an individual y iff $y = x$, and we shall normally write $y = x$ instead of $M(by)(x)(1)(y)$. In informal terms, Definition 32 guarantees that (71a, b) are logically equivalent, as are (72a,b).

(71) a. (John (run by Bill)
      b. (John run) and (John=Bill)

(72) a. (John ((kiss (by Bill)) Susan))
      b. (John kiss Susan) and (John=Bill)

Since (72b) obviously entails (*Bill* (*kiss Susan*)) our semantics for agent phrases correctly tells us that the agent $\bar{N}$ is interpreted as the subject argument of the interpretation of *kiss*. Moreover it clearly is not the subject argument syntactically of *kiss*, since it occurs as part of a Predicate Modifier of *kiss*.

Of course (72a) and (71a) seem bizarre considered as expressions of English since they present too many $\bar{N}$'s. There are only two participants in the action expressed in (72a) but there are three independently referring $\bar{N}$'s. But this just says that some expressions in L are not representations for any expression in English, something which we actually want in general (since for example we want to provide semantic representations for say relative clauses in English which violate syntactic constraints in English like the Complex NP Constraint, etc.). We return to this matter shortly, but first we want to show that we do correctly represent English passives with agent phrases. Given our analysis of *by* we may now represent English (73a) below by (73b) with the semantic analysis in (73c).

(73) a. John was kissed by Mary

b.

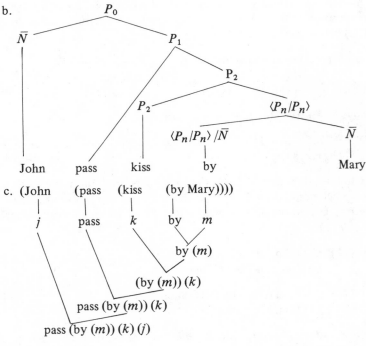

c. (John (pass (kiss (by Mary))))

$$= (\text{by } (m)) \ (k) \ (j) \ (\lor y)$$
$$= \bigvee_{y} (\text{by } (m)) \ (k) \ (j) \ (y)$$
$$= \bigvee_{y} (k \ (j) \ (y)) \land m = y$$
$$= \bigvee_{y} (k \ (j) \ (m))$$
$$= k \ (j) \ (m)$$
$$= 1 \text{ iff } (\text{Mary } (\text{kiss John})) \text{ is true}$$

Definition of M (*pass*)
(by (m)) (k) (j) in T_{p_1} is a homomorphism
Definition of M (*by*)

Substitute = for =

vacuous quantification

Thus *John was kissed by Mary* and *Mary kissed John* are logically equivalent, as desired. As further support for the empirical adequacy of our treatment we invite the reader to show that the sentences in (74) below are all logically equivalent.

(74) a. Some individual kissed John
    b. John was kissed
    c. John was kissed by some individual

Similarly the passives of P_1's with agent phrases in Latin yields essentially correct results on our analysis. That is, (75a, b) are provably logically equivalent.

(75) a. (pass (run (by John)))
    b. (John run)

Returning now to the curious excess of $\bar{N}$'s in (72), notice that we can generate sentences with 'too many' $\bar{N}$'s precisely because we introduce a semantic argument of a P_n as part of a predicate modifier and thus the resultant structure may still take a syntactic argument. Were we to derive agented passive sentences from active ones by (roughly) interchanging noun phrases and adding a *by* as part of the transformation this possibility would not arise. But this option is both syntactically and semantically misguided.

Syntactically, it would fail to account for the general fact that agent phrases are in surface presented as PM's, as previously discussed. It would also fail to account for the fact that agent phrases may occur in non-passive structures. For example, in the various nominalizations of P_1's below we clearly have agent phrases, i.e. semantic but not syntactic subjects of the nominalized predicates, but those phrases cannot have been introduced by a passive rule since P_1's don't passivize in English.

(76) a. Talking by students during examinations is forbidden
    b. The strike by the farm workers was successful

On our approach, though we do not provide a semantics for nominalized P_n's, such nominals as (76a) could be represented by a nominalizer *ing* deriving nominals from P_1's. It could of course, like *pass*, take complex P_1's as arguments. Thus the subject phrase of (76a) could be analyzed as *ing* (*talk by students during examinations*).

And semantically, deriving agented passive sentences from active ones still fails the Fregean condition, there being no regular entailment relation between actives and the corresponding agented passives. For example (77a) below does not entail (77b).

(77) a. No politician kissed every baby
      b. Every baby was kissed by no politician

Replacing *no* above by other determiners like *fewer than three, at most three*, etc. preserves the lack of entailment. Thus actives do not in general entail their agented passives. The converse holds as well, since (78a) fails to entail (78b).

(78) a. Fewer than three babies were kissed by every politician
      b. Every politician kissed fewer than three babies

Thus, from the examples above we see that we don't want to derive agented passives from actives and we do want to generate agent phrases independently of passive constructions.

Further there might be some additional motivation for independently generating agent phrases in non-passive structures as follows: observe that the *L* sentences in (79) below are logically equivalent.

(79) a. (John (walk (by John)))
      b. (John walk) and (John (be John))
      c. (John walk)

We might want to consider that (79a) is our representation in *L* for *John walks by himself* (see the section on Variable Binding Operators for an exact statement of reflexives in *L*). This would mean that *John walks by himself* and *John walks* would be logically equivalent on our representations. On the one hand that may seem incorrect since the former sentence seems to imply something like *John walks without help* whereas *John walks* at least does not so clearly imply that. Our judgments of entailment here are a little fuzzy however and we might want to impute the inference not to logical entailment but rather to some more pragmatically based interpretation of the sentence. The basis of the pragmatic inference would be that sentences which are logically redundant, as (79a) is since (see (79b)) part of its truth conditions involve the logically true statement that *John is John*, get interpreted in a more emphatic way than non-redundant ones. Perhaps then it is the 'logical' focussing of attention on John in (79a) which is responsible for the inference that John performs the action unaided. Thus, if our pragmatic analysis could be made explicit we might after all find a use for L sentences with two $\bar{N}$'s referring to the subject argument of the predicate.

Finally, let us observe that *by* phrases in English are perhaps not the only sorts of non-subject expressions which function to specify the subject argument of a predicate. For example, (80a, b) below are approximately paraphrases.

(80) a. They worship Gandhi in India
b. Inhabitants of India worship Gandhi

It seems that the PM *in India* in (80a) in effect determines the semantic argument of *worship Ghandi*. Somewhat similarly note that (81a, b) are paraphrases:

(81) a. That Fred left was strange
b. It was strange that Fred left

It appears here that the non-subject expression *that Fred left* in (80b) specifies the semantic subject of that sentence, its syntactic subject being *it*.

Extending Passive to Nominals and Other Predicative Hierarchies

Nominals

Chomsky (1970) suggests that we might want to extend the domain of Passive in order to represent the relation between *the enemy's destruction of the city* and *the city's destruction by the enemy*. We do not represent in L non-count nominals like *destruction* but we have represented nominalizations such as *swimmer, employer*, etc. and there is a natural algebraic generalization of *pass* nominalizations of the latter sort, one which, perhaps surprisingly, has a natural, if somewhat limited, linguistic expression in English. To illustrate the generalization let us note some further (somewhat curious) facts regarding passives.

THEOREM 20. For all $p \in T_{P_n}$, $n \geqslant 0$, there is a $g \in T_{P_{n+1}}$ such that $pass(g) = p$.

Proof. Let n, p arbitrary as above and define g_p in T_{Pn+1} by: $g_p\,(x_1)\ldots$ $(x_{n+1}) = p\,(x_2)\ldots(x_n)\,(x_1)$, all individuals $x_1\ldots x_{n+1}$. Then, $pass\,(g_p)\,(z_1)\ldots(z_n) = g_p\,(z_n)\,(z_1)\ldots(z_{n-1})\,(\bigvee y)$ by Definition 31,

$$= \bigvee_y g_p\,(z_n)\,(z_1)\ldots(z_{n-1})\,(y) \qquad g_p\,(z_1)\ldots(z_{n-1}) \text{ is a homomorphism}$$

$$= \bigvee_y p\,(z_1)\ldots(z_n) \qquad\qquad\qquad \text{Definition of } g_p$$

$$= p\,(z_1)\ldots(z_n) \qquad\qquad\qquad\quad \text{vacuous quantification}$$

whence by the Justification Theorem *pass* $(g_p) = p$.

Thus we may infer that *pass* restricted to T_{Pn+1} is a function *onto* T_{Pn}.

Theorem 20 is somewhat curious from the point of view of ordinary English. It says that, semantically, any element of T_{Pn} is the passive of an element of T_{Pn+1}.

Can we, for example, find a P_2 whose passive is, in effect, the P_1 *exist*? Here the answer is yes: *be* is such. Using *be* and *exist* to represent their interpretations, we note:

THEOREM 21. For all interpretation m of L, m (*pass, be*) = m (*exist*) and m (*pass, exist*) = 1 (true)

    Proof.

   (a)   for all individuals x,

$$pass\,(be)\,(x) = (be\,(x))\,(\bigcup_{y\,\in\,I_p} y) \qquad \text{Definition 31}$$

$$= \bigvee_{y\,\in\,I_p} (be\,(x))\,(y) \qquad be\,(x) \text{ is a homomorphism}$$

$$= (be\,(x))\,(x) \vee (\text{other terms}) \qquad x \text{ is one of the individuals over which the join is taken}$$

$$= 1 \qquad\qquad \text{Definition of } M\,(be)$$

$$= (exist)\,(x) \qquad \text{Definition of } M\,(exist)$$

          So *pass* (*be*) and *exist* hold of the same individuals and thus are the same elements of T_{P_1}.

   (b) $pass\,(exist) = exist\,(\bigcup_{y\,\in\,I_p} y)$ Definition 31

$$= \bigvee_{y\,\in\,I_p} exist\,(y) \qquad exist \text{ is a homomorphism}$$

$$= 1 \qquad\qquad \text{Definition } M(exist) \text{ and } I_p \neq \emptyset$$

So *truth* is the passive of *to exist* (and *false* the passive of *not exist*). Curious.

In general however it seems that English does not present the means to construct from an $e \in P_n$ an expression $d \in P_{n+1}$ such that (pass d) and e are interpreted identically. Moreover, L as so far developed also seems to be expressively deficient in this way (though the reader may check that for $e \in P_1$, (pass (e by)) and e and interpreted identically; note our assumed use of by as a verbal extensor here). Once the lambda operator, λ, is added to L (see the section on Variable Binding Operators) this deficiency is remedied however. Thus the reader may check in that section that kiss is interpreted the same as (pass λ y x z ((x (kiss y)) and (x (be z)))).

To continue our generalization of Passive to nominals, recall from Theorem 17 that $T_{P_{n+1}}$ is isomorphic to T_{N_n}, all $n \geqslant 0$, and that that isomorphism is at least partially expressible in English by -er. Thus, mixing levels, swimmer is the isomorphic image of swim, employer of employ, etc. For reference let us give an explicit definition of the interpretation of er:

DEFINITION 33. $M(er)$ is that function from $\bigcup_{n \geqslant 0} T_{P_{n+1}}$ into $\bigcup_{n \geqslant 0} T_{N_n}$ such that for all individuals $x_1, \ldots, x_n$, and I, and all $h \in T_{P_{n+1}}$,

$$M(er)(h)(x_1) \ldots (x_n) \in I \quad \text{iff} \quad h(x_1) \ldots (x_n)(I) = 1$$

So for example employer is interpreted as that element of T_{N_1} such that for all individuals x and I, (employer (of) x) is a property I has iff (employ x) holds of I.

Now, to define pass on T_{N_n} consider the following diagram which in effect defines a passive relation between elements of T_{N_n} and $T_{N_{n-1}}$ ($n \geqslant 1$).

(82)

$$
\begin{array}{ccc}
T_{P_{n+1}} & \xrightarrow{\;\;er\;\;} & T_{N_n} \\
\Big\downarrow pass & & \Big\downarrow pass \\
T_{P_n} & \xrightarrow{\;\;er\;\;} & T_{N_{n-1}}
\end{array}
$$

Thus to find the passive of an element of T_{N_n} first find the element of $T_{P_{n+1}}$ it is the isomorphic image of, take its passive, and then find the isomorphic image of that in T_{N_n}. Formally,

DEFINITION 34. For $n \geqslant 1$, $d \in T_{N_n}$, pass $(d) = er(pass(er^{-1}(d)))$

To consider a special case, suppose that $h \in T_{P_2}$. Then $er(h) \in T_{N_1}$, and by Definition 34 we have that pass $(er(h)) = er(pass(er^{-1}(er(h))))$ which is just er ($pass$ (h)) by the definition of an inverse (er^{-1}) of an isomorphism. Thus we have that $pass$ ($employer$) is er ($pass$ ($employ$)), which from Definition 33 will denote the property an individual I has iff $pass$ ($employ$) (I) = 1; that is, just in case I is employed. But this property is just the one denoted in English by $employee$. Thus we may think of $employee$ as the passive of $employer$, $advisee$ of $advisor$, etc. Note that the active/passive -er/-ee morphology can be used productively in English: *It was the killee not the killer who broke the vase, the kissee and not the kisser who had bad breath*, etc. Though these examples are somewhat strained they are good enough we feel to show that items like $employee$ are not simply independent lexical items idiosyncratically related to -er forms. We might note as well that the passive nature of -ee forms is in accordance with the etymology of -ee. The ending is borrowed from French where it functions as the distinctive morphology on passives: *Marie est employée = Mary is employed*.

We have been arguing that in a certain reasonable sense $employee$ is the passive of $employer$. But would we really want to enter -ee in L in the category $\langle N_n/N_{n+1}\rangle$ and interpret it as $pass$ restricted to the Predicative Hierarchy generated by N_0 (= N)? The answer is no. Morphologically -ee actually combines with P_2's to form N's (i.e. N_0's). The interpretation of -ee is given by:

DEFINITION 35. M (-ee) is that function from $T_{P_{n+1}}$ into $T_{N_{n-1}}$ such that M (-ee) (p) = er ($pass$ (p)), all $p \in T_{P_{n+1}}$.

The active/passive distinction in nominals then is derivative. Whenever we have an expression $d \in P_2$ for example which forms an N_1 with the -er suffix and an N_0 with the -ee suffix the resulting forms will bear the active/passive relation. But, at least for the class of nominals considered in L, we do not appear to have a way of directly passivizing N_1's to form N_0's. Thus lexically simple N_1's such as *friend* (*of*), *colleague* (*of*) etc. do not form passive N_0's. These facts should not however detract from the fact that diagram (82) did lead us to notice an active/passive distinction among nominals, albeit a derived one. We may further query whether other of the isomorphisms among the Predicative Hierarchies we have defined also determine such a distinction.

Passive Adjectives?

Recall that intersecting AP's denoted functions f from T_N into T_N such that for all $p \in T_N$, $f(p) = p \wedge f(1)$, where 1 here is the unit element in T_N, the denotation of *existent* (or *individual*). We saw (Theorem 4) that T_N was isomorphic to $T_{\underset{i}{AP}}$, whence $T_{\underset{i}{AP}}$ is isomorphic to T_{P_1}. (The function h from T_{P_1} into $T_{\underset{i}{AP}}$ such that for all g in T_{P_1}, $h(g)$ is that element of $T_{\underset{i}{AP}}$ such that $h(g)\,(1)$ is an element of an individual I iff $g(I) = 1$ is easily shown to be an isomorphism.) Moreover setting $\underset{i}{AP}_0$ equal to $\underset{i}{AP}$ and $\underset{i}{AP}_{n+1}$ to $\underset{i}{AP}_n/\overline{N}$ we have that the function h above generalizes to an isomorphism from $T_{P_{n+1}}$ onto $T_{\underset{i}{AP}_n}$ by setting $h(g)\,(x_1)\ldots(x_n)\,(1) \in I$ iff $g(x_1)\ldots(x_n)\,(I) = 1$. We may therefore extend *pass* to combine with $\underset{i}{AP}_n$'s yielding $\underset{i}{AP}_{n-1}$'s and define its interpretation as that function which makes the diagram below commute:

(83)
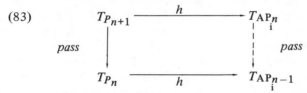

But is there any way in English (or L) to form the passive of say a one place AP? Recall that among the AP_1's (we drop the subcategorization feature i since we are only considering intersecting AP's here) we have expressions like *proud (of)*, *envious (of)*, *jealous (of)*, *respectful (of)*, etc. Note that these expressions do seem naturally interpreted by intersecting AP_1's. This will say for example that an individual has the *student proud of Billy* property iff he has the *student* property and the *individual proud of Billy* property, which seems basically correct.

Formally we define:

DEFINITION 36. For $d \in T_{\underset{i}{AP}_n}$, *pass* $(d) = h\,(pass\,(h^{-1}\,(d)))$

To find the passive of *proud of* we note first (mixing levels of notation) that h^{-1} (*proud of*) = *is proud of*. The passive of that is that P_1 which holds of an individual x iff for some y, y *is proud of* x. So we are looking for an AP_0 whose value at the *existent* property is an element of an individual I iff someone is proud of I. Once we introduce relative clauses into L (see the section on Variable Binding Operators) we can easily concoct such an AP_0. It is simply *who someone is proud of*. But there does not appear to exist in English any unitary syntactic operation on AP_1's which yields AP_0's interpreted as their passives.

The situation is so far reminiscent of the absence of direct passives relating N_1's to N_0's. So we might wonder whether there is here an analogue of -ee and -er where -ee (d) was interpreted as the passive of -er (d), for d a P_2. A near analogue of -ee would appear to be the past participle function -en. This function would derive *beaten* from *beat, kissed* from *kiss*, and it very roughly appears that a woman kissed is a woman and an individual who someone kissed. So we might plausibly regard *beaten, kissed*, etc. as passive AP_0's. But we find no plausible AP_1's of which they are the passives. That is, we appear to lack the analogue of -er which would send us from P_2 to AP_1.

One possible, if forced, candidate here is -ing. It does at least approximate to the isomorphism from P_1's to AP_0's. That is, a laughing child is a child and an individual who is laughing. We might consider that it also applies to P_2's, so that *kissing* would be a derived AP_1, combining with an unmarked $\bar{N}$ to form an AP_0 such as *kissing Bill* as it occurs in *the woman kissing Bill is drunk*. But it doesn't seem correct to regard *kissed* as the passive of *kissing*. Using -ing for h in Definition 36 for example we have that pass (ing (kiss)) = ing (pass (ing^{-1} (ing (kiss)))) which is just ing (pass (kiss)), which in turn is expressed in English by *being kissed*. So if we accept *kissing* as an AP_1 we do have a natural passive, *being kissed*, but this hardly seems interesting. For now we have only two operators, *ing* which takes us from P_{n+1}'s to AP_n's and *pass* which takes us from P_{n+1}'s to P_n's. But we have no English operator expressing *pass* which takes us from AP_n's to AP_{n-1}'s, nor do we even have the partial operator analogous to -ee which takes us from P_{n+1}'s to AP_{n-1}'s.

Rejecting *kissing* as the active AP_1 form of *kissed* then we appear to have no regular active/passive alternation within AP's even of a derived sort. There appear only to be a handful of idiosyncratic cases where we can derive an AP_1 from a P_2 in such a way that the -er form of the P_2 behaves like its passive. For example, arguably from the P_2 *envy* we can derive the AP_1 *envious of* and its passive AP_0 *envied*. Perhaps *respectful of* and *respected* from *respect* is another case.

Passive Prepositions??

The case here seems hopeless and is at most only interesting as a way of illustrating some expressive limitations of English. Recalling from Theorem 18 that $T_{P_{n+1}}$ is isomorphic to $T_{PM_n^{arg}}$ we may construct diagrams analogous to (82) and (83) and extend *pass* to derive PM_{n-1}'s from PM_n's interpreting that operator as the one which makes the diagram commute. But what in the world would the passive of say *under* mean? Simplifying slightly we may compute its passive as follows: the P_2 it corresponds to under the isomorphism is roughly *be under*. Its passive then holds of x iff for some y, y is under x. The corresponding PM_0 — call it *undered* for the nonce — would send a P_1 h to a P_1 *undered* (h) which held of x iff h (x) was true and for some y, y was under x. Thus *John sang undered* would mean *John sang* and *some individual was under John*.

Unfortunately there seems no regular, or even irregular, way of forming the passive of *under*. Perhaps the best idiosyncratic case we can think of (and it's pretty bad) is with converse prepositions such as *in front of* and *behind*. (x is in front of y iff y is behind x.) Now let us suppose (this is the dubious part) that *John sat in front (behind)* means that John sat and John was in front of (behind) someone. So *in front* and *behind* would be PM_0's, and *in front of* and *behind* would be PM_1's. Then *in front* would be the passive of *behind* (considered as a PM_1) since *John sat in front = John sat and John was in front of someone = John sat and someone was behind John*. Perhaps as well we might consider *Eastwards* a lexical passive of the PM_1 *to the West of*. However these examples are not fully accurate, but perhaps they suggest that the existence of passives of prepositions is not wholly implausible.

5. EXTENDING AND SUBCATEGORIZING THE CLASS OF DETERMINERS

In our earlier treatment of Determiners (= $\bar{N}/N$, abbreviated *Det*) we claimed (Theorem 14, Part A) that T_{Det} was just the set of conservative functions from P (= T_N) into P^* (= $T_{\bar{N}}$), where $f \in F_{P^*/P}$ is *conservative* iff for all p, $q \in P$, $p \in f$ (q) iff $(p \wedge q) \in f$ (q). But so far we have provided only four logically distinct elements of Det: *every, a, the,* and *no*. One of our tasks in this section is to significantly increase the set of expressions of category Det. Our additions will include first a variety of 'numerical' Dets such as *at least six, more than six, at most six, fewer than six, between six and ten, exactly six, infinitely many, half (of) the, the six,* and *all but six*. These expressions, like those currently in Det, will be logical constants in the sense of satisfying (84) below:

(84) For e an expression of category C, if e is a logical constant then for all ontologies $\langle P, 2 \rangle$ and all interpretations m_1, m_2 of L, m_1 $(e) = m_2$ (e)

Among these logical constants we semantically distinguish a subset which are *cardinality dependent*. That is, we define a property of functions from P into P^* and show that denotations of *at least six, exactly six*, etc. have that property while the denotations of *every, all but six*, etc. do not.

Somewhat more deeply, we add elements to Det such as *John's, no student's*, etc. as they occur in *John's house*, etc. These expressions are not logical constants — they fail (84). Moreover, we find a property of functions from P into P^* which defines the set of possible denotations of logical constants among Det. That is, we have found a *semantic* property of Dets which distinguishes 'logical' ones from 'non-logical' ones. This allows us to provide a novel analysis of certain 'vague' yet 'logical' Dets such as *several* and *a few*. It also provides the basis of some further language universals concerning Det interpretations. Namely, we can show that there is a sense in which Dets, compared to expressions of other categories, are not freely interpreted despite the existence of non-logical elements such as *John's* among the Dets. Moreover we can also, at least in part, account for why there are so many logical constants among Dets compared to other categories.

We close this section by extending the class of Det's considered in two ways. First, we extend the analysis of possessor Dets (e.g. *John's*) in several ways. And second, we extend Det to include two place Dets such as *more . . . than . . .* as it occurs e.g. in *more students than teachers*, treating it as an expression which combines with two *N*'s (*student, teacher*) to form an $\bar{N}$. The definition of conservativity is shown to naturally extend to functions from $P \times P$ into P^*.

Numerical Determiners

To enter expressions like *at least six, more than six*, etc. into L let us assume that we have defined the set K of *finite cardinal numerals*. That is, K is the set $\{zero, one, two, . . .\}$ (So we ignore whatever rules English has which forms say *two hundred forty six* from *two, four*, and *six*.) We may then enrich L as follow:

(85)   For all k, k_1, and k_2, in K, the following expressions are added to the basic vocabulary V and assigned by lexical rule to Det: *at least k, k or more, more than k, at most k, fewer than k, exactly k, between k_1 and k_2, the k, all but k, infinitely many, just finitely many, at least half (of) the.*

Adding these expressions to L as syntactically unanalyzable is merely a simplifying strategy. A more refined approach would treat K as a new primitive category whose type would be the natural numbers. Then expressions like *at least*, *at most*, etc. would be of category Det/K and thus interpreted by functions from natural numbers into T_{Det}. As we have done it however we may interpret the above expressions, which are all intuitively logical constants, by appropriately constraining the lexical interpreting function M.

We consider first expressions of the form *at least k*. In general the properties which at least k students possess are those properties p which are elements of at least k distinct individuals each having the student property. As a somewhat special case we may note that any property p is possessed by at least zero students. The following definition is then intuitive (it could have been given more elegantly to avoid the special case, but the definition would be less perspicuous):

DEFINITION 37. For all k in K, all $q \in P$,

    (a) M (*at least k*) $(q) = 1_{\text{Det}}$ if $k = zero$; otherwise,

    (b) M (*at least k*) $(q) = \bigcup \{I_1 \cap I_2 \cap \ldots \cap I_k : I_i \neq I_j$ for $j \neq i$ and $q \in I_1 \cap I_2 \cap \ldots \cap I_k\}$

Two remarks are in order here. First, recall that since T_{Det} is defined as a subalgebra of the pointwise algebra from P into P^* the unit element 1_{Det} of T_{Det} is that function sending each $q \in P$ to P itself, the set of all the properties. Second, we are assuming with our use of subscripts in part (b) of the definition that we know what number k refers to. We are in fact assuming natural number arithmetic. This assumption is harmless for our purposes, though we indicate shortly how to define Det denotations without that assumption, thereby providing in fact another type of model for natural number arithmetic.

DEFINITION 38. For all $k \in K$ and all $q \in P$, M (*more than k*) $(q) = \bigcup \{I_1 \cap I_2 \cap \ldots \cap I_{k+1} : I_i \neq I_j$ for $j \neq i$ and $q \in I_1 \cap I_2 \cap \ldots \cap I_{k+1}\}$.

Definition 38 is self explanatory, noting only that in our use of subscripts $k+1$ we assume the ordinary definition of addition of natural numbers. Relative to Definition 37 and 38 definitions for many of the other Dets in (85) is straightforward:

DEFINITION 39. For all k, k_1, $k_2 \in K$ and all $q \in P$,

(a) $M\,(k \ or \ more) = M\,(at \ least \ k)$
(b) $M\,(fewer \ than \ k) = (M\,(at \ least \ k))\,'$
(c) $M\,(at \ most \ k) = (M\,(more \ than \ k))\,'$
(d) $M\,(exactly \ k) = M\,(at \ least \ k) \wedge M\,(at \ most \ k)$
(e) $M\,(between \ k_1 \ and \ k_2) = M\,(at \ least \ k_1) \wedge M\,(at \ most \ k_2)$
(f) $M\,(strictly \ between \ k_1 \ and \ k_2) = M\,(more \ than \ k_1) \wedge M\,(fewer$
      $than \ k_2)$
(g) $M\,(infinitely \ many) = \underset{k \,\in\, K}{\bigwedge} M\,(at \ least \ k)$

(h) $M\,(just \ finitely \ many) = \underset{k \,\in\, K}{\bigvee} M\,(exactly \ k)$

To simplify the definitions of the other Dets in (85) let us use the following notation (which is not necessary, only convenient): if X is a set, $|X|$ will denote the cardinality of X, as is standard. By extension, for $p \in P$, $|p|$ will denote $|\{\alpha\colon \alpha \text{ is an atom in } P \text{ and } \alpha \leqslant p\}|$.

DEFINITION 40. For all $k \in K$ and all $q \in P$,

(a) $M\,(the \ k)\,(q) = \begin{cases} M\,(every)\,(q) & \text{if } |q| = k \\ \emptyset \ \text{otherwise} \end{cases}$

(b) $M\,(all \ but \ k)\,(q) = \underset{\substack{s \,\leqslant\, q \\ |s| \,=\, k}}{\bigvee} M\,(every)\,(q \wedge s')$

(c) $M\,(at \ least \ half \ the)\,(q) = \{p\colon |(p \wedge q)| \geqslant |(p' \wedge q)|\}$

The functions defined in Definitions 37–40 are all easily shown to be conservative. For example,

THEOREM 22. $M\,(at \ least \ k)$ is conservative.
   Proof. For $p, q \in P$, $(p \wedge q) \in M\,(at \ least \ k)\,(q)$ iff there exist k distinct individuals such that:

$$((p \wedge q) \wedge q) \in I_1 \cap I_2 \cap .., \cap I_k \quad \text{Definition 37}$$
$$\text{iff } (p \wedge q) \in I_1 \cap I_2 \cap \ldots \cap I_k \quad \text{idempotency}$$
$$\text{iff } p \in M\,(at \ least \ k)\,(q) \quad \text{Definition 37.}$$

The proof that $M\,(more \ than \ k)$ is conservative is identical to that in Theorem 22 above, replacing k by $k+1$. That the functions defined in Definition 39 are conservative follows from the fact that they are defined to be boolean functions of conservative functions and the fact that T_{Det} is closed under these boolean operations by definition and Theorem 14, Part A, which proves T_{Det} to be just the set of conservative functions from P into P^*.

As for the functions in Definition 40, the fact that M (*the k*) is conservative follows directly from the fact that M (*every*) is. Observe further that M (*every*) (*q*), by definition $\bigcap_{I \ni q} I$, is just $\{s: q \leqslant s\}$, that is, the filter generated by q (denoted F_q). Observe second that in any boolean algebra $(x \wedge y) \leqslant z$ iff $(x \wedge y) \leqslant (z \wedge x)$. Then,

THEOREM 23. M (*all but k*) is conservative.

Proof. For $p, q \in P$, $p \in M$ (*all but k*) (*q*)   iff

	For some $s \leqslant q$, $\lvert s \rvert = k$, $p \in M$ (*every*) ($q \wedge s'$)	Definition 40b
iff	for some $s \leqslant q$, $\lvert s \rvert = k$, ($q \wedge s'$) $\leqslant p$	observation above
iff	for some $s \leqslant q$, $\lvert s \rvert = k$, ($q \wedge s'$) $\leqslant (p \wedge q)$	observation above
iff	($p \wedge q$) $\in M$ (*all but k*) (*q*)	Definition 40b

And to prove that M (*at least half the*) is conservative, observe that $(p \wedge q) = ((p \wedge q) \wedge q)$ and $(p' \wedge q) = ((p \wedge q)' \wedge q)$, whence we may infer that similar Dets such as *more than half the, less than half the,* etc. are conservative as well.

Let us point out now a few properties of the new Dets. Syntactically several of the new Dets enter into boolean combinations, which gives us significantly more motivation than did our original class of Dets for wanting T_{Det} to have a boolean structure. Thus complex Dets such as *either fewer than ten or (else) more than a hundred, at least two and at most eight, either exactly two or exactly three,* etc. are reasonably natural English.

Semantically, we may observe that some of the old Dets are logically equivalent to some of the new ones. In particular M (*a*) = M (*at least one*) and M (*the*) = M (*the one*). Further, it is reasonable to extend the Dets formed from *the* along the following lines: Add *the k or more* and *the more than k* to Det and interpret them as in Definition 40a, replacing $\lvert q \rvert = k$ by $\lvert q \rvert \geqslant k$ and $\lvert q \rvert > k$ respectively. Add *the$_{pl}$* to Det and set M (*the$_{pl}$*) = M (*the two or more*). This will give us distinct representations for *the student* and *the students*, namely (*the student*) and (*the$_{pl}$ student*).

More interestingly, let us consider some of the semantic distinctions we can make among the elements of Det. First, it is natural to distinguish Det denotations according as they are *increasing, decreasing,* or neither. (Recall from Definition 29, Part A, that a subset S of an algebra B is *increasing* iff whenever $x \in S$ and $x \leqslant y$ then $y \in S$; S is *decreasing* iff whenever $x \in S$ and $y \leqslant x$ then $y \in S$; a function from S into S^* is *increasing* (*decreasing*) iff its value at every argument is increasing (decreasing).)

We invite the reader to verify that, of the syntactically unanalyzed elements of Det, *every, a, the, at least k, more than k, infinitely many, the k, the k or more, the more than k*, and *at least half the* are interpreted by increasing functions; *at most k, fewer than k* and *less than half the* are interpreted by decreasing functions; and *exactly k, between k_1 and k_2, just finitely many*, and *all but k* are interpreted by functions which are not in general either increasing or decreasing.

A less obvious distinction among Det denotations is that between those which crucially refer to cardinalities and those which don't. To specify this property more precisely let us first give an alternate characterization of conservativity.

DEFINITION 41. $f \in F_{P^*/P}$ is *meet dependent* iff for all $p, q, r \in P$,

$$\text{if } (p \wedge r) = (q \wedge r) \text{ then } p \in f(r) \text{ iff } q \in f(r)$$

THEOREM 24. For $f \in F_{P^*/P}$, f is conservative iff f is meet dependent.
    Proof. Assume first that f is conservative. Let $(p \wedge r) = (q \wedge r)$.

Then, $p \in f(r)$	iff $(p \wedge r) \in f(r)$	f is conservative
	iff $(q \wedge r) \in f(r)$	assumption
	iff $q \in f(r)$	f is conservative

Thus f is meet dependent.

Assume second that f is meet dependent. Then
if $(p \wedge q) = ((p \wedge q) \wedge q)$ then $p \in f(q)$ iff $(p \wedge q) \in f(q)$.
But $(p \wedge q) = ((p \wedge q \wedge q)$, whence f is conservative.

The intuition behind the concept of *meet dependence* is the following: an element f in T_{Det} cannot distinguish between properties p, q which have the same meet with its argument r. Either it puts both of them in $f(r)$ or it puts neither in.

Consider now the stronger notion of *cardinality dependence*. The intuition here is that the function f cannot distinguish among properties p, q at an argument r if $(p \wedge r)$ and $(q \wedge r)$ have the same cardinality. Thus,

DEFINITION 42. $f \in F_{P^*/P}$ is *cardinality dependent* iff for all $p, q, r \in P$,

$$\text{if } |(p \wedge r)| = |(q \wedge r)| \text{ then } p \in f(r) \text{ iff } q \in f(r)$$

Theorem 25 below follows immediately from Definition 42 and Theorem 24:

THEOREM 25. For all $f \in F_{P*/P}$, if f is cardinality dependent then

f is meet dependent, whence $f \in T_{Det}$.

We have defined cardinality dependence for elements of T_{Det}. By extension we shall say that $d \in$ Det is *cardinality dependent* iff for all ontologies $\langle P, 2 \rangle$ and all interpretations m relative to $\langle P, 2 \rangle$, $m(d)$ is cardinality dependent. And in general when a property of elements of T_{Det} has been defined we shall assume its extension to elements of Det as has been done above.

THEOREM 26. For k, k_1, k_2 in K, the set of finite cardinal numerals, *at least k, more than k, fewer than k, at most k, exactly k, between k_1 and k_2, infinitely many, just finitely many,* and *the k* are cardinality dependent.
   Proof hint: To see that *at least k* is cardinality dependent assume that $|(p \wedge r)| = |(q \wedge r)|$. Then $p \in M$ (*at least k*) (r) iff there are k distinct individuals such that $(p \wedge r)$ is in each of them. But by assumption $(p \wedge r)$ and $(q \wedge r)$ dominate the same number of atoms and thus are elements of the same number of individuals. Whence there must be k distinct individuals which $(q \wedge r)$ is in, so $q \in M$ (*at least k*) (r). The proof for *more than k* is similar. Most of the other cases follow from their definitions and Theorem 27 below.

THEOREM 27. The set of cardinality dependent elements of T_{Det} is a complete and atomic subalgebra of T_{Det}.

   Proof. We must show that (a) 0_{Det} and 1_{Det} are cardinality dependent (CD), (b) if f is CD then f' is CD, and (c) if K is a set of CD functions then $\wedge K$ and $\vee K$ are CD. Let $p, q, r \in P$ such that $|(p \wedge r)| = |(q \wedge r)|$. Then trivially 0_{Det} is CD since for all r, $0_{Det}(r) = \emptyset$, so $p \in 0_{Det}(r)$ iff $q \in 0_{Det}(r)$.
   Similarly 1_{Det} is CD trivially since $1_{Det}(r) = P$, all r.
   Now assume f is CD. Then f' is CD since:

$p \in (f')(r)$	iff $p \in (f(r))'$	Pointwise definition of $'$ in T_{Det}
	iff $p \notin f(r)$	Definition $'$ in $P*$
	iff $q \notin f(r)$	f is CD
	iff $q \in (f')(r)$	

Finally, let K a set of CD functions. Then $\wedge K$ is CD since:

$p \in (\wedge K)(r)$ iff $p \in \bigcap_{k \in K} k(r)$ Pointwise definition $\wedge$ in T_{Det}

iff for all $k \in K$, $p \in k \, (r)$ Definition $\bigcap$
iff for all $k \in K$, $q \in k \, (r)$ each k is CD
iff $q \in (\wedge K) \, (r)$

There are however several elements of Det as so far defined which are not CD. Thus:

THEOREM 28. *every*, *all but k*, and *more than half the* are not CD.

Proof sketch: Choose P with denumerably many atoms. Choose r to be the join of all the atoms, so $r = 1_P$. Choose $p = 1_P$ and $q = b'$ for some atom b. Then $|(p \wedge r)| = |(q \wedge r)| = \aleph_0$. But $p \in M \, (every) \, (r) = F_1$ but $q \notin F_1$ since $1 \not\leqslant (b' \wedge 1) = b'$.

Proofs for the other cases are essentially similar though more tedious.

Note that *every* only fails to be CD in cases where we have an infinite number of individuals. If P is finite then for some (finite) k, $M \, (every) = M \, (at\ least\ k)$ which was proven above to be CD. (The k in question is the one which denotes the number of individuals = the number of atoms of P). Note that from standard logic we are used to thinking of *every* and *a* (= *at least one*) as being interdefinable. Yet *a* has a semantic property which *every* fails to have, namely it is CD.

We would like now to turn to non-logical Dets. First however let us make good on a promissory note tendered earlier. Namely, we claimed that in specifying the value of M at Dets like *at least k* etc. it was not necessary to assume the ordinary development of arithmetic. Here we sketch how this can be done, and thereby provide a new model for arithmetic. We begin by defining an analogue of the successor function in arithmetic.

DEFINITION 43: $^+$ is that function from F_{P*}/P into F_{P*}/P such that for all $f \in F_{P*}/P$, and all $p \in P$,

$$f^+ \, (p) = \{(q \vee \alpha): q \in f(p) \text{ and } \alpha \text{ an atom}, \alpha \leqslant p \text{ and } \alpha \not\leqslant q\}.$$

Then we may define the finite cardinal numbers over P, Card_P as follows:

DEFINITION 44. Card_P is the least set of functions from P into $P*$ such that

(i) $1_{\text{Det}} \in \text{Card}_P$ and
(ii) Card_P is closed under $^+$.

We note without proof that if P is infinite then Card_P is isomorphic to ω, the standard set theoretical representation for the natural numbers, where 1_{Det} plays the role of 0 (the empty set) and $^+$ corresponds to the set theoretical successor function. We may now interpret the cardinality dependent Dets above in Card$_P$. M (*at least zero*) is 1_{Det}. M (*at least one*) is M (*at least zero*)) $^+$, M (*at least two*) is (M (*at least one*)) $^+$, etc. Ultimately of course the 'etc.' in this last clause would have to be replaced by an explicit statement of how complex numerical expressions in English take their denotations as a function of their parts, but this we still forego. Of course M (*more than k*) is now just (M (*k*)) $^+$. And the other cardinal Dets are defined as before in terms of *at least k* and *more than k*.

Non-Logical Determiners

As expressions like *John's car, every student's house*, etc. are clearly full noun phrases in English and *car, house*, etc. are clearly common nouns, it is reasonable to treat expressions like *John's, every student's*, etc. as being determiners. We may then enrich L as follows:

(86)   Enter $'s$ in the basic vocabulary V and assign it by lexical rule to the category $Det/\overline{N} (= (\overline{N}/N)/\overline{N})$.

It follows immediately that *John's, every student's*, etc. are elements of Det.

How shall we interpret these Dets? Intuitively we want (87a) and (87b) below to have the same interpretation:

(87) a. John's car
      b. The car which John has

Thus the interpretation of *John's*, and so ultimately of $'s$, will not be independent of the non-logical P_2 *have*. We hereby enter *have* in the basic vocabulary and assign it the category P_2.

Now we need a way of referring to the property denoted by *car which John has*. Once relative clauses are entered into L in the section on Variable Binding Operators we will be able to form such expressions directly in L. But even without relative clauses L already has enough expressive power to express *car which John has*. It will basically be $(p \wedge q)$, where p is the *car* property and q is the property an individual I has iff John has I is true. Now the P_1 (*pass* (*have* (*by John*))) is the one which holds of an individual iff John has it. Recall that *er* expresses the natural isomorphism from T_{P_1} into $P (= T_N)$. That is, for $h \in T_{P_1}$, *er* (*h*) is that element of P which is in an individual I iff h $(I) = 1$. Thus the property q mentioned above is essentially expressed by (*er* (*pass* (*have* (*by John*)))). So at least we can say that we want the value of the lexical interpreting function M at $'s$ to satisfy (88) below:

(88)   For all individuals I and all $p \in P$,
$$(M ('s)) (I) (p) = M (the) (p \wedge er (pass ((by \ I) (M (have))))).$$

Note that as before we use er, $pass$, and by to represent their own interpretations.

But of course the domain of $M ('s)$ is all of P^*, not just the individuals. So how does $M ('s)$ behave on non-individuals in P^*? Surprisingly perhaps it by and large behaves homomorphically. For example, taking $M ('s)$, which we henceforth represent simply as $'s$, as a complete homomorphism we have that (89a) is true under the conditions expressed in (89b). This is represented explicitly in (90) below.

(89)   a.   Some teacher's car exploded
        b.   There is a teacher x such that x's car exploded

(90) $((\ (\text{some} \quad \text{teacher}) \quad 's) \ \text{car}) \ \text{exploded}$

$$= h \left(\left(\bigvee_{I \ni t} ('s (I)) \right) (p) \right) \qquad \text{'s is a homomorphism}$$

$$= h \left(\bigvee_{I \ni t} 's (I) (p) \right) \qquad \text{pointwise definition } \vee \text{ in } T_{\text{Det}}$$

$$= \bigvee_{I \ni t} h ('s (I) (p)) \qquad h \in T_{P_1} \text{ is a homomorphism}$$

$= 1$ iff for some individual I with the teacher property, $h ('s (I) (p)) = 1$. That is, iff for some such I, I's car exploded.

Similarly we want (the interpretation of) $'s$ to preserve complements. If so, then (91a) will, correctly, be logically equivalent to (91b) as shown in (92).

(91) a. No teacher's car exploded
      b. It is not the case that a teacher's car exploded

(92)   (((no   teacher) $'s$) car)   exploded

$$a' \qquad t \qquad p \qquad h$$

$$a'(t)$$

$$'s(a'(t))$$

$$('s(a'(t)))(p)$$

$$h(('s(a'(t)))(p))$$

$$\begin{aligned}
&= h(('s((a(t))'))(p)) &&\text{pointwise definition } ' \text{ in } T_{\text{Det}} \\
&= h(('s(a(t)))'(p)) &&'s \text{ is a homomorphism} \\
&= h(('s(a(t))(p))') &&\text{pointwise definition } ' \text{ in } T_{\text{Det}} \\
&= (h('s(a(t))(p)))' &&h \in T_{P_1} \text{ is a homomorphism} \\
&= 1 \text{ iff } h('s(a(t))(p)) \text{ is false; that is, iff } a \textit{ teacher's car exploded}
\end{aligned}$$
   is false.

So we want $'s$ to preserve complements, whence both complements and joins, whence it is a should be a complete homomorphism from $T_{\bar{N}}$ into T_{Det}. Accordingly we may constrain M as follows:

(93) $M('s)$ is a complete homomorphism from $T_{\bar{N}}$ into T_{Det} which satisfies (88) above.

Recall from the Justification Theorem of Part A that homomorphisms on $T_{\bar{N}}$ are not only defined by stating their values on the individuals, but those values may be freely stated, that is, in any way we like. Note further that once M (*have*) is given, the values of $M('s)$ on the individuals is uniquely determined. Finally, it is easily shown that for all individuals I, $M('s)(I)$ is conservative, whence for any set of properties Q, $M('s)(Q)$ is conservative since it is a boolean function of elements of the form $M('s)(I)$ and by Theorem 14, Part A, the conservative functions are closed under the boolean operations.

Now it is clear that possessor Dets (ones of the form $\overline{N}$'s such as *John's*) are not logical constants in the sense of (84). For a given ontology $\langle P, 2 \rangle$ different interpretations may assign *John's* to different elements of T_{Det} depending upon which individual *John* is interpreted as, and depending upon which element of T_{P_2} *have* is interpreted as.

Further there appear other plausible candidates for non-logical Dets in English besides the simple possessives. One class of cases is given by extending ways of forming complex Dets from simpler ones which we have, in effect, already seen. Thus plausibly *John's three* is a Det as it occurs in *John's three cars were stolen*. In general the interpretation of *John's k* will follow that of *the k* and will not be given explicitly here.

A different sort of example is given by comparatives of the sort *more male than female, fewer French than Spanish* as they occur in *more male than female students failed the exam*. Let us define:

DEFINITION 45. MT is that function from $(T_{\mathrm{AP}})^2$ into T_{Det} such that for all $h, g \in T_{\mathrm{AP}}$ and all $p \in P$,

$$\mathrm{MT}\,(h, g)\,(p) = \{q: |q \wedge h\,(p)| > |q \wedge g\,(p)|\}.$$

It is easily checked that MT (h, g) as above is conservative (given that h and g are restricting!). We may then interpret *more male than female* as MT $(M\,(male), M\,(female))$. And clearly such Dets are not logical constants since their interpretation varies with that of the AP's they are formed from.

Characterizing 'Logical' Determiners

At this point an interesting question arises: we have been (partially at least) characterizing logical constants in terms of uniqueness of interpretation given a choice of P. But aside from giving examples we have said nothing about what elements of T_{Det} may be denoted by logical constants. Can in fact just any element of T_{Det} be a denotation for a logical constant, or rather does being a logical constant impose some constraint on which elements of T_{Det} are possible denotations? The latter option turns out to be correct.

Intuitively we would expect that interpretations of 'logical' Dets would treat properties 'with the same boolean structure' in the same way. We may represent the notion of having the same boolean structure as follows. By definition an isomorphism from an algebra B to an algebra D is a function which preserves all of the boolean structure of B, so an element of $d \in D$ may reasonably be said to have the same boolean structure as an element

$b \in B$ if there is an isomorphism $i: B \to D$ such that $i(b) = d$. (Note that if there is such an isomorphism then there is also an isomorphism from D to B which sends d to b, namely i^{-1}, so we may think of two elements p, q of P as having the same boolean structure iff for some isomorphism $i: P \to P$ we have that $i(p) = q$. An isomorphism from an algebra onto itself is called an *automorphism*.)

Now, how may we say that an element $f \in T_{\mathrm{Det}}$ treats booleanly identical elements in the same way? The idea here is that if q differs from p by an isomorphism i, that is $q = i(p)$, then the elements of $f(q)$ are just those which differ from those of $f(p)$ by the isomorphism i, that is $f(q) = \{i(s): s \in f(p)\}$. Formally then we define:

DEFINITION 46. For all $f \in F_{P*/P}$, f is *automorphism invariant* (AI) iff for all p, $q \in P$ and all automorphisms i on P, if $q = i(p)$ then $f(q) = \{i(s): s \in f(p)\}$.

(The definition is a bit long-winded. The function i above extends naturally to a function from P^* onto P^* as follows: for all $K \subseteq P$, $i(K) = \{i(k): k \in K\}$. So the last line in Definition 46 may be written: if $q = i(p)$, then $f(q) = i(f(p))$, and that in turn simply says: $f(i(p)) = i(f(p))$. We may note as well that the extended function i restricted to P^* is an automorphism on P^*.)

THEOREM 29. All elements of Det introduced before the section called *Non-logical Dets* are interpreted by automorphism invariant elements of T_{Det}.

Let us show for example that $M(every)$ is AI. We use in the proof the fact that $M(every)(p)$ is provably just F_p, the filter generated by p, that is, $\{q: p \leqslant q\}$. We also use standard observation that if i is an isomorphism from B to D, then $x \leqslant y$ iff $i(x) \leqslant i(y)$. Then, $M(every)(i(p)) = i(M(every)(p))$ as follows: For $s \in P$,

$$
\begin{aligned}
s \in M(every)(i(p)) \quad &\text{iff } i(p) \leqslant s \\
&\text{iff } i^{-1}(i(p)) = p \leqslant i^{-1}(s) \\
&\text{iff } i^{-1}(s) \in M(every)(p) \\
&\text{iff } i(i^{-1}(s)) = s \in i(M(every)(p))
\end{aligned}
$$

Similarly let us sketch the proof that $M(a)$ is AI. Recall first that an individual I is the filter generated by some atom. Moreover, by Theorem 7c of Part IA, the value of an isomorphism at an atom must itself be an atom. Then,

$s \in M(a)(i(p))$ iff for some individual I, $i(p) \in I$ and $s \in I$
                    iff for some atom α, $\alpha \leqslant i(p)$ and $\alpha \leqslant s$
                    iff for some atom α, $i^{-1}(\alpha) \leqslant i^{-1}(i(p)) = p$ and
                                   $i^{-1}(\alpha) \leqslant i^{-1}(s)$
                    iff for some atom β, $\beta \leqslant p$ and $\beta \leqslant i^{-1}(s)$
                    iff for some individual I, $p \in I$ and $i^{-1}(s) \in I$
                    iff $i^{-1}(s) \in M(a)(p)$
                    iff $i(i^{-1}(s)) = s \in i(M(a)(p))$.

To facilitate proofs for other cases we note the following theorem:

THEOREM 30. $\{f \in T_{\text{Det}}: f$ is AI$\}$ is a complete and atomic subalgebra of T_{Det}

The proof that meets, joins, and complements of AI functions are themselves AI is merely a tedious exercise and will be omitted.

We may conclude then that the Dets we have been calling logical constants are automorphism invariant. Moreover, as expected, the Dets such as *John's* which we have called non-logical are not automorphism invariant. That is, we can find interpretations m of L such that m (*John's*) is not AI. It will be instructive to exhibit a case where *John's* fails to be AI. First let us note that any two atoms of P have the same boolean structure, i.e. they can be identified by an automorphism. More generally consider Theorem 31 and its corollaries below, where At_P denotes the set of atoms of P and f is a *permutation* of At_P iff f is a one-to-one function from At_P onto At_P.

THEOREM 31. For every permutation f of At_P the function i_f from P to P defined by setting $i_f(p) = \vee \{f(\alpha): \alpha$ an atom and $\alpha \leqslant p\}$ extends f and is an automorphism. Moreover the set of automorphisms on P is just $\{i_f: f$ a permutation of $\text{At}_P\}$.

COROLLARY 1. For all atoms α, β there is an automorphism i such that $i(\alpha) = \beta$ and $i(\beta) = \alpha$.

COROLLARY 2. For all $p, q \in P$, there is an automorphism i on P such that $i(p) = q$ iff $|p| = |q|$ and $|p'| = |q'|$.

Again the proofs are straightforward algebraic exercises and will be omitted. We may now show:

THEOREM 32: *John's* is not automorphism invariant.

Proof. Choose P with at least two atoms α, β. Interpret *have* such that for all individuals x, y $m(have)(x)(y) = 1$ iff $x = I_\alpha$, the individual generated by α, and $y = M(John)$. Then $m(John's)(\alpha) = I_\alpha$ and m $(John's)(\beta) = \emptyset$. Now let i be that automorphism on P such that $i(\alpha) = \beta$ and $i(\beta) = \alpha$ and for all other atoms γ, $i(\gamma) = \gamma$. Then $i(\beta) = \alpha$ but $i((m(John's)(\beta)) = i(0) = \emptyset \neq m$ $(John's)(i(\beta)) = m(John's)(\alpha) = I_\alpha$. Thus $m(John's)$ is not AI.

To illustrate the intuitive interpretation of the proof above imagine an interpretation in which there are at least three individuals, one being John, one being the only individual with the boat property, and the third being the only individual with the car property. Suppose that John has the boat and nothing else. Then John's boat is that individual with the boat property, and John's car is the empty set. But since both *boat* and *car* are interpreted by atoms we can find an automorphism in which the boat atom is the isomorphic image of the car atom. But John's boat, an individual, is not the set of isomorphic image of elements of John's car, which is empty.

Loosely then, *John's* is not automorphism invariant, that is, it is not 'logical', because it can tell the difference between atoms, sending some to individuals and others to the empty set, elements of P^* which do not have the same boolean structure (that is, which cannot be identified by any automorphism on P^* since only the zero element of P^* (the empty set) can be identified with the zero element).

We have then distinguished among elements of T_{Det} according as they may interpret 'logical' Dets or not. We might then add the subcategorization feature *logical* to SF (L) and define:

(94) $T_{Det}_{logical} = \{f \in T_{Det} : f$ is automorphism invariant$\}$.

But is there any motivation for adding this feature to L? After all, we don't need to explicitly constrain the interpretations of *at least k, every*, etc. to lie in $T_{Det}_{logical}$ since we give their denotations explicitly and it is a theorem that they lie in that set. Similarly, all the non-logical Dets we have discussed are syntactically complex, whence their interpretations are given as a function of that of their constituents, and it is a theorem (see Theorem 32 above) that they need not lie in the set of AI elements of T_{Det}. Nevertheless some motivation for adding the feature *logical* to L may come from the analysis of 'vague' Dets, to which we now turn.

Vague Determiners

Dets such as *several, a few, many, few, a large number of*, etc. seem vague in a way in which the Dets so far considered are not. It is unclear for example just how many, or what proportion, of the Democrats must be vegetarians in order for the sentence *several Democrats are vegetarians* to be true. Limiting ourselves to *several* and *a few*, one approach to the problem of vagueness would be to simply enter these items as syntactically unanalyzed elements of Det and not constraint their interpretation. So more than one element of T_{Det} would be a possible denotation for these items. They would be vague then in the sense that since their interpretations are not a function of the interpretations of their parts (they don't have any) we have no way of knowing which elements of T_{Det} they do denote.

However this approach (so far) overshoots the mark in the sense that *several* and *a few* are surely not freely interpretable in T_{Det}. Intuitively for example they are more 'quantitative' or 'logical' than *John's*. Thus, assuming a P with only finitely many individuals for simplicity of illustration, if the number of Democrats is the same as the number of Republicans, and the number of Democrats who are vegetarians is the same as the number of Republicans who are alcoholics, we want (95a, b) below to have the same truth value.

(95) a. Several Democrats are vegetarians
      b. Several Republicans are alcoholics

This will be guaranteed (see Keenan and Stavi, 1981, for details) if we require that *several* and *a few* are interpreted by automorphism invariant elements of T_{Det}. We may than enter these expressions into the $Det_{logical}$ subcategory of Det, whence by (94) their interpretations are AI. This analysis moreover suggests the following language universal:

(96)   *Universal I*
        All syntactically simple Dets in a language which are extensional
        are automorphism invariant

Of course we probably want the interpretations of *several* and *a few* to satisfy additional constraints. Arguably for example they are cardinality dependent. For example, if the number of Democrats who are vegetarians is the same as the number of Democrats who are alcoholics then it seems that *several Democrats are vegetarians* and *several Democrats are alcoholics* should have the same truth value. We can of course require that M (*several*) etc. be CD in the same way that we required that they be AI above. Note that these two properties are completely independent:

THEOREM 33.

> (a) There exist $f \in T_{Det}$ such that f is AI and not CD
> (b) There exist $f \in T_{Det}$ such that f is CD and not AI.

Proof sketch.

> (a) M (*every*) has already been shown to be AI and not CD.
> (b) Choose P with at least two atoms α, β. Define f_α from P into P^* by:
>
> $$f_\alpha (q) = \begin{cases} P \text{ if } \alpha \leq q \\ \emptyset \text{ otherwise.} \end{cases}$$
>
> f_α as defined is easily seen to be conservative and (trivially) CD. It is not AI since it sends distinct atoms α and β to elements of P^* (P and $\emptyset$ respectively) which are not isomorphic images of each other.

Finally, it seems reasonable, though judgments are somewhat less clear for *several* than for *a few*, that M (*several*), etc. be interpreted by increasing elements of T_{Det}. Clearly if a few Democrats are vegetarians and all vegetarians are alcoholics, then a few Democrats are alcoholics. If we accept the comparable judgements for *several* then we might posit a second universal as follows:

(97)   *Universal II*
       All syntactically simple Dets in a language which are extensional are increasing.

(97) is more problematic than the first universal. At the very least it requires that *no* and *neither*, which are clearly decreasing and not increasing, be analyzed as syntactically complex. It is historically correct that they consist

of a base and a negative morpheme *ne*, and plausibly we might consider them to be synchronically bimorphemic, based on alternations like *one/none, either/neither, ever/never, ary/nary*, etc. But other plausible counter-examples exist. Bare numerals like *two* in *two students came early* are not increasing if they are interpreted in the sense of *exactly two* (but they are increasing if interpreted to mean *at least two*). Finally, *few* appears to be decreasing and not increasing, though it is argued in Keenan and Stavi (1981) that *few* (like *many*) cannot be analyzed as a function from P into P^* at all.

Determiners Compared to Other Categories

Despite the existence of non-logical constants among the Dets, Det as a category seems distinct from the other categories we have considered in that, in some sense, a heavy proportion of elements of Det are either logical constants or at least interpreted by AI elements of T_{Det}. For other categories we find the odd logical constant among their syntactically simple members, e.g. *exist, be, individual*, etc. but generally the lexical elements of N, AP, and the P_n's are not logical constants. Is this just an accident, or can we provide some reason to expect this distribution?

In fact the distribution of logical constants is not wholly unexpected. It correlates with certain semantic properties of the relevant categories. To see this in broad outline (see Keenan and Stavi, *op. cit.*, for all details and proofs) let us first note that it makes sense to speak of automorphism invariant elements in any type, not just T_{Det}. Specifically:

(98)   An automorphism i on P extends to an automorphism on all the types as follows:

(a)   We extend i to T_{P_0} by setting $i(1) = 1$ and $i(0) = 0$.

(b)   if i has been extended to an automorphism on a set X then i extends to X^* by setting $i(K) = \{i(k): k \in K\}$, all subsets K of X.

(c)   if i has been extended to sets X and Y, then i extends to $F_{Y/X}$ as follows: for all $x \in F_{Y/X}, i(f)$ is that element of $F_{Y/X}$ such that for all $x \in X, i(f)(x) = i(f(i^{-1}(x)))$.

Given (98), slightly elaborated to cover types for categories like $\langle P_1, P_2, \ldots \rangle /$ $\langle P_1, P_2, \ldots \rangle$, we may define an element $\tau \in T_C$, C any category, to be *automorphism invariant* iff $i(\tau) = \tau$, all automorphisms i on T_C which extend ones on P. The reader may check that this yields the same results as earlier for AI elements of T_{Det}. We may then show:

THEOREM 34.

(a) $T_{\bar{N}}$ prop has no elements which are automorphism invariant.

(b) Each of T_N, T_{AP}, and T_{P_1} have exactly two AI elements.

(c) T_{P_2} has at most four AI elements.

We note that Theorem 34 holds regardless of the size of P and hence of the number of individuals of the model. Thus Theorem 34 (a) says that there can be no logically constant proper nouns. Part (b) says for example that there can be at most two logically distinct logical constants among the P_1's (their simplest expressions are *exist* and *not exist*). Part (c) says that there are at most four logically distinct logical constants among the P_2's. (The only one which is lexically expressible is *be*; the others are *not be* and the zero and unit elements of T_{P_2}.) It is then no accident that we do not find more logical constants among the proper nouns, common nouns, intersecting adjectives, and one and two place predicates.

Matters are quite otherwise for T_{Det} however. There are 'typically' a rather large number of AI elements in T_{Det}. Moreover the number increases with the number of individuals and thus does not have a fixed upper bound An informal way to exemplify this is to note that for a finite P with k individuals, all the Dets of the form *at least k_1, more than k_1*, etc. for $k_1 > k$ denote the same element of T_{Det}, namely the zero element. But choosing a P with more than k individuals some of these Dets will no longer denote the zero element. As all these Dets are AI then we infer that the number of AI elements of T_{Det} increases with the size of P.

These facts are perhaps not sufficient to explain why in fact so many of the AI elements of T_{Det} are naturally expressible in English, but they do at least say that it is possible to have many logical constants among the Dets. We might note that $T_{\bar{N}}$ has even more AI elements than T_{Det} since for every AI element f of T_{Det}, $f(1)$ and $f(0)$ are AI elements of $T_{\bar{N}}$. Taking (as we have) *individual* and *non-individual* to denote the unit and zero respectively in T_N such AI elements of $T_{\bar{N}}$ are expressible whenever the AI element f in T_{Det} is. For example, *every individual, at least three individuals*, etc. denote AI elements of $T_{\bar{N}}$. These elements however are not commonly expressed by syntactically simple elements of $\bar{N}$, though indefinite pronouns such as *everyone, no one*, and *someone* are near exceptions (if we take them as syntactically simple).

Universal I suggests another related way in which Det semantically differs from other boolean categories. Namely, it imposes a severe constraint on how the lexical elements of the category may be interpreted in T_{Det}. In general, most elements of T_{Det} are not possible denotations of lexical Dets. By contrast, for an arbitrary P, an arbitrary element of T_{P_1} is denotable. Simply choose a lexical interpreting function M which interprets say *sleep* as that element. Let us say that a category C is *expressively free* if there is an expression $e \in C$ such that for any ontology $\langle P, 2 \rangle$ and any element $\tau \in T_C$ there is an interpretation m such that $m(e) = \tau$. Then P_1 is expressively free.

Is Det expressively free? The answer is not obvious, for while lexical Dets are not freely interpreted, more complex Dets such as *John's*, etc. introduce greater degrees of freedom, not being constrained to denote AI elements of T_{Det}. Nonetheless, under quite generous assumptions concerning what non-logical expressions Dets may be formed from, it is shown in Keenan and Stavi (*op. cit.*) that:

THEOREM 35. There is no element e of Det such that for any finite P and any element f of T_{Det} there is an interpretation m such that $m(e) = f$.

Generalizing Determiners

As suggested at the beginning of this section, it is not unreasonable to analyze expressions such as *more . . . than . . .* as it occurs in *more students than teachers* as ones which combine with two N's to form an $\bar{N}$. Semantically then such expressions would be interpreted by functions from $P \times P$ into P^*. For example, the obvious definition of *more . . . than . . .* is given by:

(99)   For all $p, q \in P$, *more p than q* $= \{s \in P: |s \wedge p| > |s \wedge q|\}$.

If we adopt such an analysis it is natural to wonder whether the notion of conservativity generalizes to such functions. In fact it does, the characterization in Theorem 24 forming the basis of the generalization:

DEFINITION 47. For all $n > 0$, all functions f from P^n into P^*, f is *conservative* iff for all $p, q \in P$ and all n-tuples $\langle r_1, r_2, \ldots, r_n \rangle \in P^n$, if $(p \wedge r_i) = (q \wedge r_i)$, all r_i in the n-tuple, then $p \in f(r_1, r_2, \ldots, r_n)$ iff $q \in f(r_1, r_2, \ldots, r_n)$.

This obviously coincides with our earlier definition for the case where $n = 1$. Further, the reader may easily check that *more . . . than . . .* as defined in (99) is a two place conservative function. Other expressions of this sort

whose natural interpretations are easily shown to be conservative are *fewer*...
than..., *exactly as many*...*as*..., *twice as many*...*as*...,etc.

There are at least two properties of interest concerning such two place
Dets. First, we *cannot* treat them as one place functions from P into T_{Det}.
If we did, the appropriate definition would be:

(100)   For each $q \in P$, (*more than* q) is that function f from P into P^*
such that for all $p \in P$, $f(p) = \{s: |(s \wedge p)| > |(s \wedge q)|\}$.

But clearly the function f above is not conservative (so *more than* q does
not lie in T_{Det}) since if it were it would follow that for all properties s, p
$|(s \wedge p)| > |(s \wedge q)|$ iff $|((s \wedge p) \wedge p)| > |((s \wedge p) \wedge q)|$ which is obviously
false.

The second point of interest is that two place Dets give us a way to
represent a certain ambiguity, or variation in interpretation of noun phrases
consisting (apparently) of an ordinary Det and a conjunction or disjunction
of common noun phrases. The subject noun phrase of (101a) below is perhaps
most naturally interpreted as synonymous with that in (101b), whereas that
in (102a) is more naturally thought of as synonymous with that in (102b).

(101) a. A man and woman came to see me today
      b. A man and a woman came to see me today

(102) a. A professor and civil rights activist will speak this afternoon
      b. An individual who is both a professor and a civil rights activist
         will speak this afternoon.

If we analyze such constructions as consisting of a Det and a conjunction
of N's, the only interpretation we represent is that in (102). To represent
the interpretation in (101) we can extend the class of two place Dets by
treating a ... *and* ... as a two place Det and interpreting a p *and* q as
$a(p) \cap a(q)$. More generally:

DEFINITION 48. For $f \in F_{P^*/P}$,

(a)   (f *and*) is that function from P^2 into P^* such that for all p, $q \in P$,
       (f *and*) $(p, q) = f(p) \cap f(q)$
(b)   (f *or*) is that function from P^2 into P^* such that for all p, $q \in P$,
       (f *or*) $(p, q) = f(p) \cup f(q)$.

THEOREM 36. If $f \in F_{P*/P}$ is conservative then so are $(f \ and)$ and $(f \ or)$.
  Proof. Let s and t have the same meet with p and the same meet with q. Then,

$$s \in (f \ and) \ (p, q) \quad \text{iff } s \in f(p) \cap f(q) \qquad \text{Definition of } (f \ and)$$

$$\text{iff } s \in f(p) \text{ and } s \in f(q) \quad \text{Definition of } \cap$$

$$\text{iff } t \in f(p) \text{ and } t \in f(q) \quad f \text{ is conservative}$$

$$\text{iff } t \in (f \ and) \ (p, q)$$

The proof that $(f \ or)$ is conservative is completely analogous. Moreover both proofs generalize easily to the case where f is a function from P^n into $P*$.

Extending Possessive Determiners

We have been treating $'s$ as having the category $Det/\bar{N} \ (= (\bar{N}/N) \ /\bar{N})$. Here we shall extend its category in a variety of ways which are of syntactic and semantic interest. First, we argued in Keenan and Faltz (1978) that $'s$ should be able to combine directly with N's to form expressions of category $\bar{N}/\bar{N}$. On this view, *John's house* would be analyzed as $(John \ ('s \ house))$. Semantically, $'s$ would send a property p to that complete homomorphism from $T_{\bar{N}}$ into $T_{\bar{N}}$ such that for all individuals I, $'s \ (p) \ (I) = ('s \ (I)) \ (p)$ as previously given. We shall not pursue that analysis here, but only want to note that both analyses of $'s$ may be incorporated into our system by assigning $'s$ to the category $\langle (\bar{N}/N), (\bar{N}/\bar{N}) \rangle \ / \ \langle \bar{N}/N \rangle$.

A more important extension concerns the use of $'s$ in expressions such as *John's friend, every country's president*, etc. Since *friend, president*, etc. are of category $N_1 \ (= N/\bar{N})$ it appears that we should allow Dets like *John's* to combine directly with N_1's as well as N_0's (that is, N's) to form $\bar{N}$'s. For simplicity of presentation let us think of *John's* for the nonce as have only the category $\bar{N}/N_1$ and let us take the type for that category as simply the entire set of functions from T_{N_1} into $T_{\bar{N}}$, regarded as a (complete and atomic) algebra where the operations are defined pointwise. Then $'s$ would be of category $(\bar{N}/N_1) \ /\bar{N}$ and would be interpreted as follows:

(103) $M \ ('s)$ is that complete homomorphism from $T_{\bar{N}}$ into $F_{T_{\bar{N}}/T_{N_1}}$ such that for all individuals I and all $f \in T_{N_1}$, $M \ ('s) \ (I) \ (f) = M \ (the) \ (f(I))$.

We may then extend the previous analyses of $'s$ to accommodate this usage by assigning $'s$ the category in (104).

(104) $\langle\langle\bar{N}/\bar{N}\rangle \,/\, \langle N_1, N_0\rangle,\ \bar{N}/\bar{N}\rangle \,/\, \langle\bar{N}/N\rangle$

Note that on this analysis *John's friend* and *the friend of John* will be logically equivalent, that is, always interpreted by the same element of $T_{\bar{N}}$. But this will fail for *every student's friend* and *the friend of every student*. To see the difference, imagine a state of affairs in which each student has exactly one friend. Then *every student's friend* will be the intersection of those individuals. But *the friend of every student* will denote the unique individual who has the property that for every student he is a friend of his. If there is no such individual then it will denote the empty set. Arguably in fact the English expression *the friend of every student* is ambiguous, having either of the interpretations noted above (though *every student's friend* is not ambiguous, having only the interpretation given). The second reading, on which it is a paraphrase of *every student's friend*, cannot be represented in L at the moment, but it can be once variable binding operators are introduced in the next section. There the wide scope reading may be represented by *(every student)* $(\lambda\, x\ the\ friend\ (of)\ x)$.

Finally, a somewhat more subtle use of *'s* concerns the ambiguity in (105a) below:

(105) a. Every student's bike was stolen
　　　b. For each student, his bike was stolen
　　　c. Every bike of the student variety was stolen

Only the reading in (105b) is currently represented in L. To represent the (105c) reading we shall extend *'s* to allow it to combine with N's (*student*) to form something which combines with an N (*bike*) to yield an N (*student's bike*). The (105c) reading then will be represented as *(every ((student 's) bike))*. We will think of *student's bike* as merely specifying a subtype of bike, so in effect *student's* will be interpreted by a restricting function from P into P, that is, an element of T_{AP}. Thus on this view, M (*'s*) will send a property p to an arbitrary element of T_{AP} since we have no substantive way of saying what we mean by 'bike of the student variety'. nor have we investigated whether M (*'s*) in this use should have any particular properties other than yielding a restricting function from P into P. This analysis can be made compatible with our previous analyses by assigning *'s* the category in (106).

(106) $\langle\langle\bar{N}, N\rangle \,/\, \langle\bar{N}, N\rangle,\ \langle\bar{N}, \bar{N}\rangle \,/\, \langle N, N_1\rangle\rangle \,/\, \langle N, \bar{N}\rangle$

6. VARIABLES AND VARIABLE BINDING OPERATORS

We shall now extend L to include variables and variable binding operators (VBO's). The VBO's are λ, *self*, and *suchthat*. The variables are $x_1, x_2, \ldots$; they will have category $\bar{N}$. Arbitrary variables will often be denoted simply x and y.

Our motivation for extending L in this way is twofold. First, we shall be able to represent English expressions such as relative clauses and reflexives not currently representable in L (or its previous extensions). And second, we can represent alternate readings (ambiguities) of English expressions in cases where only one reading is currently representable in L. Below we informally illustrate some typical cases of these extensions and then turn to their formal statement.

The *suchthat* operator is used to represent English relative clauses. Thus (107a) below will be represented as in (107b).

> (107) a. every doctor (who(m)) Mary saw
> b. (every (doctor (x suchthat (Mary (saw x)))))).

In (107b), x is of the category $\bar{N}$ so (*Mary saw x*) is of category P_0. Our syntax for *suchthat* will tell us that (x *suchthat* (*Mary saw x*)) is an intersecting AP. It thus forms an N when combined with the N *doctor*. And since *every* is a Det ($\bar{N}/N$), the entire expression in (107b) is an $\bar{N}$.

The *self* operator forms reflexives, as illustrated in:

> (108) a. No doctor shot himself
> b. (no doctor) (self x (shoot x)).

Since *shoot* is a P_2 and x an $\bar{N}$, *shoot x* in (108b) is a P_1. Our syntax for *self* will tell us that (*self x* (*shoot x*)) is also a P_1, whence the entire expression in (108b) is a P_0.

Our syntax for *self* is general enough that it can 'bind' positions other than the two argument positions of P_2's. We may for example represent object controlled reflexives as in (109):

> (109) a. John saved Mary from herself
> b. (John ((self x (save from x)) Mary)

In (109b) *from x* is a Predicate Modifier and *save* a P_2, whence *save from x* is a P_2. Our syntax for *self* will tell us that (*self x save from x*) is also a P_2; it combines then with the $\bar{N}$ *Mary* to form a P_1, and the result combines with the $\bar{N}$ *John* to form a P_0.

Finally the λ operator is used to represent ambiguities of quantifier scope as well as variable binding which cannot be expressed by the syntactically more restricted operators *suchthat* and *self*. Thus the classical scope ambiguity in (110a) below can be represented in our extended language. (110b) represents the 'natural' reading of (110a) in which *every student* has wide scope over *some book*. (110c) represents the reading in which *some book* has wide scope over *every student*.

(110) a. Every student read some book
      b. (every student) (read (some book))
      c. (some book) (λx ((every student) (read x))).

In (110c) the expression (*every student read x*) is of category P_0; the result of combining it with λ and x is a P_1, which combines then with *some book* to form a P_0.

We note that our treatment of λ is general enough to represent similar scope ambiguities within $\bar{N}$'s. Thus the two readings of (111a) are represented as in (111b, c) below:

(111) a. some friend of every senator
      b. (some (friend (every senator)))
              of
      c. (every senator) (λx (some (friend x)))
                         of

In (111c) the expression (*some friend x*) is an $\bar{N}$ and (λx *some* friend x) is an $(\bar{N})_1$, that is, an $\bar{N}/\bar{N}$, so the whole expression in (111c) is an $\bar{N}$.

As an example of variable binding expressible with λ but not with the other operators consider (112a) below which has a reading expressed in (112b) in which informally *his* is bound by *every child*.

(112) a. Every child and his father
      b. ((every child) (λx (x and x's father)))

Since x is a $\bar{N}$ we have that (*x and x's father*) is an $\bar{N}$, so the result above of combining it with λ and x is a $\bar{N}/\bar{N}$, which combines with the $\bar{N}$ *every child* to yield an $\bar{N}$.

Another use of the lambda operator, whose formal statement must await the intensional logic of Part II, is the creation of transparent or *de re* structures. Thus in Part II the transparent reading of (113a), in which we understand that there is a unicorn and John sought it, may be represented as in (113b). The more natural reading, in which the existence of a unicorn is not implied, will be represented directly, that is, without the use of a lambda operator, as in (113c).

(113) a. John sought a unicorn
   b. (John ((λx (seek x)) (a unicorn))
   c. (John) (seek (a unicorn)

We turn now to the formal statement of the syntax and semantics of VBOs.

First, variables are added to L as follows. Put *var* in the set of subcategorization features for L, whence for all $C \in \text{CAT}$, C_{var} is a subcategory of C. Potentially, therefore, we allow variables of every category; in practice we shall limit our variables to $\bar{N}_{\text{var}}$. Thus, for every positive integer n we add the symbol x_n to the basic vocabulary V. (we may think of x_n as an abbreviation for $\langle 'x', n \rangle$ if we like.) By lexical rule we set $\{x_n : n$ a positive interger$\} = \bar{N}_{\text{var}}$.

Semantically we expect that the type for $\bar{N}_{\text{var}}$ will be a subset of the type for $\bar{N}$. In fact we limit our variables to range over individuals. Thus.

DEFINITION 49. $T_{\bar{N}_{\text{var}}} = I_P$.

Recall that I_P is the set of individuals over P (= T_N). The type for the variables then is not closed with respect to the boolean operations on $T_{\bar{N}}$ and we do not enter $\bar{N}_{\text{var}}$ into our list of boolean categories, just as we did not enter $\bar{N}_{\text{prop}}$ into that list.

Note that L as so far extended provides expressions like (x_3 *sleep*). Our principle interest in such expressions, as in standard logic, is the role they play in defining the interpretation of expressions containing a VBO in which they occur such as (x_3 *suchthat* (x_3 *sleep*)). Such expressions however have some independent interest which we shall note but not pursue. Namely, there is a sense in which they correspond to English expressions like *he is sleeping* in which the denotation of *he* is understood to be provided in some way by the context of utterance. Such expressions contrast with ones like *John is sleeping* in which, in an ordinary discourse, social conventions of some sort determine the denotation of *John* and typically different occurrences of *John* are interpreted as the same individual. Different occurrences of *he* however may be interpreted more easily as different individuals, especially if accompanied by overt acts of ostension, as in *he is drunk and he is merely exhausted*.

It would be linguistically interesting to pursue the difference in context dependency between definite pronouns like *he, she, it*, and proper nouns like *John* by formally distinguishing how they are interpreted. For example we might represent a context (minimally at least) by functions which assign appropriate values to variables and then interpret expressions in L relative to such assignments; that is, we would interpret expressions not directly as elements of the appropriate type but rather as functions from assignments into the appropriate type. In this way the interpretation of (x_3 *sleep*) would vary with the context.

Later in this section we shall sketch this approach in somewhat more detail as it overcomes a technical awkwardness in our formal definition of the interpretations of VBOs. A full treatment however would lead us to the study of the context dependency of English expressions in general, something we shall eschew for purely practical reasons: it would be a long study, requiring for example a serious treatment of tense in English, and the novelty and interest of our work here does not in any specific way concern such context dependencies.

Let us turn now to the treatment of the VBOs themselves. To present their semantics it will be helpful to recall first the way in which a full interpretation of L is defined.

We have defined a model to be a triple $\langle P, 2, M \rangle$, where 2 is the boolean algebra of truth values, P is an arbitrary complete atomic boolean algebra, and M is a lexical assignment function. Let us denote by V^+ the subset of the set of vocabulary items V consisting of interpretable expressions. The expressions of V which are *not* themselves interpreted are the boolean combiners *and, or*, and *not*, and, now that we are adding them, the VBOs *suchthat, self*, and λ. Thus, we simply have $V^+ = V - \{$and, or, not, suchthat, self, $\lambda\}$. We can now say that V^+ is the domain of M, and if $e \in V^+$ and e is of category C, then $M(e)$ is an element of T_C.

Now, given the triple $\langle P, 2, M \rangle$, there is a unique function m defined whose domain is the set of all expressions of the language L. If e is an expression of L, then we just have $m(e) = M(e)$ if $e \in V^+$. If e is a complex expression, then $m(e)$ is calculated according to the principles we have been using all along. Thus, if e is a boolean combination of expressions then $m(e)$ is the appropriate boolean function of the interpretations of the constituents of e.

And if e is composed of an expression of a functional category and an expression of its argument category, then $m\,(e)$ is calculated by applying the interpreting function to the interpreting argument. Now that we are adding the VBOs to our language, of course, we must define how $m\,(e)$ is calculated in the case that e is constructed using a VBO. We will do this in a moment. But here, let us note that, with P fixed, the functions m are in one-to-one correspondence with the lexical assignment functions M. For, distinct Ms lead to distinct ms (since, for M_1 and M_2 to be distinct, we must have $M_1(e)$ $\neq M_2(e)$ for some $e \in V^+$; but then, since $m_i(e) = M_i(e)$ ($i = 1$ or 2), we have $m_1(e) \neq m_2(e)$ for this expression e). On the other hand, given M, there is a unique m defined, as we have already indicated. Finally, we note that if m is an interpretation function, then the restriction of m to V^+ is the lexical assignment function M which gave rise to it.

In order to give the definitions of the interpretations of the VBOs we will need the notions defined as follows:

DEFINITION 50. Let M_1 and M_2 be two lexical assignment functions relative to a given ontology $\langle P, 2 \rangle$, and let $x \in \bar{N}_{\mathrm{var}}$. Then M_1 is an x-variant of M_2 iff for every $y \in V^+$ such that $y \neq x$, $M_1(y) = M_2(y)$.

Thus, M_1 is an x-variant of M_2 iff M_1 interprets every lexical item the same as M_2, with the possible exception of the variable x. Note, therefore, that if M_2 is given, and if we specify that M_1 is an x-variant of M_2, then M_1 is completely and uniquely determined by assigning a value to $M_1(x)$.

DEFINITION 51. Let m_1 and m_2 be two functions which interpret the language L; assume that m_i restricted to V^+ is the lexical assignment function M_i ($i = 1$ or 2), again with the same P chosen for both. Then m_1 is an x-variant of m_2 iff M_1 is an x-variant of M_2.

By the fact that the interpretation functions of the language are in one-to-one correspondence with the lexical assignment functions, we conclude that if m_2 is an interpretation function and if m_1 is specified as an x-variant of m_2, then m_1 is completely defined by giving a value for $m_1(x)$.

We are now in a position to give the syntax and semantics of the VBOs.

The Lambda Operator

Syntactically we enrich L by adding (114) below to the formation rules for complex expressions in L:

(114) For each expression e in a boolean category C, and each variable x, $(\lambda x\, e)$ is an expression of category $C/\bar{N}$.

Thus, where x and y are variables (elements of $\bar{N}_{\text{var}}$) we have that $(x\, (kiss\, y))$ is a P_0, whence $(\lambda x\, (x\, (kiss\, y)))$ is of category $P_0/\bar{N}$, that is, P_1, and $(\lambda y\, (\lambda x\, (x\, (kiss\, y))))$ is of category $P/\bar{N}\,(= P_2)$. Similarly, since $(some\, (friend\, x))$ is a $\bar{N}$ we have that $(\lambda x\, (some\, friend\, x))$ is of category $\bar{N}/\bar{N}$.

Semantically an expression of the form $(\lambda x\, e)$ will be interpreted by an element of $T_{C/\bar{N}}$, where e is of category C and C is boolean. Thus T_C is a complete and atomic algebra and $T_{C/\bar{N}}$ is the set of complete homomorphisms from $T_{\bar{N}} = P^*$ into T_C. By the Justification Theorem we can define such homomorphisms by stating their values on the individuals. This we do as follows:

DEFINITION 52. For $\langle P, 2, M \rangle$ a model, $x \in \bar{N}_{\text{var}}$ and $e \in C$, C boolean, $m\,(\lambda x\, e)$ is that complete homomorphism from $T_{\bar{N}}$ into T_C such that for all individuals I, $m(\lambda x\, e)\,(I) = m'(e)$, where m' is that x-variant of m such that $m'(x) = I$.

So for example $m\,(\lambda x_1\, (every\, boy\, kiss\, x_1))$ is that complete homomorphism which assigns to an individual I the truth value of $(every\, boy\, kiss\, x_1)$ where x_1 has now been interpreted as I. (We refer the reader to the end of this section for further technical comments on Definition 52.)

We now go through several examples to illustrate how expressions involving λ are actually interpreted with this definition (writing $(\lambda x\, e)$ indifferently as $(x\, \lambda\, e)$, which we may do since derived expressions are sets). First, starting with the formula $John\, (kiss\, x)$ we may form the expression $(x\, \lambda\, (John\, (kiss\, x)))$ of category $P_0/\bar{N} = P_1$. Combining this with an $\bar{N}$, say $Mary$, we form a new formula (P_0). Since $Mary$ is a proper noun, its interpretation in any model, say, the model $\langle P, 2, M \rangle$, will be an individual, say I_m. Thus we have $m\,(Mary) = M\,(Mary) = I_m$.

Now, by the way interpretations are constrained on functional expressions, we have that $m((Mary)\, (x\, \lambda\, John\, (kiss\, x))) = (m\, (x\, \lambda\, John\, (kiss\, x)))\, (m(Mary)) = (m\, (x\, \lambda\, John\, (kiss\, x)))\, (I_m)$. But by the definition above, this is simply equal to $m'\, (John\, (kiss\, x))$, where m' is the x-variant of m such that $m'\, (x) = I_m$. Since m' is an x-variant of m, we have that $m'\, (John) = m\, (John) = I_j$ (say), and $m'(kiss) = m(kiss) = k$ (say). Thus, since $m'(x) = I_m$, we have that $m'(kiss\, x) = k\, (I_m)$, and therefore $m'(John\, (kiss\, x)) = (k\, (I_m))\, (I_j)$. We have thus shown that the interpretation in the model $\langle P, 2, M \rangle$ of

(*Mary*) (*x* λ *John* (*kiss x*)) is ($k(I_m)$) (I_j), where k, I_m, and I_j are the inter-pretations in this model of *kiss, Mary*, and *John* respectively. The reader can easily check that this is also the interpretation in this model of the formula *John* (*kiss Mary*). Thus, (*Mary*) (*x* λ *John* (*kiss x*)) and *John* (*kiss Mary*) are logically equivalent (since the model ⟨*P*, 2, *M*⟩ was arbitrary). Examining these two expressions we can see the sense in which the λ effects a substitution of the $\bar{N}$ *Mary* for the variable *x*.

As a somewhat less trivial example, let us start with the formula (*every boy*) (*kiss x*) and form the expression (*x* λ (*every boy*) (*kiss x*)), which is again a member of category $P_0/\bar{N} = P_1$. Let us calculate the interpretation of the formula which results when this P_1 is combined with the $\bar{N}$ *a girl*.

Letting ⟨*P*, 2, *M*⟩ be the model we are working in, we have, say, $m(kiss) = M(kiss) = k$, $m(boy) = M(boy) = b$, and $m(girl) = M(girl) = g$. Next, we have that $m(a\ girl) = a(g) = \bigcup_{g \in I} I$. We therefore have that $m((a\ girl)\ (x\ \lambda$ (*every boy*) (*kiss x*))) = (*m* (*x* λ (*every boy*) (*kiss x*))) (*m* (*a girl*)) = (*m* (*x* λ (*every boy*) (*kiss x*))) ($\bigcup_{g \in I} I$) = $\bigvee_{g \in I}$ (*m* (*x* λ (*every boy*) (*kiss x*))) (*I*), where the last equation follows because $m(x\ \lambda$ (*every boy*) (*kiss x*)) is a homomorphism and so preserves joins.

Now, by Definition 52 above, m (*x* λ (*every boy*) (*kiss x*)) (*I*) = *m'* ((*every boy*) (*kiss x*)), where *m'* is the *x*-variant of *m* such that $m'(x) = I$. Since *m'* is an *x*-variant of *m*, we have $m'(boy) = m(boy) = b$ and $m'(kiss) = m(kiss) = k$. Thus,

$$m'((every\ boy)\ (kiss\ x)) = (k\ (I))\ (\bigcap_{b \in J} J) \text{ (from the definition of } m(every))$$

$$= \bigwedge_{b \in J} (k\ (I))\ (J) \text{ (since } k\ (I) \text{ is a homo-morphism).}$$

(*J* ranges over individuals of course). Substituting this in the expression obtained above for $m((a\ girl)\ (x\ \lambda$ (*every boy*) (*kiss x*))), we arrive at the conclusion that this is equal to $\bigvee_{g \in I} \left[\bigwedge_{b \in J} (k\ (I))\ (J) \right]$. This expression is true iff there is some individual who is a girl which is such that every individual who is a boy kisses her. In other words, the interpretation of (*a girl*) (*x* λ (*every boy*) (*kiss x*)) differs from the interpretation of (*every boy*) (*kiss* (*a girl*)) precisely in that, in the latter formula, the quantifier combined with *boy* has wide scope, whereas in the former formula, the quantifier combined with *girl* has wide scope. Thus, the effect of the λ to render the object argument position of *kiss* accessible after *kiss x* is combined with a subject $\bar{N}$ also includes the effect of giving that now-accessible object

$\bar{N}$ wide scope over the subject $\bar{N}$. The λ therefore enables us to represent in our logical language the possible but less-common scope relationship of the English sentence *every boy kissed a girl* in which only one girl is involved.

Note that the more common reading of *every boy kissed a girl* is the one with the simplest representation in our system, namely (*every boy*) (*kiss* (*a girl*)), whereas the less common reading is the one which requires the use of the λ: (*a girl*) (x λ (*every boy*) (*kiss x*)). It is surely not an accident that the more common reading is represented in the simpler way. Rather, it is evidence that our system, more than being merely logically adequate, reflects something of the way real English is interpreted. Of course, the correlation between simplicity of representation and priority of reading would have to be verified in a wide variety of cases, something we do not do here. Nevertheless, it seems promising to us that such a correlation may exist, based on several particular cases such as the one we have just seen.

The examples of the use of λ that we have looked at all involved combining it with a formula. However, the definitions given for the syntax and semantics of this VBO are quite general. For example, if e is an expression of category P_n or N_n, then (x λ e) is a well-formed and interpretable expression of category P_{n+1} or N_{n+1} respectively. For example, (x λ (*kiss x*)) is a P_2. By Definition 52, the interpretation of this expression as applied to an individual I, that is, ($m(x$ λ (*kiss x*))) (I), is $m'(kiss\ x)$, where m' is the x-variant of m such that $m'(x) = I$. However, we have $m'(kiss\ x) = (m'(kiss))\ (m'(x)) = (m(kiss))\ (I)$, since $m'(kiss) = m(kiss)$. Since the equation ($m(x$ λ (*kiss x*))) (I) $= (m(kiss))\ (I)$ holds for an arbitrary individual I, we can conclude that $m(x$ λ (*kiss x*)) $= m(kiss)$, and since *kiss* was an arbitrarily chosen P_2, subject only to the condition that $m'(kiss) = m(kiss)$, we can conclude further that if e is a P_2 which does not contain any free occurrence of x, then the interpretation of the P_2 (x λ (e x)) is always the same as the interpretation of e; that is, e and (x λ (e x)) are logically equivalent. In particular, this holds if e is a lexical P_2. The reader may easily show that the logical equivalence of e and (x λ (e x)) remains true if e is any expression (in a boolean category of the form $C/\bar{N}$) not containing a free occurrence of x. This suggests that our definitions may be too general.

However, in addition to those cases in which e does contain a free occurrence of x so that e and (x λ (e x)) are logically distinct, let us point out here that in the intensional system it will turn out that e and (x λ (e x)) are *not* in general logically equivalent, even if e does not contain a free occurrence of x. In particular, if e is, say, a P_2 such as *seek* which is properly intensional on its object, then the interpretation of e as combined with an object $\bar{N}$ will always represent the *de dictu* interpretation, whereas the interpretation of the P_2 (x λ (e x)) as combined with an object $\bar{N}$ will represent the *de re* interpretation. Thus, it appears that the generality of our definitions is indeed necessary in order for the significant distinction between *de dictu* and *de re* readings to be representable in our logic.

Note finally the case of expressions (λ x e) where e is not in a category of the form $C/\bar{N}$; for example, e may be a P_0. In such a case the reader may prove that m (λ x e) is that complete homomorphism whose value at each I is just $m(e)$. So $m(\lambda$ x e) is constant on the individuals. Surprisingly perhaps such expressions with 'vacuous' variable binding may be of some utility in representing English expressions. For example, while (115b, c) are logically equivalent, we may want to choose (115b) as a representation for (115a) on grounds of better correspondence between surface form and logical form.

(115) a. As for John, everybody loves him
     b. (John (λ x (everybody (love x)))))
     c. (everybody (love John)).

Now, while the variable binding in (115b) is not vacuous since (*everybody love x*) contains a free occurrence of the variable introduced with the lambda operator, we may concoct other examples, somewhat less natural admittedly, in which the binding is vacuous. Imagine for example a discussion of a new university complex in which someone says "The classrooms are barely tolerable, and *as for the auditorium, you can't even hear the speaker from the podium*". It is not unreasonable here to represent the second conjunct above by (*the auditorium* (λ x e)), where e represents *you can't even hear the speaker from the podium*.

The Reflexive Operator

The VBO *self* will serve to bind a variable which occurs in an expression that takes an $\bar{N}$ argument in such a way that that variable has the same interpretation as that argument when it is an individual. We thus enrich L as follows:

(117)   For C a boolean category, e an expression of category $C/\bar{N}$, and for $x \in \bar{N}_{\text{var}}$, ($x$ *self* e) is an expression of category $C/\bar{N}$.

Note that e and (x *self* e) above have the same category. Thus since (*cut* x_1)

is a P_1, so then is $(x_1 \; self \; (cut \; x_1))$. And if $(save \; (from \; x))$ is a P_2 then so is $(x \; self \; (save \; (from \; x)))$. Semantically we define:

DEFINITION 53. For $(x \; self \; e)$ as in (117), $m(x \; self \; e)$ is that complete homomorphism from $T_{\bar{N}}$ into T_C such that for all individuals I, $m(x \; self \; e) \; (I)$ $= m'(e) \; (I)$, where m' is that x-variant of m such that $m'(x) = I$.

From the above definition it follows that for m an interpretation of L and I an individual, $m(x \; self \; (cut \; x)) \; (I) = m(cut) \; (I) \; (I)$. In more detail:

(118) $m(x \; self \; (cut \; x)) \; (I)$

$= m'(cut \; x) \; (I)$, where $m'(x) = I$	Definition 53
$= m'(cut) \; (m'(x)) \; (I)$	m' is an interpretation and $(cut \; x)$ is generated by the rules of functional applications
$= m'(cut) \; (I) \; (I)$	$m'(x) = I$
$= m(cut) \; (I) \; (I)$	m' is an x-variant of m and so differs from m on lexical expressions only at x.

We may then calculate the interpretation of our representation for *every student cut himself* in (119) below as follows, where we take $m \; (student)$ to be the property s and I ranges over individuals:

(119) $m(every \; student) \; (x \; self \; (cut \; x)))$

$= m(x \; self \; (cut \; x)) \; m(every \; student)$

$= m(x \; self \; (cut \; x)) \; (\underset{I \; \ni \; s}{\cap} \; I)$

$= \underset{I \; \ni \; s}{\wedge} \; m(x \; self \; (cut \; x)) \; (I) \quad m(x \; self \; cut \; x)$ is a homomorphism

$= \underset{I \; \ni \; s}{\wedge} \; m(cut) \; (I) \; (I) \qquad$ by (118 above).

Note that the corresponding representation for *every student cut every student* would be as in (120) below, where I and J range over individuals:

(120) $\underset{I \; \ni \; s}{\wedge} \left[\underset{J \; \ni \; s}{\wedge} \; m(cut) \; (J) \; (I) \right]$

Thus the effect of the VBO *self* is not to mechanically substitute the argument expression for the variable x, a procedure which would incorrectly lead to the conclusion that *every student cut every student* is logically equivalent to $(every \; student) \; (x \; self \; (cut \; x))$.

Note that the analysis in (118) remains essentially unchanged if *cut x* is replaced by any expression (with a free occurrence of *x*) in any category of the form $C/\bar{N}$. Thus if expressions such as *safe from x* or *tell about x* are analyzed as complex P_2s we may compute that m (x *self* (*save* (*from x*))) is that homomorphism whose value at an individual I is m(*from* (I) m(*save*) (I). Thus (x *self* (*save* (*from x*))) is an appropriate representation in L for the English *to save from oneself*. Similarly, making use a few more times of the definition of an interpretation at expressions generated by the rules of functional applications, we may compute the value of m(x *self* (*love* (x's *mother*))) at an individual I to be m (*love*) [('s) (I) (m (*mother*)) (I)] , whence that P_1 is an appropriate representation for *to love one's own mother*. (we note that many languages, such as Hindi and Japanese, present reflexive possessives, somewhat imperfectly realized in English as *one's own*).

This essentially completes our analysis of reflexives. The following reflections on that analysis suggest ways we might want to extend or restrict that analysis.

First, some languages appear not to permit object controlled reflexives of the *save Mary from herself, tell Mary about herself* sort. One might suggest that the semantic representations for those languages would present a more restricted *self* operator in which in (x *self e*) e was required to be a P_1. But if the logic for those languages has an unrestricted lambda operator of the sort we have presented, the restriction on (x *self e*) will not in fact guarantee that 'inherently' non-subject noun phrases cannot control reflexives. Thus in (121) below the object argument y of *tell about x* controls the reference of x:

(121)

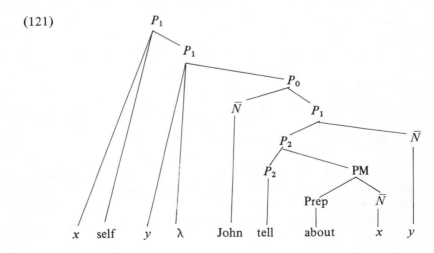

Second, note that $(x\ self\ e)$ is logically equivalent to $(\lambda x\ (e\ x))$. So the reflexive operator *self* does not contribute anything to the expressive power of L as extended. But it does give us structures which correspond better to natural English. Thus in the lambda representation for reflexives *John cut himself* would be represented as $(John\ (\lambda\ x\ (x\ (cut\ x))))$. This expression contains an embedded P_0, $(x\ (cut\ x))$ and a $\bar{N}$, the subject of $(x\ (cut\ x))$, not present in any way in the English expression. The representation with *self* localizes the complexity of reflexives in the P_1 and does not present the additional $\bar{N}$ expression. It thus provides a better correspondence with the English expression whose logical properties it represents. It also provides more natural representations (present in the intensional logic) for reflexive P_n's in which no subject is present in English, as in *to shave oneself in the dark is difficult*.

Third, our semantics for reflexives crucially (it appears) uses the fact that e in $(x\ self\ e)$ is interpreted by a function taking elements of $T_{\bar{N}}$ as arguments. Thus e cannot be a PM (*in x's garden*) or an AP_i (*proud of x*) since these expressions are interpreted by functions taking properties and $n > 0$ place predicate denotations as arguments respectively. Equally e cannot be an N (*friend of x*) since Ns are not interpreted by functions at all. Yet e can be a P_1 and the types for PM (whether subject or argument oriented), AP_i and N are isomorphic to the type for P_1. Thus it is a straightforward matter to extend the domain of the reflexive operator to apply to expressions in these categories. The mechanism for the extension is given informally by the diagram in (122) below, where C is any category whose type is isomorphic to that for P_1 and h is such an isomorphism. Then for $e \in C$, $(x\ self\ e)$ is interpreted as that element of T_C which makes the diagram commute as indicated by the dotted line:

(122)

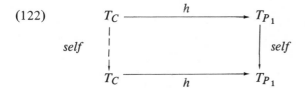

For example, taking *critic* as an N_1 $(= N/\bar{N})$ and thus $(critic\ (of)\ x)$ as an N, we have that the isomorphic image of $m\ (critic\ of\ x)$ is $m\ (criticize\ x)$. That is, $m\ (critic\ of\ x)$ is the property an individual I has iff $m\ (criticize\ x)\ (I)$ is true, whence from (122) we infer in effect that $m\ (x\ self\ (critic\ of\ x))$ is the property an individual I has iff $m\ (x\ self\ (criticize\ x))\ (I)$ is true, that is, the individual I criticizes himself. Thus $(x\ self\ (critic\ of\ x))$ is a natural representation of *critic of oneself*.

Similarly the intersecting AP $(x\ self\ (proud\ of\ x))$ is a reasonable representation of *proud of oneself* as it is interpreted by that function from P into P whose value at the unit property (the denotation of *individual*) is a member of an individual I iff $m\ (x\ self\ (be\ (proud\ of\ x)))$ holds of I. That is, the individual I is proud of himself.

Finally, a reflexive PM such as $(x\ self\ (in\ x$'s $garden))$ will denote that element of $T_{PM_{arg}}$ whose value at the unit element in T_{P_1} (the denotation of *exist*) is the denotation of $(x\ self\ (exist\ (in\ x$'s $garden)))$. Thus $(x\ self\ (in\ x$'s $garden))$ is a reasonable representation for *in one's own garden*.

We might note that extending the domain of *self* in this way allows us to represent a sort of binding which is known to be difficult to represent in a way which preserves some reasonable correspondence between logical form and surface form. (123a) below illustrates the type of problem (matching subscripts indicating binding), and (123b) is our representation for it:

(123) a. a man$_i$ with a scar on his$_i$ face
      b. (a (man $(x$ self (with a scar on x's face))))).

(Note that we have assumed here that the domain of PMs has been extended to include N. This assumption is unproblematic since T_N is isomorphic to T_{P_1} which is already included in the domain of PMs.)

The Relative Clause Operator

Adding (124) below to the formation rules of L allows us to generate relative clauses straightforwardly:

(124)   if e is an expression of category P_0 and x a variable then $(x\ suchthat\ e)$ is a phrase of category $\underset{i}{AP}$.

To interpret such expressions recall first that a property (an element of $P = T_N$) is defined by stating just what individuals it is an element of (see the earlier discussion in Part A). And secondly, recall that T_{AP} is the set of intersecting functions from P into P and that any such function is defined by stating its value at the unit property. We may then straightforwardly interpret expressions of the form $(x\ suchthat\ e)$ as follows:

DEFINITION 54. For *e, x* as in (124), and for any model $\langle P, 2, M \rangle$, $m(x$ *suchthat e*) is that intersecting function from P into P such that for each individual I, $m(x$ *suchthat e*) (1) $\in I$ iff $m'(e) = 1$, where m' is the x-variant of m such that $m'(x) = I$.

To exemplify this definition let us assume an arbitrary model $\langle P, 2, M \rangle$ and calculate the interpretation of (125) below:

(125)   student (*x* suchthat (Dorothy (hug *x*))).

This phrase is formed by combining the *N student* with the AP (*x suchthat* (*Dorothy* (*hug x*))) and so is itself of category *N*. Its interpretation is therefore an element of P. For convenience, let us set $m(x$ *suchthat* (*Dorothy* (*hug x*))) $= f$. Then the interpretation of the phrase (125) is $f(s)$, where $s = m(student)$. Our task is to determine just what property $f(s)$ actually is. We will do this by indicating for each arbitrary individual I whether or not I contains $f(s)$.

First, since f is intersecting, we have that $f(s) = s \wedge f(1)$. By the Meets Condition on individuals (Part A), the individual I contains $f(s)$ if and only if I contains both s and $f(1)$.

Next, we apply Definition 54 above. Set $m(Dorothy) = I_d$ and $m(hug) = h$. If m' is the x-variant of m such that $m'(x) = I$ (where I is an arbitrary individual), then $m'(Dorothy$ (*hug x*)) $= (m'(hug \, x)) \, (m'(Dorothy)) = (h \, (I)) \, (I_d)$ (since $m'(hug) = m(hug)$ and $m'(Dorothy) = m(Dorothy)$). Thus, the individual I contains $f(1)$ if and only if $(h \, (I)) \, (I_d) = 1$.

Combining this result with the previous paragraph, we conclude that the property $f(s)$ is the one which is contained in the individual I just in case I contains s and $h \, (I) \, (I_d) = 1$. Informally, (125) denotes the property an individual has iff that individual is a student and Dorothy hugs that individual. Thus (125) appears to be an adequate representation of the somewhat stilted English (126) below, as well as of the more natural expressions in (127).

(126)   student such that Dorothy hugged him

(127)   student $\left\{ \begin{array}{l} \text{who (m)} \\ \text{that} \\ \emptyset \end{array} \right\}$ Dorothy hugged

Obviously (125) exhibits a better correspondence with (126) than with

(127) since (126) presents an overt pronoun, *him*, in the position corresponding to the bound occurrence of x in (125). We shall not consider the problem
of systematically relating structures like (127) to their L-representations,
noting only that in many languages, e.g. Persian, Fijian, Margi, Arabic, etc.
the natural expression of (125) would present an overt 'resumptive' pronoun
in surface. (128) below from Hebrew is illustrative.

> (128)   talmid še-   Dorit   xibka   oto
>   student that- Dorothy hugged him
>   'student who Dorothy hugged'

We may note as well that the superficial similarity in structure between
(126) and (127) is perhaps misleading, suggesting that *such that* in English
is a relativizer with the same status as *whom(m)*, *that*, etc. In more complex
relatives however *such that* tends to force a wide scope reading of the head
N compared with *who(m)*, *that*, etc. Contrast for example (129a, b):

> (129) a. the language that everyone here speaks best (is an Indo-European
>   language)
>   b. the language such that everyone here speaks it best . . .

(129b) rather forces the interpretation that everyone here speaks the same
language best, whereas (129a) seems to allow that different people here
may speak different languages best; it is true as long as in each case that
language is an Indo-European one.

Moreover the *such that* construction, analyzed as an AP in L, functions
naturally as an AP in predicate position, illustrated in (130a) below and
represented in L by (130b). The wh-relatives function less naturally in predicate position, as indicated in (131).

> (130) a. No one is such that everyone likes him
>   b. (no individual (be (x suchthat (every individual like x))))

> (131)   *No one is who(m) everyone likes

Notice also that the *such that* construction in English, especially when
functioning predicatively, does not always force the sentence it combines
with to contain a bound $\bar{N}$ position, as in *the acoustics of the auditorium
were such that no one could hear the speaker from the podium.*

Observe further that the VBO *suchthat* allows us to construct relatives in *L* which correspond to ungrammatical wh-relatives in English due to the violation of island constraints. Thus (132) below corresponds to the ungrammatical (133) in English as well as to the grammatical but stilted (134) in English and the grammatical though slightly cumbersome (135) in Hebrew:

(132)   student (x suchthat (Dan (know (a girl (y suchthat (y hug x))))))

(133)   *student who Dan knows a girl who hugged

(134)   student such that Dan knows a girl who hugged him

(135)   talmid   še-   Dan   makir   baxura   še-   xibka   oto
         student that- Dan   knows   girl   that- hugged him

The expressions (134) and (135) are sufficient to show that we want logical representations for natural language expressions to contain structures which violate island constraints. Thus the motivation for such constraints in English does not arise from any difficulty with their logical semantics and must then be otherwise motivated.

Finally, we note that since an expression like (x *suchthat* e) is a member of the boolean categories AP and AP, it is possible to construct and interpret expressions like (136) and (137) in our logical language:

(136)   (Albanian and (x suchthat Dorothy (hug x))) student

(137)   (tall and (x suchthat Dorothy (hug x))) student.

In English, there are no expressions like *Albanian and who* (*m*) *Dorothy hugged a student*, *student Albanian and who* (*m*) *Dorothy hugged*, *tall and who* (*m*) *Dorothy hugged a student*, etc. However, as in the case of the island constraints, we do not want to claim that the difficulty with such expressions resides in their logical semantics since the normal interpretations of English phrases like *Albanian student that Dorothy hugged* and *tall student that Dorothy hugged* are just (136) and (137) respectively.

This essentially completes our treatment of VBOs in *L*. Let us however indicate how a (standard) awkwardness in our basic definitions may be corrected. In defining the value of an interpretation *m* at for example (λ x e) we refer to the values of all x-variants m' of *m* at e. But strictly speaking the only x-variant of *m* we are allowed to refer to is *m* itself, the others having not yet been defined.

There are a variety of ways this difficulty can be overcome. One which, as indicated earlier, will prove useful in a more detailed treatment of context dependency of English expressions will be sketched here.

First, let us use for the nonce A to denote the set of functions from $\bar{N}_{\mathrm{var}}$ into I_P, the set of individuals of the model. Elements of A will be called *assignments* (*of values to the variables*). If a is an assignment and x is a variable and I an individual then $a_{x,\,I}$ will be that x-variant of a which sends x to I. Now given an ontology $\langle P, 2 \rangle$ we define a model to be a triple $\langle P, 2, M \rangle$ as before, except that the variables do not lie in the domain of M. We shall then interpret expressions of L in general not directly as elements of the appropriate types, but rather as functions from A into the types. So the interpretation of an expression will depend on what assignment is being considered. It will turn out that expressions containing no free occurrences of variables will be constant functions, that is, they will not in fact depend on how the variables are interpreted. Typically however, expressions containing free occurrences of variables will depend on the assignment, that is, they will send different assignments to different elements of the appropriate type.

Somewhat more formally, given a model $\langle P, 2, M \rangle$ we define m to be an interpretation of L iff m is a function from L into the set of functions from A into the union of the types such that the following conditions are satisfied for all $a \in A$ and all individuals I:

(i)   for e in the domain of M, $m\,(e)\,(a) = M\,(e)$.

(ii) for e a variable, $m\,(e)\,(a) = a\,(e)$.

(iii) for e_1, e_2 in any boolean category C, $m\,(e_1\ and\ e_2)\,(a) = m\,(e_1)\,(a) \wedge m\,(e_2)\,(a)$, and analogously for other boolean combinations.

(iv) for e_1 in X/Y and e_2 in Y, $m\,(e_1\ e_2)\,(a) = (m\,(e_1)\,(a))\,(m\,(e_2)\,(a))$

(v)   for e in any boolean catefory C, $m\,(\lambda\ x\ e)$ is that complete homomorphism from $T_{\bar{N}}$ into T_C such that $m\,(\lambda\ x\ e)\,(a)\,(I) = m\,(e)\,(a_{x,\,I})$.

(vi) for e in a boolean category of the form $C/\bar{N}$, $m\,(x\ self\ e)\,(a)\,(I) = m\,(e)\,(a_{x,\,I})\,(I)$

(vii) for e of category P_0, $m\,(x\ suchthat\ e)\,(a)\,(1) \in I$ iff $m\,(e)\,(a_{x,\,I}) = 1$.

Note that this approach does overcome the awkwardness alluded to since, for example, the value of m at $(\lambda\ x\ e)$ does not refer to the values of other interpretations m' at e but only to the value of m at e; analogously for the interpretations of the other VBOs.

This concludes our treatment of VBOs in L. It also essentially concludes our treatment of the extensional additions to L. Below we consider (but reject) a final addition to L which has doubtless occurred to many, namely, the addition of predicates which do not behave homomorphically on their arguments.

7. NON-HOMOMORPHIC PREDICATES?

There are a variety of English predicates which appear to behave non-homomorphically on their arguments. Several such are surveyed below. The natural suggestion for incorporating such predicates into L would be to introduce a subcategorization feature for P_ns into L, say $+hom$, and define the type for $P_{n_{+hom}}$ to be T_{P_n} as previously defined. Then predicates not in this subcategory would not be required to be interpreted by homomorphisms. On closer examination however the apparent non-homomorphic predicates do not appear to be adequately treated in this way. Rather, to the extent that we understand their (pre-theoretical) semantics it seems that the domain of these predicates is not properly taken to be sets of properties of individuals but rather something at least as complicated as sets of properties of sets of individuals. Once the domain of these predicates is properly defined, something we do not do rigorously here, it appears that, in fact, the predicates do behave homomorphically.

Let us consider first some apparent non-homomorphic predicates. For a more thorough discussion we refer the reader to Gil (1982) and Busby (1983) and references cited there. We shall draw examples freely from those works below; moreover, our classification of non-homomorphic predicates is intended as mnemonic only. The classes are not exhaustive or mutually exclusive.

Numerical Predicates

Predicates such as *be two teachers, be the two students John knows best, be the only survivors*, etc. appear non-homomorphic since (138a, b) below are not logically equivalent, whence such predicates appear not to preserve meets.

(138) a. John and Bill are the two students I know best
b. John is the two students I know best and Bill is the two students I know best

Collective Predicates

Predicates such as *be a bore, be a happy couple, constitute a quorum*, etc. also appear to fail to preserve meets, as illustrated in (139a, b) below which are not logically equivalent.

(139) a. John and Mary are a happy couple
      b. John is a happy couple and Mary is a happy couple

Predicates such as *solve the problem together* and *read ten plays between them* probably also fall into this category. In any event (140a) below does not mean anything like (140b).

(140) a. John and Mary read ten plays between them
      b. John read ten plays (between him) and Mary read ten plays (between her)

Reciprocal Predicates

Obviously P_1s such as *love each other* cannot be represented as homomorphisms from P^* into 2 since (150a, b) are not paraphrases:

(150) a. John and Mary love each other
      b. John loves each other and Mary loves each other

Into this category as well we might include a large variety of nominal and adjectival predicates which, in one way or another, involve a reciprocal meaning even though no overt use is made of the reciprocal pronoun *each other*. Thus (151a, b) are not paraphrases:

(151) a. John and Bill are partners/friends/enemies
      b. John is a partner/friend/enemy and Bill is a partner/friend/enemy

Similar predicates crucially involving adjectives would be *live in neighboring villages, work on parallel streets, attend the same school, work for different employers*, etc. So called symmetric predicates such as (intransitive) *meet, be parallel*, etc. also fall into this category.

Intensional Predicates

Non-extensional predicates such as *seek, look for, need*, etc. appear not to preserve joins since *I'm looking for the owner or the manager* is not (at least on one reading) logically equivalent to *I'm looking for the owner or I'm looking for the manager*. Similarly the complex non-extensional P_1 in (152) below also fails (on one reading) to preserve joins:

> (152) a. The President or the Vice-President is required to be a citizen
> b. The President is required to be a citizen or the Vice-President is required to be a citizen

((152a) is true if the constitution stipulates that 'Either the President or the Vice-President must be a citizen', whereas that condition is not sufficient to guarantee the truth of either disjunct of (152b) and thus it does not guarantee the truth of the disjunction.)

Of the predicates considered above the intensional ones are treated in Part II of this monograph and are in fact interpreted there by non-homomorphic elements of the appropriate type. The other predicates however are extensional and it is tempting to want to add them to L but not require that they be interpreted by homomorphisms. It appears to us however that no such approach is likely to succeed. To support this claim let us consider the case of overt reciprocal predicates such as *love each other*.

If *love each other* were interpreted by some sort of function, not necessarily a homomorphism, from P^* into 2 this would necessitate a very thorough going redefinition of the interpretations of $\bar{N}$s. For example, conjunctions of $\bar{N}$s would no longer be both commutative and associative since the natural reading of (153a) below is a paraphrase of (153b) and not of (153c). Yet by the commutativity and associativity of meets, (153a, c) are logically equivalent since their subject $\bar{N}$s are interpreted as the same element of P^*.

> (153) a. Both John and Mary and also Bill and Sue love each other
> b. John and Mary love each other and Bill and Sue love each other
> c. Both John and Bill and also Mary and Sue love each other

Further, determiner denotations would have to be redefined. Consider for example a model with at least three individuals, John, Bill, and Harry, in which Bill and Harry are the only students. Then *every student* is interpreted as the same element of P^* as *Bill and Harry*, whence (154a) should have the same truth value in that model as (154b). But this is incorrect. (154a) is a paraphrase of (154c) and does not, as judged pre-theoretically, entail (154d). (154b) does however entail (154d).

(154) a. John and every student love each other
     b. John and (Bill and Harry) love each other
     c. John and Bill love each other and John and Harry love each other
     d. Bill and Harry love each other

Now we can find no way of reinterpreting *and* and *every* in such a way that the $\bar{N}$s they form take their denotations in P^* and the entailments we have previously modelled correctly by L are still correctly represented.

Additional reasons for not taking *love each other* as a function on P^* could be adduced but it seems needless to belabor the point since in fact our initial pre-theoretical intuitions concerning a correct approach to the semantics of reciprocals are clear: *love each other* does not express a property of individuals, but rather of (at least) *sets* of individuals. Roughly the set {John, Mary} has the love-each-other property iff John loves Mary and Mary loves John. Minimally then we want the domain of the love-each-other function to include sets of individuals, or pursuing the general approach taken here, sets of properties of sets of individuals. Once the domain of reciprocal predicates is correctly defined it appears, contra our initial intuitions, that reciprocal predicates do behave homomorphically on their arguments. For example, (155a, b) below are logically equivalent, whence *love each other* preserves joins.

(155) a. Either John and Mary or Bill and Sue love each other
     b. Either John and Mary love each other or Bill and Sue love each other

Similarly the equivalence of (156a, b) shows that reciprocal predicates preserve meets and complements:

(156) a. John and Mary but not Bill and Sue love each other
     b. John and Mary love each other and it is not the case that Bill and Sue love each other

Pursuing this approach would probably require that we distinguish two *and*'s in English, the lower order *and* we have been using which forms intersections and a higher order one which (roughly) forms sets. Using *and* for the lower order one and & for the higher order one, we might represent (157a) below as (157b).

(157) a. Both John and Mary and also Bill and Sue love each other
     b. ((John & Mary) and (Bill & Sue)) (love each other)

We shall not however pursue this approach here since it seems clear that we cannot adequately represent reciprocal predicates (or the other non-extensional ones discussed above) merely by extending the types for the predicates to include non-homomorphisms. Rather we must seriously extend the domains of the predicates in our system in such a way as to introduce the full apparatus of higher order logic. And while this is a much needed enterprise, it would surely encompass another monograph. Instead we turn now to the revisions of L necessary to accommodate properly non-extensional expressions of English.

PART II: THE INTENSIONAL LOGIC

1. INTRODUCTION TO THE INTENSIONAL SYSTEM

We now wish to address ourselves to the task of constructing a logical system which can represent facts of the sort referred to as properly intensional, facts which cannot be handled by the extensional system developed earlier. We begin with some basic discussion which will set the stage for the more detailed developments to come.

Our motivation in wanting to construct an intensional system should be clear at this point. Even while developing the extensional system, we often came across phrases or constructions for which an extensional interpretation was in principle unable to represent the logical facts adequately. For example, an adjective like *skillful* cannot be correctly interpreted in a purely extensional manner. For if it were, then its interpretation would be a function which would take as its argument the extensional interpretation of the *N* with which it is combined. Now, this would mean that in a world in which the individuals who are lawyers are exactly the same as the individuals who are doctors, so that *lawyer* and *doctor* have the same extensional interpretation, the interpretation of *skillful lawyer* and of *skillful doctor* would automatically be the same, since the function which interprets *skillful* would have been applied to the same argument. But this is unsatisfactory: even if the lawyers and the doctors in some state of affairs are the same individuals, the skillful lawyers and the skillful doctors clearly need not be so. Similar situations exist in the case of other modifier categories. Thus, we noted earlier that PMs like manner adverbs (*skillfully*) or comitative phrases (*with Mary*) cannot be adequately represented extensionally.

The difficulty is not restricted to modifiers, of course. A classic example of a transitive verb which cannot be handled extensionally is *look-for*. Extensionally, this verb would be interpreted by a homomorphism whose argument is the extensional interpretation of its object $\bar{N}$. This means that, in a world in which, say, *Mary* and *the queen* refer to the same individual (so that their extensional interpretations are the same), *look for Mary* and *look for the queen* would automatically have the same interpretation, since the interpretation of either would be obtained by applying the *look-for* homomorphism

272

to the common interpretation of the two noun phrases. But, again, this is incorrect: John could be looking for Mary without looking for the queen (he might not know that Mary is in fact the queen).

In order to handle examples such as these (and many others as well), we will enrich the semantic system of our language. But before we set about to do this, let us note that syntactically, we will not change our language in any way, except to enlarge the membership of certain categories and to refine the subcategorizations. Thus, the slash, bar, and bracket notations of the extensional language are defined and used exactly the same for the intensional system, categories such as P_n and N_m have the same definition, etc., and a complex expression is still an unordered set of other expressions.

The sort of enlargement that will be involved can be illustrated by the verb *look-for*. This verb cannot be a member of P_2 in the extensional language, for the reason indicated above. In the intensional language, however, P_2 will contain this verb, along with others whose interpretations may be properly intensional (such as *criticize*). Moreover, such verbs will be subcategorized in such a way that they are part of a different subcategory of P_2 from verbs like *kiss* or *hit*. The interpretations of expressions of category P_2 will then be arranged so that expressions of the latter subcategory will never be interpreted in a properly intensional manner.

In addition, there are categories which are definable but which have no members in the extensional language. The intensional system will allow us to treat expressions which are members of certain of these. Thus, for example, the categories $\bar{P}_0$, $\bar{P}_0/P_0$, and $P_1/\bar{P}_0$ are definable but uninhabited in the extensional language. In the intensional language, these categories will contain expressions such as *that Bill kiss Mary, that*, and *believe*, respectively.

The method of presentation here will be the same as for the extensional system. That is, we will discuss the system category by category, beginning with a core language consisting of (at least) the categories N, $\bar{N}$, $\bar{N}/N$, and P_n (for all nonnegative integers n). In the remainder of this section we lay the groundwork for our intensional semantics.

It will be recalled that, in our extensional system, for each category C, a set T_C, the type for C, was defined. Moreover, the definition of each T_C depended on the pair $\langle P, 2 \rangle$, where 2 is the boolean algebra of two elements, representing the set of possible truth values of a formula, and P was an arbitrary complete atomic boolean algebra, representing the set of (extensional) properties, that is, the set of possible denotations of a common noun. In our intensional system, we again will define a type for each category C, which we again denote T_C. However, rather than depending on the pair

$\langle P, 2 \rangle$, the definition of the intensional types will depend on the triplet $\langle P, 2, J \rangle$, where, as before, 2 is the boolean algebra of two elements and P is an arbitrary complete atomic boolean algebra, but now J is an arbitrary set. The set J is to be understood as a set which indexes the possible worlds which are involved in a particular intensional interpretation.

Having chosen the triplet $\langle P, 2, J \rangle$ on which to base our definitions of the types, we could, of course, construct the extensional types which our earlier system associated with the categories on the basis of just 2 and P (that is, ignoring the set J). The sets so constructed will be henceforth denoted T_C^e. We are thus promulgating a change of notation: sets which previously were denoted T_C are now going to be denoted T_C^e, whereas the symbol T_C will be used for the intensional type of C. In general, we will be free to use the superscript e to create a symbol which will denote an object defined in our extensional system.

Our general task will be to create a system of model-theoretic interpretation for our logical language which will preserve the advantages and insights revealed by our extensional system while allowing properly intensional facts to be represented. Loosely speaking, we want the extensional system that we have already developed to be embedded, in some sense, inside the intensional system we are constructing. Exactly how we propose to do this will become clear in the course of the presentation. However, we would like to point out that there is no a priori reason to assume that there is only one viable way to extend our extensional system to an intensional one. The system we will present here seems to us to be a natural one; and it certainly is capable of representing a substantial range of properly intensional phenomena. Nevertheless, it may be that a different system could be constructed which would be superior in some respects, but would still incorporate the extensional system given earlier.

A question we could raise immediately is the following: given the category C, what is the relationship between T_C and T_C^e? A conceivable answer is that T_C^e is a subset of T_C. Thus, for example, if $C = P_2$, we can imagine that the interpretation function will be restricted so that, while verbs like *look-for* and *criticize* could take their (intensional) denotations anywhere in the set T_{P_2}, verbs like *kiss* or *hit* would have to take their denotations inside the subset $T_{P_2}^e$. As it turns out, it will be the case for no category that T_C^e is a subset of T_C, although for some categories (P_2 included) properly extensional expressions *will* be restricted to take their denotations in a proper subset of T_C.

Since we have already mentioned that the intensional types are to be defined on the basis of $\langle P, 2, J \rangle$, the reader may have guessed another possible relationship between T_C and T_C^e, namely that $T_C = FT_C^e/J$, that is, that the elements of T_C are just all the functions with domain J and with range the extensional type T_C^e. This by now standard notion of intension captures the idea that to know the meaning of an expression is equivalent to knowing its extension in any possible world. This is in fact how the intensional types of categories are defined in classical Montague grammar.

In the system we shall propose, we shall indeed take T_C to be equal to FT_C^e/J, but only for certain categories C, rather than for all of them, as is done in Montague grammar. In the core language, for example, the types for the categories P_0, N, and $\overline{N}$ will be so defined. However, functional categories will be handled differently. Suppose, say, that $C = B/A$. Then, rather than taking $T_C = FT_C^e/J$, we will in general take T_C to be some subset of FT_B/T_A. Thus, if f is a possible (intensional) denotion of an expression of category C, then f is indeed a function, but its argument, rather than being the index of a possible world, is just the intension of the expression with which the original expression was combined. It will turn out that a relationship between FT_B/T_A and FT_C^e/J can often be established; how this is done will become clear later on.

Suppose that C is one of those categories for which we have $T_C = FT_C^e/J$. If f is a possible intensional denotation of an expression of category C (which we abbreviate by calling f a *C-intension*), then, given $j \in J$, $f(j)$ is a well-defined member of T_C^e. We will call $f(j)$ the *extension of f in the world j*.

Next, suppose that C is a category for which it is *not* the case that $T_C = FT_C^e/J$, and let f be a C-intension. Now, of course, if $j \in J$, the expression $f(j)$ is undefined. However, in certain cases, it will be possible to associate with f a set $\{f_j : j \in J\}$, where each f_j is a member of T_C^e. This association will be biunique; this is, given f, a unique $f_j \in T_C^e$ will be defined for each $j \in J$, and, conversely, given the set $\{f_j : j \in J\}$, where each $f_j \in T_C^e$, there will be a unique $f \in T_C$ associated with it. In such cases, we will call f_j the *extension of f in the world j*. (Again, we ask the reader's patience: *how* a C-intension f can be associated with a set $\{f_j : j \in J\}$ will become clear later on.)

Now, let f be a C-intension, where C is any category. Then we will say that f is *extensional* iff, for each $j \in J$, f has an extension in the world j. In general, we will use the notation f_j to denote this extension. Thus, by what we have said above, if f is a C-intension for a category C such that $T_C = FT_C^e/J$, then f is necessarily extensional, and $f_j = f(j)$. For other categories, a particular intension f may or may not be extensional depending on whether the association of f with a set $\{f_j: j \in J\}$ discussed in the previous paragraph can be defined. Thus, for these categories, we can expect that the extensional intensions will form a proper subset of T_C. Let us denote the subset of T_C which consists of all the extensional intensions by T_{Ce}. Then, we have $T_{Ce} = T_C$ if $T_C = FT_C^e/J$, and in general $T_{Ce} \subseteq T_C$.

We pointed out above that in the case that a C-intension f is extensional, we want the association of f with the set $\{f_j: j \in J\}$ to be biunique. Let us formulate this as a definition:

DEFINITION 1. Given the category C, T_{Ce} is *total* iff for every set $\{x_j: j \in J\} \subseteq T_C^e$, there exists a unique $f \in T_{Ce}$ such that $f_j = x_j$.

Note that, a priori, a set T_{Ce} might not be total. That is, it might be possible to define $f_j \in T_C^e$ for each $j \in J$, given a C-intension f, in such a way that distinct C-intensions have the same extensions in all the worlds. Or again, it might be the case that not every set $\{x_j: j \in J\}$ of j-indexed elements of T_C^e is the set of extensions of some C-intension. These possibilities are ruled out when T_{Ce} is total.

For all the cases of interest to us, T_{Ce} will turn out to be total. Of course, this will have to be proved for each category or class of categories as we study it. However, we can say at least the following right now:

(1)   If the category C is such that $T_C = FT_C^e/J$, then T_{Ce} ($= T_C$) is total.

The reader will recall that at several places in the development of the extensional system, we used the term *transparent* to denote an expression whose denotation could be defined as a function which takes an extensional denotation as an argument. Transparent expressions were in contrast to properly intensional ones. In our intensional system, transparent expressions and properly intensional ones of the same category will be interpreted by intensions of the same general sort. In order to represent the different logical behavior of these two sorts of expressions, we will want to require that the intension of a transparent expression be dependent extensionally on its argument, in some sense. We are able to give a precise formulation of what this means, using what we have already developed in this section, as follows:

DEFINITION 2. Let C_1 and C_2 be arbitrary categories, and let $f: T_{C_1 e} \to T_{C_2 e}$ be an arbitrary function. Then f is *transparent* iff for each $j \in J$, if $x, y \in T_{C_1 e}$ are such that $x_j = y_j$, then $(f(x))_j = (f(y))_j$.

Thus, for the function f (which maps intensions onto intensions) to be transparent, it must be the case that the extension of the value of f in any world depend only on the extension of the argument of f in that world.

As an example, consider the transitive verbs *kiss* and *look-for* as applied to the $\bar{N}$s *Mary* and *the queen*. In our intensional system, all four expressions will be interpreted by intensions. In general, *Mary* and *the queen* will be interpreted by different intensions, say, x and y respectively; but in some particular world, say j, Mary and the queen might be the same individual, that is, $x_j = y_j$. Now, although the intensions of *kiss Mary* and *kiss the queen* can be expected to be different, in general, we would want the extension of *kiss Mary* in j to be the same as the extension of *kiss the queen* in j, since, in j, Mary and the queen are the same person. But if the function f which interprets *kiss* is transparent, then this is exactly what happens; since $x_j = y_j$, the definition insures that $(f(x))_j$ (the extension in j of *kiss Mary*) equals $(f(y))_j$ (the extension in j of *kiss the queen*). On the other hand, if g interprets *look-for*, we would not, in general, want this to be the case: even though $x_j = y_j$, the extensions of *look for Mary* and *look for the queen* might be different in world j. Thus, if the function which interprets an ordinary extensional transitive verb like *kiss* is required to be transparent, while the function which interprets a properly intensional transitive verb like *look-for* is not so required, these basic facts will automatically be represented.

Definition 2 is formulated only to apply to a function whose domain and range are sets T_{Ce}. It is convenient to use the term *transparent* for a function with any domain and range to mean that the restriction of that function to the subset of extensional arguments is transparent in the sense of Definition 2. An important special case is:

DEFINITION 3. Let $f: T_{C_1} \to T_{C_2}$ be an arbitrary function (where C_1, C_2 are arbitrary categories) such that whenever $x \in T_{C_1 e}$, then $f(x) \in T_{C_2 e}$. Then f is *transparent* iff its restriction to $T_{C_1 e}$ is transparent.

We can now give the following important theorem, which, in essence, relates the notions of transparency and extensionality:

THEOREM 1. *General Extensionality Theorem* . Let C_1 and C_2 be categories such that $T_{C_1 e}$ and $T_{C_2 e}$ are total. Let $f: T_{C_1} \to T_{C_2}$ be such that whenever $x \in T_{C_1 e}$, $f(x) \in T_{C_2 e}$. If f is transparent, then, for each $j \in J$, the equation $f_j(x_j) = (f(x))_j \ \forall x \in T_{C_1 e}$ uniquely defines an element f_j of $F T_{C_2}^e / T_{C_1}^e$.

Conversely, if for each $j \in J$ a function $f_j \in FT^e_{C_2}/T^e_{C_1}$ is given, then there is a unique transparent $f: T_{C_1 e} \rightarrow T_{C_2 e}$ such that $(f(x))_j = f_j(x_j)$.

There are two points of detail that the reader should keep in mind about the general extensionality theorem. The first is that the theorem does not assert that there is a unique function $f: T_{C_1} \rightarrow T_{C_2}$ defined when extensions f_j are given. What is unique is the restriction of such a function f to $T_{C_1 e}$; but if $T_{C_1 e}$ is a proper subset of T_{C_1}, then the values of f for nonextensional arguments are not in any way constrained, a priori. Thus, there could be distinct functions f_1 and f_2, which took different values on nonextensional arguments, but whose restrictions to $T_{C_1 e}$ were the same; these functions would have the same extensions in all the worlds (if they were transparent, of course). However, in the special case that $T_{C_1 e}$ is all of T_{C_1} (a situation which happens often enough to be of interest to us), we *can* conclude that a unique transparent function $f: T_{C_1} \rightarrow T_{C_2}$ is defined by giving its extensions in all the worlds.

The second point is that the function $f: T_{C_1 e} \rightarrow T_{C_2 e}$ whose existence and uniqueness is guaranteed if extensions f_j are given cannot be assumed to be a member of $T_{C_2/C_1 e}$. The reason is that, in addition to being a function from $T_{C_1 e}$ into $T_{C_2 e}$, a member of $T_{C_2/C_1 e}$ might have to satisfy other restrictions, such as being a homomorphism, being restricting or intersecting, etc. Even if each extension of such a function lies in $T^e_{C_2/C_1}$ and hence satisfies the appropriate restrictions it is not automatically guaranteed that the intensional function will also do so. In particular cases, it *will* happen that an extensional intension inherits properties of its extensions, and hence will be a member of $T_{C_2/C_1 e}$; but this will have to be proven in addition to appealing to the general extensionality theorem.

In developing the extensional system, we argued that the types for many categories should have the structure of boolean algebras. The same arguments show that the intensional types for many categories should be boolean algebras. The following theorem will prove useful in many cases for defining boolean structure:

THEOREM 2. *Lifting Theorem.* Let C be a category for which T_{Ce} is total. If T^e_C is a boolean algebra, then T_{Ce} is a boolean algebra under the operations $\wedge$, $\vee$, and $'$ defined as follows:

(a) If $f, g \in T_{Ce}, f \wedge g$ is that element of T_{Ce} such that for each $j \in J$, $(f \wedge g)_j = f_j \wedge g_j$.

(b) If $f, g \in T_{Ce}$, $f \vee g$ is that element of T_{Ce} such that for each $j \in J$, $(f \vee g)_j = f_j \vee g_j$.

(c) If $f \in T_{Ce}$, f' is that element of T_{Ce} such that for each $j \in J$, $(f')_j = (f_j)'$.

Moreover, if T_C^e is complete, then T_{Ce} is complete, and if T_C^e is atomic, then T_{Ce} is atomic.

The operations on T_{Ce} defined in the lifting theorem may be described as operating 'pointwise on the worlds'; that is, the extension in some world of the boolean combination of intensions is just the (extensional) boolean combination of their extensions in that world. In this sense, the boolean structure of T_C^e is 'lifted' up to T_{Ce}.

We note that in the case that C is a boolean category such that $T_C = F_{T_C^e/J}$, the lifting theorem automatically assigns boolean structure to T_C ($= T_{Ce}$). In the case that T_{Ce} is a proper subset of T_C, the lifting theorem does *not* assign structure to the whole of T_C, but only to T_{Ce}. The question of whether it is possible to make all of T_C a boolean algebra, or even whether it is desirable to do so, is somewhat difficult, and will be taken up in connection with certain specific categories.

Having laid this much of a foundation, we are ready to proceed to the construction of the intensional system for the core language.

Proofs of the Theorems

Statement (1) in the text is an obvious consequence of the definitions. Here we shall prove the general extensionality theorem and the lifting theorem.

THEOREM 1. *General Extensionality Theorem.* Let C_1 and C_2 be categories such that $T_{C_1 e}$ and $T_{C_2 e}$ are total. Let $f: T_{C_1} \to T_{C_2}$ be such that whenever $x \in T_{C_1 e}$, $f(x) \in T_{C_2 e}$. If f is transparent, then, for each $j \in J$, the equation $f_j(x_j) = (f(x))_j$ $\forall x \in T_{C_1 e}$ uniquely defines an element f_j of $F_{T_{C_2}^e / T_{C_1}^e}$. Conversely, if for each $j \in J$ a function $f_j \in F_{T_{C_2}^e / T_{C_1}^e}$ is given, then there is a unique transparent $f: T_{C_1 e} \to T_{C_2 e}$ such that $(f(x))_j = f_j(x_j)$.

Suppose first that C_1, C_2, and f satisfy the assumptions of the first part of the theorem. Let ξ be an arbitrary element of T_C^e. For a fixed $j \in J$, there must be an $x \in T_{C_1 e}$ such that $x_j = \xi$, since $T_{C_1 e}$ is total. We define $f_j(\xi)$ by setting it equal to $(f(x))_j$. Note that $(f(x))_j$ is indeed an element of $T_{C_2}^e$.

Moreover, if some $y \neq x$ were chosen from $T_{C_1 e}$ such that $y_j = \xi$, then $(f(y))_j$ would be equal to $(f(x))_j$, since $y_j = x_j$ and f is transparent. Thus, $f_j(\xi)$ is well defined. Since $x_j = \xi$, the equation $f_j(x_j) = (f(x))_j$ holds. This proves the first part of the theorem.

Next assume that functions $f_j \in FT^e_{C_2}/T^e_{C_1}$ have been given. For an arbitrary $x \in T_{C_1 e}$, $f_j(x_j) \in T^e_{C_2}$. Thus the set $\{f_j(x_j): j \in J\}$ (for this fixed x) is a subset of $T^e_{C_2}$, and so, since $T_{C_2 e}$ is total, there is a unique element $z \in T_{C_2 e}$ such that $z_j = f_j(x_j)$, $\forall j \in J$. Set $f(x) = z$. Then, the equation $(f(x))_j = f_j(x_j)$ holds, by the way f was defined. Moreover, f is transparent, as follows directly from this equation: if, for some j, $y_j = x_j$, then $(f(y))_j = f_j(y_j) = f_j(x_j) = (f(x))_j$. Finally, the equation $(f(x))_j = f_j(x_j)$ determines f uniquely. For, if there was a function g such that $(g(x))_j = f_j(x_j)$, then, for each x, $f(x)$ and $g(x)$ would have exactly the same extension in all worlds. Since $T_{C_2 e}$ is total, this would mean that $f(x) = g(x)$; and since x is arbitrary, we would have $f = g$.

THEOREM 2. *Lifting Theorem.* Let C be a category for which T_{Ce} is total. If T^e_C is a boolean algebra, then T_{Ce} is a boolean algebra under the operations $\wedge$, $\vee$, and $'$ defined as follows:

(a) *If f, $g \in T_{Ce}$, $f \wedge g$ is that element of T_{Ce} such that for each $j \in J$, $(f \wedge g)_j = f_j \wedge g_j$.*

(b) If f, $g \in T_{Ce}$, $f \vee g$ is that element of T_{Ce} such that for each $j \in J$, $(f \vee g)_j = f_j \vee g_j$.

(c) If $f \in T_{Ce}$, f' is that element of T_{Ce} such that for each $j \in J$, $(f')_j = (f_j)'$.

Moreover, if T^e_C is complete then T_{Ce} is complete, and if T^e_C is atomic, then T_{Ce} is atomic.

We note first that the totality of T_{Ce} guarantees that the operations are in fact well defined by the statements in (a), (b), and (c).

Next, the fact that the boolean axioms are satisfied in T_{Ce} follows almost trivially from the fact that they are satisfied in T^e_C. For example, suppose we want to prove the distributive law for T_{Ce}. Letting f, g, and h be arbitrary elements of T_{Ce}, we have:

$$
\begin{aligned}
(f \wedge (g \vee h))_j &= f_j \wedge (g \vee h)_j && \text{(by (a))} \\
&= f_j \wedge (g_j \vee h_j) && \text{(by (b))}
\end{aligned}
$$

$$= (f_j \wedge g_j) \vee (f_j \wedge h_j) \quad \text{(by the distributive law in } T_C^e)$$
$$= (f \wedge g)_j \vee (f \wedge h)_j \quad \text{(by (a))}$$
$$= ((f \wedge g) \vee (f \wedge h))_j \quad \text{(by (b))}$$

for an arbitrary $j \in J$. Since T_{Ce} is total, we conclude that $f \wedge (g \vee h) = (f \wedge g) \vee (f \wedge h)$.

The other boolean axioms may be proved in exactly the same way. We leave it to the reader to supply the details. Here, we simply point out that the zero element of T_{Ce} is that element 0 such that $0_j = 0_{T_C^e}$ for each $j \in J$; similarly, the unit element of T_{Ce} is that element 1 such that $1_j = 1_{T_C^e}$ for each $j \in J$. Thus, the zero is that intension whose extension in any world is zero, and the unit is that intension whose extension in an world is the unit.

Similarly, by a proof similar to the proof of the distributive law above, it follows from the definitions that, for arbitrary $f, g \in T_{Ce}$, $f \leqslant g$ iff $f_j \leqslant g_j$ for each $j \in J$. That is, for one extensional intension to bear the relation $\leqslant$ to another, it is necessary and sufficient that all its extensions bear this relation to the extensions of the other intension, in all the worlds.

Now, suppose that T_C^e is complete. Let $K \subseteq T_{Ce}$ be an arbitrary subset. We define $\wedge K$ by setting $(\wedge K)_j = \wedge_{f \in K} f_j$ for each $j \in J$. The right hand side of this equation is well defined, since T_C^e is complete. Since T_{Ce} is total, this equation defines the element $\wedge K$. We claim that $\wedge K$ so defined is in fact the glb of K.

First, let $f_0 \in K$ be arbitrary. Then we have $(\wedge K)_j = \wedge_{f \in K} f_j \leqslant f_{0j}$ for each $j \in J$, since $\wedge_{f \in K} f_j$ is the glb of the set $\{f_j : f \in K\}$, and f_{0j} is a member of this set. But then $\wedge K \leqslant f_0$, since j was arbitrary. Since f_0 was an arbitrary member of K, this shows that $\wedge K$ as defined above is a lower bound for the set K.

Secondly, suppose that $g \leqslant f$ holds for every $f \in K$. Then, for arbitrary $j \in J$, $g_j \leqslant f_j$ for every $f \in K$, whence g_j is a lower bound for the set $\{f_j : f \in K\}$. But this means that $g_j \leqslant \wedge_{f \in K} f_j = (\wedge K)_j$, since, again, $\wedge_{f \in K} f_j$ is the glb. Since this is true for arbitrary $j \in J$, we have $g \leqslant \wedge K$, showing that $\wedge K$ is the glb.

The proof that any subset of T_{Ce} has a lub is of course just the dual of this one.

Finally, suppose that T_C^e is atomic. Given an atom $a \in T_C^e$ and a world index $j \in J$, let us define an element $f_{aj} \in T_{Ce}$ as follows. For each $j' \in J$ such that $j' \neq j$, set $(f_{aj})_{j'} = 0_{T_C^e}$; and set $(f_{aj})_j = a$. Then, since T_{Ce} is total, f_{aj} is a well defined element of T_{Ce}. Moreover, f_{aj} is an atom; for, if $g \leqslant f_{aj}$ then, for each $j' \neq j$, $g_{j'} \leqslant (f_{aj})_{j'} = 0$ so that $g_{j'} = 0$ if $j' \neq j$. And, $g_j \leqslant (f_{aj})_j = $

a, so g_j is either 0 or a, since a is an atom. If $g_j = 0$, then $g = 0$, since all of its extensions are zero. If $g_j = a$, then $g = f_{aj}$, since g and f_{aj} then have the same extensions in all the worlds. Thus, f_{aj} is an atom. The reader may show easily that any atom of T_{Ce} is of the form f_{aj}, for some atom a of T_C^e and some $j \in J$.

Now, if $g \in T_{Ce}$ and $g \neq 0$, we can show that T_{Ce} contains some atom less than or equal to g. For, since $g \neq 0$, there must be at least one $j \in J$ such that $g_j \neq 0$. Since T_C^e is atomic, we can find an atom a such that $a \leqslant g_j$. The element f_{aj} of T_{Ce} is an atom, as we just showed above, and moreover $f_{aj} \leqslant g$, since, as the reader can easily verify, $(f_{aj})_{j'} \leqslant g_{j'}$ for every $j' \in J$. Thus, T_{Ce} is atomic.

It is worth remembering that an extensional intension is an atom iff its extensions are zero in all worlds but one, and in that exceptional world its extension is an atom.

2. THE INTENSIONAL SYSTEM FOR THE CORE LANGUAGE

We begin by defining the intensional type for the category P_0 of formulas:

DEFINITION 1. $T_{P_0} = FT_{P_0}^e / J \ (= F_2/J)$

Thus, a formula intension is a function which assigns a truth value for each world. By the developments of the previous section, formula intensions are always extensional, that is, $T_{P_0 e} = T_{P_0}$. Moreover, since 2 is a complete atomic boolean algebra, the lifting theorem enables us to conclude that T_{P_0} is also a complete atomic boolean algebra.

The effect of the pointwise definition in the lifting theorem is to allow the calculation of the interpretation of boolean combinations of formulas on a 'world-by-world' basis. For example, suppose that e and e' are formulas. Then, their interpretations $M(e)$ and $M(e')$ in some model will each be a formula intension, that is, a function from J into 2. If j is a particular world, then the truth value of the formula e in j is just the value of the function $M(e)$ applied to the argument j, that is, $M(e)\,(j)$. Similarly, the truth value of e' in j is the value of $M(e')\,(j)$. Now, if we form the boolean combination e *and* e', then this too is a formula, and so its interpretation $M(e \ and \ e')$ must also be a function from J into 2. Thus, the truth value of e *and* e' in j is $M(e \ and \ e')\,(j)$. But, since boolean combinations of expressions are interpreted as boolean combinations of interpretations, $M(e \ and \ e') = M(e) \wedge M(e')$, Now, by (a) of the lifting theorem, we have $M(e \ and \ e')\,(j) =$

$(M(e) \wedge M(e'))$ $(j) = M(e)$ $(j) \wedge M(e')$ (j). This says that the truth value of *e and e'* in *j* is just the ordinary boolean meet (that is, truth table combination) of the truth values of *e* and of *e'* in *j*.

Let us briefly examine the atoms of T_{P_0}. By the discussion in the proof of the lifting theorem, these are exactly those formula intensions which are true in exactly one world. In other words, if the formula intension *f* is an atom, then there is exactly one world, say j_f, such that $f(j_f) = 1$; for all worlds $j \neq j_f$, $f(j) = 0$.

The atoms of T_{P_0} will not play a significant role in the sequel. However, one can imagine ways in which these atoms may become relevant. Suppose, for example, that the set *J* is conceived of as indexing moments of time. An atomic formula would then be one true at an individual moment. Thus, we would be able to distinguish formulas like *John died* or *the door opened*, which are understood as occurring at individual moments, from formulas like *John worked*, or even *John wrote the letter*, which appear to be true during intervals consisting of many moments, if they are true at all. Momentary formulas would somehow have their interpretations restricted in such a way that they would always be atoms, whereas the interpretations of non-momentary formulas would not be atoms. Since we do not impose any structure or special interpretation on the set *J* in this study, we will not pursue this approach here.

Let us now move on to the categories *N* and $\bar{N}$. As in the case of formulas, we define the intensional type of *N* to be the set of functions from *J* into the extensional type:

DEFINITION 2. $T_N = FT_N^e/J \ (= F_{P/J})$,

where *P* is an arbitrary complete atomic boolean algebra, representing as before the set of (extensional) properties. Thus, the intension of an *N* like *student* will associate an element of *P* to each world *j*. Again, all *N* intensions are extensional, and, by the lifting theorem, T_N is a complete atomic boolean algebra. By the definitions of the operations in T_N, boolean combinations of *N*s are interpreted on a world-by-world basis using the operations in *P*.

The intensional type for $\bar{N}$s will be defined in the same way:

DEFINITION 3. $T_{\bar{N}} = FT_{\bar{N}}^e/J \ (= F_{P*/J})$.

An $\bar{N}$ intension associates an element of $P*$ to each world *j*. All $\bar{N}$ intensions are extensional, and, by the lifting theorem, $T_{\bar{N}}$ is a complete atomic boolean algebra, with boolean operations on $\overline{N}$ intensions calculated on a world-by-world basis using the operations in $P*$.

However, let us note at this point that an alternate definition for $T_{\overline{N}}$ might suggest itself. Namely, since $T_N = F_{P/J}$ is the set which represents (intensional) properties, and since we argued, in our development of the extensional system, that an $\overline{N}$ is reasonably interpreted as the set of all properties which hold of its referent, we might wish to have the denotation of an $\overline{N}$ be a subset of $F_{P/J}$. This would mean that, instead of $F_{P*/J}$, $T_{\overline{N}}$ would be taken to be equal to $(F_{P/J})^*$. In preliminary support of this idea, we note that since $F_{P/J}$ is a complete atomic boolean algebra, the entire algebraic development which we constructed earlier for $P*$ carries over unchanged to $(F_{P/J})^*$. In particular, $(F_{P/J})^*$ has individuals, the justification theorem allows a unique homomorphism from $(F_{P/J})^*$ into an arbitrary boolean algebra to be specified by arbitrarily assigning values to these individuals, etc. (Thinking ahead, we will need some such theorem in order to handle P_1 intensions properly.)

Nevertheless, problems arise as soon as we attempt to consider the extensions which such $\overline{N}$ intensions would have. Presumably, the extension in world j of a set of (intensional) properties is the set of extensions of these properties in j. Formally:

DEFINITION 4. Let $Q \in (F_{P/J})^*$ be an arbitrary element, and let $j \in J$ be an arbitrary world index. Then $Q_j = \{p(j): p \in Q\}$.

Note that $Q_j \in T_{\overline{N}}^e (= P*)$.

With this definition, all elements of $(F_{P/J})^*$ are extensional. However, the set of extensional elements of $(F_{P/J})^*$ is not total. To see this, suppose that $Q \in (F_{P/J})^*$ is such that, for some particular j, $Q_j = \emptyset$. By the definition above, this can only happen if $Q = \emptyset$. But then $Q_j = \emptyset$ for *all* j. What this means is that there could be no $\overline{N}$ intension whose extension in some worlds is $\emptyset$ and whose extensions in other worlds is not $\emptyset$. Thus, it would be possible to give a set of extensions $\{Q_j\}$ such that these are the extensions for no intension. But this does not seem reasonable. Surely, we want to allow for the possibility that a particular $\overline{N}$ is interpreted as $\emptyset$ in some worlds but not in others. (The reader may also check that, in general, it is possible for distinct intensions to have the same extensions in *all* worlds, using Definition 4.) Because of this nontotality, it does not seem that $(F_{P/J})^*$ is the appropriate candidate for $T_{\overline{N}}$.

Having fixed on Definition 3 as the proper definition for $T_{\overline{N}}$, let us consider what the interpretation of a proper noun should be. Extensionally, a proper noun is interpreted as an individual in P^*, so we will naturally want the intension f of a proper noun to be such that $f(j)$ is an individual for every world j. Moreover, since individuals are conceived of as being defined by the properties which hold of them, and since the property set P is chosen a priori and is independent of the set J, it seems not unreasonable to require that the extension of a proper name be the same *individual in every world*. Let us define the notion *intensional individual* thus:

DEFINITION 5. The function $f \in F_{P^*/J}$ is an *intensional individual* iff there exists an individual $I \in P^*$ such that $\forall j \in J, f(j) = I$.

We now define the type for proper nouns to be the set of intensional individuals:

DEFINITION 6. $T_{\bar{N}\mathrm{prop}} = \{f \in T_{\bar{N}} : f \text{ is an intensional individual}\}$.

Algebraically, intensional individuals are somewhat different from ordinary individuals. Recall that the individuals of P^* are in one-to-one correspondence with the atoms of P; in fact, each individual contains exactly one atom as a member, and distinct individuals contain distinct atoms. However, intensional individuals are, first of all, not sets of extensional or intensional properties, so they cannot be said to contain atoms of any algebra. Moreover, they are not in one-to-one correspondence with the atoms of T_N. From the proof of the lifting theorem, we know that the atoms of T_N are those functions f_{aj} which map the particular world j into the atom a of P, and which map all other worlds into the zero property. Recalling that an atom of P may be thought of as the property of being a particular individual, we can think of f_{aj} as being the (intensional) property of existing only in world j and being a particular individual in that world. If P has n atoms, say, then the number of atoms in T_N is therefore $n|J|$. But there are only n intensional individuals, corresponding to the n individuals in P^* (and to the n atoms of P, of course).

We can say that the intensional individuals are in one-to-one correspondence with the functions $f_a \in T_N$, where, for each atom a of P, f_a is defined by $f_a(j) = a$ for every j in J. In fact, if f is an intensional individual, then for exactly one atom a of P, $f_a(j) \in f(j)$ for each j in J. But, of course, f_a is not an atom in T_N; in fact, for each j in J, we have $f_{aj} \leqslant f_a$.

Having defined T_N and $T_{\bar{N}}$ as in Definitions 2 and 3, let us consider the definition of T_{Det}. Restricting our attention to the few simple determiners in the core language, we can use the second part of the general extensionality theorem to define intensional interpretations for these logical constants.

For example, let us take the determiner *every*. We would like the intension of this determiner to have the extension $every^e$ in each world, where $every^e$ is as defined in Definition 25 of Part IA (note the superscript 'e' to indicate an object defined within our extensional system). By the general extensionality theorem, there is a unique transparent function *every*, mapping T_N into $T_{\bar{N}}$, such that, for every $j \in J$, $(every(x))_j = every^e(x_j)$, for each $x \in T_N$. We will now restrict any (intensional) model of our language in such a way that the logical constant *every* is always interpreted as *every*.

The other logical constant determiners in the core language are handled in exactly the same way. Note that the intensions which interpret these determiners are all transparent, which is what we want, since the interpretation of an $\bar{N}$ formed by combining such a determiner with an N, in a given world, depends only on the extension of the N in that world. In general, of course, properly intensional determiners do exist. Thus, when properly defined, T_{Det} cannot consist entirely of transparent functions from T_N into $T_{\bar{N}}$. However, the question of a general definition of T_{Det} will not be further considered here.

We are now ready to turn to the category P_n of n-place predicates. As earlier, we begin by considering the category P_1, and then examining how our considerations can be extended to the general case.

Let us note at the outset that the category P_1 will have to be subdivided into two subcategories, namely, those expressions which are 'extensional' in their arguments (that is, in their subject $\bar{N}$s), and those which are properly intensional. All the examples of P_1s we have dealt with up until now have been examples of the former type; but properly intensional P_1s exist as well. For example, consider the P_1 *is required to be over 35 years old*. We surely do not want the two sentences

(1)   The president is required to be over 35 years old

and

(2)   Franklin Pierce is required to be over 35 years old

to have the same truth value in any world in which *the president* and *Franklin Pierce* happen to have the same extension. But this means that this P_1 cannot be interpreted by a function which takes as its argument the extensional denotation of its subject. This is in contrast to P_1s like *kiss Mary*; we certainly do want to claim that

(3)   The president kissed Mary

and

(4)   Franklin Pierce kissed Mary

necessarily have the same truth value in any world in which *the president* and *Franklin Pierce* have the same extension.

The way in which this can be handled was indicated in the previous section. The type for P_1 in general will be a certain set of functions from $T_{\bar{N}}$ into T_{P_0}. A P_1 like *kiss Mary* will always be interpreted as a transparent such function. By the definition of transparency, the value returned by such a function in a particular world depends only on the extension of its argument in that world. Properly intensional P_1s will in general not be interpreted as transparent functions. Thus, if f interprets *be required to be over 35 years old,* f might return distinct truth values in world j when applied to distinct arguments, even if those arguments happen to have the same extension in j.

We will say that P_1s like *kiss Mary* belong to the subcategory of *transparent* P_1s; we denote this category $P_1 \atop t$. Similarly, properly intensional P_1s will be said to belong to the subcategory of *nontransparent* P_1s; this category will be denoted $P_1 \atop nt$. To insure that expressions of these categories are properly interpreted, there are two things we must do.

Firstly, lexical members of the category P_1 must be specified as being either transparent or nontransparent. The interpreting function will then be restricted so that lexical members of $P_1 \atop t$ will be interpreted only by transparent members of T_{P_1}. As it turns out, all of the lexical members of P_1 that we are accounting for in our language are transparent. In fact, we do not know of a clear example of an English intransitive verb, semantically a one-place predicate, which is properly intensional on its subject.

Secondly, the interpretation of nonlexical P_1s must be calculated in such a way that the correct transparency always results. For example, the (intensional) function which interprets *kiss* in any model must be such that, when applied to an $\bar{N}$ intension, the resulting P_1 intension is automatically transparent. Each construction which results in a P_1 will have to be dealt with separately.

Let us restrict our attention now to transparent P_1s. In our development of the extensional system, we showed that the denotation of a P_1 should be a homomorphism. Clearly, the evidence cited there is just as relevant here: we would like the intensional denotation of a transparent P_1 to be a homomorphism. Note that such a denotation is a function, in fact, a transparent function, from $T_{\bar{N}}$ (= $T_{\bar{N}e}$) into T_{P_0} (= $T_{P_0 e}$), which are both boolean algebras, as we have seen, so it makes sense to require that it be a homomorphism. However, by our earlier development, it would appear rather that what we want is for the extensions of such a function in all the worlds to be homomorphisms. We might ask if there is any connection between an intension being a homomorphism and its extensions being homomorphisms. The answer to this is provided by the following theorem:

THEOREM 1. *Homomorphic Inheritance Theorem.* Let C_1 and C_2 be categories such that $T_{C_1 e}$ and $T_{C_2 e}$ are total and $T_{C_1}^e$ and $T_{C_2}^e$ are boolean algebras. Then, a transparent function $f \colon T_{C_1 e} \to T_{C_2 e}$ is a homomorphism iff $\forall j \in J$, $f_j \colon T_{C_1}^e \to T_{C_2}^e$ is a homomorphism.

(Note that the lifting theorem guarantees that $T_{C_1 e}$ and $T_{C_2 e}$ are boolean algebras.) The content of this theorem can be paraphrased by saying that a transparent function inherits the property of being a homomorphism from its extensions; and conversely, the extensions inherit the property of being homomorphisms from their intension.

In the case of transparent P_1's, the effect of this theorem, together with the general extensionality theorem, is to insure that a transparent homomorphism f from $T_{\bar{N}}$ into T_{P_0} is determined by a set of homomorphisms f_j from $T_{\bar{N}}^e$ into $T_{P_0}^e$, one for each world j. That is, any transparent homomorphism f determines such a set $\{f_j\}$, and conversely, if an arbitrary set of such homomorphism $\{f_j\}$ is given, there is a unique transparent homomorphism $f \colon T_{\bar{N}} \to T_{P_0}$ which has those f_js as extensions. All this being so, it is clear that we want to define the type for transparent P_1s as follows:

DEFINITION 7. $T_{P_1 \atop t} = \{f \in F_{T_{P_0}/T\bar{N}} \colon f \text{ is a transparent homomorphism}\}$.

And, as we just saw, by the homomorphic inheritance theorem and the general extensionality theorem, $T_{P_1 \atop t} = T_{P_1 e \atop t}$ is total. But note now that $T_{P_1 \atop t}^e$ is a boolean algebra (in fact, a complete atomic one). Thus the lifting theorem can be applied to conclude that $T_{P_1 e \atop t}$ is a complete atomic boolean algebra under the operations defined pointwise on the worlds.

At this point, it may be instructive to illustrate how our intensional system is used to calculate truth values for formulas of the sort which our extensional system was able to handle. Let us take the formula *every student laughs or cries*. The calculation here should be compared with the discussion of (42) in Part IA. We have:

(5)

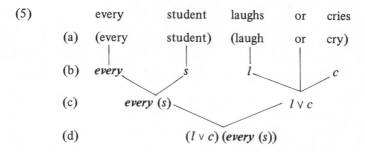

	every	student	laughs	or	cries
(a)	(every	student)	(laugh	or	cry)
(b)	*every*	*s*	*l*		*c*
(c)	*every (s)*				*l* ∨ *c*
(d)		(*l* ∨ *c*) (*every* (*s*))			

Line (a) gives the representation of the given English sentence in our logical language. In line (b), the lexical expressions are replaced by their interpretations; but note that these are now *intensional* denotations. Lines (c) and (d) just involve combining these in the usual way. Line (d), therefore, is the intensional denotation of the entire formula.

Now, suppose that, given a world $j \in J$, we wish to know the truth value of the formula in j. Clearly, all we need to do is to apply the formula intension to j, giving us

(6) $((l \vee c) (every\ (s)))\ (j)$.

By using the theorems and definitions we have developed, we can express the truth value (6) in terms of the extensions of s, l, and c in j. To do this, we first note that since $l \vee c$ is transparent (see below), we have the equation:

(7) $((l \vee c)\ (every\ (s)))\ (j) = (l \vee c)_j\ (every\ (s))_j$.

Next, we recall that the lifting theorem defines the boolean operations in $T_{P_1}^{t_1}$ pointwise on the worlds. This means that we have:

(8) $(l \vee c)_j = l_j \vee c_j$.

Also, the function *every* was defined earlier by means of the following equation:

(9) $(every\ (s))_j = every^e\ (s_j) = \underset{s_j \in I}{\cap} I,$

where we have added on the equation which defines $every^e$ in the extensional system. Substituting (8) and (9) into (7), we get:

(10) $((l \vee c)\ (every\ (s)))\ (j) = (l_j \vee c_j)\ (\underset{s_j \in I}{\cap} I).$

Note that (10) expresses the truth value of the formula in j in terms of the extensions of *student, laugh*, and *cry* in j. The remainder of the calculation proceeds exactly as in the extensional system. We have:

(11) $((l \vee c)\ (every\ (s)))\ (j) = (l_j \vee c_j)\ (\underset{s_j \in I}{\cap} I)$

$$= \underset{s_j \in I}{\wedge}\ [(l_j \vee c_j)\ (I)]$$

$$= \underset{s_j \in I}{\wedge}\ [l_j(I) \vee c_j(I)]$$

where the second equality follows since $l_j \vee c_j$ is a homomorphism, and the third equality follows from the definition of $\vee$ in $T^e_{P_1}$. The right hand side of the third equality in (11) should be compared with (42f) of Part IA.

The reader may find it instructive to calculate the truth value of ((*every student*) *laugh*) *or* ((*every student*) *cry*), and to show that in any world in which this formula is true, the formula (*every student*) (*laugh or cry*) must be true, but not conversely.

In our illustrative example above, we made use of the fact that $l \vee c$ was transparent (in fact, a transparent homomorphism). Let us briefly review the justification for this conclusion.

First, l and c are transparent homomorphisms, since they are the interpretations of the lexical P_1s *laugh* and *cry*. Recall that lexical P_1s are always transparent, and hence their interpretations are required to be in the set $T_{P_1}^t$ defined in Definition 7.

Secondly, $T_{P_1}^t$ is a boolean algebra, by the lifting theorem. Therefore, boolean combinations of transparent homomorphisms from $T_{\bar{N}}$ into T_{P_0} are always themselves transparent homomorphisms from $T_{\bar{N}}$ into T_{P_0}. But this means that the interpretation of a boolean combination of transparent P_1s is automatically an appropriate denotation for a transparent P_1, which is what we want. In particular, $l \vee c$ is a well-defined transparent homomorphism.

Since the only transparent P_1s we can handle so far in a formal way are either lexical P_1s or else boolean combinations of transparent P_1s, these considerations show that, so far, a transparent P_1 will always be interpreted by a transparent homomorphism, as desired.

Let us now turn our attention to the nontransparent P_1s. So far, the only thing we have said concerning their interpretation is that a nontransparent P_1 intension is a function from $T_{\overline{N}}$ into T_{P_0} which is not required to be transparent. Let us examine the question of whether such an intension should be a homomorphism.

Comparing the sentences

(12)   The president and the vice-president are required to be over 35 years old.

and

(13)   The president is required to be over 35 years old and the vice-president is required to be over 35 years old.

it certainly seems that the truth of one of these in some world necessarily entails the truth of the other. The logical equivalence of these sentences suggests that the intension which interprets the P_1 should preserve meets.

However, when we examine the situation with regard to joins, the matter is not so simple. Consider the following two sentences:

(14)   The president or the vice-president is required to be over 35 years old.
(15)   The president is required to be over 35 years old or the vice-president is required to be over 35 years old.

Sentence (14) is ambiguous. In the reading which appears to us to be the most natural one, the sentence asserts that there is a requirement to the effect that, of the two individuals who are serving as president and as vice-president, at least one be over 35 years old. The less natural reading of (14) is logically equivalent to (15); in this reading, what is asserted is that there is either a requirement for the president to be over 35 years old, or else there is a requirement for the vice-president to be over 35 years old. Clearly, these two readings are not logically equivalent, and, in fact, neither entails the other. The second reading is the one which results if the P_1 *is required to be over 35 years old* is assumed to preserve joins.

Similar facts obtain in the case of a subject $\overline{N}$ quantified by a determiner of the sort that we are representing in our language by a. In the case of the sentence

(16)   An elected official is required to be over 35 years old.

it is virtually impossible not to interpret the subject generically. However, the following are ambiguous the way that (14) above is:

(17) $\begin{Bmatrix} \text{Some} \\ \text{At least one} \end{Bmatrix}$ elected official is required to be over 35 years old.

On one reading, (17) asserts a requirement that among all the individuals who are elected officials, at least one be over 35 years old; on the other reading, (17) asserts that of all the elected offices, at least one has on it the requirement that the person who fills that office must be over 35 years old. It is this second reading which corresponds to the preservation of joins by the interpretation of the P_1. Again, this reading neither implies nor is implied by the first reading.

The chief embarrassment to our system provided by these sentences is their ambiguity; but perhaps it is made worse by the fact that the more common reading is the one which does not preserve joins. The ambiguity means that these sentences will ultimately have to have two representations in our logical language. However, it would be preferable if the simpler representation corresponded to the more common reading. Here, however, it is clear that the simpler representation of, say, (14), will just be something like

(18)   ((the president) or (the vice-president)) (be required . . .).

It will surely be easier to impose join-preservation on the P_1 (which corresponds to the second, less-likely reading) than to somehow guarantee that the P_1 interpretation in (18) can reference the internal structure of the interpretation of its subject $\overline{N}$, which is what would be needed in order to represent the first, more common, reading. Nevertheless, as a first approximation, it does not seem too unreasonable to assume that even nontransparent P_1s preserve joins, and to hope that the other reading of (14) can be represented by a structure in which the highly derived character of the P_1 (involving as it does passive, as well as an embedded P_1) will form the basis for the way the more common interpretation is calculated.

The fact that nontransparent P_1s preserve complements seems relatively unproblematic, for surely (19) and (20) are logically equivalent:

(19)   The president but not the vice-president is required to be over 35 years old.

(20)   The president is required to be over 35 years old but it is not the case that the vice-president is required to be over 35 years old.

We therefore might propose that nontransparent P_1s be interpreted by homomorphisms, just as transparent P_1s are. If so, we can define the intensional type for P_1s as follows:

DEFINITION 8. $T_{P_1 \atop \langle t \rangle} = \{f \in H_{TP_0}/T_{\bar{N}} : \langle f \text{ is transparent} \rangle\}$

where the angle bracket notation indicates, as usual, that the presence of the subcategorization feature t correlates with the presence of the condition that f be transparent.

Note that if $f \colon T_{\bar{N}} \to T_{P_0}$ is not transparent, there is no natural way to define extensions of f in the various worlds. On the other hand, we saw earlier that $T_{P_{t^1}e} = T_{P_{t^1}}$, and that $T_{P_{t^1}e}$ is total. We conclude that the extensional members of T_{P_1} are just the transparent members. That is, $T_{P_1 e} = T_{P_1}$; and, of course, $T_{P_1 e}$ is total, since $T_{P_{t^1}e}$ is. Note moreover that $T_{P_1 e}$ is a proper subset of T_{P_1}. The category P_1 is the first category we have encountered (with the exception of Det, whose full intensional type we have not actually defined yet) where this is the case.

There remains to be considered the matter of the category P_1 and its subcategories being boolean. In the case of P_{t^1}, we have seen that the lifting theorem provides a boolean structure for $T_{P_{t^1}}$. We now consider the following two questions: (i) should the subcategory of nontransparent P_1s be a boolean category, and, if so, how should boolean structure be defined for its type?; and (ii) should the category of all P_1s be boolean, and, if so, how should boolean structure be defined for its type?

To take up the first of these questions, we first take note of sentences such as:

(21)   The president is required to be over 35 years old $\left\{ \begin{array}{l} \text{and is} \\ \text{or is} \\ \text{but isn't} \end{array} \right\}$ required to be an American citizen.

While stylistically a bit awkward, these sentences seem both grammatical and perfectly interpretable. We conclude that we would like the category of nontransparent P_1s to be boolean.

To define boolean structure on the type for nontransparent P_1s, there are two sorts of considerations to bring to bear: the interpretation of English sentences involving boolean combinations of nontransparent P_1s, and the mathematical possibilities and consequences of various definitions of boolean structure. Let us first look at the interpretation of English sentences.

The first thing we can say is that the sentences in (21) above are clearly logically equivalent to:

(22)   The president is required to be over 35 years old $\left\{\begin{array}{l}\text{and} \\ \text{or} \\ \text{and it is not}\end{array}\right.$

the case that $\Big\}$the president is required to be an American citizen.

If g and h are the intensions of the two P_1s in (21) and if f is the intension of *the president*, this shows that we must have $(g \wedge h)(f) = g(f) \wedge h(f)$ in this case, where, of course, $g \wedge h$ is the intension of the P_1 formed by conjoining the two P_1s of (21) with *and*; and similar equations hold for $g \vee h$ and for g'.

This being so, there are two conceivable approaches we might take towards the definition of boolean structure on the type for nontransparent P_1s. One would be to define $g \wedge h$ by simply setting $(g \wedge h)(f) = g(f) \wedge h(f)$ for every $\bar{N}$ intension f; and similarly for the other operations; call this the *pointwise approach*. This would certainly define $g \wedge h$ as a function from $T_{\bar{N}}$ into T_{P_0}. However, let us recall that this is *not* the way that the boolean combinations of P_1 interpretations were defined when we were developing the extensional system. In fact, with such a definition, $g \wedge h$ is not in general a homomorphism. What was actually done there is to define $g \wedge h$ by setting $(g \wedge h)(f) = g(f) \wedge h(f)$ just in case f was an individual, and then use the justification theorem to show that this in effect defined a unique homomorphism $g \wedge h$ from $T_{\bar{N}}^e$ into $T_{P_0}^e$; call this the *individual approach*. In the case of the nontransparent P_1s, however, it is not a priori obvious which of these two approaches is the correct one.

We can try to clear up the matter by examining sentences in which nontransparent P_1s that are boolean combinations of P_1s are combined with $\bar{N}$s that are themselves boolean combinations of $\bar{N}$s, and seeing how the resulting sentences are interpreted. Unfortunately, such sentences tend to be unwieldy, and it is difficult to judge what interpretation is the most natural. Consider, for example, the sentence:

(23)   Every elected official is required to be over 35 years old or is
          required to be an American citizen.

With the pointwise approach, this sentence would be logically equivalent
to (24), whereas with the individual approach, it would presumably be
equivalent to (25):

(24)   Every elected official is required to be over 35 years old or
          every elected official is required to be an American citizen.

(25)   For each elected official, there is a requirement on that official
          to the effect that he/she must either be over 35 years old or else
          be an American citizen.

It is unclear to us which of these is or ought to be the interpretation of (23).[1]
A similarly difficult sentence is:

(26)   At least one elected official is required to be over 35 years old
          and is required to be an American citizen.

With the pointwise approach, this sentence would be equivalent to (27),
whereas with the individual approach, it would be equivalent to (28):

(27)   At least one elected official is required to be over 35 years old
          and at least one elected official is required to be an American
          citizen.

(28)   For at least one elected official, that official is required to be over
          35 years old and is also required to be an American citizen.

Again, our judgments are unclear.

However, if we examine the mathematics involved, it appears that we
can make a decision. To see what the situation is, let us recall the way the
individual approach was developed in the extensional system.

The justification theorem says that homomorphisms from $T_{\bar{N}}^{e}$ into an
arbitrary boolean algebra are uniquely determined by giving arbitrary values
on the individuals. But this requires that $T_{\bar{N}}^{e}$ contain individuals in the first
place. If the definitions are examined, it is seen that the individuals of $T_{\bar{N}}^{e}$
exist by virtue of the fact that $T_{\bar{N}}^{e}$ is a power set P^{*} of a set P which *itself*
is a boolean algebra. There are two things to note about this.

The first is that the definition of which elements of P^{*} are individuals makes use of the algebraic structure of P. Thus, if B is an abstractly defined boolean algebra which happens by accident to be isomorphic to some P^*, there is no way to define individuals in B making use only of its own algebraic structure. In general, if B is isomorphic to some P^*, then there is more than one isomorphism of P^* onto B, and distinct isomorphisms will associate distinct sets of elements of B with the individuals of P^*.

The second is that it is possible for a boolean algebra B to not be isomorphic to any P^* at all. In the finite case, this is very easy to see by a counting argument. Since P is an arbitrary boolean algebra, if P is finite, then P has 2^n elements, and so P^* has 2^{2^n} elements. Now, an arbitrary finite boolean algebra B has 2^k elements, for some integer k. But, if $k \neq 2^n$ for some n, then B cannot be isomorphic to any P^*. For such a B there is no way that the definitions which were set up to apply to P^* can be made to apply.

Actually, we can say even more. Suppose that B is a boolean algebra for which the justification theorem holds. Then, the development of Part IA can be applied to conclude that the set of all homomorphisms from B into an arbitrary algebra X itself forms an algebra. Now, let us take $X = \{0, 1\}$. If B is a finite boolean algebra of 2^k elements, it can be easily shown that the number of distinct homomorphisms from B into X is just k.[2] Since the number of elements of a finite boolean algebra is always a power of 2, if k is not a power of 2, there is no way that the set of homomorphisms from B into X can be made into a boolean algebra. Thus, if k is not a power of 2, the justification theorem does not apply to an algebra with 2^k elements.

Returning to the matter of defining boolean structure on the type for nontransparent P_1s, what all this means is simply that, since $T_{\bar{N}}$ is not the power set of an algebra, there is no way to define individuals in $T_{\bar{N}}$ (individuals in the sense of Definitions 10 and 21 of Part IA), and, in addition, the justification theorem may not apply to $T_{\bar{N}}$ at all. In fact, if J is finite with, say, m members, and if P has 2^n members, then $T_{\bar{N}}$ has $2^{m 2^n}$ members. Thus, if m is not a power of 2, then, by the argument above, the justification theorem cannot apply to $T_{\bar{N}}$.

It appears, therefore, that there is good mathematical reason for rejecting the individual apporach to defining boolean structure on the type for non-transparent P_1s. This may seem unfortunate: there is a sense in which an $\bar{N}$ like the *president* should be interpreted as an individual, and that an $\bar{N}$ like *every elected official* should be interpreted as the intersection of individuals, each one of which is the intension of some particular elected official. Of course, it may still be possible to do this, provided that we do not insist that these 'individuals' have all the properties of individuals as defined in Part IA.

The notion of *intensional individual* defined above for the purpose of providing interpretations for proper nouns is surely too strong. We might propose that an $\bar{N}$ like *the president* have an intension whose extension in any particular world is either an (extensional) individual or else $\emptyset$, with distinct individuals permitted as extensions of the same intension in different worlds. This seems satisfactory as a first approximation, but we caution that an arbitrary function which gives values for such intensions in a boolean algebra cannot be presumed to define a unique homomorphism from all of $T_{\bar{N}}$ into that algebra. The individual approach could perhaps be salvaged by changing the definition of $T_{\bar{N}}$, but we will not pursue that here.

The pointwise approach is mathematically unproblematical. Of course, with this approach, we must admit nonhomomorphisms as possible P_1 intensions, so that Definition 8 must be rejected. One possibility would be to take all of $F_{TP_0/T\bar{N}}$ as the type for nontransparent P_1s. Note that this set is indeed a boolean algebra with the operations defined pointwise; in fact, this follows essentially from the lifting theorem, with $T_{\bar{N}}$ here playing the role of the set J in that theorem. However, it might be claimed that any nontransparent P_1 intension either is a homomorphism or else is a boolean combination of homomorphisms. This suggests that we restrict the type of nontransparent P_1s to the subalgebra of $F_{TP_0/T\bar{N}}$ generated by the homomorphisms. (Another way of saying the same thing is that we would take the type of nontransparent P_1s to be the smallest subalgebra of $F_{TP_0/T\bar{N}}$ that contains $H_{TP_0/T\bar{N}}$.) Using the symbol $\hat{H}_{TP_0/T\bar{N}}$ to denote this subalgebra, we could therefore make the following definition:

DEFINITION 9. $T_{P_1 \atop nt} = \hat{H}_{TP_0}/T_{\bar{N}}$.

In general, $\hat{H}_{TP_0}/T_{\bar{N}}$ is a proper subset of $F_{TP_0}/T_{\bar{N}}$,[3] so that this definition does narrow down the class of possible denotations of nontransparent P_1s when compared with the idea of taking the type of $P_{1 \atop nt}$ to be simply $F_{TP_0}/T_{\bar{N}}$.

If we do this, however, a new problem arises. The difficulty is that since the set of homomorphisms from $T_{\bar{N}}$ into T_{P_0} is contained in T_{P_1}, then in particular, the set of all transparent homomorphisms, that is, $T_{P_1 \atop t}^{nt}$, is contained in T_{P_1}. There is nothing wrong with this in itself; we surely want to allow the ^{nt} possibility that in some model a nontransparent P_1 happens to get interpreted transparently. However, while $T_{P_{t1}}$ is a subset of T_{P_1}, it is not the case that $T_{P_{t1}}$ is a subalgebra of T_{P_1}. In particular, the boolean ^{nt} operations in $T_{P_{t1}}$ are defined differently from the boolean operations in $T_{P_1 \atop nt}$. What this means is that if f and g are transparent homomorphisms from

$T_{\bar{N}}$ into T_{P_0}, then, for example, there are two distinct definitions for $f \vee g$, depending on whether f and g are regarded as members of $T_{P_{t1}}$ or of $T_{P_{1_{n:}}}$. This in turn means that the interpretation of a boolean combination of P_1s cannot be defined on the basis of the intensions of the constituent P_1s alone: it is also necessary to know whether the P_1s are transparent or non-transparent. That is, the semantics of the constituent P_1s are not sufficient to determine the interpretation of the combination, since reference has to be made to the syntactic category membership of the constituents, a situation we would hope to avoid.

We can avoid this problem in the following, somewhat mechanical, way. We define two distinct and disjoint copies of $F_{T_{P_0}}/T_{\bar{N}}$, indexed, say, by the features t and nt. Let us denote these copies by $F^t_{T_{P_0}}/T_{\bar{N}}$ and $F^{nt}_{T_{P_0}}/T_{\bar{N}}$ respectively. We then require that transparent P_1s take their intensions in $F^t_{T_{P_0}}/T_{\bar{N}}$, and that nontransparent P_1s take their intensions in $F^{nt}_{T_{P_0}}/T_{\bar{N}}$. We define $T_{P_{t1}}$ as the subset of $F^t_{T_{P_0}}/T_{\bar{N}}$ consisting of exactly the transparent homomorphisms, with a boolean structure as defined earlier. We define $T_{P_{1_{nt}}}$ as the subset $\hat{H}_{T_{P_0}}/T_{\bar{N}}$ of the distinct set $F^{nt}_{T_{P_0}}/T_{\bar{N}}$, as defined above. If we do this, then even if the intension f of a nontransparent P_1 happens to be a transparent homomorphism, f will be a member of $F^{nt}_{T_{P_0}}/T_{\bar{N}}$ and not of $F^t_{T_{P_0}}/T_{\bar{N}}$: Boolean operations applied to such an intension f will therefore automatically follow the definitions as in $T_{P_{1_{nt}}}$ rather than as in $T_{P_{t1}}$.

To conclude, we can say that the category of nontransparent P_1s should be taken to be boolean. With the individual approach to the definition of boolean structure on the type for nontransparent P_1s, there are mathematical problems, at least if the definition of $T_{\bar{N}}$ is the one given earlier. With the pointwise definition, a mathematically coherent system can be set up, but we now run into the problem that syntactic information has to be accessed in order for the interpretation of boolean combinations of P_1s to be carried out. This problem can be mechanically solved by interpreting transparent and nontransparent P_1s in disjoint copies of $F_{T_{P_0}}/T_{\bar{N}}$. Here we shall opt for this latter solution, but the question deserves further study.

Let us turn our attention now to the question of whether the category of all the P_1s should be regarded as boolean, and, if so, how boolean combinations are to be interpreted. Given two P_1s, if both are transparent, or if both are nontransparent, then the matter of the interpretation of a boolean combination of which they are the constituents has already been discussed. There remains the question of what happens if a transparent and a nontransparent P_1 are combined. An example of such a situation might be:

(29)   The president is required to be over 35 years old and is kissing
         Mary.

The awkwardness of such a combination is evident. If (29) can be interpreted
at all, it seems that the properly intensional P_1 is given its *de re* rather than
de dictu reading (see Note 1). We will see later that in our system the *de re*
reading of what in English is normally a properly intensional expression will
be represented in our system by means of a λ operator which will create a
transparent expression. Thus, in our language, the representation of (29)
will not actually involve the combination of a nontransparent P_1 with a
transparent P_1, but rather the combination of two transparent P_1s. If we
assume that combinations such as (29) in general require a *de re* reading for
the properly intensional constituent, then, in our system, we need never have
to deal with a transparent and a nontransparent P_1 being combined. Thus,
the category P_1 will *not* be a boolean category, and we are not faced with
the task of defining a boolean structure on all of T_{P_1}.

Let us summarize what we have done regarding the intensional type for
the category P_1 and its subcategories. We take $T_{P_1 t}$ to be the set of transparent
homomorphisms from $T_{\bar{N}}$ into T_{P_0}. This set is a boolean algebra by the
lifting theorem; the boolean operations are carried out on a world-by-world
basis on the extensions of its members. For the nontransparent P_1s, we define
boolean structure on the set of all functions from $T_{\bar{N}}$ into T_{P_0} by pointwise
operations. We then take $T_{P_1 nt}$ to be the subalgebra of this generated by
the homomorphisms. The sets $T_{P_1 t}$ and $T_{P_1 nt}$ are defined to be disjoint. T_{P_1} is
simply the union of these sets. No boolean structure is defined on T_{P_1}.

There remains one relatively minor difficulty. If we ask which elements
of T_{P_1} are extensional, we find that not only are all the members of $T_{P_1 t}$
extensional, but, by the general extensionality theorem, so are those elements
of $T_{P_1 nt}$ which are transparent functions. This means that the set of all extensional elements of T_{P_1} is not total. In particular, if $\{f_j\}$ is a set of elements
of $T_{P_1}^e$, one for each world $j \in J$, then there are *two* intensions in T_{P_1} which
have these extensions, one in $T_{P_1 t}$ and one in $T_{P_1 nt}$. In the sequel, we can avoid
any difficulty which might arise from this simply by defining $T_{P_1 e}$ to be
the set $T_{P_1 t}$. This set is total, as indicated earlier, and moreover, it is the set
of possible intensions for those P_1s which are necessarily extensional, as
opposed to those P_1s which might be interpreted extensionally in some
particular model. Still, the fact that there is a problem of this sort suggests
that further study is needed here.

Let us turn now to the consideration of the intensional type for P_2s. Since

$P_2 = P_1/\bar{N}$, T_{P_2} will consist of functions from $T_{\bar{N}}$ into T_{P_1}. As usual, our task is to determine which such functions are appropriate interpretations of P_2s.

Let us first examine the P_1s which are created by combining a P_2 with its argument $\bar{N}$. Since there are two subclasses of P_1s, namely, the transparent ones and the nontransparent ones, we can automatically divide the P_2s into two classes, namely: those P_2s which always yield a transparent P_1 when combined with any $\bar{N}$, and those which can yield a nontransparent P_1 when so combined. However, when we examine lexical transitive verbs in English or boolean combinations of these, it appears that there are no cases of the latter. That is, it is always the case that when any P_2 (even one which itself is properly intensional on its own argument, like *look-for*) is combined with its argument $\bar{N}$, the P_1 which results is transparent. This being so, we can already narrow down the class of functions which could possibly make up T_{P_2}; namely, T_{P_2} can only consist of functions from $T_{\bar{N}}$ into T_{P_1} which actually take values in $T_{P_1}_t$.

Now, since $T_{P_1 e} = T_{P_1}_t$, and $T_{\bar{N}e} = T_{\bar{N}}$, all the functions which are potentially members of T_{P_2} can be viewed as functions from $T_{\bar{N}e}$ into $T_{P_1 e}$. Definition 2 of Part II.1 can be applied to divide these functions into two subclasses: those that are transparent and those that are not. As in the case of the P_1s, we make use of this distinction in setting up the interpretations of two subclasses of P_2s. Namely, those P_2s which depend extensionally on their argument will be called transparent, whereas those which are properly intensional on their argument will be called nontransparent. The interpretation of a transparent P_2 will always be a transparent function, whereas the interpretation of a nontransparent P_2 will not be so restricted.

To insure that each P_2 is correctly interpreted, we must, first of all, mark all lexical P_2s as being either transparent or nontransparent. Unlike the case with the P_1s, there are nontransparent lexical P_2s, such as *look-for, need*, or *criticize*. The correct interpretation of complex P_2s will result if the principles for calculating them are properly set up.

Let us restrict our attention for the moment to the transparent P_2s. These will be interpreted as transparent functions from $T_{\bar{N}}$ into $T_{P_1 e}$, as we have seen. By the general extensionality theorem, any such function has extensions in all the worlds; in fact, a transparent function $f\colon T_{\bar{N}e} \to T_{P_1 e}$ is in one-to-one correspondence with a set $\{f_j\}$ of functions each mapping $T_{\bar{N}}^e$ into $T_{P_1}^e$. Moreover, by the homomorphic inheritance theorem, since $T_{\bar{N}e}$ and $T_{P_1 e}$ are total and $T_{\bar{N}}^e$ and $T_{P_1}^e$ are boolean algebras, $f\colon T_{\bar{N}e} \to T_{P_1 e}$ is a homomorphism iff each $f_j\colon T_{\bar{N}}^e \to T_{P_1}^e$ is a homomorphism. Now, we surely want the interpretation of a transparent P_2 to be a homomorphism, for the reasons given earlier in our development of the extensional system. Thus, we conclude that, if $T_{P_2}^t$ consists exactly of the transparent homomorphisms from $T_{\bar{N}e}$ into $T_{P_1 e}$, then the elements of $T_{P_2}^t$ are in one-to-one correspondence with sets $\{f_j\}$ of homomorphisms from $T_{\bar{N}}^e$ into $T_{P_1}^e$, that is, with sets of elements of $T_{P_2}^e$. This already shows that T_{P_2} is total. But now, since $T_{P_2}^e$ is a complete atomic boolean algebra, we can apply the lifting theorem to conclude that $T_{P_2}^t$ is a complete atomic boolean algebra, with the boolean operations in $T_{P_2}^t$ defined on a world-by-world basis.

Before we consider the question of the type for nontransparent P_2s, let us note that our treatment of the type for transparent P_2s can be generalized, by induction, to transparent n-place predicates. To see this, we first note that the type for n-place predicates, or for any subcategory thereof, is a set of functions from $T_{\bar{N}}$ into $T_{P_{n-1}}$, where we can assume by induction that $T_{P_{n-1}}$ has already been defined. However, we claim further that an n-place predicate intension actually maps $T_{\bar{N}}$ into $T_{P_{n-1}}^t$, that is, into the type for transparent $n - 1$ place predicates.

The evidence supporting this claim is conclusive to a greater or lesser degree depending on the way we analyze certain constructions involving predicates that take three or more arguments. What we want to show, of course, is that there do not exist any expressions of category P_n which are properly intensional in more than one argument; and, moreover, if such an expression is properly intensional in one argument, then that argument is its 'first' argument, that is, the argument with which it is directly combined to create an expression of category P_{n-1}.

Restricting our attention to three place predicates, we note that the verbs discussed in Part IB in connection with our representation of ditransitive verbs in the extensional system are indeed extensional in all arguments. Thus, for example, in a world in which the novels are exactly the same individuals as the books, the sentence *John gave a novel to Mary* must have the same truth value as *John gave a book to Mary*. Similarly, if *Mary* and *the queen* refer to the same individual in some world, then *John gave a book to Mary* has the same truth value as *John gave a book to the queen*.

Ditransitive verbs which are extensional in all arguments support our claim, but they do so in a weak way. It would be more revealing to find ditransitive verbs which are properly intensional in (at least) one argument. Verbs such as *give, hand, send*, which refer to acts of physical transfer, as well as *sell, lend*, etc. which involve change of (permanent or temporary) ownership, will not exhibit any proper intensionality.

A candidate for a ditransitive verb with a properly intensional argument is *tell*. We do not mean the verb *tell* with an ordinary $\bar{N}$ object. Such combinations appear to be extensional; thus, if in some world the stories and the jokes are exactly the same, then *John told Mary a story* and *John told Mary a joke* surely have the same truth value (and, the extensionality of *tell* in its other two arguments is obvious). However, if *tell* is combined with a *that* clause, as in *John told Mary that Bill kissed Sally*, it seems reasonable to consider *tell* to be properly intensional in the *that* clause.

In order to make use of this as a piece of evidence which bears on our hypothesis, we first must show that *tell* in this construction is indeed a member of P_3. If *tell* is a member of P_3, then a formula is constructed by combining *tell* successively with three $\bar{N}$s. But is a *that* clause an $\bar{N}$? Note that, so far, we have not discussed $\bar{N}$s whose structure appears anything like that of a *that* clause. In fact, we will suggest later that a *that* clause is *not* an $\bar{N}$, but rather a member of the category $\bar{P}_0$. If this analysis is accepted, then *tell* in this construction is not a P_3 at all, and hence provides no evidence for our hypothesis.

However, let us suppose for the sake of argument that the *that* clause is an $\bar{N}$. Then our hypothesis is supported if the *that* clause is combined directly with *tell* as its first argument, to create a complex P_2, to which the remaining two arguments are added; otherwise, our hypothesis is argued against, for, say, the P_2 created by combining *tell* with one of its extensional arguments would then be properly intensional in its own argument, namely, in the *that* clause. Now, if we analyze *tell* as being analogous to *give*, and if the Patient analysis, chosen for verbs like *give* in Part IB, is adopted for *tell*, then indeed the *that* clause (which is clearly analogous to the patient) is the direct argument of *tell*, confirming our hypothesis. This is further strengthened by examining the scope relations in sentences like *John told every professor that a student failed* or *John told a professor that every student failed*. The Patient analysis predicts that the quantifier associated with the recipient (*professor* in these two sentences) has wide scope over the quantifier associated with the patient (the *that* clause in these sentences). This is indeed the case, provided we assume that the quantifier in the subject of the *that* clause somehow can be viewed as quantifying the *that* clause itself, not an unreasonable assumption, since the quantifier of a subject $\bar{N}$ does quantify the sentence of which it is the subject (since the P_1 it combines with is interpreted as a homomorphism). It would seem, therefore, that, to the extent that verbs like *tell* are at all relevant for our claim, our claim is supported.

If we could find a ditransitive verb which is properly intensional in two of its three arguments, this would be clear counterevidence to our claim. We know of no unimpeachable example of such a verb. However, a case to be considered might be the verb *criticize*, as used in a construction like *John criticized the queen for supporting the tax plan*. Here it might be claimed that the direct object and the *for* phrase constitute two arguments in both of which the verb is properly intensional. Again, we suggest that the *for* phrase is not in fact an $\bar{N}$, so that *criticize* in this construction is not a P_3. Moreover, the fact that the subject of the verb in the *for* phrase is understood to be coreferent with the direct object of *criticize* shows that the two arguments in question are not independent of each other, suggesting further that we are not dealing with a P_3 here. The relevance of this example to our claim seems to us sufficiently doubtful that we are content to proceed with the general definition for the type for n-place predicates on the assumption that an n-place predicate intension does indeed map $T_{\bar{N}}$ into $T_{P_{n-1}}$.

Now, by the inductive assumption, $T_{P_{n-1}}$ is a total set of extensional homomorphisms; moreover, it is a boolean algebra. Clearly, T_{P_n} should be the set of all transparent homomorphisms from $T_{\bar{N}}$ into $T_{P_{n-1}}$. By the general extensionality theorem and the homomorphic inheritance theorem, each such function f has extensions f_j in every world which are themselves homomorphisms, and conversely, given a set $\{f_j\}$ of homomorphisms from $T_{P_n}^e$, one for each world $j \in J$, there is a unique transparent homomorphism f from $T_{\bar{N}}$ into $T_{P_{n-1}}$ which has that set as its extensions. Thus, the set of all these transparent homomorphisms is total, and so the lifting theorem can be applied to define a boolean structure for this set using the boolean structure of $T_{P_n}^e$ to calculate boolean combinations of n-place predicate intensions on a world-by-world basis. Thus, T_{P_n} is defined as a boolean algebra for any positive integer n.

Let us now restrict our attention to the P_2s again, and let us consider the type for nontransparent P_2s. Our earlier discussion concerning the nontransparent P_1s carries over to the P_2s. We briefly go through the important points, with some examples.

First, is a nontransparent P_2 intension a homomorphism? As in the case of the P_1s, the evidence that a nontransparent P_2 preserves meets and complements seems unproblematic. Thus, the sentences (30) are logically equivalent to the sentences (31) respectively:

(30)   John is looking for a unicorn $\begin{Bmatrix} \text{and} \\ \text{but not} \end{Bmatrix}$ a leprechaun.

(31)   John is looking for a unicorn $\begin{cases} \text{and is looking} \\ \text{but is not looking} \end{cases}$ for a leprechaun.

However, preservation of joins is less clear. Sentence (32) is ambiguous:

(32)   John is looking for a unicorn or a leprechaun.

One reading has (32) logically equivalent to:

(33)   John is looking for a unicorn or is looking for a leprechaun.

With this reading, *look-for* preserves joins. On the other hand, (32) has an-other reading which appears to us to be much more natural. Namely, (32) can mean that John is engaging in a search which will be satisfied if John either finds a unicorn or a leprechaun. Unlike the parallel situation with the P_1s discussed earlier, we cannot here hope to represent this ambiguity by making use of any internal structure of the P_2, since *look-for* is, in our system, an unanalyzable lexical item. On the other hand, it is clearly inade-quate not to represent the more common reading of (32), and it is clear that this will require that the English expression *look for* will have to be indicated as being equivalent to something like *search with an aim towards finding* at some level of the description. One way this could be done would be to assume that the English P_2 *look for* has two translations in our logical language. One would be the single lexical item *look-for*, whose intension would be a homomorphism; this would enable us to represent the less com-mon reading of (32). The other translation would be a complex P_2, perhaps something like *try to find*, whose interpretation would be set up in such a way that the more common reading of (32) would be represented.

But such an approach has drawbacks. First of all, it represents a retreat from the idea of having the constituent structure in our logical language be parallel to the constituent structure in English. If the English P_2 is a (relatively) simple expression, or at least an expression without the internal syntactic structure of an embedding or an infinitive, then we want its trans-lation in our logical language to be equally simple.

More seriously, this approach would leave unrepresented and unexplained the fact that the ambiguity of (32) is *due to* the semantics of the expression *look for*. That is, it is *because* the expression *look for* has a meaning involving the fulfillment of a desire that (32) can be ambiguous. Note that other verbs involving desire, including *want*, are similarly ambiguous. Thus, (34) can mean either (35), or, more commonly, (36):

(34)   John wants a unicorn or a leprechaun.
(35)   John wants a unicorn or wants a leprechaun.
(36)   John has a desire which will be fulfilled if he can get either a unicorn or a leprechaun.

Ideally, therefore, *look for* (like *want* and all verbs of this sort) should be represented by a single lexical item in our language whose semantic interpretation would have properties leading to the ambiguity of (32). If we insisted that our logical language be unambiguous, it would still be better if the interpretation of the simplest translation of (32) were the more common interpretation, which would mean that the intension of *look-for* would not be a homomorphism, since it would not preserve joins.

We will not present a solution to this issue here, noting only that we should allow for the possibility that a nontransparent P_2 intension might not be a homomorphism. Thinking ahead, and recalling our discussion of the nontransparent P_1s, we note that the interpretation of boolean combinations of nontransparent P_2s may also be nonhomomorphisms in general, so that we will need to allow for this anyway.

In fact, turning our attention to the matter of boolean combinations of nontransparent P_2s, we see that we are faced with exactly the same issue as we were when we considered boolean combinations of nontransparent P_1s, namely, whether the interpretations of such combinations should be defined by means of the pointwise approach or the individual approach. In the case of the P_2s, the evidence from the interpretations of real English sentences seems to favor the pointwise approach somewhat more clearly than in the case of the P_1s. Thus, (37) seems to mean (38) rather than (39), which, it seems to us, is rather difficult, if not impossible, to interpret *de dictu*:

(37)   John needs or is looking for every unicorn.
(38)   John needs every unicorn or is looking for every unicorn.
(39)   For each unicorn, John needs that unicorn or is looking for that unicorn.

The mathematical arguments, of course, are exactly the same in the case of the P_2s as in the case of the P_1s, since we are again dealing with functions whose domain is $T_{\bar{N}}$, an algebra for which the justification theorem does not in general apply. We conclude that the type for the nontransparent P_2s should be a subalgebra of the algebra of functions from $T_{\bar{N}}$ into $T_{P_t^1}$ where the operations are defined pointwise; that is, giving g and h such functions and any $f \in T_{\bar{N}}$, $(g \wedge h)$ $(f) = g(f) \wedge h(f)$, and similarly for $\vee$ and $'$. We could perhaps further specify that $T_{P_2 \atop n\tilde{t}}$ should be $\hat{H}T_{P_1 \atop t}/T\bar{N}$, the subalgebra of $F_{T_{P_1 \atop t}}/T\bar{N}$ generated by the homomorphisms. However, given the uncertainly surrounding the correct interpretation of lexical P_2s like *look-for*, this might be premature.

Again, since the interpretation of nontransparent P_2s might in some model be transparent homomorphisms, whereas the boolean combinations of these interpretations are defined differently for nontransparent P_2 intensions from the way they are defined for transparent P_2 intensions, we postulate that $T_{P_2 \atop t^2}$ and $T_{P_2 \atop n\tilde{t}}$ be regarded as disjoint sets.

As far as the category P_2 as a whole is concerned, we take its type T_{P_2} to be simply the disjoint union of $T_{P_2 \atop t}$ and $T_{P_2 \atop n\tilde{t}}$, with no boolean structure. Thus, P_2 is not a boolean category in our intensional language. We are thus claiming that boolean combinations of two P_2s, one transparent and one nontransparent, do not occur. Actually, it seems possible in real English to get sentences like

(40)   John looked for and found a unicorn.

where the first verb is understood *de dictu*. The meaning of (40) is apparently the same as that of

(41)   John looked for a unicorn and found a unicorn.

(with *looked for a unicorn* understood *de dictu*). We could represent this in our system if all P_2 intensions (transparent and nontransparent) were elements of the same copy of $F_{T_{P_1 \atop t}}/T\bar{N}$, and if boolean operations were defined pointwise in this set. However, this would lead us back to the same difficulty we discussed earlier in connection with the interpretation of nontransparent P_1s whose intensions happened to be transparent homomorphisms; namely, boolean operations would have to make reference to the syntactic category of the expressions that were being interpreted in order to calculate combinations of transparent homomorphisms, since the definition of these operations would be different depending on whether these homomorphisms were intensions of transparent or of nontransparent P_2s. For the present, we simply will not form sentences such as (40) in our logical language.

This construction of the type for nontransparent P_2s (and for the entire category of P_2s) can be easily generalized to the case of n-place predicates.

Recall that we have already defined the type for the transparent n-place predicates as the set of transparent homomorphisms from $T_{\bar{N}}$ into T_{Pn-1}. For the nontransparent n-place predicates, we start with a copy of the set of all functions from $T_{\bar{N}}$ into T_{Pn-1} which is disjoint from T_{Pn}, and we impose boolean structure by means of the pointwise definition of the operations. Some subalgebra of the resulting algebra will then be taken to be T_{Pn}, perhaps the subalgebra generated by the homomorphisms from $T_{\bar{N}}$ into T_{Pn-1}. The type for all n-place predicates will then be the disjoint union of T_{Pn} and T_{Pn} with no boolean structure defined. Thus, P_n as a whole is not a boolean category.

Proof of the Theorems

In this section we have only the following theorem:

THEOREM 1. *Homomorphic Inheritance Theorem.* Let C_1 and C_2 be categories such that $T_{C_1 e}$ and $T_{C_2 e}$ are total and $T_{C_1}^e$ and $T_{C_2}^e$ are boolean algebras. Then, a transparent function $f\colon T_{C_1 e} \to T_{C_2 e}$ is a homomorphism iff $\forall j \in J$, $f_j\colon T_{C_1}^e \to T_{C_2}^e$ is a homomorphism.

Let f be a transparent function from $T_{C_1 e}$ into $T_{C_2 e}$, let $j \in J$ be arbitrary, and let x and y be arbitrary elements of $T_{C_1 e}$. Note that x_j and y_j are well defined elements of $T_{C_1}^e$, and that $(x \wedge y)_j = x_j \wedge y_j$ by the lifting theorem applied to $T_{C_1 e}$.

Now, since f is transparent, we have $(f(x \wedge y))_j = f_j((x \wedge y)_j) = f_j(x_j \wedge y_j)$. Suppose that f preserves meets. Then we have:

$$
\begin{aligned}
(f(x \wedge y))_j &= (f(x) \wedge f(y))_j \\
&= (f(x))_j \wedge f(y))_j \quad \text{(by the lifting theorem in } T_{C_2 e}) \\
&= f_j(x_j) \wedge f_j(y_j) \quad \text{(since } f \text{ is transparent)}
\end{aligned}
$$

Substituting this into the equation $(f(x \wedge y))_j = f_j(x_j \wedge y_j)$, we get $f_j(x_j \wedge y_j) = f_j(x_j) \wedge f_j(y_j)$. That is, f_j preserves meets.

We have just proved that if f preserves meets, then so does f_j, for arbitrary $j \in J$. Exactly parallel proofs show that if f preserves joins or complements, then f_j preserves joins or complements respectively, for arbitrary $j \in J$. Thus, if f is a homomorphism, then each f_j is a homomorphism.

Conversely, choosing f, j, x, and y as before, and having $(f(x \wedge y))_j = f_j(x_j \wedge y_j)$ as before, suppose that f_j preserves meets. Then we have:

$$(f(x \wedge y))_j = f_j(x_j) \wedge f_j(y_j)$$
$$= (f(x))_j \wedge (f(y))_j \quad \text{(since } f \text{ is transparent)}$$
$$= (f(x) \wedge f(y))_j \quad \text{(lifting theorem applied to } T_{C_2 e}).$$

Since this last equation is true for all j, we conclude, since $T_{C_2 e}$ is total, that $f(x \wedge y) = f(x) \wedge f(y)$, that is, that f preserves meets. Corresponding proofs show that if each f_j preserves joins or complements, then f preserves joins or complements, respectively. Thus, if each f_j is a homomorphism, then f is a homomorphism. This completes the proof of the theorem.

NOTES FOR II.2

[1] The judgments concerning the interpretation of (23) are complicated by the fact that sentences with a nontransparent P_1 exhibit a *de dictu/de re* ambiguity. With a *de re* reading the individual interpretation is clearly right, but we are trying for the *de dictu* reading here; similarly for (26).

[2] B has k atoms $a_1, \ldots, a_k$. If $h: B \to 2$ is a homomorphism, then $h(a_i) = 1$ for at least one atom, for otherwise $h(1_B) = h(a_1 \vee \ldots \vee a_k) = h(a_1) \vee \ldots \vee h(a_k) = 0$, a contradiction to $h(1_B) = 1$ (since h is a homomorphism). However, h cannot map two distinct atoms onto 1. For, if, say, $h(a_i) = 1$, then if $j \neq i$, we have $a_j \leqslant a_i'$, whence $h(a_j) \leqslant h(a_i') = (h(a_i))' = 1' = 0$. For each i, the equations $h(a_i) = 1$, $h(a_j) = 0$ $(j \neq i)$, can be easily seen to define a unique homomorphism $h: B \to 2$.

[3] By a simple induction argument, if f is a boolean combination of homomorphisms from $T_{\bar{N}}$ into T_{P_0} (boolean operations defined pointwise), then either $f(1_{T_{\bar{N}}}) = 1_{T_{P_0}}$ or $f(1_{T_{\bar{N}}}) = 0_{T_{P_0}}$. This might not be true for an arbitrary function from $T_{\bar{N}}$ into T_{P_0}.

3. THE INTENSIONAL LOGIC FOR APs

As in the extensional system, the category AP is defined by

DEFINITION 1. AP = N/N.

The justification for this is exactly the same as it was in our earlier development. Syntactically, the only difference between the category AP as we shall discuss it here and the category AP as discussed previously is that we now permit AP to contain properly intensional expressions. In particular, lexical expressions such as *skillful, severe, fake, alleged*, etc. which were pointed out earlier as being impossible to represent within the structure of an extensional logic are now assumed to be legitimate members of AP.

In the discussion of the extensional logic for AP, we examined several distinct subcategories of this major category. We will do the same here. Of course, since we are now permitting properly intensional expressions to be part of our system, there will be more such subcategories, and there will be more things to say about the relationships among the types for these subcategories.

Since AP is a slash category, we know that T_{AP} will consist of functions. In particular, T_{AP} will be some subset of the set F_{T_N/T_N} $(= F_{F_{P/J}/F_{P/J}}$; see Definition 2, Part II.2). In fact, different subcategories of AP will have types which are different subsets of this set. Our principal task is to determine which subsets these types ought to be. Most of the mathematical developments needed to do this have already been done. It will be recalled, for example, that in Part IB we gave definitions for a number of subsets of $F_{B/B}$, where B is an arbitrary boolean algebra, and we proved some theorems about these subsets. Now, T_N is a boolean algebra, and so these definitions and theorems can be applied directly.

Recall further that $T_N = T_{Ne}$, and that, in fact, T_N is a boolean algebra by virtue of the lifting theorem. In order to formulate statements of greater generality than just for the category AP, it will be handy to have the following definition:

DEFINITION 2. The boolean algebra B is *J-lifted* iff there exists a boolean algebra B^e such that B is isomorphic to $F_{B^e/J}$.

Note that although we are not viewing $F_{B^e/J}$ as the type for any particular category in this definition, it nevertheless makes sense to view $F_{B^e/J}$ as a set of objects each of which has an extension in each world indexed by J. In this sense, $F_{B^e/J}$ satisfies Definition 1 of Part II.1 for totality, and hence the lifting theorem can be applied to conclude that $F_{B^e/J}$ is a boolean algebra. Thus, it is reasonable to require that B be isomorphic to this algebra, as we do in the definition above.

As in our extensional discussion earlier, it is useful to consider various subcategories of APs one at a time. The first such subcategory we will discuss is the subcategory of restricting APs.

By a *restricting AP* we mean here exactly the same as in our earlier discussion. Adjectives like *Albanian, tall*, and *skillful* are restricting, since, for example, an individual who can be truthfully described as an Albanian doctor, a tall doctor, or a skillful doctor, in some world, is necessarily a doctor in that world. In our extensional system, the category of APs was limited to restricting expressions, since, as far as we can tell, all APs which are not properly intensional are restricting. Here, we do not want to do this, since there are a number of properly intensional nonrestricting APs, such as *alleged* and *fake*, as we have seen. However, there is a sense in which the prototypical function of a modifying expression is to be restricting; and, statistically, nonrestricting adjectives certainly appear to be a small minority, limited to a few particular classes of expressions. Therefore, it does not seem incorrect to regard the set of restricting APs as being 'almost' the whole set of APs.

Let us assume that there is a feature r, and that the restricting APs are all members of the subcategory $\underset{r}{\text{AP}}$. Lexical members of $\underset{r}{\text{AP}}$ will be marked with the feature r. As in the cases of subcategorization we have already seen, we will require that lexical restricting APs have intensions which lead to the correct entailment. Complex APs will have to be interpreted as a combination of the interpretations of their constituent expressions in such a way that a complex restricting AP will automatically have an appropriate intension.

Which elements of F_{T_N/T_N} are appropriate interpretations of restricting APs? The answer is easily given, using Definition 2 in Part IB: a restricting AP should be interpreted by means of a restricting member of F_{T_N/T_N} (since T_N is a boolean algebra, Definition 2 can be applied.) In other words, using the notation introduced in Theorem 2 of Part IB, we can define:

DEFINITION 3. $T_{\underset{r}{\text{AP}}} = R_{T_N/T_N}$

To see that this corresponds to the desired notion of restrictingness, we reason as follows. First, we note that if p and q are elements of T_N, then $p \leqslant q$ iff for each $j \in J$, $p_j \leqslant q_j$. Slightly more generally, we have:

THEOREM 1. Let B be a J-lifted boolean algebra and let $p, q \in B$ be arbitrary. Then $p \leqslant q$ iff $\forall j \in J$, $p_j \leqslant q_j$ (in B^e).

Theorem 1 is an almost trivial consequence of the lifting theorem.

Now, to say that $f \in F_{T_N/T_N}$ is restricting means just to say that $f(p) \leqslant p$ for any $p \in T_N$. By Theorem 1 above, this is equivalent to saying that for each world j, $(f(p))_j \leqslant p_j$. But this is just what we want. If, say, p is the intension of *doctor* and f is the intension of *skillful*, then this would mean that for each world j, if an individual is a skillful doctor in that world, then that individual is a doctor in that world.

We will see in a moment that intensions which interpret APs that can be represented in the extensional system will be required to be transparent (in the sense of Definition 2, Part II.1). However, it is important to notice that the considerations above do not require in any way that f be transparent. Suppose, for example, that the N intensions p and q have the same extensions in world j, that is, that $p_j = q_j$. If f is a restricting AP intension, we can conclude that $(f(p))_j \leqslant p_j = q_j$ and that $(f(q))_j \leqslant q_j = p_j$. However, it might still be the case that $(f(p))_j \neq (f(q))_j$. In other words, even though in some world the lawyers and the doctors are exactly the same individuals, and even though, in that world, a skillful lawyer is a lawyer (and a doctor), and a skillful doctor is a doctor (and a lawyer), a skillful lawyer need not be a skillful doctor, and vice versa.

Let us turn next to those APs which can be handled in the extensional system. By the general extensionality theorem, the functions which interpret these APs should be required to be transparent. We assume a feature t, therefore, and we regard these APs as members of the subcategory $\underset{t}{\text{AP}}$. Lexical members of $\underset{t}{\text{AP}}$ will be required to be interpreted by transparent functions from T_N into T_N.

Conceptually, the features r and t are independent of each other. We thus have, at this point, a four-way classification of APs, namely: restricting, transparent APs, restricting APs which are not transparent, transparent APs which are not restricting, and APs which are neither restricting nor transparent. However, it appears to us that there may be no members of the third sort. We could therefore, if we wished, include the notion of restricting-ness as part of the notion of transparency for APs. But it does not seem advisable to do so; not only would such a procedure be entirely ad hoc, but it would also add confusion to the notion of transparency. After all, transparency is relevant to many categories, some of which lack the notion of restrictingness (e.g. the categories P_n). It seems better, therefore, to allow r and t to remain independent, and to leave unexplained the fact that there are no transparent nonrestricting APs.

Given this, we would want to make the following definition:

DEFINITION 4. $T_{\underset{\langle t \rangle_2}{\underset{\langle r \rangle_1}{\text{AP}}}} = \{f \in F_{T_N/T_N}:\ \langle f \text{ is restricting} \rangle_1\}$
$\phantom{DEFINITION 4. T_{AP} = \{f \in F_{T_N/T_N}:\ }$ $\langle f \text{ is transparent} \rangle_2$

There is one potential source of difficulty. We would certainly want our definition here to reduce to the definitions given earlier in the case of transparent APs. However, restrictingness for an AP intension was defined without any reference to the properties, let alone existence, of its extensions in the worlds. Specifically, if f is a transparent restricting AP intension, can we be sure that its extensions are restricting (as AP extensions in the sense of the extensional system)? As it turns out, there is no problem at all, as shown by the following theorem:

THEOREM 2. *Restrictingness Inheritance Theorem*. Let B be a J-lifted boolean algebra and let $f \in F_{B/B}$ be transparent. Then f is restricting iff $\forall j \in j, f_j$ is restricting.

The restrictingness inheritance theorem was given in a slightly more general statement than is needed just for the APs. Note that since B is J-lifted, the definition of transparency applies directly to the elements of $F_{B/B}$, and, by the general extensionality theorem, the extensions f_j of f are elements of F_{B^e/B^e}. In the present case, of course, T_N plays the role of B. We conclude that an AP intension is restricting and transparent just in case it has restricting extensions (in the sense of the extensional system) in every world.

In our extensional system, we defined a particular subclass of the extensional (here: transparent and restricting) APs called the intersecting APs. Loosely speaking, an intersecting AP is one which determines a property independent of a particular N. Thus, in a particular world, an Albanian athlete is an individual who is simultaneously an athlete and an Albanian. We clearly want to distinguish these APs in our intensional system as well, so we posit a feature i, and we take intersecting APs to be members of the subcategory $\underset{i}{\text{AP}}$ of AP.

To determine which elements of F_{T_N/T_N} are the appropriate interpretations of intersecting APs, we turn to Definition 5 in Part IB. Letting T_N play the role of B in that definition, we can say that an intersecting AP should be interpreted by means of an intersecting member of F_{T_N/T_N}. Noting that the meet operation in that definition here corresponds to *and* as conjoining N intensions and that 1 in that definition here corresponds to the intension of being an entity, we see that, if, say, f is the intension of *Albanian* and x is the intension of *athlete*, then the equation $f(x) = x \wedge f(1)$ translates directly to the requirement that the intension of *Albanian athlete* must be the same as the intension of *athlete* conjoined with the intension of *Albanian entity*. Using the notation introduced in Theorem 3, Part IB, we can alternatively define:

DEFINITION 5. $T_{\underset{i}{\text{AP}}} = I_{T_N/T_N}$.

Can anything be said about the relationship between intersecting APs and, on the one hand, restricting APs, and, on the other hand, transparent APs?

Theorem 1, Part IB can be applied directly, with T_N playing the role of B, to conclude that an intersecting AP intension is automatically restricting. We thus have:

(1) $T_{\underset{i}{\mathrm{AP}}} \subseteq T_{\underset{r}{\mathrm{AP}}}.$

However, we can show more. Suppose that f is an intersecting AP intension, that x is an N intension, and that j is the index of some world. We have that $(f(x))_j = (x \wedge f(1))_j = x_j \wedge (f(1))_j$, where the first equality follows by the definition of intersectingness and the second equality follows from the fact that, since $T_N = T_{Ne}$ is total, meets in T_N are calculated on a world by world basis. Now, suppose that x and y are N intensions with the same extension in j, that is, that $x_j = y_j$. Then $(f(x))_j = x_j \wedge (f(1))_j = y_j \wedge (f(1))_j = (f(y))_j$. But this just means that f satisfies the definition of transparency. We have thus shown that an intersecting AP intension is necessarily transparent. In other words, we have:

(2) $T_{\underset{i}{\mathrm{AP}}} \subseteq T_{\underset{t}{\mathrm{AP}}}.$

Thus, there are no new expressions of category AP when we pass from the extensional to the intensional system. In addition, we have the following theorem:

THEOREM 3. *Intersectingness Inheritance Theorem.* Let B be a J-lifted boolean algebra and let $f \in F_{B/B}$ be transparent. Then f is intersecting iff $\forall j \in J$, f_j is intersecting.

As in the case of the restrictingness inheritance theorem, the definition of transparency applies to $F_{B/B}$ since B is J-lifted, and the extensions f_j of f are elements of F_{B^e/B^e}. In the case of the intersecting APs, T_N plays the role of B in this theorem.

Summarizing what we have so far, we can extend Definition 4 above to read as follows:

DEFINITION 6. $T_{\mathrm{AP}} = \{f \in F_{T_N/T_N}: \quad \langle f \text{ is restricting} \rangle_1 \}$
$\quad\quad\quad\quad\quad\quad \begin{matrix} \langle r \rangle_1 \\ \langle t \rangle_2 \\ \langle i \rangle_3 \end{matrix} \quad\quad\quad\quad\quad \langle f \text{ is transparent} \rangle_2$
$\quad\quad\quad\quad\quad\quad\quad\quad\quad\quad\quad\quad\quad\quad\quad \langle f \text{ is intersecting} \rangle_3$

Moreover, the sets T_{AP}, $T_{\underset{r}{\mathrm{AP}}}$, $T_{\underset{t}{\mathrm{AP}}}$, and $T_{\underset{i}{\mathrm{AP}}}$ are related as in the diagram:

(3)

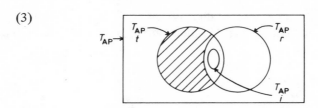

with the shading in $T_{AP_t} - T_{AP_r}$ indicating that these intensions are apparently not the intensions of any actual APs. Finally, for transparent AP intensions, the properties of being restricting or intersecting are equivalent to having restricting or intersecting extensions in all the worlds.

Let us turn next to the small class of negative APs, which includes adjectives like *fake*. It is convenient to make the following definition:

DEFINITION 7. Let B be a boolean algebra. The function $f \in F_{B/B}$ is *negative* iff $\forall x \in B, f(x) \leqslant x'$.

If we now require that negative APs are members of the subcategory $\underset{n}{AP}$, we can insure that the correct entailments result by taking the type for $\underset{n}{AP}$ to be the set of negative functions from T_N into T_N. Note that if f is such a negative function and x is an N intension, then, by Theorem 1, we have that, for each world j, $(f(x))_j \leqslant (x')_j = (x_j)'$ (the last equality following by the lifting theorem applied to T_N). Thus, if f interprets *fake* and x interprets *gun*, then, in any world, if an individual is a fake gun, that individual is not a gun.

Finally, there is the class of APs, including the adjectives *alleged, putative,* etc., which are neither negative nor restricting. The logical characteristic of these APs, which we call conjectural APs, is a negative one: none of the entailments which can be made on the basis of an AP being restricting, transparent, intersecting, or negative, can be made for these APs. Therefore, we define the type for this group of APs as being the entire set F_{T_N/T_N}. Note that we do not want to forbid the intension of a conjectural AP to be transparent, restricting, etc. It might happen that in a particular interpretation, some conjectural AP could in fact exhibit one or another of these special properties. For example, it might happen that in some interpretation an alleged thief always (or never) turned out to be a thief. For such an interpretation, the interpretation of *alleged* would be restricting (or negative). However, this would be an accidental fact about that interpretation; in general, an alleged thief is neither necessarily a thief nor necessarily a non-thief.

The interpretation of *alleged* can therefore not be restricted to lie in any of the special subsets of FT_N/T_N that we have defined above.

Because of this, it is perhaps simplest if we assume that conjectural *AP*s just do not carry any of the four subcategorization features that we have defined for *AP*s. If so, then a complete definition of the types for the category *AP* and its subcategories can be given as follows:

DEFINITION 8. $T_{AP} = \{f \in FT_N/T_N: \langle f \text{ is restricting} \rangle_1 \}$
$$\langle r \rangle_1$$
$$\langle t \rangle_2 \qquad\qquad \langle f \text{ is transparent} \rangle_2$$
$$\langle i \rangle_3 \qquad\qquad \langle f \text{ is intersecting} \rangle_3$$
$$\langle n \rangle_4 \qquad\qquad \langle f \text{ is negative} \rangle_4$$

As pointed out following the previous version of this definition, namely Definition 6, there are relationships among the subsets defined above. Here we need only add that T_{AP_r} and T_{AP_n} are almost disjoint by their very definition: there is only one function which is a member of both these sets, namely, the function which maps every N intension into the zero N intension.

At this point we are in a position to illustrate how the interpretation of sentences with APs can be carried out. Let us calculate the interpretation of *John kissed a skillful doctor*:

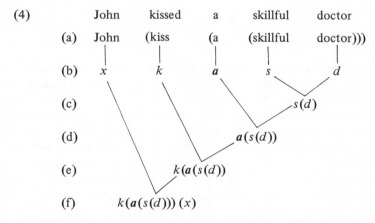

(4)   John   kissed   a   skillful   doctor

(a)   John   (kiss   (a   (skillful   doctor)))

(b) x k a s d

(c) $s(d)$

(d) $a(s(d))$

(e) $k(a(s(d))$

(f) $k(a(s(d)))\,(x)$

Line (a) gives the representation of the given English sentence in our logical language. In line (b), the lexical expressions are replaced by their interpretations, which are, of course, intensions. In particular, x is an $\bar{N}$ intension whose extension in every world is some individual, say I_1. The remaining lines involve combining the intensions in the usual function-argument manner. Line (f) is therefore the intension of the whole sentence.

In a particular world j, the following calculation can be made:

$$(5) \quad (k(a(s(d)))\,(x))_j = (k(a(s(d))))_j\,(I_1) \qquad (x_j = I_1;\ k(a(s(d)))\ \text{is transparent})$$

$$= k_j(a(s(d)))_j\,(I_1) \qquad (k\ \text{is transparent})$$

$$= k_j(a_j(s(d))_j)\,(I_1) \qquad (a\ \text{is transparent})$$

$$= k_j\big(\bigcup_{(s(d))_j\,\in\,I} I\big)\,(I_1) \qquad (\text{definition of }a)$$

$$= \big(\bigvee_{(s(d))_j\,\in\,I} k_j(I)\big)\,(I_1) \qquad (k_j\ \text{is a homomorphism})$$

$$= \bigvee_{(s(d))_j\,\in\,I} k_j(I)\,(I_1) \qquad (\text{definition of } \vee \text{ in } T_{P_1}^{e})$$

(This should be compared with the calculation in (1) in Part IB.) Now, since *skillful* is a lexical member of the category $\underset{r}{\text{AP}}$, its intension s is required to be restricting. Thus, $s(d) \leqslant d$, whence, by Theorem 1, $(s(d))_j \leqslant d_j$. But $(s(d))_j$ and d_j and N extensions, that is, elements of P. Since an N extension is a member of an individual iff the atom associated with that individual is contained in that N extension, we conclude that:

$$(6) \qquad \bigvee_{(s(d))_j\,\in\,I} k_j(I)\,(I_1) \leqslant \bigvee_{d_j\,\in\,I} k_j(I)\,(I_1).$$

Since the right hand side of (6) is the extension in j of *John* (*kiss* (*a doctor*)), as the reader can easily verify, we conclude that *John* (*kiss* (*a* (*skillful doctor*))) implies *John* (*kiss* (*a doctor*)) in any world. Note that in our discussion we never made use of any assumption of transparency for s; indeed, since *skillful* is not a member of $\underset{t}{\text{AP}}$, we must allow the possibility that s is *not* transparent, and therefore that there are no such things as extensions of s in the worlds.

Of course, if we replace *skillful* in (4) with *tall*, which *is* a member of $\underset{t}{\text{AP}}$, then, assuming that t is the intension of *tall*, the extension of *John* (*kiss* (*a* (*tall doctor*))) in j is equal to

$$(7) \qquad \bigvee_{(t(d))_j\,\in\,I} k_j(I)\,(I_1) = \bigvee_{t_j(d_j)\,\in\,I} k_j(I)\,(I_1)$$

since t is transparent. The right hand side of (7) should be compared to (1i) in Part IB; the situation reduces to precisely what we had in the extensional system.

If we replace *skillful* in (4) with *fake*, then, assuming that f is the intension of *fake*, the extension of *John* (*kiss* (*a* (*fake doctor*))) in j is equal to

$$(8) \qquad \bigvee_{(f(d))_j \in I}^{n} k_j(I)(I_1).$$

Since *fake* is a member of the subcategory $\underset{n}{\text{AP}}$, we must have $f(d) \leqslant d'$, whence $(f(d))_j \leqslant (d')_j = (d_j)'$. From this we can conclude that any individual I which contains $(f(d))_j$ cannot contain d_j (since the atom associated with I would have to be contained in $(f(d))_j$, and hence in $(d_j)'$, and so that atom could not be contained in d_j). Since (8) implies that John kisses an individual with the property $(f(d))_j$ in world j, we see that *John* (*kiss* (*a* (*fake doctor*))) implies that John kisses at least one individual who is not a doctor. No conclusion can be drawn concerning whether John kisses any doctors in world j or not, of course.

Finally, if we replace *skillful* in (4) with *putative*, then, assuming that p is the intension of *putative*, the extension of *John* (*kiss* (*a* (*putative doctor*))) in j is equal to

$$(9) \qquad \bigvee_{(p(d))_j \in I} k_j(I)(I_1).$$

Since *putative* does not carry any of the features r, t, i, or n, no particular relationship can be assumed to hold between $(p(d))_j$ and d_j. Thus, not only can we conclude neither the truth nor the falsity of *John* (*kiss* (*a doctor*)) from the truth of *John* (*kiss* (*a* (*putative doctor*))), but, assuming this latter sentence to be true in a world, we cannot conclude that any of the individuals kissed by John either is or is not a doctor.

It is interesting to consider the question of what interpretation results if *kiss* in (4) is replaced by a nontransparent P_2, say, by *look-for*. If the intension of *look-for* is l, then, parallel to (4f), we obtain $l(a(s(d)))(x)$ as the intension of *John* (*look-for* (*a* (*skillful doctor*))). Since this latter is the translation, in our logical language, of the English sentence *John is looking for a skillful doctor*, let us examine the implications of this sentence and see if they match of predictions made by our system.

As a preliminary fact, let us note that since *skillful* is restricting, we have, for an arbitrary $j \in J$, that $(s(d))_j \leqslant d_j$. Since a is an increasing determiner, we can conclude that $a_j(s(d))_j \leqslant a_j(d_j)$ for each $j \in J$. Finally, since a is transparent, we have that $(a(s(d)))_j \leq (a(d))_j$ for each $j \in J$, whence by Theorem 1, $a(s(d)) \leq a(d)$.

Having obtained this, what can we conclude about the relationship, if any, between $l(a(s(d)))$ and $l(a(d))$? Clearly, this depends on what we assume about l. In Part II.2, we discussed the question of whether or not a nontransparent P_2 intension ought to be a homomorphism, tentatively concluding that, since we wanted to use pointwise defined boolean operations on the nontransparent P_2 intensions, we could *not* restrict these intensions to being homomorphisms. However, it was suggested that, perhaps, the algebra of the nontransparent P_2 intensions is *generated* by the homomorphisms.

Specifically, we discussed the logic of some sentences involving the lexical P_2 *look-for*, deciding that there was some doubt whether the intension of this expression could be restricted to be a homomorphism. In the present circumstance, we note that if l is a homomorphism, we could conclude that $l(a(s(d))) \leq l(a(d))$. However, if l is not a homomorphism, it still might be the case that, whenever $x \leq y$, it would be the case that $l(x) \leq l(y)$. In Keenan and Faltz (1978), it was proposed that P_2s like *look-for* carry a feature +*additive*, and that the intensions of such P_2s be required at least to preserve the $\leq$ relation, even though they could not be required to be homomorphisms. If we take this approach, then we can indeed claim that $l(a(s(d))) \leq l(a(d))$. If this is so, then, since two transparent P_1 intensions are being compared, we can conclude directly (since transparent P_1 intensions are uncontroversially homomorphisms) that $l(a(s(d)))\ (x) \leq l(a(d))\ (x)$. Since the latter is the interpretation of *John* (*look-for* (*a doctor*)), this would mean that *John* (*look-for* (*a* (*skillful doctor*))) implies that *John* (*look-for* (*a doctor*)). Is this correct?

At first blush, this seems to be exactly what we want. Surely, if John is looking for a skillful doctor, we can conclude that John is looking for a doctor. However, if we examine carefully the way *look for* sentences are actually used in English, we can detect an ambiguity which calls this 'obvious' claim into question.

The ambiguity we mean is not the *de dictu–de re* ambiguity; this we shall discuss in a later chapter, where we shall see that the direct interpretation of *look-for* sentences as we have set things up always corresponds to a *de dictu* reading, and that *de re* readings always involve a λ operator in the translation of the English sentence into our logical language. What we have in mind here is rather the following. In one sense, the sentence *John is looking for a doctor* means that John is engaging in activity based on the desire to find some entity, and that this desire of his will be satisfied if he finds *any* entity which has the property of being a doctor in the world in question. Now, we *cannot* conclude that John is looking for a doctor in this sense if we know that it is the case that John is looking for a skillful doctor. The reason is simply that finding an entity which has the property of being a doctor is not enough to satisfy John's desire. The entity which will satisfy this desire must in fact be a member of the presumably smaller set of skillful doctors. If we saw John engaging in a search, finding a number of doctors, but rejecting them and continuing his search, we would surely say that it is *not* the case that *John is looking for a doctor* is true in the sense just indicated.

On the other hand, it appears that the English sentence *John is looking for a doctor* is sometimes open to the following looser interpretation: John is engaged in a search, the search will be satisfied if John finds any entity satisfying a certain property, and any such entity is a doctor. Note that this means that the set of entities any one of which will satisfy John's search is a subset of the set of doctors, but is not necessarily the whole set of doctors. In other words, this looser interpretation of *John is looking for a doctor* is equivalent to the tighter interpretation (as defined above) of a sentence like *John is looking for a doctor satisfying some (perhaps contextually defined) additional property*. It is this looser sense that we are using when we conclude ('obviously') that John is looking for a doctor on the basis of knowing that John is looking for a skillful doctor.

However, this suggests that the looser interpretation actually involves ellipsis. It is certainly the case that the tighter interpretation is the preferred (or possibly only) interpretation of *John is looking for a doctor* if this sentence is used out of context. Presumably, the problem of ellipsis is one which is appropriately handled by the component of grammar which mediates between English sentences and sentences in our logical language. If so, then we do *not* want *John (look-for (a (skillful doctor)))* to imply *John (look-for (a doctor))*, since these logical sentences will correspond unambiguously to the tighter interpretation. But this means that we do not want it to be automatically the case that $(l(a(s(d))) \leqslant l(a(d))$. This is not only further evidence that we had better *not* require nontransparent P_n intensions to be homomorphisms, it is evidence that we had better not require nontransparent P_n intensions even to preserve the $\leqslant$ relation. This matter clearly deserves further investigation. For now, however, we do not pursue it any further.

Let us return now to the types for the various subcategories of the category AP. In Definition 8, we indicated what these types are insofar as being sets of intensions. However, there remains the task of deciding which of these types ought to carry boolean structure and what that structure ought to be.

The case of restricting APs is easily handled. We clearly want boolean combinations of these to be constructed and interpreted, in order to handle English $\bar{N}$s such as *a skillful and (but)/or/but not severe teacher*. If we define $\underset{r}{AP}$ to be a boolean category, then the way to define boolean structure is indicated in Theorem 2 of Part IB. In fact, since $T_{\underset{r}{AP}} = R_{T_N/T_N}$ (in the notation of that theorem), we can conclude directly that $T_{\underset{r}{AP}}$ is a boolean algebra (in fact, a complete atomic one) with operations as defined in that theorem. We leave it to the reader to verify that those operations correspond correctly to the interpretations of English $\bar{N}$s such as the ones just mentioned.

Since the types for transparent and intersecting APs are each subsets of the type for restricting APs, we may ask whether or not they are subalgebras of $T_{\underset{r}{AP}}$. The case of the intersecting APs follows directly from Theorem 3 of Part IB; note that $T_{\underset{i}{AP}} = I_{T_N/T_N}$ in the notation of that theorem. The issue of transparency (in the technical sense) was not discussed in Part IB, so we need an additional theorem. First, we define:

DEFINITION 9. Let B be a J-lifted boolean algebra. Then

$$T_{B/B} = \{f \in F_{B/B} : f \text{ is transparent}\}.$$

We now have the following theorem:

THEOREM 4. Let B be a J-lifted boolean algebra. Then $T_{B/B} \cap R_{B/B}$ is a subalgebra of $R_{B/B}$. Moreover, if B is complete, then $T_{B/B} \cap R_{B/B}$ is complete.

In Part IB we discussed the fact that boolean combinations of APs of different subcategories are sometimes odd. Similar facts obtain when nontransparent restricting APs are combined with APs of other categories. Combinations of such APs with transparent nonintersecting APs seem mostly to be all right:

$$(10) \qquad \text{a skillful} \begin{cases} \text{and (but)} \\ \text{?or} \\ \text{but not} \end{cases} \text{fat geisha (or: a skillful, fat geisha).}$$

Combining a nontransparent restricting AP with an intersecting one is worse:

(11)   a skillful $\begin{cases} ?* \text{ and} \\ ?? \text{ or} \\ ? \text{ but not} \end{cases}$ Albanian dancer (but ok: a skillful, Albanian

dancer).

Our earlier remarks appear to apply to the same degree here that they did in Part IB. Note, incidentally, that since intersecting APs are transparent, Theorem 5 in that discussion holds on a world by world basis, and hence, also, of intersecting intensions.

We come now to the question of whether boolean combinations of other subclasses of APs ought to be formed, and, if so, what the interpretations of such combinations ought to be.

Consider first the negative APs. Some lexical expressions of category AP_n are, perhaps, *false, fake, phony, artificial*. Combinations involving these and restricting APs combined with *and* sound odd:

(12)   ? an artificial and heavy diamond
         ? a fake and Albanian gun

although these seem to become all right if comma intonation is substituted for *and*:

(13)   an artificial, heavy diamond
         a fake, Albanian gun

However, if we try to think what the expressions in (13) might mean, we may detect an odd sense of contradiction in them. We can get some insight into this if we try to construct a formal interpretation for these expressions.

To interpret the conjunction of APs in (12), it seems reasonable to try to use Definition 7 of Part IB. Supposing f and g to be the intensions of *artificial* and *heavy* respectively and x to be the intension of *diamond*, the intension of (*artificial and heavy*) *diamond* would be $(f \wedge g)(x) = f(x) \wedge g(x)$. Now, since *artificial* is negative, we have $f(x) \leqslant x'$, whence (since $f(x) \wedge g(x) \leqslant f(x)$) $(f \wedge g)(x) \leqslant x'$. However, g is restricting, so that $g(x) \leqslant x$, whence (since $f(x) \wedge g(x) \leqslant g(x)$) $(f \wedge g)(x) \leqslant x$. Thus, $(f \wedge g)(x) \leqslant x' \wedge x = 0$. What we have just proved shows that, according to our interpretation, there are no entities which have the property which interprets (*artificial and heavy*) *diamond* in any world. While our intuitions are a bit vague as to the meaning of the expressions in (13), this seems to have a reasonable chance of being correct.

The argument above would not hold, of course, if Definition 7 Part IB were used with the intensions of two negative APs. If the corresponding expressions are actually formed, we still have the sense of oddness when *and* is used:

(14)   ? a fake and phony diamond

If a comma is used instead, the expression exudes a feeling of redundancy, due to the similarity in the meanings of the two APs:

(15)   a fake, phony diamond.

However, our intuition is that the contradiction hovering within the meaning of the expressions in (13) is absent from (15). It appears, therefore, that Definition 7 Part IB may reasonably be extended to apply to the intensions of restricting and of negative APs.

Disjunctions of negative APs with other APs tend to sound odd, especially when the second AP is intersecting:

(16)   ? an artificial or heavy diamond
(17)   ?? a fake or Albanian gun

However, such expressions do seem interpretable. If a disjunction is formed with two negative APs, the *or* seems to be rhetorical rather than logical. That is, in an expression like

(18)   a fake or phony diamond

there is a sense that *or* indicates the speaker's hesitation concerning which *word, fake* or *phony* best applies, rather than indicating that the speaker is interested in referring to an entity which either satisfies the *fake diamond* property or else the *phony diamond* property. This, too, is due to the similarity in the meanings of the two negative APs. In any case, if disjunctions involving negative APs are allowed, the reader can see easily that Definition 8 of Part IB provides acceptable interpretations of such combinations.

Turning finally to the matter of negations of negative APs, we first examine expressions like

(19)   a green but not fake diamond
        an Albanian but not phony doctor.

These expressions, though odd sounding, are perfectly interpretable. More-over, our intuition is that, although the expressions *not fake diamond* and *not phony doctor* are not used by themselves as *N*s in English, they ought to be interpreted as meaning something like *real diamond* and *real doctor* respectively. In particular, this would mean that the negation of a negative AP is a restricting AP. How should this negation be interpreted?

Suppose that *f* is the intension of a negative AP and that *p* is the intension of an *N* that it is combined with. If we apply Definition 9 of Part IB to determine *f*′, we would have that $f'(p) = p \wedge (f(p))'$. But, since *f* is the interpretation of a negative AP, $f(p) \leqslant p'$, whence $p = p'' \leqslant (f(p))'$. But this means that $f'(p) = p$. That is, to be a not phony doctor (or a non-phony doctor) would be equivalent to being a doctor.

If we think of *not phony doctor* as equivalent to *real doctor*, this is not unreasonable. Surely, in any world, the set of real doctors is precisely the same as the set of doctors. The function of the adjective *real* seems to be solely discoursal, calling the hearer's attention to the fact that a certain entity is indeed a member of the set of doctors, perhaps contrary to some presupposition or expectation, rather than narrowing down the set of doctors to a properly smaller set.

Accepting this, we see that if Definitions 7, 8, and 9 of Part IB are ex-tended to negative AP intensions, then the resulting interpretations appear to be reasonable. However, if we do this, the boolean axioms are *not* satisfied. In particular, if *f* is a negative AP intension, it is not necessarily the case that $(f')'$ is equal to *f*. For, according to what we showed above, $f'(p) = p$, whence $(f')'(p) = p \wedge (f'(p))' = p \wedge p' = 0$. But, while we do require that $f(p) \leqslant p'$, we certainly cannot assume that $f(p) = 0$, as would have to be the case if $f(p) = (f')'(p)$, by what we have just seen. We are now faced with three choices:

(i) Abandon the requirement that boolean-like operations always satisfy the classical axioms. That is, with this choice, we would admit certain types as being sets with boolean-like operations but not being boolean algebras. We would certainly want to investigate what deviations from boolean-algebra-hood were permitted.

(ii) Change the definitions of the operations as they apply to negative AP intensions in such a way that the boolean axioms are indeed satisfied.

(iii) Abandon the idea of extending the boolean operations to negative AP intensions altogether.

Each of these choices has its appeal as well as its drawbacks. For now, we simply leave this issue open.

Given the fact that we have not resolved the matter of boolean operations for negative AP intensions, it is perhaps academic to consider the question of whether a single set of boolean operations can or should be defined on the entire type T_{AP}. However, let us note a few points relevant to this issue.

Defining a boolean structure on all of T_{AP} would allow the interpretation of combinations of APs at least one of which was a conjectural AP. However, the English expressions corresponding to conjunctions of this sort sound quite bad, whether the conjunction is expressed by the word *and*, as in:

$$(20) \qquad \text{an alleged and} \left\{ \begin{array}{l} \text{phony} \\ \text{skillful} \\ \text{Albanian} \end{array} \right\} \text{doctor}$$

or by a comma (as seems to be the way such conjunction is normally handled in English for prenominal adjectives), as in:

$$(21) \qquad \text{an alleged,} \left\{ \begin{array}{l} \text{phony} \\ \text{skillful} \\ \text{Albanian} \end{array} \right\} \text{doctor}$$

There are two points we should note about these.

First of all, the expressions in (21) should not be confused with expressions such as the following in which there is no comma:

$$(22) \qquad \text{an alleged} \left\{ \begin{array}{l} \text{phony} \\ \text{skillful} \\ \text{Albanian} \end{array} \right\} \text{doctor}$$

which are acceptable and interpretable. These are, of course, interpreted not as boolean combinations of adjectives, but rather as applications of the *alleged* function to the combinations *phony doctor* (or *skillful doctor*). In other words, the translation of the expressions in (22) into our logical language will be *a* (*alleged* (*phony doctor*)) (and, similarly, *a* (*alleged* (*skillful doctor*)), etc.). Such expressions are already taken care of by what we have set up in our system, and need no further comment.

Secondly, there appears to be an inherent contradiction in the expressions in (21), a contradiction of a sort not expressible in our logic. A speaker who refers to an entity by means of the $\bar{N}$

$$(23) \qquad \text{an alleged, skillful doctor}$$

seems to be committed to the idea that that entity could be referred to simultaneously by means of the $\bar{N}$

(24)   an alleged doctor

and by the $\bar{N}$

(25)   a skillful doctor

Now, since *skillful* is restricting, the use of (25) commits the speaker to the belief that the entity he wishes to refer to is indeed a doctor. However, the proper use of (24) involves the idea that the speaker is precisely *not* committing himself to the doctorhood of the intended referent. This is different from saying that the extensional referent of (24) is not required to be a doctor (but is not required to be a non-doctor, either). In terms of the relationship between the $\bar{N}$s (24) and (25) and their extensions, there is no inherent contradiction; if both are proper $\bar{N}$s to use to refer to the same entity, then it simply must be that that entity, which/who *might* be a doctor (by (24)), genuinely *is* a doctor (by (25)). However, there *is* a contradiction between the required presence of a speaker-commitment with (25) and the required absence of a speaker-commitment with (24). In other words, the locus of the contradiction inherent in the $\bar{N}$ (23) is the matter of speaker commitment, an area totally distinct from the concerns which our logical system addresses. Since this is the case (and since, as the reader may easily check by forming expressions himself, disjunctions and negations involving conjectural APs sound equally peculiar), we feel it is reasonable, at least provisionally, not to suggest a general definition for boolean structure on T_{AP}.

This completes our discussion of T_{AP} and the subsets of this set relevant to the intensional interpretation of various classes of APs. However, before moving on to the next major topic to be discussed, let us briefly look at a few special issues that relate to APs.

We would like our system to be able to handle expressions which serve to modify APs. Such expressions would include lexical items like *very* and *somewhat*, as well as, ultimately, complex expressions like *to a certain extent*. We will not make a serious proposal here concerning the syntax of such expressions. However, we can easily say something about their interpretation.

Note first that these modifiers can probably be safely restricted to combining only with restricting APs:

(26)   a $\left\{\begin{array}{l}\text{*very alleged}\\ \text{?very phony}\\ \text{very skillful}\end{array}\right\}$ doctor

This means that they are of category AP/AP, and therefore their interpretations are functions from T_{AP} into T_{AP}.

Next, these modifiers are probably all restricting. Thus, a somewhat skillful doctor is, perhaps, a skillful doctor. If so, then the type for such modifiers can be taken to be the set of restricting functions from T_{AP} into itself. Note that since T_{AP} is a boolean algebra, the notion of restrictingness is defined for such functions. (If there turn out to be clear examples of nonrestricting AP modifiers, we simply can enlarge the type to include other functions.)

Finally, we can perhaps define the interpretation of one such modifier, regarding it as a logical constant. The modifier we have in mind is *very*, and the interpretation we can give is the same one we suggested earlier in our discussion of extensional APs. Namely, we can require that in any model *very* be interpreted as **very**, where **very** $(f) = f^2$ for any $f \in T_{AP}$. The reader can check easily that Theorems 7 and 8 of Part IB are still true even if we are dealing with AP intensions rather than AP extensions. We conclude that this definition interprets *very* as a restricting AP modifier. Moreover, if f is intersecting, then **very** $(f) = f$, so that the discussion in Part IB of the awkwardness and reinterpretation of intersecting APs combined with *very* still goes through. Incidentally, there is nothing particularly problematic about combining *very* with a nontransparent AP like *skillful*. If the intension of *skillful* is f, then the intension of *very skillful* will be just f^2, itself a nontransparent restricting function, in general.

Returning to the APs themselves, recall that in Part IB we discussed the extensional interpretations of scalar adjectives. One approach suggested there was that the extensions of scalar adjectives be required to satisfy three conditions, called coherence, transitivity, and order-consistency. Since an AP intension is a restricting function from a complete atomic boolean algebra (namely T_N) into itself, the same definitions can be mechanically adopted for AP intensions. However, it is not clear that the correct notion of scalarity emerges from this procedure.

To see the problem, note first that the atoms of T_N do not correspond to individuals or entities, but rather to individuals-per-world. That is, an atom of T_N is determined uniquely not by an atom a of P, but by a pair $\langle a, j \rangle$, where a is an atom of P and $j \in J$ is an arbitrary world. This by itself is not necessarily a problem; the procedure of Part IB will impose a scalarity on individuals-per-world, allowing the (probably desirable) possibility of comparing individuals in different worlds with respect to some scale. If worlds correspond to points in time, this would allow us to make sense of a sentence like *John is smarter than he was last year*.

However, in the case of a properly intensional AP like *skillful*, the property of order-consistency will not work correctly. To see this, let f be the intension which interprets *skillful*, let a and b be two atoms of P, let j and k be two worlds, and let $q \in T_N$ be such that $q(j) = a$, $q(k) = b$, and $q(i) = 0$ for every world i where $i \neq j$ and $i \neq k$. Suppose that $f(q)$ is the N intension which maps every world except k into 0 and which maps k into b. Intuitively, then, this should correspond to the idea that the only skillful 'q' is to be found in world k, and that the only individual in world k who is a skillful 'q' is the individual corresponding to the atom b.

Now, suppose that the individual corresponding to a is a doctor in world j, and that the individual corresponding to b is a doctor in world k. Suppose further that a is a skillful doctor in world j. By the property of order consistency as defined in Definition 15 of Part IB, it would necessarily be the case that b is a skillful doctor in world k. Clearly, we do not want to be able to come to such a conclusion.

The difficulty, of course, is that there is no particular connection between being a 'q' and being a doctor. Thus, a properly intensional AP like *skillful* must be expected to behave randomly different when modifying distinct N intensions. Note that if we replace *skillful* with *tall* in the above paragraph, the problem disappears. We could, perhaps, then retain the earlier analysis, but restrict it to transparent scalar APs only. But this still would leave the problem of the scalarity of nontransparent APs like *skillful* to be dealt with; note that the chief motivation which led us to want to formalize scalarity, namely, the existence of comparatives, applies to these nontransparent cases as well. This too is a question which we leave unresolved for now.

Finally, let us briefly consider a situation in which APs enter into a structure as arguments. What we have in mind are expressions such as *seem happy, look Albanian, appear rested and content* in which an expression like *seem, look, appear, sound*, etc. is combined with an AP to produce a complex P_1. By the way we have been setting up our syntax, we see that, as a first approximation, *seem, look*, etc. are members of category P_1/AP. However, we can tighten this up somewhat.

First of all, not every AP can be an argument of such a verb. In particular, conjectural APs cannot be used this way:

(27)   * The thief seemed/looked/sounded alleged/putative.

However, negative APs, as well as all subclasses of restricting APs, can be freely combined with these verbs:

$$
(28) \quad \text{The thief} \left\{ \begin{array}{l} \text{seemed} \\ \text{looked} \end{array} \right\} \left\{ \begin{array}{l} \text{phony} \\ \text{skillful} \\ \text{tall} \\ \text{Albanian} \end{array} \right\}
$$

We can therefore say more specifically that *seem*, etc. are members of the category $P_1/(\underset{r}{AP} \cup \underset{n}{AP})$.

Secondly, the P_1^n that is created when such a combination is made is always transparent. Thus, in a world in which *the thief* and *John* are the same individual, the truth values of the sentences in (28) are necessarily the same as the truth values of:

$$
(29) \quad \text{John} \left\{ \begin{array}{l} \text{seemed} \\ \text{looked} \end{array} \right\} \left\{ \begin{array}{l} \text{phony} \\ \text{skillful} \\ \text{tall} \\ \text{Albanian} \end{array} \right\}
$$

Note that, as in the case of *be* (see our discussion in Part IB), we feel compelled to neglect the role of context in the interpretation of such sentences. For example, if we compare (30) and (31):

(30)   The doctor seems skillful
(31)   The lawyer seems skillful

we have the sense that, in its most expected context, sentence (30) would be used to indicate that the individual referred to by the $\bar{N}$ *the doctor* seems skillful *as a doctor*, whereas sentence (31) would be used to indicate that the individual referred to by the $\bar{N}$ the *lawyer* seems skillful as a lawyer. In a world in which there is precisely one doctor and precisely one lawyer and in which the one doctor and the one lawyer are the same individual, it might appear, therefore, that although the extensions of the subjects of (30) and (31) are the same, the truth values of these sentences needn't be the same, and hence that *seem skillful* is not transparent. However, if we factor out the effect of context, this problem does not arise. Specifically, we imagine the meaning of *seem skillful* as applied to an individual to be that that individual exhibits an appearance from which one may deduce that he is skillful at some (contextually determined) activity. Since this activity is contextually determined, we are not in a position to take it into consideration in our representation of the semantics; for our purposes, we have to imagine that *seem skillful* means exhibit an appearance of skill at some activity. If so, then (30) and (31) do necessarily have the same truth value in the world we sketched out. Note, in support of this, that, say, (31) could be perfectly well uttered to indicate that the individual described as being the lawyer seems skillful as he gives medical attention to someone, i.e., as he acts in the capacity of being a doctor, even though he is being referred to as the lawyer.

This being the case, we can further state that the category of *seem*, etc. is $P_{t_1}/(\underset{r}{AP} \cup \underset{n}{AP})$. From this, we can deduce that the type of this class of words is some subset of $FT_{P_{t_1}}/(T_{\underset{r}{AP}} \cup T_{\underset{n}{AP}})$. The question now arises as to which subset of this set is the appropriate type for the category $P_{t_1}/(\underset{r}{AP} \cup \underset{n}{AP})$.

We have seen that when an expression of type P_{t_2} is combined with an argument to create a transparent P_1, the interpretation of that P_2 depends homomorphically on the interpretation of its argument. We might therefore expect that when a verb like *seem* is combined with an AP argument, its interpretation depends homomorphically on the interpretation of the AP. As it happens, this is not so.

First of all, if the argument AP is negative, we have the problem that the boolean operations have not been defined for negative APs. Thus, $T_{\underset{r}{AP}} \cup T_{\underset{n}{AP}}$ is simply not a boolean algebra, as things now stand, and so no function which has this set as its domain can be described as being a homomorphism.

However, it still might be the case that the restriction of the interpretation of *seem* to $T_{\underset{r}{AP}}$ is a homomorphism (recall that $T_{\underset{r}{AP}}$ is a boolean algebra; in fact, it is the restricting algebra RT_N/T_N). This would mean that the (a) and (b) sentences in the following pairs would necessarily have the same truth value in any world:

(32) (a) John seems happy and successful
     (b) John seems happy and seems successful
(33) (a) John seems happy or successful
     (b) John seems happy or seems successful
(34) (a) John seems successful but not happy
     (b) John seems successful but doesn't seem happy

While it might seem at a causal glance that the (a) and (b) sentences in each of these pairs are indeed synonymous, a closer examination reveals that this is probably not so. Consider for example (33a) and (33b). Sentence (33a) appears to state that John exhibits a certain appearance, and that that appearance suggests that either happiness or success can be truthfully predicated of John. Sentence (33b) on the other hand states that John exhibits one of two appearances, one of which suggests happiness, the other of which suggests success. While our judgments here are not secure, it seems possible that (33b) might be true in a world in which (33a) is false. (The reverse situation seems less likely.)

The nonequivalence of (34a) and (34b) is perhaps clearer. From sentence (34a) we definitely derive the sense that John's appearance suggests actual unhappiness, whereas (34b) merely states that John lacks the appearance of happiness. Thus, (34b) could easily be true in a world in which (34a) is false.

The case of the pair of sentences in (32) is less clear. Possibly, (32a) predicates a single appearance while (32b) predicates two appearances. In any case, we prefer not to assume any algebraic properties to hold of the intensions of words like *seem*. Provisionally, then, we take the type of category $P_{t^1}/(\underset{r}{AP} \cup \underset{n}{AP})$ to be the full set of functions from $T_{\underset{r}{AP}} \cup T_{\underset{n}{AP}}$ into $T_{P_{t^1}}$.

Incidentally, the situation here is clearly reminiscent of the situation involving nontransparent P_2s as they are applied to their object $\bar{N}$s. Here too we have a nontransparent intension (transparency being here defined according to the more general Definition 3 of Part II.1 rather than Definition 2): in a world in which the happy individuals are precisely the successful individuals, it need not be the case that the individuals who seem happy are exactly the individuals who seem successful. The algebraic properties of such intensions are unclear; they may depend on meaning postulates which relate these intensions to the interpretations of complex expressions. In the case of *seem*, we will return to this question briefly later, when we consider the interpretation of sentences like *John seems to be happy* and *it seems that John is happy*.

However, in the one case of the logical constant *be*, we can easily give an interpretation. What we do is simply to take the definitions already worked out in the extensional system and embed them into our intensional logic. As before, *be* is viewed as a member of category $\langle P_1, P_1 \rangle / \langle \bar{N}, AP \rangle$. When combined with an $\bar{N}$, *be* is interpreted as $\mathbf{be}_1$, where $\mathbf{be}_1$ is that element of $T_{P_{t^2}}$ such that, for every $j \in J$, $(\mathbf{be}_1)_j$ is the element of $T_{P_2}^e$ defined to be the extension of *be* in our earlier discussion; recall that, by the General

Extensionality Theorem and the Homomorphic Inheritance Theorem, this uniquely defines an element of T_{P_2}.

When combined with an AP, *be* is interpreted as be_2, where be_2 is that element of FT_{P_1}/T_{AP} such that given $f \in T_{AP}$ and $j \in J$, $(be_2(f))_j$ is that homomorphism from P^* into 2 such that, for any individual I, $((be_2(f))_j(I)$ $= 1$ iff $\bigvee_{p \in T_N}(f(p))_j \in I$. The reader may check easily that this definition reduces to the one given in the extensional system on a world by world basis in case f is transparent. However, f need not be transparent for this definition to be applied. If f is the interpretation of *skillful*, then, with this definition, *be skillful* is still true of an individual in a particular world iff, roughly, *be a skillful e* is true of that individual, for some actual or potential N *e*.

Proofs of the Theorems

THEOREM 1. Let B be a J-lifted boolean algebra and let p, $q \in B$ be arbitrary. Then $p \leqslant q$ iff $\forall j \in J$, $p_j \leqslant q_j$ (in B^e).

We have $p \leqslant q$ iff $p \wedge q = p$ (definition of $\leqslant$)
                 iff $(p \wedge q)_j = p_j$, $\forall j \in J$ (B is J-lifted)
                 iff $p_j \wedge q_j = p_j$, $\forall j \in J$ (lifting theorem)
                 iff $p_j \leqslant q_j$, $\forall j \in J$ (definition of $\leqslant$)

THEOREM 2. *Restrictingness Inheritance Theorem.* Let B be a J-lifted boolean algebra and let $f \in F_{B/B}$ be transparent. Then f is restricting iff $\forall j \in J$, f_j is restricting.

We have that f is restricting   iff $f(b) \leqslant b$ $\forall b \in B$ (definition of restricting)
                 iff $(f(b))_j \leqslant b_j$ $\forall b \in B$, $\forall j \in J$ (Theorem 1)
                 iff $f_j(b_j) \leqslant b_j$ $\forall b \in B$, $\forall j \in J$
                 (f is transparent; B is J-lifted; general extensionality theorem)
                 iff $f_j(x) \leqslant x$ $\forall x \in B^e$, $\forall j \in J$ (B is J-lifted)
                 iff f_j is restricting $\forall j \in J$ (definition of restricting)

THEOREM 3. *Intersectingness Inheritance Theorem.* Let B be a J-lifted boolean algebra and let $f \in F_{B/B}$ be transparent. Then f is intersecting iff $\forall j \in J$, f_j is intersecting.

We have that f is intersecting

iff $f(b) = b \wedge f(1)$ $\forall b \in B$	(definition of intersecting)
iff $(f(b))_j = (b \wedge f(1))_j$ $\forall b \in B$, $\forall j \in J$	(B is J-lifted)
iff $(f(b))_j = b_j \wedge (f(1))_j$ $\forall b \in B$, $\forall j \in J$	(lifting theorem)
iff $f_j(b_j) = b_j \wedge f_j(1)$ $\forall b \in B$, $\forall j \in J$	(f is transparent; B is J-lifted; general extensionality theorem)
iff $f_j(x) = x \wedge f_j(1)$ $\forall x \in B^e$, $\forall j \in J$	(B is J-lifted)
iff f_j is intersecting $\forall j \in J$	(definition of intersecting).

THEOREM 4. Let B be a J-lifted boolean algebra. Then $T_{B/B} \cap R_{B/B}$ is a subalgebra of $R_{B/B}$. Moreover, if B is complete, than $T_{B/B} \cap R_{B/B}$ is complete.

Let f, $g \in T_{B/B} \cap R_{B/B}$. We can show that the latter set is a subalgebra of $R_{B/B}$ if we show that $f \wedge g$, $f \vee g$, and f' are transparent, using the operations as defined in $R_{B/B}$.

Let x, $y \in B$ be such that $x_j = y_j$ for some particular $j \in J$. Then

we have that $((f \wedge g)(x))_j = (f(x) \wedge g(x))_j$	(definition of $\wedge$ in $R_{B/B}$)
$= (f(x))_j \wedge (g(x))_j$	(lifting theorem)
$= (f(y))_j \wedge (g(y))_j$	(f and g are transparent)
$= ((f \wedge g)(y))_j$	(definition of $\wedge$ in $R_{B/B}$)

This shows that $f \wedge g$ is transparent. The proof that $f \vee g$ is transparent is completely parallel. Finally we have

$(f'(x))_j = (x \wedge (f(x))')_j$	(definition of $'$ in $R_{B/B}$)
$= x_j \wedge ((f(x))')_j$	(lifting theorem)
$= x_j \wedge ((f(x))_j)'$	(lifting theorem)
$= y_j \wedge ((f(y))_j)'$	(f is transparent)
$= y_j \wedge ((f(y))')_j$	(lifting theorem)
$= (y \wedge (f(y))')_j$	(lifting theorem)
$= (f'(y))_j$	(definition of $'$ in $R_{B/B}$)

If B is complete then $R_{B/B}$ is complete (Theorem 2 of Part IB). If the set $K \subseteq R_{B/B}$ contains only transparent functions, proofs parallel to the ones above show that $\wedge K$ and $\vee K$ are transparent, and hence $T_{B/B} \cap R_{B/B}$ is complete.

This completes the proof of the theorem. Incidentally, the reader may check that if B is atomic, so that $R_{B/B}$ is atomic, the atoms of $R_{B/B}$ are not in general transparent . . . .

4. PREDICATE MODIFIERS AND PREPOSITIONS IN THE INTENSIONAL SYSTEM

In extending the intensional system, we find it convenient at this stage to discuss the predicate modifiers (PMs) and prepositions together.

Syntactically, the category PM is defined to be $\langle P_n \rangle \, / \, \langle P_n \rangle$, just as in the extensional system. Prepositions are then members of the category PM/$\bar{N}$. As in the extensional system, we are interested in distinguishing various subcategories of these categories. However, we will not consider further the matter of argument-orientation and subject-orientation, which we feel we treated in the earlier chapter as deeply as we wish to do so at this time. Here we are interested in discussing the question of transparency as it applies to these categories.

But first, let us consider the intensional type for the category PM as a whole. By our general procedure, we want the type of PM to be some subset of the set of functions from the union of the sets T_{P_n} into itself. In fact, based on the development found in Definitions 22 through 25 in Part IB, we might wish to define T_{PM} to be $\text{PR}_{A/A}$, where $A = \{ T_{P_n} : n \geqslant 1 \}$; that is, T_{PM} would be the set of proper restricting functions from the union of the T_{P_n} into itself. However, given our discussion of the nature of T_{P_n} in the intensional system, we are not in a position to do this, simply because we are not assuming that the types T_{P_n} are boolean algebras.

The way around this problem which we shall adopt here is to restrict the PMs so that they may only combine with transparent n-place predicates. In other words, the category PM is now defined to be $\langle P_n \rangle_t \, / \, \langle P_n \rangle_t$. If we take A to be the collection of sets $T_{P_{n_t}}$, we can apply the development of Part IB to define T_{PM} as being $\text{PR}_{A/A}$, since each $T_{P_{n_t}}$ is a boolean algebra. In terms of the ability of our system to represent English sentences, this will not actually constitute a serious restriction. A sentence like *John is looking for a unicorn with a magnifying glass* will simply have only the translation in (1):

(1)   John (look-for (a unicorn)) (with (a magnifying glass))

as opposed to the two translations of *John sees a unicorn with a magnifying glass* in (2):

(2) (a) John (see (a unicorn)) (with (a magnifying-glass))
     (b) John (see (with (a magnifying-glass))) (a unicorn)

Still, this difference in behavior could be claimed to lack any correlation with linguistic facts. If this is the case, we would have to regard the difference between (1) and (2) as a defect in our system, albeit a minor one.

Since we are not considering argument or subject orientation here, we are faced with a small issue which we should resolve before proceeding. Namely, we certainly want the following two P_1s to be logically equivalent:

(3) (a) (kiss Mary) skillfully
     (b) (kiss skillfully) Mary

If *skillfully* is interpreted as an arbitrary proper restricting function, this need not be the case. This is very easily taken care of, however. We make the following definition:

DEFINITION 1. The function $f \in \mathrm{PR} \cup T_{P_n} / \cup T_{P_n}$ is *consistent* iff for each $p \in T_{P_n}$ and for each $g \in T_{\overline{N}}$ whose extension in any world is an individual we have $f(p(g)) = (f(p))(g)$.

If f interprets *skillfully*, p interprets *kiss*, and g interprets *Mary*, then the equation in Definition 1 says precisely that (3a) and (3b) are logically equivalent. Note, incidentally, that, in the left hand side of this equation, f is applied to an element of $T_{P_{n-1}}$, whereas on the right hand side, it is applied to an element of T_{P_n}. The equation thus constrains the behavior of f as it applies to predicates of different valences, which is just what we want. Incidentally, the reader may easily check that argument-oriented and subject-oriented PMs (in the sense of Part IB) are necessarily consistent.

Letting A be a set of total boolean algebras, we use the notation $\mathrm{CPR}_{A/A}$ to represent the set of all consistent proper restricting functions from the union of the algebras in A into itself. It now seems reasonable to define.

DEFINITION 2. $T_{\mathrm{PM}} = \mathrm{CPR}_{A/A}$, where A is the set of algebras T_{P_n}.

It is not immediately obvious that T_{PM} defined this way is itself a boolean algebra. However, this is indeed the case. To show that it is, we need only show that the boolean operations already defined in $\mathrm{PR}_{A/A}$ yield consistent functions when they are applied to consistent functions. We indicate the proof for this here in the case of complementation; the proofs for the other operations are similar (and, if anything, slightly simpler), and are left to the reader.

Let f, p, and g have the meanings they have in Definition 1 above. We have then:

$$
\begin{aligned}
(4) \quad f'(p(g)) &= p(g) \wedge (f(p(g)))' && \text{(definition of ' in PR}_{A/A}\text{)} \\
&= p(g) \wedge ((f(p))'\,(g)) && \text{(extensions of } g \text{ are individuals)} \\
&= (p \wedge (f(p))')\,(g) && \text{(extensions of } g \text{ are individuals)} \\
&= (f'(p))\,(g) && \text{(definition of ' in PR}_{A/A}\text{)}
\end{aligned}
$$

Thus, f' is a consistent function. Note that since we require that p and $f(p)$ be transparent n-place predicate intensions, boolean operations involving them can be performed on a world by world basis. Thus, if the extension of g in any world is an individual, it is permissible to unpack boolean combinations of n-place predicate intensions pointwise, as we did in the second and third steps of (4) above.

Let us turn now to the prepositions. Since T_{PM} and $T_{\bar{N}}$ are boolean algebras and since prepositions are predicatives, we expect to define T_{Prep} to be the set of homomorphisms from $T_{\bar{N}}$ into T_{PM}. Generally speaking, this approach gives reasonable answers. For example, if the interpretation of *with* preserves meets, then the phrases *with the hammer and the chisel* is logically equivalent to *with the hammer and with the chisel*, a reasonable thing to suppose; surely if John sculpts this statue with the hammer and the chisel, then he sculpts it with the hammer and with the chisel, and conversely. Similarly, if, in a particular world, the only tools are the hammer and the chisel, if John sculpts this statue with a tool, it must be that he sculpts it with the hammer or with the chisel, and conversely.

However, defining T_{Prep} as $H_{T_{\text{PM}}/T_{\bar{N}}}$ leads to difficulties as soon as we turn to the matter of transparency. By the definitions of II.1, in order for a preposition intension to be transparent, it would be necessary for it to map every $\bar{N}$ intension into a transparent PM intension. Thus, a transparent preposition would be one which creates a transparent prepositional phrase. Recalling our discussion in Part IB of extensional versus properly intensional PMs, this would mean that locative prepositions, and, possibly, source prepositions, would be the only transparent prepositions.

The problem with leaving things this way is that there are differences in the logical behavior of other prepositions which seem to have to do with transparency but which are not captured with this approach. To see this, let us compare the prepositions *with* (in its instrumental sense) and *about* (in the sense of 'concerning'). Surely, in a world in which the hammers and the metal tools are precisely the same entities, the phrase *with a hammer* should have the same extension as *with a metal tool*. However, in a world in which Mary is the queen, we certainly do not want the phrase *about Mary* to be interpreted the same as *about the queen*; surely John could be talking about the queen without saying a word about Mary (he might not even know that Mary is the queen).

To see how this may be handled, let us examine more closely the transparency of instrumental *with*. If w is the function which interprets *with*, we have just seen that in a world j in which the $\bar{N}$ intensions f and g have the same extension, that is, in a world j such that $f_j = g_j$, the PMs $w(f)$ and $w(g)$ are, in some sense, the same. But what does it mean for these to be the same in j? If these PMs had extensions in j, the meaning is simple: we would simply be requiring that $(w(f))_j = (w(g))_j$; this is just our ordinary definition of transparency. But by the General Extensionality Theorem, this would require that $w(f)$ and $w(g)$ be transparent PMs. However, we have already seen that *with* phrases modify n-place predicates in a properly intensional way. Therefore, it cannot be the case that *with* phrases have extensions at all.

However, we can still give meaning to the idea that $w(f)$ and $w(g)$ are the same in world j. Namely, if p is an arbitrary transparent n-place predicate intension, then the extensions $((w(f))\,(p))_j$ and $((w(g))\,(p))_j$ are well defined. Clearly, to say that $w(f)$ and $w(g)$ are the same in world j means (at least) that these two extensions are equal. As an example: in a world in which the hammers and the metal tools are precisely the same entities, while the phrases *with a hammer* and *with a metal tool* would not themselves have extensions, P_1s like *fix the door with a hammer* and *fix the door with a metal tool* would necessarily have the same extension.

Formally, we can make the following definition:

DEFINITION 3. Let X and Y be sets of extensional intensions, and let Z be a subset of $F_{Y/Y}$. A function f from X into Z is *modifyingly transparent* (or *m-transparent*) iff, whenever for some $x_1, x_2 \in X$ and $j \in J$ we have $x_{1j} = x_{2j}$, then for each $y \in Y$ it is the case that $((f(x_1))\,(y))_j = ((f(x_2))\,(y))_j$.

Using this definition, we can describe the intensional interpretation of different classes of prepositions as follows. All prepositions take their interpretations in the set $H_{T_{PM}/T_{\bar{N}}}$. Some prepositions, such as the locatives like *in*, are subcategorized as transparent; their interpretations are required to be transparent (in the usual sense). Another group of prepositions (including instrumental *with*) are subcategorized as being *m*-transparent; these are required to take *m*-transparent intensions as their interpretations. Finally, prepositions like *about* would carry neither subcategorization feature, their interpretations would be unconstrained, allowing P_1s like *talk about Mary* and *talk about the queen* to have different extensions even in a world in which *Mary* and *the queen* have the same extension.

It may be objected that the definition of *m*-transparency above is inelegant, in that reference must be made to the nature of the elements of the set Z, rather than merely to abstract properties of that set. In the case of prepositions, we are making crucial use of the fact that when a preposition is combined with an $\bar{N}$, the resulting expression is an *n*-place predicate modifier. This can be avoided, but other problems arise.

One way of avoiding this difficulty is to regard prepositions not as expressions which combine with $\bar{N}$s to create PMs, but rather as expressions which combine with *n*-place predicates to create *n*-place predicates of valence one higher (that is, a preposition would combine with an *n*-place predicate to create an $n + 1$-place predicate). This was essentially the approach taken in Keenan and Faltz (1978), where prepositions were called 'verbal extensors'. Some discussion was provided (pp. 181–191) to convince the reader that such an approach was not as bad linguistically as it might seem if only ordinary notions of English phrase structure are considered. In addition to that discussion, the reader may check that the kind of inelegance illustrated by Definition 3 does not arise if the verbal extensor approach is taken. Nevertheless, for English at least, the phrase structure evidence does seem to point strongly to a notion of prepositional phrase. Thus, the approach outlined here yields a better match between the syntactic structure of our logical language and the syntactic structure of real English.

As a further point of comparison between the two approaches, we might ask whether interpreting a preposition as a homomorphism from $T_{\bar{N}}$ into T_{PM} is algebraically equivalent to the verbal extensor approach. Specifically, let us attempt to make the following definition:

(5) Given any $f \in HT_{PM}/T_{\bar{N}}$, f_* is defined as that function from T_{P_n} into $T_{P_{n+1}}$ such that, for any $p \in T_{P_n}$ and any $g \in T_{\bar{N}}$, $(f_*(p))(g) = (f(g))(p)$.

It is clear that the equation in (5) defines $f_*(p)$ as a function from $T_{\bar{N}}$ into T_{P_n}. However, before we can claim that $f_*(p)$ is really a member of $T_{P_{n+1}}$, it is necessary to show that it is a homomorphism. Since f is assumed to be a homomorphism, and since the argument of f is the same as the argument of $f_*(p)$, we might guess that this is indeed the case. We leave it to the reader to show that with f_* defined as in (5), $f_*(p)$ does preserve meets and joins. In the case of complements, however, we have the following:

$$
\begin{aligned}
(6) \quad (f_*(p))\,(g') &= (f(g'))\,(p) && \text{(definition (5))} \\
&= (f(g))'\,(p) && \text{(f is a homomorphism)} \\
&= p \wedge [(f(g))\,(p)]' && \text{(definition of $'$ in T_{PM})} \\
&= p \wedge [(f_*(p))\,(g)]' && \text{(definition (5))}
\end{aligned}
$$

Now, if $f_*(p)$ preserved complements, then instead of the result in (6) we would have:

$$
(7) \qquad (f_*(p))\,(g') = [(f_*(p))\,(g)]'.
$$

Thus, the function f_* defined in (5) does not correspond to a verbal extensor intension, since such an object would be *defined* as taking its values in $T_{P_{n+1}}$. In other words, the approach outlined here is not equivalent, algebraically, to the verbal extensor approach.

This being the case, it ought to be possible to decide between the two approaches by examining data from real English. Since the distinction shows up in the case of taking a complement of the $\bar{N}$ argument which corresponds to the object of the preposition, we are led to an example such as the P_1:

(8)   work with that saw but not this hammer.

The difference between (5) and (7) is that (5) predicts that when a preposition is combined with a complemented $\bar{N}$, it remains the case that the P_1 which the resulting prepositional phrase is modifying must still be entailed; this is not the case with the analysis in (7). Now, in the case of (8), it is certainly true that if John works with that saw but not this hammer, we can conclude that John works. However, this does not mean that (5) is definitely the correct analysis rather than (7). The problem is that the object of the preposition in (5) is a conjunction of a complemented $\bar{N}$ and one which is not complemented. Thus, on the verbal extensor analysis, (8) should be equivalent to (9):

(9)   work with that saw but not work with this hammer.

Assuming that *that saw* is an individual, we can suppose that the verbal extensor analysis predicts that *work with that saw* entails *work*. Thus, (8) is predicted to entail *work* by both analyses, and hence we cannot as yet distinguish between them.

To avoid this problem, we clearly have to get rid of the noncomplemented part of the object of the preposition in (8). If we do this, the result is not acceptable English:

(10)   work with not this hammer

That is, we cannot say **John works with not this hammer*. In the case of (10), our two analyses make different predictions; the approach here leads to the claim that (10) entails *work*, while the verbal extensor approach does not lead to that claim. However, since (10) is not an acceptable English P_1, we have no intuitions concerning whether or not it ought to entail *work*.

Normally, it is acceptable in English to negate an $\bar{N}$ without conjoining it to a non-negated $\bar{N}$, if the negated $\bar{N}$ itself contains a quantifier like *every* or *a*. However, although not as bad as (10), such combinations sound sufficiently odd as objects of a preposition, that we do not have intuitions as to whether the P_1s:

(11)   work with not every hammer
(12)   work with not a hammer

entail *work* or not. If we replace *not a hammer* with *no hammer* in (12), we obtain:

(13)   work with no hammer

which seems perfectly acceptable. However, it is *still* unclear whether *John works with no hammer* entails *John works* or not. Here, our intuition is slightly in favor of this entailment. To the extent that this is a valid intuition, this constitutes slight evidence in favor of the approach taken here over the verbal extensor approach.

(We note in passing that the fact that, say, *John works without a hammer* clearly entails that *John works* does not decide unequivocally in favor of the approach here. The reason is simply that the relationship between the interpretation of *without* and the interpretation of *with*, mediated by means of a meaning postulate, say, will not be the same with the two approaches.

In the verbal extensor approach, the interpretation of *without* would be defined not so that *without* $\bar{N}$ and *with not* $\bar{N}$ are equivalent, but rather so that *without* is restricting (as required on that approach; see Keenan and Faltz, 1978, p. 223) as well as entailing *with* − *not*. In the approach here, we could simply require that *without* $\bar{N}$ be equivalent to *with not* $\bar{N}$ (which is equivalent to *not* (*with* $\bar{N}$), since *with* is interpreted as a homomorphism.))

Summarizing, we can say that the following definition for the type for prepositions is acceptable, providing we can live with a subcategorization feature which is associated with the *m*-transparency condition given in Definition 3:

DEFINITION 4. $T_{\text{Prep}} = H_{T_{\text{PM}}/T_{\bar{N}}}$.

Before leaving the matter of PMs and prepositions, let us say a brief word about the relationship between adjectives and adverbs in *ly*.

For many adjectives in English, there exists an abverb formed by suffixing -*ly* whose meaning is related to the meaning of the corresponding adjective in a regular way. The logical content of this relationship can be illustrated by the judgment that (14) is true iff (15) is true:

(14)   John is a skillful worker.
(15)   John works skillfully.

To represent such a fact in our system, we can proceed as follows.

First, let us assume that there is an expression *ly* of category **PM/AP**. Then, *ly* will combine with restricting adjective phrases to form predicate modifiers. Of course, this will lead to overgeneration; but that seems to be a relatively harmless defect at this stage, which, hopefully, could be cleared up in subsequent investigation.

Next, we will want to interpret *ly* as a logical constant. To see what the interpretation of *ly* should be, we must first look at the relationship between the phrases which an AP and its corresponding PM modify.

In the above example, the *ly* adverb modifies the P_1 *work*, while the adjective from which it is formed modifies *worker*, an *N* related morphologically and logically to *work*. Morphologically, *worker* is formed by combining the P_1 *work* with the suffix -*er*; and logically, in any particular world, *work* is true of an individual just in case the property which interprets *worker* is a member of that individual.

The relationship between *work* and *worker* is easy to handle in our system.

If we wish to include expressions like *worker* in our logical language, we need only posit an expression *er* of category N/P_{t1} (which, like *ly*, will over-generate, but harmlessly). Whether or not we do this, we can still elucidate the relationship between P_1s like *work* and Ns like *worker*, which is all we have to do in order to be able to handle the interpretation of *ly*. The key is Theorem 20 of Part IA, which shows that there exists a canonical isomorphism from $T^e_{P_{t1}}$ onto T^e_N. Let us call this isomorphism φ^e.

Now, since $T_{P_{t1}}$ (= $T_{P_1 e}$) and T_N (= T_{Ne}) are total, the isomorphism φ^e can be 'lifted' to an isomorphism φ from $T_{P_{t1}}$ onto T_N. We leave to the reader the easy demonstration that the equation

(16) $(\varphi(p))_j = \varphi^e(p_j)$

defines such an isomorphism (where p is an arbitrary element of $T_{P_{t1}}$ and j is an arbitrary world). Clearly, if p is the intension of *work*, then $\varphi(p)$ is the intension of *worker*.

We can now define the interpretation of the logical constant *ly* as follows:

DEFINITION 5. In any interpretation, *ly* is interpreted as the function **ly**: $T_{PM} \to T_{AP_t}$ defined by $(\textbf{ly}(h))(p) = \varphi^{-1}(h(\varphi(p)))$, where $h \in T_{PM}$ and $p \in T_{P_{t1}}$ are arbitrary.

(In Definition 5, φ^{-1} refers to the inverse isomorphism of φ; that is, φ^{-1} maps T_N isomorphically onto $T_{P_{t1}}$.) Thus, what **ly**(h) does to a P_1 intension p corresponds algebraically with what h does to the corresponding N intension $\varphi(p)$.

Unfortunately, Definition 5 does not settle the matter. While it provides an acceptable interpretation for *ly* in the case that the adverb it forms combines with a P_1, there remains the question of how to interpret such adverbs when they combine with an n-place predicate, for arbitrary n. However, it is not difficult to see how the approach given above for P_1 modification can be generalized. The steps are as follows. First, show that there exists a canonical isomorphism φ^e_n from $T^e_{P_n}$ onto $T^e_{N_{n-1}}$ (where N_n is the category of n-place common nouns; the category $N = N_0$ is regarded as the first member of a predicative hierarchy; see Chapter IB.3). Next, lift this isomorphism to an isomorphism φ_n from T_{P_n} onto $T_{N_{n-1}}$. And finally, define *ly* to be interpreted as **ly**, where, for each $h \in T_{PM}$ and each $p \in T_{P_n}$, $(\textbf{ly}(h))(p) = \varphi_n^{-1}(h(\varphi_n(p)))$.

5. VARIABLES AND VARIABLE BINDING OPERATORS
IN THE INTENSIONAL SYSTEM

As in the extensional system, we assume that variables are expressions of category $\underset{var}{C}$, where C is any category and *var* is a subcategorization feature. We continue to restrict our attention to those variables which are members of the category $\underset{var}{N_0} = \underset{var}{\bar{N}}$, assuming as before that there are variables x_1, $x_2, \ldots$ of this category. Again, for convenience, specific such variables may be denoted x, y, etc.

Our first task is to define the intensional type for these variables. Recalling that in the extensional system we have

(1) $\qquad \underset{var}{T_{\bar{N}}^e} = I_P = \underset{proper}{T_{\bar{N}}^e}$

the following two definitions suggest themselves:

DEFINITION 1. $\underset{var}{T_{\bar{N}}} = \underset{proper}{T_{\bar{N}}}$

DEFINITION 2. $\underset{var}{T_{\bar{N}}} = F_{I_P/J}$

Let us call Definition 1 the *intensional individual definition* of variable interpretation, and Definition 2 the *strict definition* of variable interpretation (this latter term will become clear in a moment). Note that with either of these definitions, a variable intension is extensional, and its extension in any world is an individual, so that, in either case, the situation we had earlier with our extensional definition is recovered if we are working inside one particular world.

In comparing these two definitions, it seems reasonable to reject the intensional individual definition. The reason is this. Although we are not specifying in this work what precisely the ultimate functioning of the distinction between worlds is to be, we surely expect that the extension of a variable should be allowed to vary from one world to the next. Certainly this is the case if distinct worlds are thought of as representing distinct contexts, a common notion often applied to the idea of distinct worlds.

This leave us with the strict definition of variable interpretation, apparently settling the issue. However, in integrating the intensional interpretation of variables with the intensional interpretation of variable binding operators, we will see that there is some evidence in favor of a third definition of the type for variables, namely:

DEFINITION 3. $T_{\bar{N} \atop \mathrm{var}} = T_{\bar{N}}$.

Let us call Definition 3 the *loose definition* of variable interpretation. We note that if this definition is adopted, then variable intensions are still all extensional, but the extension of a variable intension in a particular world need not be an individual, and hence this definition does not reduce to the situation we had previously with our extensional system. In order to evaluate the relative merits of the strict and loose definitions of variable interpretation, we need to consider the matter of the intensional interpretation of variable binding operators, to which we now turn.

We take over the syntax and general structure of models from the extensional system unchanged. We have three variable binding operators (VBOs), namely, λ, *suchthat*, and *self*. Recall that we use V to denote the set of vocabulary items and V^+ to denote the set $V - \{and, or, not, \lambda, suchthat, self\}$. V^+ is the domain for lexical assignment functions M which define models. That is, a model is now a quadruple $\langle P, 2, J, M \rangle$, where M is a function whose domain is V^+ and for which, given any x of category C, $M(x)$ is an element of T_C, here the intensional type, of course. As before, $M(x)$ is an arbitrary element of T_C except in the case that x is a logical constant, in which case $M(x)$ is defined a priori for all models.

Given the model $\langle P, 2, J, M \rangle$, we want to extend M uniquely to a function m whose domain is the set of all expressions of the language such that if $e \in V^+$ then $m(e) = M(e)$. If e is a boolean combination of expressions or else a function-argument combination of expressions, then $m(e)$ is defined the usual way. Our task here is to define $m(e)$ in the case that e is a complex expression formed with the aid of a VBO. As before, the functions m and M are in one-to-one correspondence. We take over the definitions of x-variance (for a given $x \in \bar{N} \atop \mathrm{var}$) unchanged (see Part IB, Definitions 50 and 51). We begin our detailed discussion of the VBOs with the λ.

As far as the syntax of λ is concerned, we make one change in the definition given earlier for our extensional system. If $x \in \bar{N} \atop \mathrm{var}$, then, in order for (x, λ, e) to be a well formed expression, we require that e be not only a member of a boolean category B, but in addition, e must be extensional (that is, the intensions which could legitimately interpret e must be extensional). In practice, this will be fulfilled by e being either a member of a category like P_0, all of whose possible intensions are extensional, or else a transparent expression, that is, an expression which must be interpreted by a transparent (hence extensional) intension. As earlier, (x, λ, e) will be a member of category $B/\bar{N}$; in fact, it will be a transparent member of this category.

The intensional semantics of expressions of the form (x, λ, e) must now be defined. To do so, we find it convenient to make the following definition:

DEFINITION 4. Let $a \in P$ be an atom, and let $j \in J$ be a world. Then, $D_{aj} = \{g \in T_{\bar{N}}^{\text{var}}: g_j = I_a\}$.

In the above definition, I_a refers to the individual (in P) which contains the atom a. We see that D_{aj} is a set of variable intensions; that is, $D_{aj} \subseteq T_{\bar{N}}^{\text{var}} \subseteq T_{\bar{N}}$. In fact, D_{aj} is exactly the set of those variable intensions which have as their extension in the world j the individual associated with atom a.

We now define the intensional interpretation of expressions like (x, λ, e) as follows:

DEFINITION 5. Let e be an expression of the boolean extensional category B and let $x \in \underset{\text{var}}{\bar{N}}$. Then the interpretation $m(x, \lambda, e)$ of (x, λ, e) in the model $\langle P, 2, J, M \rangle$ is the transparent function from $T_{\bar{N}}$ into T_B defined by the fact that, for each $j \in J$, $(m(x, \lambda, e))_j$ is the homomorphism from $T_{\bar{N}}^e$ into T_B^e such that, for each atom $a \in P$, $(m(x, \lambda, e))_j(I_a) = \underset{g \in D_{aj}}{\vee} (m_g(e))_j$. Here, I_a denotes the individual containing the atom a, and m_g denotes the x-variant of m such that $m_g(x) = g$.

(As in the corresponding extensional definition, there is here, strictly speaking, a circularity which can be eliminated by inductively defining extensions of the function M on expressions of increasing length; we leave it to the reader to construct the routine, but rather tedious, correct definition.)

In this definition, we are of course appealing to the General Extensionality Theorem when we define a transparent function from $T_{\bar{N}}$ into T_B by giving its extensions, and to the Justification Theorem when we define a homomorphism from $T_{\bar{N}}^e$ into T_B^e by giving its values on the individuals.

We can see that if the expression e is such that its interpretation depends transparently on the interpretation of x, then the definition above reduces to the extensional definition given earlier on a world by world basis. The reason is that the union in the definition above is taken over a set of variable intensions whose extensions in world j are all the same. To say that the interpretation of e depends transparently on the interpretation of x just means that $(m_g(x))_j$ would be the same extension for all of the g's. Thus, in this case, we have a union of identical elements, which is just equal to that element. Finally, since $m_g(x) = g$, we have $(m_g(x))_j = g_j = I_a$, so that the extension $(m_g(e))_j$ can be identified with the extensional x-variant interpretation of e which interprets x as I_a.

Definition 5 above makes use of the set D_{aj}. Now, the definition of D_{aj} (Definition 4) is itself relative to $T_{\bar{N}}^{\text{var}}$; that is, depending on whether we choose the strict or the loose definition of variable interpretation (or some other definition), we will end up with different definitions for the intensional interpretation of λ. It will be useful to examine here what these interpretations involve in a typical case. By what we have said above, if the interpretation of e depends transparently on the interpretation of x, the interpretation of λ reduces to what we had earlier in the extensional system no matter what the definition of $T_{\bar{N}}^{\text{var}}$ is, since, in either case, D_{aj} is a set of $\bar{N}$ intensions whose extensions in world j are in individual. Thus, to determine the effect of the definition of $T_{\bar{N}}^{\text{var}}$, it will be necessary to examine a case in which e does not depend transparently on x. Such a case would be the situation in which the variable appears as the object of a properly intensional transitive verb.

Specifically, let us examine the interpretation of

(2)   (a unicorn) $(x \ \lambda$ (John (look-for x)))

which would be a possible translation into our logical language of the English sentence:

(3)   John is looking for a unicorn.

First of all, it follows from Definition 5 that no matter how the intensional interpretation of variables is defined, the intension of the formula in (2) depends transparently on the intension of the expression *a unicorn*. In particular, if (2) is true in a certain world, then there must exist at least one unicorn in that world. In short, it will be the case that (2) represents the *de re* reading of (3).

Before proceeding with (2), let us stop a moment and see what happens if (3) is interpreted in the more straightforward way shown in (4):

(4)   John (look-for (a unicorn))

If the intensions of *John, unicorn*, and *look-for* are g, u, and f respectively, then the intension of the P_0 in (4) is $(f(a(u)))$ (g), by our general functional application procedure. (Recall that a is defined a priori as the intension of a in any model; since a is a logical constant; see II.2.) If $j \in J$ is the index of some world, then the truth value of (4) in world j is given by:

(5) $((f(a(u)))\,(g))_j = (f(a(u)))_j\,(g_j) = (f(a(u)))_j\,(I_{\text{john}})$

(where I_{john} is the individual which is the extension of g in any world). The equation in (5) is valid because of the General Extensionality Theorem. Recall also that whenever a P_n intension is applied to an $\bar{N}$ intension, the resulting P_{n-1} intension is transparent. Thus, the P_1 *look-for* (*a unicorn*) in (4) is transparent, so that the General Extensionality Theorem can indeed be applied.

However, in the case of (5), we can go no further. In particular, the General Extensionality Theorem cannot be applied to unpack $(f(a(u)))_j$, since f is not (necessarily) transparent. This should be compared to the situation that arises when we do have a transparent transitive verb, as in the case of the sentence

(6)   John is kissing a unicorn.

which may be translated into our logical language as

(7)   John (kiss (a unicorn))

If the intension of *kiss* is k, then the intension of formula (7) is $(k(a(u)))(g)$. In world j, we have in this case:

(8) $((k(a(u)))(g))_j = (k(a(u)))_j(g_j)$ (General Extensionality Theorem)

$= (k(a(u)))_j(I_{\mathrm{john}})$ (I_{john} is the extension of g in any world)

$= (k_j(a(u))_j)(I_{\mathrm{john}})$ (General Extensionality Theorem)

$= (k_j(a^e(u_j)))(I_{\mathrm{john}})$ (General Extensionality Theorem)

$= (k_j(\bigcup_{u_j \in I} I))(I_{\mathrm{john}})$ (Definition of a^e)

$= (\bigvee_{u_j \in I} k_j(I))(I_{\mathrm{john}})$ (k_j is a homomorphism)

$= \bigvee_{u_j \in I} (k_j(I))(I_{\mathrm{john}})$ (Definition of $\vee$ in $T_{P_1}^e$)

The third equality in (8) is a valid step since k is a transparent P_2 intension (since *kiss* is subcategorized as being transparent). The fourth equality follows from the (definitional) transparency of a (see II.2); the remainder of the development in (8) is as in the extensional system. Note that, say, the truth of (7) in world j requires that there exist at least one individual which contains the unicorn property in j, by the last line of (8). Again, if Mary (interpreted as I_{mary}) is a unicorn, and if *John* (*kiss Mary*) is true in j (so that $(k_j(I_{mary}))$ $(I_{john}) = 1$), then, by the last line in (8) it must be the case that John kisses a unicorn in world j. In other words, the argument:

(9)   John (kiss Mary))
        Mary (be (a unicorn))
        _____
        ∴ John (kiss (a unicorn))

is valid.

Returning to (5), we see that the development shown in (8) cannot be carried out here, since f is not (necessarily) transparent, as we have said. In particular, the intension of the $\bar{N}$ *a unicorn* is trapped inside the intension of the verb phrase. An immediate consequence of this is that, whereas in order for (7) to be true in world j it is necessary that at least one individual have the property u_j (that is, at least one unicorn has to exist in world j), (4) could be true in world j even though *no* individual has property u_j, that is, even though there are no unicorns in world j. This is the intuitively desired result.

To pursue the matter a little further, the P_0 *John* (*look-for* (*Mary*)) would have as its extension in world j

(10) $(f(h))_j (I_{john})$

where h is the intension of *Mary*. Set $h_j = I_{mary}$, and suppose that I_{mary} contains property u_j (that is, Mary is in fact a unicorn in world j). Because $a(u)$ in (5) and h in (10) are buried inside the P_1 intension, there is no way to use the fact that I_{mary} contains u_j in order to relate the formulas *John* (*look-for* (*a unicorn*)) and *John* (*look-for* (*Mary*)) logically. This strongly suggests that the argument in (11) is invalid:

(11)   John (look-for (Mary))
         Mary (be (a unicorn))
         _____
         ∴ John (look-for (a unicorn))

To show that the argument is indeed invalid, we need only note that since f (the intension of *look-for*) is an arbitrary member of T_{P_2}, it can be chosen such that $f(a(u))$ and $f(h)$ are different members of $T_{P_{t1}}$. But then, for some world j, $(f(a(u)))_j$ and $(f(h))_j$ are distinct, whence (by the Justification Theorem) they must differ for some individual.

Note that, intuitively, we *want* the argument in (11) to be invalid if *look-for* is given the *de dictu* interpretation: John may be indeed looking for a being named Mary without knowing that Mary is a unicorn. Even if Mary *is* a unicorn, we would not want to conclude that John is looking for a unicorn if the property of being a unicorn is not the property which defines how John's search is satisfied.

Suppose, however, that we interpret *look for* in the *de re* manner, in the following argument:

(12)   John is looking for Mary
         Mary is a unicorn
         _____

    ∴ John is looking for a unicorn.

The *de re* interpretation arises if the phrases *Mary* and *a unicorn* are the speaker's descriptions (rather than John's descriptions) of the object of John's search. In this case, we would want (12) to be valid. We have already seen that the argument in (11) is invalid; we cannot, therefore, use the P_0s in (11) to translate the English sentences in (12) (if these are to be interpreted *de re*). However, if we translate the sentences of (12) by means of P_0s such as the one in (2), then the resulting arument is valid. Specifically,

(13)   (Mary $(x\ \lambda$ (John (look-for x))))
         Mary (be (a unicorn))
         _____

    ∴ (a unicorn) $(x\ \lambda$ (John (look-for x)))

is valid. In fact, the reader may easily show that (13) is valid no matter which definition we use for $T_{\bar{N}}^{\text{var}}$. Here, let us look carefully at the interpretation of (13) as provided by Definition 5.

First, assume again that *John* and *look-for* are interpreted by the intensions g and f respectively. Let j be a world and let I_a be an arbitrary individual ($a \in P$ an atom). By Definition 5,

(14) $(m(x\ \lambda$ (John (look-for x))))$_j$ (I_a) = $\underset{h\ \in D_{aj}}{\vee}$ $(m_h$ (John (look-for)))$_j$

That is, John looks for the individual I_a in a *de re* sense if and only if there is a variable intension h whose extension in j is I_a such that, loosely speaking, *John looks for 'h'*, in the *de dictu* sense, is true in j.

Let us consider this a bit more carefully. If the individual I_a happens to be named Mary, under what conditions might we want to say that

(15)   John is looking for Mary.

is true, with the *de re* reading? Suppose, for example, that in world j, Mary is the queen, and suppose that John is looking for the queen (*de dictu*). Surely, we would want to conclude that (15) holds in the *de re* sense.

However, in order for this to follow from our analysis, there would have to be some *variable* intension h which could equally well interpret the $\bar{N}$ *the queen*. Now, while the extension of *the queen* in some worlds would surely be an individual, we must allow for the possibility of a world in which there is no queen. In such a world, the extension of *the queen* would be the zero element of $T_{\bar{N}}^e$. This shows that, all other things being equal, variable intensions should not be restricted to having individuals as their only possible extensions.

Should variable intensions be allowed to range over all of $T_{\bar{N}}$? The evidence is a little unclear. Suppose, for example, that John is looking (*de dictu*) for a unicorn, and that in world j there is exactly one unicorn and that unicorn's name is Mary. Can we conclude that John is looking (*de re*) for Mary? The issue does not seem as clear cut as the case in which John is looking (*de dictu*) for the queen. Here, we tentatively take the position that this conclusion can be validly drawn. On the basis of such examples, we propose that the loose interpretation of variables is the correct definition for $T_{\bar{N}}^{var}$. We emphasize that this is a tentative proposal which should be carefully reexamined.

We remind the reader that the validity of the argument in (13) above is independent of our choice for the interpretation of variables. The reader may also check that the following arguments are valid, independently of how we choose to interpret variables:

(16)   John is looking for Mary   (*de dictu*)

∴ John is looking for Mary   (*de re*)

(17)   John is looking for Mary   (*de dictu*)
         Mary is a unicorn

∴ John is looking for a unicorn   (*de re*)

Similarly, the following arguments are invalid, independently of how we choose to interpret variables:

(18)   John is looking for a unicorn   (*de dictu*)

∴ John is looking for a unicorn   (*de re*)

(cf. (16), which is valid!)

(19)   John is looking for a unicorn   (*de re*)

∴ John is looking for a unicorn   (*de dictu*)
(20)   John is looking for Mary   (*de re*)

∴ John is looking for Mary   (*de dictu*)

These results agree completely with our intuitions. Note that the validity of (16) stems from the fact that the extension of a proper noun is an I_a (in fact, the same I_a) in any world. That is, the semantics we have proposed does not allow for the possibility that Mary does not exist in a world. If the semantics were changed to allow for this possibility (certainly, a conceivable idea), then (16) would no longer be valid.

In the examples we have examined so far, λ was used to bind a variable in a P_0. Definition 5 is more general, however; we have defined an interpretation for expressions in which λ binds a variable in any boolean extensional expression. Therefore, it might be thought that an additional reading could be assigned to a sentence like 'John is looking for Mary' by combining λ with the P_1 *look-for* x rather than with the P_0 *John* (*look-for* x). This is actually not the case; the reader should verify the following logical equivalence:

(21)   (Mary (x λ (John (look-for x)))) ⟺
        (John) ((Mary) (x λ (look-for x)))

Similarly, no new additional reading is assigned to 'John is looking for a unicorn', because of the following equivalence:

(22)   (a unicorn) (x λ (John (look-for x))) ⟺
        (John) ((a unicorn) (x λ (look-for x)))

This is to be expected, since the difference between the left and the right sides of the equivalences in (21) and in (22) do not involve crossing one quantifier over another. However, when both the subject and the object of *look for* are quantified, the situation is a little different.

Consider the English sentence:

(23)   Every man is looking for a woman.

There are two sources of logical ambiguity in this sentence. On the one hand, there is the matter of quantifier scope: either *every* has wide scope or else *a* does. On the other hand, there is the *de dictu/de re* ambiguity associated with the verb *look for*. We can therefore imagine that (23) might be capable of four logical readings. In fact, however, there seem to be only three, the forbidden combination being the case where *a* has wide scope together with the *de dictu* reading. The fact that this reading is forbidden follows directly from the syntax and semantics of λ in our system. On the one hand, in order for *a woman* to have wide scope over *every man* in (23), it is necessary to use λ in order to extract *a woman* from inside the P_1. On the other hand, a λ always creates a transparent expression. Thus, if *a woman* has wide scope in (23), it is necessarily the case that the interpretation of (23) as a whole be transparent in the interpretation of *a woman*. But this just means that the *de re* reading results. The three actually occurring readings of sentence (23) are represented in our language as follows:

(24)   (every man) (look-for (a woman))   (*de dictu, every* has wide scope)

(25)   (every man) ((a woman) (x λ (look-for x)))   (*de re, every* has wide scope)

(26)   (a woman) (x λ ((every man) (look-for x)))   (*de re, a* has wide scope)

With this, we complete what we shall say here concerning the intensional interpretation of λ and of variables. Let us briefly consider the matter of the intensional interpretation of *self* and of *suchthat*.

In order to be able to interpret *self* intensionally, we must restrict its syntax slightly, in the same way we did in the case of λ. Specifically, if B is any boolean category and e is any extensional expression of category $B/\bar{N}$, then $(x, self, e)$ is a well formed expression. As in the case of the extensional *self*, we interpret *self* intensionally in such a way that $(x, self, e)$ and $(x, \lambda, (e, x))$ are logically equivalent. Specifically:

DEFINITION 6. Let e be an extensional expression of category $B/\bar{N}$, where B is a boolean category, and let $x \in \bar{N}_{\text{var}}$. Then the interpretation $m(x, \text{self}, e)$

of (x, self, e) in the model $\langle P, 2, J, M \rangle$ is the transparent function from $T_{\bar{N}}$ into T_B defined by the fact that, for each $j \in J$, $(m(x, \text{self}, e))_j$ is the homomorphism from $T_{\bar{N}}^e$ into T_B^e such that, for each atom $a \in P$, we have $(m(x, \text{self}, e))_j (I_a) = \bigvee_{g \in D_{aj}} (m_g(e))_j (I_a)$.

Here, I_a denotes the individual containing the atom a, and m_g denotes the x-variant of m such that $m_g(x) = g$.

We will not discuss *self* any further here.

Finally, let us turn to the VBO *suchthat*. We do not have to change anything concerning the syntax of this element in order to be able to interpret it intensionally. The definition of that interpretation can be given as follows:

DEFINITION 7. Let e be an expression of category P_0 and let $x \in \bar{N}_{\text{var}}$. Then the interpretation $m(x, \text{suchthat}, e)$ of $(x, \text{suchthat}, e)$ in the model $\langle P, 2, J, M \rangle$ is the element of T_{AP}^i such that, for each $j \in J$, $(m(x, \text{suchthat}, e))_j$ is the element of T_{AP}^e such that, for each atom $a \in P$, $(m(x, \text{suchthat}, e))_j$ (1) $\in I_a$ iff $\bigvee_{g \in D_{aj}} (m_g(e))_j = 1$. Again, I_a is the individual containing the atom a, and m_g is the x-variant of m such that $m_g(x) = g$.

That an element of T_{AP}^i is actually defined here follows from the Intersectingness Inheritance Theorem. The discussion of the definition of the extensional interpretation of *suchthat* (Definition 54 of Part IB) should be reviewed for the justification that $(m(x, \text{suchthat}, e))_j$ is properly defined as an element of T_{AP}^e.

As in the case of λ and *self*, expressions created with *suchthat* are necessarily transparent in their $\bar{N}$ arguments. In particular, if we relativize out of a nontransparent context (such as the object of a non-transparent P_2 like look for), the *de re* reading is automatically produced. Thus, for example, the *de re* reading of *look for* is created in the interpretation of the relative clause in (27):

(27)   (a (unicorn (x suchthat (John (look-for x))))) (kiss Mary).

If (27) is the translation into our logical language of the English sentence:

(28)   A unicorn which John is looking for is kissing Mary.

then this is reasonable: as far as we can tell, only a *de re* reading can be given to *look for* in (28). However, if we change the determiner used with *unicorn*, it appears that a *de dictu* reading becomes possible:

(29)   Every unicorn which John is looking for is kissing Mary.
(30)   The unicorn which John is looking for is kissing Mary.

Suppose for example that in a certain world it is true that John is looking (*de dictu*) for a unicorn which is kissing Mary. It seems that there is a reading of (30) according to which that sentence is true even if there is no such unicorn. The *de dictu* possibility is even clearer in the case of sentences with a modal, such as:

(31)   The unicorn which John is looking for must have a golden horn.

In fact, not only is the *de dictu* reading possible, but the interpretation of *look for* is linked to the interpretation of *must*; roughly, the necessity expressed by *must* is understood as a requirement to be met by any world in which John's search is satisfied. At the present time, we are not proposing any way of handling this sort of thing. A more structured conception of the notion of world is undoubtedly needed.

6. SENTENTIAL PREDICATES IN THE INTENSIONAL SYSTEM

The by now classical non-extensional treatments of natural language semantics were initially proposed to handle 'sentence taking' predicates like *is necessary, is possible,* etc. on the one hand, and predicates expressing propositional attitudes like *believe, think,* etc. on the other. Below we extend our intensional logic to include such predicates. The initial treatment we provide is more adequate than 'standard' treatments, e.g. Montague (1974), in several respects. In particular, our boolean approach to semantics generalizes nicely to such predicates and allows us to represent certain ambiguities not captured on other approaches. It also allows us to capture generalizations concerning similarities between sentence taking predicates and more 'ordinary' $\bar{N}$ taking ones. More specifically, we show that there is a semantic unity to the notion *argument category* which includes ordinary $\bar{N}$'s, sentential complements, and certain sorts of infinitival complements.

On the other hand, our initial treatment of sentence taking predicates does preserve one basic inadequacy of 'standard' treatments — one for which different solutions are proposed in Thomason (1980) and Ben-Chorin (1982). We indicate how our approach may be generalized along the lines in Ben-Chorin (*op. cit.*) without disturbing the advantages we have established for it.

Syntax of Sentence Taking Predicates

Within the tradition of philosophical logics (specifically, modal logic) the syntactic arguments of predicates like *is necessary* have been treated as ordinary sentences (for which we use the symbol S rather than the typographically more cumbersome P_0 in this section). In categorial notation, then, *is necessary* would be of category S/S. By extension, *believe* would be of category $(S/\bar{N})/S$; it would combine with an S to yield an ordinary one place predicate, one taking an ordinary $\bar{N}$ argument to form an S. Similarly, predicates like *surprise*, as it occurs in *that Fred left surprised John*, would be of category $(S/S)/\bar{N}$, and one like *mean, imply, entail*, etc. which take two sentential arguments would be of category $(S/S)/S$.

By contrast, early work in generative grammar treated the direct objects of verbs like *kiss* and *believe* in (1) as having the same category, NP.

(1) (a) Mary kissed John
    (b) Everyone believed (that) the Earth was flat

The motivation for this treatment was strictly syntactic, not semantic as in the case of the philosophical approach. For example, by treating the objects of *kiss* and *believe* above as having the same category, NP, it was possible to formulate the Passive transformation in a reasonably general way: it moved NPs around in sentences, and since the objects of *kiss* and *believe* were both NPs the same rule derived (2) from (roughly) their corresponding sources in (1).

(2) (a) John was kissed by Mary
    (b) That the Earth was flat was believed by everyone

However, on both syntactic and semantic grounds this early linguistic approach seemed ill advised. Syntactically, for example, the grammar generated such apparent non-sentences as *Mary kissed that the Earth was flat*. More important for our purposes, such strings seem to be semantic nonsense, instantiating some sort of category mistake. We surely do not want expressions like *John* and *(that) the Earth was flat* to be able to denote the same sort of objects. Semantically, then, the philosophical approach seems preferable.

More recent linguistic approaches, however, assign the sentential objects of *believe*, etc. to a new category, $\bar{S}$, which is distinct both from S and from

NP (our $\bar{N}$). Thus, ignoring many details, a reasonably current structural description of (1b) above would be:

(3)

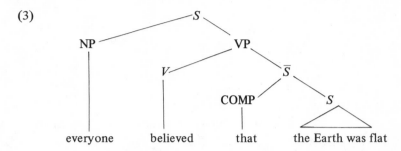

It is this latter approach which we shall adopt here. Since it is more complicated than the standard philosophical approach, we must justify in basically semantic terms why we want to make a category distinction between S and $\bar{S}$. Such justification, while somewhat subtle, is not hard to come by.

Consider first what sorts of expressions we want to be members of the category $\bar{S}$. Obviously, we want expressions of the form *that+S*. But we want much else besides. In particular, given the strongly boolean nature of natural language so far discussed, we would expect boolean combinations in *and, or*, and *not* to be included in this category. This is correct, as illustrated in (4) below:

(4) (a)   John believes (both) that Fred left and that Mary stayed.
     (b)   John believes (either) that Fred left or that Mary stayed.
     (c)   John believes that Fred left but not that Mary stayed.
     (d)   John believes neither that Fred left nor that Mary stayed.

Thus the direct object of *believe* in (4a) is a conjunction of two $\bar{S}$'s, both of the form *that+S*. In (4b) it is a disjunction, etc.

Thus, the syntax of our extended intensional logic treats the complementizer *that* as having the category $\bar{S}/S$, and treats both S and $\bar{S}$ as boolean; in each of those categories boolean combinations may be formed to yield complex expressions in those categories. We therefore structurally distinguish between the result of conjoining two $\bar{S}$'s, each of the form *that+S*, to form a complex $\bar{S}$, and the result of conjoining two S's to form a complex S and combining the result with *that* to fom an $\bar{S}$. The difference is illustrated in (5) below:

(5)   (a)

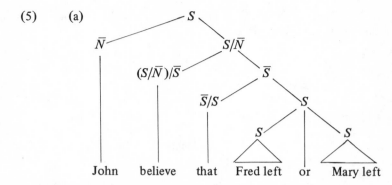

'John believes that (either) Fred left or Mary left'

(b)

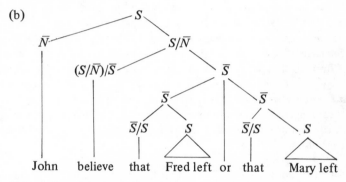

'John believes (either) that Fred left or that Mary left'

Crucially, the syntactic distinction forced in (5a, b) corresponds to a semantic distinction: (5a) says that John believes that a certain disjunction holds; he may have no opinion as to which disjunct it is (as might naturally be the case if the second disjunct were the negation of the first). In (5b), however, we assert that John does believe one of the disjuncts though we do not commit ourselves as to which. (5b) is a paraphrase of

(6)   John believes that Fred left or John believes that Mary left

Clearly (5a) can be true in circumstances in which (5b) is false, whence the two are not paraphrases.

Thus, we have motivated making a distinction between the categories

S and $\bar{S}$, since by so doing we can provide distinct representations for the English sentences in (5a) and (5b) and thus can assign them different truth conditions, ones which for example guarantee that (5b) entails (6) but that (5a) does not. (In the next section we provide a semantics for $\bar{S}$ and $\bar{S}$-taking predicates which does just that.) By contrast, the philosophical approach we outlined above does not make a distinction between S and $\bar{S}$ and thus would appear inadequate to express the meaning difference between (5a) and (5b), since it would have to assign them the same logical form.

One might object to our informal analysis above on the grounds that English speakers do not in fact rigidly observe the meaning/form distinction we have given for (5a, b). Might not a speaker utter (5a), even without the *that*, intending the meaning we have attributed to (5b)? Quite plausibly the answer here is yes. But even for such speakers we feel it is reasonable to say that (5a) is ambiguous, having the distinct meanings we have ascribed to (5a) and (5b). On the reading in (5b), for example, the utterance might be naturally followed in discourse by 'I can't remember which'. In any event, if (5a) is regarded as ambiguous, we are obliged in our logical syntax to have two structures, one for each of the two readings. Thus we shall stick with the syntactic course we have charted so far, leaving open the questions concerning how we match up surface forms and logical forms.

Let us note finally that, for some speakers at least, additional support of a syntactic nature argues in favor of the distinction between boolean combinations of $\bar{S}$'s and the result of combining *that* with boolean combinations of S's. Specifically, for some speakers, conjunctions of $\bar{S}$s in subject position may trigger plural agreement in the predicate whereas this is not the case for *that* combined with a conjunction of Ss:

(7)   (Both) that Fred passed and (also) that Mary failed were/*was strange
(8)   That Fred passed and Mary failed was/*?were strange

Again, the syntactic difference between (7) and (8) corresponds to a semantic difference: (7) says that there were two strange things, Fred's passing and Mary's failing; (8) says that there was only one strange thing, the fact that a certain conjunction holds (as would be the case for example if Mary is known to be much more knowledgeable than Fred — they might both pass if the exam was easy, both fail if the exam was hard, but it is surprising to find an exam which allows Fred to pass and Mary to fail).

Overall, we find it more enlightening as regards the semantic system of

English to elucidate somewhat subtle distinctions than to ride roughshod over them, whence we shall formally incorporate the distinction between S and $\bar{S}$ in our logical syntax. Formally this is done, almost trivially, as follows.

First we note that S is already a category and is in our list of boolean categories, so boolean combinations of S's are S's. Moreover $\bar{S}$ (= $\bar{P}_0$) is already a category, but to date has no expressions in it. So we add *that* to the basic vocabulary and by lexical rule assign it the category $\bar{S}/S$. This guarantees that expressions of the form $\{that, e\}$ are of category $\bar{S}$, where e is an expression of category S. Finally we include $\bar{S}$ in the list of boolean categories, whence boolean combinations in *and*, *or*, and *not* are also expressions of category $\bar{S}$. We shall not add further expressions to the category $\bar{S}$, though a more detailed treatment of this category than we give here would probably do so. For example, the direct objects in (9) should probably be assigned this category:

(9) (a) John believes whatever Fred says
     (b) John proved everything that Fred conjectured
     (c) John believes the Axiom of Choice

Thus the expressions in $\bar{S}$ are just the expressions of the form $\{that, e\}$ for e of category S, together with all boolean combinations formed recursively beginning with these expressions.

We then add to the basic vocabulary expressions like *is necessary* (which we do not for the nonce analyse into its component parts), *believe, surprise, mean*, etc. and add lexical rules to the grammar assigning these expressions to the appropriate category; e.g., *is necessary* is put in the category $S/\bar{S}$, *believe* in the category $(S/\bar{N})/\bar{S}$, etc. We shall also include these categories in the list of boolean ones enabling us to generate booleanly complex elements in these categories such as (*both*) *hope and believe*, as in *John both hoped and believed that Fred would win; surprise and annoy* as in *That Fred failed both surprised and annoyed Bill*, etc.

A Semantics for $\bar{S}$ and $\bar{S}$-Taking Predicates

Our problem here is to define the types for $\bar{S}$ and the various categories of $\bar{S}$-taking predicates. Once that is done, complex expressions formed from these, such as *believe that Fred left* will be assigned an interpretation according to the rule of functional applications already given. We consider first the type for $\bar{S}$ and then that of the relevant predicates.

Recall that the type for S $(= P_0)$ is already given as the set of functions from J, the set of possible worlds of the model, into 2, the set of truth values. We shall refer to this set as Prop, and refer to its elements by lower case letters p, q, r, and s. Prop is, recall, a complete and atomic boolean algebra isomorphic to J^*, the power set of J. The boolean operations on Prop are defined pointwise on J, e.g. $(p \vee q)(j) = p(j) \vee q(j)$, etc.

What now can we say about the type for $\overline{S}$? It seems clear that, as expected, we want it to be a boolean algebra in order to provide interpretations for boolean combinations of $\overline{S}$'s. Further, where e is of category S, we want e and $\{that, e\}$ to have different interpretations for the reasons already given. e will be interpreted as an element of Prop, so it remains to find a possible denotation for $\{that, e\}$. We may construct such a denotation by analogy with the way denotations for proper nouns (in the extensional logic) were constructed, namely as the set of properties which the proposition expressed by e has. Intuitively this is reasonable. Taking e for example to be *Fred left*, we naturally consider that under a given interpretation e has the property that John believes it, that Bill doubts it, that it is surprising, not logically true, etc. Thus where e is interpreted as a proposition p, we shall interpret $\{that, e\}$ as I_p, the set of properties which p has. More explicitly, a property of propositions is a function from Prop into 2, so I_p is the set of functions from Prop into 2 which assign p value 1. Formally,

DEFINITION 1. For all $p \in \text{Prop}$ $(= F_{2/J})$, $I_p = \{f \in F_{2/\text{Prop}} : f(p) = 1\}$

Recalling that the set of functions from Prop into 2 is isomorphic to Prop*, the power set of Prop, we have that, up to isomorphism, an I_p is a subset of Prop*, that is, an element of Prop**, the power set of Prop*. Since the I_ps must be among the elements of $T_{\overline{S}}$ it appears sufficient to take that type to be Prop**. We may then naturally interpret the complementizer *that*, of category $\overline{S}/S$, as that function from T_S into $T_{\overline{S}}$ which sends each $p \in \text{Prop}$ $(= T_S)$ to I_p. And finally, since the elements of $T_{\overline{S}}$ are sets (of properties of propositions) we may naturally interpret boolean combinations of $\overline{S}$'s as intersections, unions, and complements (relative to the set of all properties of propositions) of their conjuncts, disjuncts, etc.

Note that on this approach p and I_p are always distinct objects, whence for e a sentence, e and $\{that, e\}$ are always interpreted as different formal objects. Further, it also turns out that a boolean combination of $\overline{S}$'s and the result of combining *that* with the corresponding boolean combination of sentences generally are interpreted differently. For example, suppose that

Fred passed and *Mary failed* are interpreted by propositions p and q respectively, and assume further for simplicity of illustration that p and q are completely independent, in the sense that neither is $\leqslant$ to the other (i.e. there is a possible world j in which p holds and q fails and another world k in which q holds and p fails). Then the conjunction of the $\bar{S}$'s *that Fred passed and that Mary failed* is interpreted as $I_p \cap I_q$ as illustrated below:

(10)

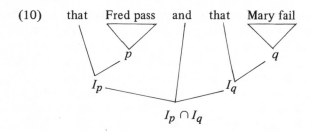

On the other hand, the result of first conjoining the two S's and then forming the $\bar{S}$ with *that* is interpreted as follows:

(11)

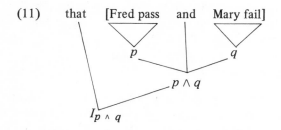

Clearly $I_{p \wedge q}$ and $I_p \cap I_q$ are distinct sets of properties. For example, $I_{p \wedge q}$ contains the function which assigns $p \wedge q$ value 1 and all other propositions value 0. Since p and q are completely independent, $p \wedge q$ is a different proposition from p, hence that function is not in I_p and so not in $I_p \cap I_q$. So given that *be strange* (*be necessary*, etc.) of category $S/\bar{S}$ will be interpreted as a *function* (about which more in a moment) from $T_{\bar{S}}$ into T_S, it can easily be the case that (7) and (8), repeated below as (12) and (13), are interpreted as different elements of Prop, since the *be strange* function is applying to different arguments and so may naturally take different values.

(12)   that Fred passed and that Mary failed were strange
(13)   that Fred passed and Mary failed was strange

This essentially completes our construction of $T_{\bar{S}}$. Before giving a more formal statement let us note the deep and most non-obvious similarity between the type for $\bar{S}$ and the (extensional) type for $\bar{N}$. (Note that we have not made an extension/intension distinction in the type for $\bar{S}$.) The most crucial similarity is that both types possess distinguished subsets whose elements we have called *individuals*. In each case the individuals are *generators* for the whole type, in the sense any element of the type is some boolean combination of individuals. So, relative to the boolean operations, the elements of the type are, in some sense, determined by the individuals. Moreover, these sets of generators have a very special property — they are *free* (for complete and atomic algebras), or *ca-free* for short. What this means, informally, is that anything that can be said about elements of the entire type is determined by what can be said about the individuals in the type. For the extensional type for $\bar{N}$, the n-place predicates express what we can say about the elements of that type; these predicates are just the complete homomorphisms on $T_{\bar{N}}$, and by the Justification Theorem the complete homomorphisms from $T_{\bar{N}}$ into any *ca*-algebra D are unique functions which extend functions from the individuals in $T_{\bar{N}}$ into D. So we can define an n-place predicate just by stating its values on the individuals, and we can state those values freely. In this sense, what we can say about $\bar{N}$ denotations is determined by what we can say about the individuals among those denotations.

Similarly in $T_{\bar{S}}$ the I_p's are easily shown to be a set of *ca*-free generators for $T_{\bar{S}}$. This subset of $\bar{S}$ may naturally be called the proper $\bar{S}$'s in the same way that the subset of $\bar{N}$ whose possible denotations *ca*-free generate $T_{\bar{N}}$ are the proper $\bar{N}$'s. For later reference let us formally define:

DEFINITION 2. $\bar{S}_{\text{prop}}$ = {(*that, e*): e of category S}

THEOREM 1. $T_{\bar{S}}{}_{\text{prop}}$ is a set of *ca*-free generators for $T_{\bar{S}}$ (= Prop**).

Thus, if predicates on $\bar{S}$ denotations are judged to behave homomorphically, as with $T_{\bar{N}}$, what can be said of $\bar{S}$ denotations is determined by what can be said of sentential individuals, the I_p's (the proper $\bar{S}$ denotations). Now, $\bar{S}$ taking predicates do behave homomorphically on their $\bar{S}$ arguments. For example, *believe either that S or that T* holds of the same individuals as does *either believe that S or believe that T*, and thus *believe* preserves joins. Similarly it is easy to see that it preserves meets and complements, that is, *believe* is interpreted by a homomorphism. Notice here that we are only claiming that (14a) and (14b) must be interpreted by the same function:

(14) (a) . . . believe (either) that S or that T

    (b) . . . (either) believe that S or believe that T

We are not claiming that (15a) and (15b) must be interpreted by the same function:

(15) (a) . . . believe that ((either) S or T)

    (b) . . . (either) believe that S or believe that T

(14a) and (14b) must be semantically identical since the argument of *believe* in (14a) is a disjunction of $\bar{S}$'s and must be interpreted then as a join of $\bar{S}$ denotations, in this case of sentential individuals, I_p's. Since *believe* is to be interpreted by a homomorphism it must preserve joins and thus be semantically identical to the interpretation of (14b). But in (15a) the argument of *believe* is not a join, in fact not even a boolean combination, of $\bar{S}$'s. It is merely an expression of the form $\{ that,\ e\}$ where e has category S. So the argument expression of *believe* in (15a) is interpreted as a generator, an I_p, and the complete homomorphisms take their values freely — in any way we like — on the generators.

Thus the homomorphic nature of $\bar{S}$ taking predicates is only clear once the distinction between S and $\bar{S}$ is made clear. Similarly it is clear that other $\bar{S}$ taking predicates behave homomorphically on their $\bar{S}$ arguments. Thus *be strange* must preserve meets since (16a) and (16b) below are logically equivalent:

(16) (a) (Both) that Fred passed and that Mary failed are strange.

    (b) That Fred passed is strange and that Mary failed is strange.

Again of course treating *be strange* as a homomorphism does not commit us to the logical equivalence of (17a) and (17b) below, since the argument of (17a) is not a boolean combination of $\bar{S}$'s, so the homomorphic nature of *be strange* does not commit us in any way as to what proposition it yields when applied to it.

(17) (a) That ((both) Fred passed and Mary failed) is strange

    (b) (Both) that Fred passed and that Mary failed are strange

Thus the similarity between $\bar{N}$ and $\bar{S}$ is non-trivial. Their types are both *ca*-free generated algebras, and major classes or predicates on them behave homomorphically what they say about elements of the types is determined by what they say about the individuals in those types. Let us codify these observations with the following definition; note that we have given a general, that is category independent, characterization of the semantic interpretation of the subcategorization feature *proper*.

DEFINITION 3. A complete boolean algebra B is said to be an *argument algebra* iff it has a set of *ca*-free generators. By extension, a category C is an *argument category* iff T_C is an argument algebra.

(18)   *Constraint on the feature 'proper'*
         If A is an argument category then $T_{A_{\text{Prop}}}$ is a set of *ca*-free generators for T_A.

As regards the last constraint it is worth noting perhaps that there may be expressions in $\bar{S}$ in addition to the ones of the form $\{that, e\}$, for e a sentence, which bear some resemblance to proper nouns, in the sense of denoting somewhat arbitrarily a fixed object. Such expressions would include *Fermat's Last Theorem* (which is not a theorem), *Zorn's Lemma* (a specific one of the many he proved), etc.

Formal Definitions of the New Types

Relative to a model $\langle P, 2, J \rangle$ we define the types for the new categories discussed above as follows:

DEFINITION 4. $T_S = F_{2/J}$ as before but now called Prop, regarded as a *ca*-algebra, the boolean operations being defined pointwise on J.

DEFINITION 5. $T_{\bar{S}} = $ Prop** regarded as a power set boolean algebra.

DEFINITION 6. $T_{\bar{S}_{\text{prop}}} = \{I_p : p \in \text{Prop}\}$.

Recall that, by Theorem 1, $T_{\bar{S}_{\text{prop}}}$ is a set of *ca*-free generators for $T_{\bar{S}}$, whence $\bar{S}$ is an argument category.

To give a generalized semantics for n-place predicates regardless of whether the ith argument category is $\bar{N}$ or $\bar{S}$ (or any of the other argument categories to be suggested shortly) we introduce the following systematic abbreviatory convention:

for $C, C_1, \ldots, C_n$ any elements of CAT, $C_1, \overset{C}{\ldots}, C_n$ abbreviates $C_1, \overset{C}{\ldots}, C_{n-1}/C_n$. For example, the category to which *believe* belongs will be abbreviated $\frac{S}{N}\overline{S}$, which by the above convention abbreviates $\frac{S}{N}/\overline{S}$, which in turn abbreviates $(S/\overline{N})/\overline{S}$, the category to which *believe* belongs.

We may then define:

DEFINITION 7. For all argument categories $A_1, \ldots, A_n$, the type for $A_1, \overset{S}{\ldots}, A_n$ is the set of complete homomorphisms from T_{A_n} into the type for $A_1, \ldots, A_{n-1}$ regarded as a boolean algebra where the operations are defined pointwise on $T_{A_{n_{\text{prop}}}}$.

For example, the above definition together with the rule for interpreting boolean combinations tells us that $m(hope$ and $believe)$ is that complete homomorphism from $T_{\overline{S}}$ into $T_{S/\overline{N}}$ whose value at any propositional individual I_p is $m(hope)(I_p) \wedge m(believe)(I_p)$, the meet here being taken in the algebra $T_{S/\overline{N}}$ understood to be the algebra of *transparent* homomorphisms from $T_{\overline{N}}$ into T_S.

Note that our subcategorization abbreviations have *not* adequately reflected the transparency distinctions discussed earlier in our intensional logic. It is unproblematic to enrich our abbreviatory conventions to include them; e.g. we might write the category for *believe* as $\frac{S}{N}\overline{S}_{+t}$, but we shall not make sufficiently elaborate use of the notation to require the detailed spelling out of these conventions here. We shall assume where relevant that predicative categories are understood to be transparent unless indicated otherwise.

Lexical Constraints on the Interpreting Function m

The new categories in our system present a variety of expressions which are in the standard sense logical constants. Thus, as before, the class of interpreting functions m considered for the language must be restricted so that these expressions have fixed denotations relative to the primitives of the model. In giving examples below we ignore the assignment function a of values to variables as these are not relevant to the present discussion.

In addition to the constraints on the acceptable interpreting functions m already presented we now require that:

(19) $m(be$ $true)$ is that complete homomorphism from $T_{\overline{S}}$ into T_S defined by:
$h(I_p)(j) = p(j)$, all $p \in$ Prop, all $j \in J$.

Thus, informally, *that Fred sings is true* holds in a world j iff *Fred sings* holds in j. Note that (19) is a well definition in virtue of the one-to-one correspondence between sentential individuals (I_p's) and propositions. Thus if I is a sentential individual there is exactly one proposition p such that $I = I_p$. Given the individual I then we may unambiguously refer to its proposition as p_I; the equation in (19) could then read: for all sentential individuals I and all possible worlds j, $h(I)(j) = p_I(j)$. Having noted this point we shall use the somewhat less correct but easier to read notation in (19).

$$(20) \qquad m(be\ false) = (m(be\ true))'$$

Thus *that Fred sings is false* holds in j iff the complement of *that Fred sings is true* fails in j.

$$(21) \qquad m(be\ necessary) \text{ is that complete homomorphism } h \text{ from } T_{\overline{S}} \text{ into }$$
$$T_S \text{ such that for all } p \in T_S \text{ and all } j \in J, h(I_p)(j) = \bigwedge_{k \in J} p(k).$$

Thus *that Fred sings is necessary* holds in j iff *Fred sings* holds in all worlds k.

$$(22) \qquad m(be\ possible) \text{ is that complete homomorphism } h \text{ such that for}$$
$$\text{all } p, j \text{ as above}, h(I_p)(j) = \bigvee_{k \in J} p(k)$$

Thus *that Fred sings is possible* holds in j iff for some world k *Fred sings* holds in k.

Note that on our approach, as in more standard ones, necessity and possibility are treated as properly modal predicates quantifying over possible worlds, with necessity universal quantification and possibility existential quantification. The propositions which interpret the sentences these predicates form are constant (in any given model): they have the same value at all $j \in J$.

We may note as well that there are two place logical predicates with the same properties — quantifying over worlds and being constant at all worlds in a given model. Thus (23) below is as plausible a semantics for *imply* as (21) above is for *be necessary*.

$$(23) \qquad m(imply) \text{ is that complete homomorphism } h \text{ from } T_{\overline{S}} \text{ into } T_{S/\overline{S}}$$
$$\text{such that for all } p, q \in \text{Prop and all } j \in J, h(I_p)(I_q)(j) = 1 \text{ iff for}$$
$$\text{all } k \in J, p(k) \leqslant q(k).$$

Subcategories of $\bar{S}$ Taking Predicates

The semantic difference between S and $\bar{S}$ we have developed allows us to represent meaning differences between various syntactically similar $\bar{S}$ taking predicates in ways we find enlightening. Let us consider again the case of a model in which we have completely independent propositions p and q. Then I_p, I_q, $I_{p \wedge q}$, and $I_{p \vee q}$ are distinct generators of $T_{\bar{S}}$; so the values of homomorphisms on these generators may be randomly assigned. Thus while we have $(p \wedge q) \leqslant p$, it does not follow that $h(I_{p \wedge q}) \leqslant h(I_p)$, for h a homomorphism on $T_{\bar{S}}$. (It does of course follow that $h(I_p \cap I_q) \leqslant h(I_p)$, but that is not the case we are considering.) For example, correctly, *that Fred passed and Mary failed is ironic* might be true in a world j even though *that Fred passed is ironic* is not.

However it appears that not all $\bar{S}$ taking predicates are insensitive to the difference between I_p and $I_{p \wedge q}$, I_p and $I_{p \vee q}$, etc. For example if the denotation of *is probable* holds of I_p in some world j then it should hold of $I_{p \vee q}$ in j. And if it holds of $I_{p \wedge q}$ in j it ought to hold of I_p in j and also of I_q. That is to say, (24a) below is judged to entail (24b), and (25a) (25b):

(24) (a) That Fred left is probable
　　　(b) That (Fred left or Mary fainted) is probable
(25) (a) That (Fred left and Mary stayed) is probable
　　　(b) That Fred left is probable

But if *probable* above is replaced by *doubtful* or *improbable* the entailments fail to hold; in fact that seem to be reversed. We may then distinguish semantic subcategories of $\bar{S}$ taking predicates according as entailments such as the above hold or fail to hold.

These and similar facts are naturally accommodated in our system by adding a subcategorization feature *upward entailing* (adapted from Ladusaw, 1979) to our language, assigning *be probable* to the category $S/\bar{S}_{\text{up}}$ by lexical rule, and defining the type as follows:

DEFINITION 8. $T_{S/\bar{S}_{\text{up}}} = \{h \in T_{S/\bar{S}}:$ for all $p, q \in \text{Prop}$, if $p \leqslant q$ then $h(I_p) \leqslant h(I_q)\}$.

The entailments in (24) and (25) then follow automatically. The corresponding feature *downward entailing* can be added in a similar way with the obvious semantics.

We might note that the predicates for which such subcategorization features seem to give correct results are 'impersonal' predicates like *probable, improbable*, etc. rather than 'psychological' ones like *believe*, etc. Thus it is not clear that (26a) below entails (26b).

(26) (a) John believes that Fred left
     (b) John believes that ((either) Fred left or Mary stayed)

At least one snag in inferring (26b) from (26a) is that John may never have considered the proposition expressed by the disjunction in (26b) and thus in some sense have no opinion about it, even though if he is rational he presumably would believe it if he did consider it. And the assumption of rationality in the latter case actually gives additional reason for doubting the entailment. For to say that (26a) entails (26b) is to say that whenever (26a) is true (26b) is. If this may fail in the case of irrational John then the entailment fails. We are inclined then not to want to assign psychological predicates to upward or downward entailing subcategories of $\bar{S}$ taking predicates.

On the other hand, another subcategory of $\bar{S}$ taking predicates which we feel we can represent in a reasonable if not totally adequate way are *factives* (see Kiparsky and Kiparsky, 1970, and Keenan, 1969, for more detailed discussion). Thus we judge that each of (27a) and (27b) below entails (27c).

(27) (a) That Fred left early was strange
     (b) That Fred left early wasn't strange
     (c) Fred left early

But if *strange* (*ironic, surprising*, etc.) is replaced by any of *true, false, probable, likely, necessary*, etc. at least one of the two entailments fails.

We may easily account for the entailment from (27a) to (27c) by assigning *be strange*, etc. to a subcategory of $S/\bar{S}_{\text{fact}}$ whose type is defined as follows:

DEFINITION 9. $T_{S/\bar{S}_{\text{fact}}} = \{h \in T_{S/\bar{S}}: \text{for all } p \in \text{Prop}, h(I_p) \leqslant p\}$.

It follows immediately then that if (27a) is true in j then (27c) is; and conversely if (27c) fails in j then so must (27a).

The problem however is to account for the inference from (27b) to (27c). Assuming that the predicate in (27b) is just the negation of that in (27a) and noting that *be strange* is interpreted by an element of $T_{S/\bar{S}}$ we have that the predicate in (27b) is interpreted by the complement of that in (27a). And complements in $T_{S/\overline{S}}$ are defined pointwise on individuals (see Definition 7), whence (27b) is true iff (27a) is false. Since (27a) may be false if (27c) is, it follows that (27b) does not entail (27c).

The solution we tentatively propose to this problem is as follows. Define the type for the factives as in Definition 9 above but assign it a boolean structure as follows: meets and joins are defined pointwise as before, but complements are defined by the equation $h'(I_p) = p \wedge (h(I_p))'$; the unit element sends each I_p to p, and the zero element is as in $T_{S/\overline{S}}$, it sends each I_p to the zero element of Prop, that function which sends each j in J to the zero element of 2. The reader may verify that the operations so defined satisfy the axioms of boolean algebra. But now we have a possible ambiguity in the interpretation of *not be strange*. We get one result if we consider *be strange* as an element of $S/\overline{S}$, for there $h'(I_p)$ is directly $(h(I_p))'$, and another result if we consider it an element of $\underset{\text{fact}}{S/\overline{S}}$, where $h'(I_p) = p \wedge (h(I_p))'$. To circumvent this problem we must add a rider to the general rule which interprets boolean combinations. Namely, $m(not\ e) = (m(e))'$, complements taken in the smallest subcategory to which e belongs. Similarly $m(e_1\ and\ e_2)$ $= m(e_1) \wedge m(e_2)$, meets taken in the smallest subcategory to which both e_1 and e_2 belong. For the nonce this approach seems to us satisfactory since $\underset{\text{fact}}{S/\overline{S}}$ is a subcategory of $S/\overline{S}$ and in that sense smaller than it. And more generally the smallest subcategory of a category to which an expression e belongs is the one which includes all the subcategorization features which e is overtly required to satisfy. So for the crucial case of complements we always know in what algebra to evaluate $m(not\ e)$.

Though much more could and should be said concerning subcategories of $\overline{S}$ taking predicates we turn now to the generalization inherent in our notion of *argument category*.

Argument Categories in Addition to $\overline{N}$ and $\overline{S}$

We have argued earlier that $\overline{N}$ and $\overline{S}$ should be treated as distinct categories. They nonetheless have much in common syntactically. As EST theorists have pointed out (Chomsky, 1970), there are some similarities (and also some differences) in internal structure. Externally, both categories are ones whose expressions may, depending on the language, trigger predicate agreement and be marked for case and/or thematic role (e.g. Patient, Stimulus, Cause, etc.). They are categories affected (or mentioned) be relation changing rules like Passive and Extraposition (about which more later); they are categories whose expressions can be quantified and bound, as by relativization operators (*everyone who John saw and invited to the party, everything that John believes and tries to prove*, etc.) and question operators (*What did John see?, What does John believe?*, etc.)

Above we adduced a semantic property which $\bar{N}$ and $\bar{S}$ had in common and which thus correlates with this similarity in syntactic behavior, namely, their types are (extensionally, where relevant) *ca*-freely generated algebras. This property doubtless seems esoteric when stated algebraically, but on intuitive grounds, as discussed earlier, it means that these types have individuals, a property which distinguished $\bar{N}$ and $\bar{S}$ from other major categories which are not generally arguments of predicates. For example, the types for Modifiers, categories of the form C/C, are not *ca*-freely generated algebras. Similarly, the types for predicates are not *ca*-freely generated, nor are the types for Specifiers (= Determiners). Detailed arguments to this effect would require more space than we can devote to them here, but the basic characterization theorem which is used in all such proofs is the following theorem:

THEOREM 2. A complete boolean algebra B has a set of *ca*-free generators iff B is isomorphic to the power set of a power set.

Note that $T_{\bar{S}}$ is Prop**, the power set of a power set, and $T_{\bar{N}}$ is extensionally P^*, the power set of T_N, itself taken to be a *ca*-algebra and thus isomorphic to the power set of its atoms by Theorem 6 of Part IA. We omit the proof of Theorem 2, which uses completely standard techniques.

Are there other categories of English whose types are argument algebras? The natural place to look is at categories which loosely function as arguments of predicates. To the extent that types for these categories are argument algebras we may conclude that our semantic characterization of the notion 'argument of a predicate' in English is a good one. Preliminary investigation here suggests in fact the answer to our query is affirmative.

One such category are embedded questions, such as the direct object expressions in (28) below:

(28)   John knows/remembers/forgot whether Fred left.

Tentatively assigning such expressions to the category $\bar{Q}$, and limiting ourselves for expository purposes to embedded yes-no $\bar{Q}$'s, we may note that simple expressions in this category appear to have the form *whether*+S. We want these expressions to have a different category from $\bar{S}$, however, since

(29a) and (29b) are not paraphrases, whence their direct objects must denote differently.

    (29) (a) John knows whether Fred left.
         (b) John knows that Fred left.

Clearly if John knows that Fred didn't leave then (29a) is true and (29b) not true.

    Further, for reasons similar to those given earlier for $\overline{S}$, we want $\overline{Q}$ to be a different category from $\overline{N}$. In addition, we want $\overline{Q}$ to be different from S, for otherwise sentences such as (30a) and (30b) below would be logically equivalent, which they are not.

    (30) (a) John knows both whether S and whether T
         (b) John knows whether both S and T

Clearly (30b) says that John knows whether a certain conjunction holds — which he might easily know if T is chosen as the negation of S — But it does not claim, as does (30a), that he knows whether each conjunct holds or not. Further, (30a) supports the idea that we want $\overline{Q}$ to form complex members in *and*, and (31) below that we want to form them with *or* and *not*, whence we want $\overline{Q}$ to be a boolean category having a boolean algebra as its type.

    (31) (a) John knows either whether S or whether T (I can't remember
            which)
         (b) John knows whether S but not whether T

In the essential respects, then, an adequate type for $\overline{Q}$ can be constructed along lines completely similar to those for $\overline{S}$, with *whether* playing the role of *that*. Let us assume, as it does not enter into our construction, that the type for Q, the category of yes-no questions, has been defined. (Note the obvious one-to-one correspondence between the declarative sentence S and the yes-no question *Is it the case that S?*) Then we interpret *whether*+S to be the individual generated by the denotation of the corresponding question denotation, that is, the set of properties (functions from T_Q into 2) which hold of that question denotation, and we define the type for $\overline{Q}$ to be the complete boolean closure of those individuals, an algebra provably isomorphic to $(T_Q)^{**}$, a power set of a power set and thus by Theorem 2 a *ca*-freely generated algebra. Note here, as with $T_{\overline{S}}$, that it doesn't matter what set is chosen as T_Q; $T_{\bar{Q}}$ is a power set of a power set and so *ca*-freely generated.

It seems to us likely that $\bar{N}$, $\bar{S}$, and $\bar{Q}$ (the latter enriched to include the full range of embedded wh-questions) constitute the major, most productive, categories of English with which predicates combine to form sentences. If so, our semantic characterization of argument categories as ones whose types have individuals seems reasonably good. However, other categories of expression besides those considered may function as arguments of predicates and these would have to be investigated, as their semantics is even less well understood than that of the argument categories so far considered. One possible candidate here are infinitival nominals, as illustrated in the subject phrase in (32).

(32)   To be very rich is troublesome/pleasant/fun, etc.

It seems reasonable to expect that a minimally adequate semantics for infinitival nominals can be obtained along lines fully analogous to that for $\bar{S}$ and $\bar{Q}$. Semantically, *to* would map a P_1 denotation onto the individual it determines, i.e. the set of properties which hold of it. The type for these nominals would have to be booleanly closed to provide denotations for boolean combinations of such nominals, as illustrated below:

(33) (a) (Both) to be very rich and to be very poor are troublesome
     (b) (Either) to leave early or to leave late is forbidden
     (c) To dance but not to sing is dangerous

We may take the type for infinitival nominals, call it $\bar{P}_1$, to be the complete boolean closure of the P_1 individuals, provably isomorphic to $(T_{P_1})^{**}$. (P_1 here is assumed for simplicity of illustration to be $S/\underset{+t}{N}$.) This would again yield an argument algebra, one which is distinct from T_{P_1} itself. This latter point is justified by showing that *to*, like *that* and *whether*, introduces alternative scopes involving boolean operators. For example, a disjunction of infinitives is not equivalent to the infinitive of a disjunction, so that (34a) and (34b) are not logically equivalent. Similarly, (35a) and (35b) are not equivalent.

(34) (a) To (either come early or leave late) is forbidden
     (b) (Either) to come early or to leave late is forbidden (I can't remember which)

(35) (a) (Both) to come early and to leave late are forbidden
     (b) To (both come early and leave late) is forbidden

In short, it seems as though the basic facts which motivated our analysis of $\bar{S}$ obtain here for $\bar{P}_1$, and thus $\bar{P}_1$ is properly an argument category in our semantic sense of the term. However, much more study of the semantic properties of $\bar{P}_1$ taking predicates would have to be done before any certitude could be attached to that conclusion.

Let us consider now some syntactic and semantic operations which concern argument categories in general and $\bar{S}$ in particular.

Extraposition

Sentences such as (36a) and (36b) below are logically equivalent, and moreover, appear to be syntactically related in a regular way.

(36) (a) That Fred left early is clear
     (b) It is clear that Fred left early

Early work in generative grammar derived (roughly) (36b) from (36a) by 'extraposing' the $\bar{S}$ subject of (36a) to the end of the sentence leaving a 'dummy' *it* behind (Rosenbaum, 1967). Later work, beginning perhaps with Emonds (1976), preferred to treat (36b) as somewhat more basic and derived (36a) from it by intraposition.

Our concern here is to provide a logical structure for (36b) which corresponds as closely as possible to its surface form and which is logically equivalent to the one assigned to (36a). Now, (36b) appears to be superficially in a predicate-argument form, with *it* as the argument and the rest of the sentence as the predicate. This judgment is confirmed by less superficial analysis. For example, it appears that the argument *it* 'raises', as do clear cases of $\bar{N}$ arguments. More specifically, (37a) and (37b) below seem to be syntactically related in the same way as (38a) and (38b).

(37) (a) John believes that Fred is clever
     (b) John believes Fred to be clever
(38) (a) John believes that it is clear that Fred left early
     (b) John believes it to be clear that Fred left early

Accordingly we shall treat (36b) as being of a predicate-argument form with *it* as argument.

But to what category should we assign this *it*? It appears to be a sort of pronominal place holder for the semantic subject of *is clear*, expressed by *that Fred left early*. It contributes nothing to the meaning of (36b), which is identical to that of (36a) which is *it*-less. Semantically, then, *it* is 'dumb', and we shall, adopting a terminology from Relational Grammar (Perlmutter and Postal, 1977), treat *it* as a 'dummy for category $\bar{S}$'. Note that *it* functions as a dummy for $\bar{Q}$, and $S/\bar{N}$ as well:

(39) (a) Whether John left is unknown
    (b) It is unknown whether John left
(40) (a) To leave early would be annoying
    (b) It would be annoying to leave early

And while *it* does not function as a dummy for ordinary $\bar{N}$'s, it does seem as though *there* does (as argued in the Relational Grammar framework cited above):

(41) (a) Unicorns exist
    (b) There exist unicorns

Thus, perhaps, for every argument category C we want some notion of 'dummy of category C' in our logical syntax. Since we are going to treat such dummies as arguments of predicates we need some way of forming 'dummy taking predicates' from the expressions which would 'normally' combine via the rule of functional applications to yield an S. While there are doubtless many ways to do this, the option we tentatively propose is illustrated in (42) below.

(42)

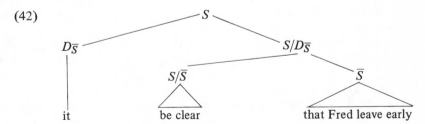

'It is clear that Fred left early'

Incorporating such structures formally in our logic will be done as follows. First we add dummy categories to our definition of CAT, the set of category

names, as per Definition 10a below, and assign them the type indicated in
Definition 10b:

DEFINITION 10.

(a) If C is an element of CAT then D_C is an element of CAT.
(b) $T_{D_C} = T_C$

With this addition to CAT the direct expansion of S in (42) is achieved by
the rule of functional applications.

The main problem now is how to generate {*be clear, that Fred leave early*}
in the category $S/D_{\overline{S}}$. To do this we add another rule to our grammar along-
side the rules of subcategorization, functional application, boolean combinations, and variable binding operators. (43) gives the rule we propose:

(43)   *Dummy Rule* (Syntax)
         For all possible expressions e_1, e_2 and A any argument category,
         if $e_1 \in n(S/A)$ and $e_2 \in n(A)$, then $\{e_1, e_2\} \in n(S/D_A)$.

Note that (43) might appear to 'contradict' the rule of functional applications which says that for e_1, e_2 as above the set $\{e_1, e_2\}$ has category S,
not S/D_A. A careful reading of our formal syntax however shows that there
is in fact no conflict. We have defined the naming function n to be the least
function from CAT, the set of category names, into $(PE_V)^*$, the collection
of all sets of possible expressions over V, which meets certain conditions. In
particular, it must meet the conditions given by both the rules of functional
application and now the dummy rules. Thus, its value at the symbol S must
include $\{e_1, e_2\}$ as an element, and its value at $S/D_{\overline{S}}$ must also include
$\{e_1, e_2\}$ as an element. This only means that $n(S)$ and $n(S/D_{\overline{S}})$ are not
disjoint sets, which is not in and of itself problematic.

It does mean however that we have *derived* expressions, such as {*be clear,
that Fred left early*} in more than one category, so we must be careful in
stating the constraints on the interpreting function m so that we are not
attempting to assign the same (derived) expression to elements in disjoint
types (for the types for S and $S/D_{\overline{S}}$ are indeed disjoint). The interpretation
of the Dummy rule in (45) below shows that this is also not problematic,
once we have modified slightly the statement of the interpretation of the
rule of functional applications, as we do now in (44).

(44)   *Modified Interpretation for Functional Applications*

If e_1 has category X/Y, e_2 has category Y, and $\{e_1, e_2\}$ has category X, then $m(\{e_1, e_2\}) = m(e_1)(m(e_2))$.

(45) *Dummy Rule (Semantics)*

If e_1 has category S/A (for A an argument category), e_2 has category A, and $\{e_1, e_2\}$ has category S/D_A, then for all $x \in T_{D_A} (= T_A), m(\{e_1, e_2\})(x) = m(e_1)(m(e_2))$.

Note that we have in a certain sense 'weakened' our semantics, in that we cannot uniquely determine the denotation of a derived expression if we only know the types of the expressions from which it is derived. We must now also know the category of the derived expression. Until now we did not have to mention the category of the derived expression in the interpretative rule since it was uniquely determined given the categories of its immediate constituents. Now that is no longer the case, so the category of the derived expression must be mentioned in the interpretative rule. So this is a modification of our system, but not one which is particularly problematic. It merely allows us to put derived expressions in more than one category.

It does not, however, allow us to put basic expressions, ones in the basic vocabulary, in more than one category (with disjoint types). For here the interpreting functions m are constrained to interpret basic expressions e of category C as elements of the type for C. If a given basic expression e was in two categories with disjoint types there would be no *functions m* satisfying the condition on basic expressions. This means for example that we cannot assign *it* to $S/D_{\overline{S}}$ and $S/D_{\overline{Q}}$ by lexical rule. An easy, though not particularly elegant, solution to this problem is to simply add artificially distinct *it*'s to the basic vocabulary and assign say it_1 by lexical rule to the category $S/D_{\overline{S}}$, it_2 to the category $S/D_{\overline{Q}}$, etc. It would perhaps be somewhat more natural to subscript the *it*'s with the category name they are dummies for. We shall adopt this latter solution. Thus the basic vocabulary is hereby enriched to include *there*, $it_{\overline{S}}$, $it_{\overline{Q}}$, etc. Lexical rules assign *there* to the category $D_{\overline{N}}$, $it_{\overline{S}}$ to $D_{\overline{S}}$, etc. The logical structure we assign to *it is clear that Fred left* then is:

(46)

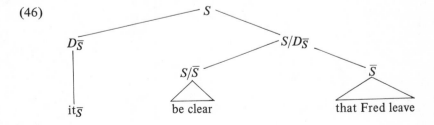

The dummy rule expands the node $S/D_{\overline{S}}$; otherwise the only rules that have been used are functional applications and lexical rules.

To see that (46) is correctly interpreted as a paraphrase of the logical representation of (*that Fred leave*) (*be clear*) we must technically assign a type to $S/D_{\overline{S}}$. This we do generally as follows:

DEFINITION 11. For all categories C, $T_{S/D_C} = F_{T_S/T_{D_C}}$.

To show that (46) is correctly interpreted, let m be an arbitrary interpretation of our extended language. $m(it_{\overline{S}})$ is an arbitrary element in $T_{D_{\overline{S}}}$ (= $T_{\overline{S}}$), since $it_{\overline{S}}$ is a lexical element in $D_{\overline{S}}$ and *it* has not been treated as a logical constant. Since the conditions for the interpretative Dummy rule (45) are met, we have that the interpretation of (46) is given by:

$$(47) \quad m(\{be\ clear,\ that\ Fred\ leave\})\ (m(it_{\overline{S}}))$$
$$= m(be\ clear)\ (m(that\ Fred\ leave))$$

And this latter is just the interpretation of (*that Fred leave*) (*be clear*). Our semantics then is correct, and dummies have been technically treated as arguments and their types are argument algebras. Hence other processes, such as Raising, which are sensitive to arguments, could treat *it*, *there*, etc. as they do other arguments.

Note, finally, that we have not had to take a position on whether the sentence pairs we are generating are generated by extraposition or by intraposition. We have in fact independently generated each element of the pair.

BIBLIOGRAPHY

Anderson, S. R.: 1971, 'On the Role of Deep Structure in Semantic Interpretation', *Foundations of Language* 7, 387–396.

Bach, E.: 1980, 'In Defense of Passive', *Linguistics and Philosophy* 3, 297–342.

Bartsch, R.: 1976, 'Subcategorization of Adnominal and Adverbial Modifiers', in E. L. Keenan (ed.), *Formal Semantics of Natural Language*, Cambridge University Press, Cambridge, England.

Barwise, J. and R. Cooper: 1980, 'Generalized Quantifiers and Natural Languages', in *Stanford Working Papers in Semantics*, Vol. 1, pp. 1–80.

Ben-Chorin, S.: 1982, 'Sentence Meanings as a Formal Basis for Intensional Logic', in *Proc. of the First West Coast Conference on Formal Linguistics*, D. Flickinger, M. Macken, and N. Wiegand (eds.), Dept. of Linguistics, Stanford University, Stanford, pp. 82–93.

Bloom, L.: 1973, *One Word at a Time*, Mouton, The Hague, Paris.

Boole, G.: 1854, *An Investigation of the Laws of Thought*, Cambridge.

Bresnan, J.: 1978, 'A Realistic Transformational Grammar', in M. Halle, J. Bresnan, and G. Miller (eds.), *Linguistic Theory and Psychological Reality*, MIT Press, Cambridge, Mass.

Busby, S.: 1983, *A Semantics for Plural Noun Phrases and Higher Order Predicative Functions*, M.A. Diss., Dept. of Linguistics, UCLA.

Chomsky, N.: 1966, *Cartesian Linguistics*, Harper and Row, New York.

Chomsky, N.: 1970, 'Remarks on Nominalizations', in Roderick A. Jacobs and Peter S. Rosenbaum (eds.), *Readings in English Transformational Grammar*, Ginn and Co., Waltham, Mass.

Chomsky, N.: 1973, 'Conditions on Transformations', in *A Festschrift for Morris Halle*, S. R. Anderson and P. Kiparsky (eds.), Holt, Rinehart and Winston, New York.

Dowty, D.: 1978, 'Governed Transformations as Lexical Rules in Montague Grammar', *Linguistic Inquiry* 9, 393–427.

Emonds, J.: 1976, *A Transformational Approach to English Syntax*, Academic Press, New York.

Faltz, L.: 1982, 'On the Non-Bal(l)m(i)er Character of Keenan–Faltz Grammar', in *Theoretical Linguistics* 9, 221–246.

Gil, D.: 1982, 'Quantifier Scope, Linguistic Variation, and Natural Language Semantics', *Linguistics and Philosophy* 5, 421–473.

Gordon, L.: 1978, 'Raising in Bauan Fijian', ms., Dept. of Linguistics, UCLA.

Jake, J. and D. Odden: 1978, 'Cross Clausal Movement Rules in Kipsigis', presented at the 10th Annual African Linguistics Conference.

Keenan, E. L.: 1969, *A Logical Base for a Transformational Grammar of English*, Ph.D. diss., Dept. of Linguistics, Univ. of Pennsylvania.

Keenan, E. L.: 1979, 'On Surface Form and Logical Form', in B. B. Kachru (ed.),

Linguistics in the Seventies: Directions and Prospects, Univ. of Illinois, Dept. of Linguistics, Champaign–Urbana, pp. 163–203.

Keenan, E. L.: 1980, 'Passive is Phrasal (not Sentential or Lexical)', in T. Hoekstra *et al.* (eds.), *Lexical Grammar*, Foris Publications, Dordrecht, pp. 343–379.

Keenan, E. L.: 1981, 'Passive in the Languages of the World', to appear in T. Shopen (ed.), *Language Typology and Syntactic Description*, Cambridge University Press, Cambridge, England.

Keenan, E. L.: 1982a, 'Parametric Variation in Universal Grammar', in *Issues in the Theory of Universal Grammar*, R. Dirven and G. Radden (eds.), Gunter Narr Verlag, Tubingen.

Keenan, E. L., 1982b, 'Eliminating the Universe: A Study in Ontological Perfection', in *Proc. of the First West Coast Conference on Formal Linguistics*, in D. Flickinger, M. Macken, and N. Wiegand (eds.), Dept. of Linguistics, Stanford Univ., pp. 71–82.

Keenan, E. L. and L. Faltz: 1978, *Logical Types for Natural Language*, UCLA Occasional Papers in Linguistics, No. 3, Dept. of Linguistics, UCLA.

Keenan, E. L. and J. Stavi: 1981, 'A Semantic Characterization of Natural Language Quantifiers', to appear in *Linguistics and Philosophy*.

Kiparsky, P. and C. Kiparsky: 1970, 'Fact', in M. Bierwisch and K. Heidolph (eds.), *Progress in Linguistics*, Mouton, the Hague.

Ladusaw, W.: 1979, *Polarity Sensitivity as Inherent Scope Relations*, Ph.D. diss., Univ. of Texas at Austin, to be published by Garland Press.

Mendelson, E.: 1970, *Boolean Algebra and Switching Circuits* (Schaum's Outline Series), McGraw Hill Book Co.

Montague, R.: 1970, 'English as a Formal Language', reprinted in *Formal Philosophy*, R. Thomason (ed.), 1974, Yale University Press, New Haven.

Montague, R.: 1973, 'The Proper Treatment of Quantification in Ordinary English', in J. Hintikka, J. Moravcsik, and P. Suppes (eds.), *Approaches to Natural Language*, Reidel, Dordrecht.

Moravcsik, E.: 1978, 'Ergative and Accusative Patterns', ms., Dept. of Linguistics, Univ. of Wisconsin.

Partee, B.: 1975, 'Montague Grammar and Transformational Grammar', *Linguistic Inquiry* VI, 203–300.

Perlmutter, D. and P. Postal: 1979, 'Towards a Universal Characterization of Passivization', in *Proc. of the Third Annual Meeting of the Berkeley Linguistics Society*, Berkeley, Ca.

Rosenbaum, P.: 1967, *The Grammar of English Predicate Complement Constructions*, MIT Press, Cambridge, Mass.

Thomason, R.: 1976, 'Some Extensions of Montague Grammar', in B. Partee (ed.) *Montague Grammar*, Academic Press.

Thomason, R.: 1980, 'A Model Theory for Propositional Attitudes', *Linguistics and Philosophy* 4, 47–71.

Trithart, L.: 1977, *Relational Grammar and Chi-cewa Subjectivization Rules*, M.A. Diss., Dept. of Linguistics, UCLA. Also in the Publications of the Indiana University Linguistics Club.

INDEX